AND THE
VIETNAM
WARS
1950–1975

THE NEW COLD WAR HISTORY

John Lewis Gaddis, editor

CHINA AND THE VIETNAM WARS
1950-1975

Qiang Zhai

The University of North Carolina Press

Chapel Hill and London

Library of Congress
Cataloging-in-Publication Data
Zhai, Qiang.
China and the Vietnam wars, 1950–1975 /
Qiang Zhai.
    p. cm. — (The new cold war history)
Includes bibliographical references and index.
ISBN 0-8078-2532-8 (alk. paper). —
ISBN 0-8078-4842-5 (pbk. : alk. paper)
1. China—Foreign relations—Vietnam
(Democratic Republic) 2. Vietnam
(Democratic Republic)—Foreign relations—
China. 3. China—Foreign relations—1949–
1976. 4. Vietnamese conflict, 1961–1975.
I. Title. II. Series.
DS777.8.z388   2000   99-016884
959.704—dc21   CIP

04   03   02   01   00   5   4   3   2   1

Portions of Chapters 1, 2, 6, and 7 appeared
earlier, in somewhat different form,
respectively, in Qiang Zhai, "Transplanting
the Chinese Model: Chinese Military Advisers
and the First Vietnam War, 1950–1954,"
Journal of Military History 57 (October 1993)
(reprinted by permission); "China and the
Geneva Conference of 1954," *China Quarterly*,
no. 129 (March 1992) (reprinted by permission of Oxford University Press); "Beijing and
the Vietnam Conflict, 1964–1965: New
Chinese Evidence," *Cold War International
History Project Bulletin*, nos. 5 and 6 (Winter
1995–96) (reprinted by permission); and
"Opposing Negotiations: China and the
Vietnam Peace Talks, 1965–1968," *Pacific
Historical Review* 68, no. 1 (February 1999)
(© 1999 by American Historical Association,
Pacific Coast Branch; reprinted by permis-
sion of the University of California Press
Journals).

For Zhai Shutao and Jin Xingzao

CONTENTS

MAPS, ILLUSTRATIONS, & TABLES

FOREWORD

Qiang Zhai's *China and the Vietnam Wars, 1950–1975* is a remarkable contribution to Cold War international history generally, and to the international history of the Vietnam War in particular. Historians have long speculated about the relationship between the People's Republic of China and the Democratic Republic of Vietnam during the quarter century of conflict in Indochina that extended from 1950 to 1975. It is only with the publication of this book that we are in a position to know.

In an admirably thorough and clearly written account, Qiang Zhai has used an impressive array of recently released Chinese archival sources, memoirs, diaries, and documentary collections to tell the story of China's support for the Vietnamese Communists in their struggle, first against the French, later against the Americans. Several striking findings emerge from his research:

That Mao Zedong viewed the Vietnamese national liberation movement in both ideological and geopolitical terms. It deserved strong support as part of his larger strategy of creating an anti-imperial world order, but at the same time he was unwilling to separate that cause from China's interest in balancing the Soviet Union and the United States against one another. This is, then, a revealing study of how, in Mao's mind, revolutionary zeal intersected with Realpolitik.

That Chinese military assistance was critical to the Viet Minh in their war against the French prior to the Geneva settlement of 1954. The extent of this assistance was all the more surprising given China's simultaneous involvement in the Korean War.

That the Russians and the Chinese did, as we have long suspected, force the Viet Minh to accept the 1954 division of the country but that the Chinese later regretted this, a sentiment that contributed both to the Sino-Soviet split and to Beijing's support for the North Vietnamese escalation of the war against South Vietnam and the Americans in the early 1960s.

That the Chinese sent some 320,000 support troops to North Vietnam during the 1965–68 period, that over a thousand of them were killed there, and that Mao would have been prepared to fight the Americans directly had they attempted a ground invasion of North Vietnam.

That the North Vietnamese failed to consult the Chinese when they began negotiations with the Americans in 1968, and that Chinese influence over North Vietnam diminished from that point, with that of the Soviet Union growing.

That the Chinese had great difficulty in explaining Nixon's 1972 Beijing visit to the North Vietnamese, that they tried to compensate by stepping up military supplies to Hanoi during the final stages of the cease-fire negotiations, and that—despite his rapprochement with the Americans—Mao strongly supported the coming to power of Pol Pot and the Khmer Rouge in Cambodia in 1975.

That the roots of the Sino-Vietnamese War of 1979 lie in what we can now see to have been the fragmentation of the Sino-Vietnamese alliance during the late 1960s and early 1970s.

These are only a few of the insights that come out of this pathbreaking monograph, which for the first time illuminates the critical role that China played in the Vietnam War. The "New Cold War History" depends, more than anything else, upon the revisions in what we thought we knew that result from access to archives on the "other side." This book is a model for such studies. It is bound to shape our understanding of the Cold War in Southeast Asia for decades to come.

John Lewis Gaddis
May 1999

ACKNOWLEDGMENTS

A large number of individuals and institutions have helped to bring this book about. John Lewis Gaddis, Steven I. Levine, and Robert McMahon read the entire manuscript. I am grateful to them for their critical suggestions. Chen Jian, who shared numerous Chinese documents with me, was a regular provider of insight and advice. I wish to express my gratitude to the following scholars who commented on earlier versions of several chapters when they were first presented as conference papers: David Anderson, Anthony Edmonds, Fredrik Logevall, Edwin Moïse, John Prados, Michael Schaller, William Stueck, Allen Whiting, and Zhang Xiaoming. Over the years, Cai Jiahe, Gordon Chang, John Garver, Li Danhui, Li Haiwen, Liu Yawei, Niu Jun, Ren Donglai, Shen Zhihua, Michael Sheng, Shi Yinhong, James Tang, Wang Jisi, Odd Arne Westad, Xu Yan, Yang Kuisong, Yu Fenglan, Zhang Baijia, and Shu Guang Zhang have aided my understanding of Chinese Communist foreign policy and Sino-American relations both in conversations and through their writings. I am grateful to Mark Bradley, William Burr, Timothy Castle, Jim Hershberg, Christian Ostermann, Carlyle Thayer, and Xue Litai for their help to my research. I also greatly benefited from the valuable comments of the readers for the University of North Carolina Press.

The Committee for Scholarly Communication with China, the American Philosophical Society, and Auburn University Montgomery awarded me research grants to carry forward my project. Michael P. Fitzsimmons, my department chair, has been most helpful as a colleague and critic. He is a great friend for all seasons.

I am indebted to several librarians at Auburn University Montgomery, especially Carolyn Johnson and Debra West, who have long since learned to brace themselves when they see me coming. I owe a similar debt to several people at the University of North Carolina Press for their help in publishing this book: Lewis Bateman, Mary Laur, and Alison Waldenberg. Mary Caviness did a superlative job of copyediting, saving me from more errors than I can count.

Portions of Chapters 1, 2, 6, and 7 first appeared in the *Journal of Military History* (October 1993), *China Quarterly* (March 1992), *Cold War International History Project Bulletin* (Winter 1995–96), and *Pacific Historical Review* (February 1999). My thanks to these journals for permitting me to include the published parts in this volume.

I owe a great deal to my children, David and Kevin, who have brought so much joy into my life. Many of their "quality hours" were deprived by my immersion in the Vietnam War, and they have spent their childhood tripping over books and documents. They realize how much this book means to me; I hope they understand how much more they mean. My wife, Hui, has remained my biggest fan, and her love and pride has fortified my desire to do a good job.

This book is dedicated to my parents, Zhai Shutao and Jin Xingzao, who taught me the importance of history.

ABBREVIATIONS

ARVN	Army of the Republic of Vietnam
CCP	Chinese Communist Party
CIA	Central Intelligence Agency
CMAG	Chinese Military Advisory Group
COSVN	Central Office for South Vietnam
CPAG	Chinese Political Advisory Group
CPK	Communist Party of Kampuchea
DRV	Democratic Republic of Vietnam
FLN	Front de Liberation Nationale
ICC	International Control Commission
ICP	Indochinese Communist Party
JCP	Japanese Communist Party
KMT	Kuomintang
LPP	Lao People's Party
MAAG	Military Assistance Advisory Group
NLF	National Liberation Front of South Vietnam
NUFK	National United Front of Kampuchea
PAVN	People's Army of Vietnam
PEO	Program Evaluation Office
PKI	Indonesian Communist Party
PLA	People's Liberation Army
POW	Prisoner of War
PRC	People's Republic of China
PRG	Provisional Revolutionary Government
RGNUK	Royal Government of National Union of Kampuchea
SEATO	Southeast Asia Treaty Organization
UN	United Nations
USOM	United States Operations Mission
USSR	Union of Soviet Socialist Republics
VWP	Vietnam Workers' Party

CHINA
AND THE
VIETNAM
WARS
1950–1975

INTRODUCTION

The rise and fall of the Sino-Vietnamese alliance is one of the most crucial developments in the history of the Cold War in Asia in general and Chinese foreign relations in particular.[1] In the quarter century after the founding of the People's Republic of China (PRC) in 1949, Beijing assisted the Democratic Republic of Vietnam (DRV) in its struggle against two formidable foes, France and the United States. In the 1950s Chinese formulas served as a model for the Vietnam Workers' Party (VWP) in its war against France and in its efforts to rebuild the north. In the 1960s, Beijing provided extensive aid to help Ho Chi Minh fight the United States. China's support was crucial in the VWP's defeat of the French in 1954 and in its ability to resist the American pressure in the Second Indochina War. At the height of Chinese-DRV solidarity, Ho characterized the relationship as "comrades plus brothers." In the early 1970s, however, as the war in Vietnam began to wind down and as China adjusted its strategic priorities by opening to the United States to balance against Soviet threats, Beijing's relations with Hanoi started to deteriorate, culminating in a direct clash in 1979.

In general, the importance of China in the two Vietnam wars has been overlooked or underrated in both Vietnamese and Western writings.[2] Vietnamese writers have tended to disregard the Chinese role in the interest of producing "national history,"[3] while lack of access to Chinese archival sources has handicapped the treatment of Beijing in the Western scholarship on the Indochina conflict.[4] No comprehensive study on China's relations with the DRV between 1950 and 1975 exists. This book attempts to redress this deficiency by drawing on fresh Chinese documents to present a full-length treatment of the evolution of the Sino-DRV relationship between the two Indochina wars, focusing on its strategic, political, and military aspects.

This study analyzes the sources of Beijing's Indochina policy by placing it in the historical, domestic, and international contexts within which it was made. It investigates the reasons for the fluctuation of the Sino-DRV relationship.

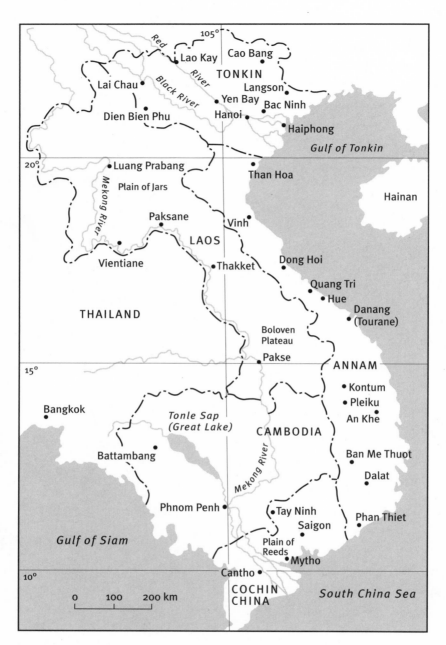

INDOCHINA

Source: Jacques Dalloz, *The War in Indo-China, 1945–54* (Dublin: Gill & Macmillan, 1987).

Specifically, it addresses a number of important questions concerning China's involvement in Indochina. Some of those relate to the nature of Beijing's objectives in Vietnam and the execution of its policies. Why did Mao decide to recognize the DRV and provide military advisers and aid to the Viet Minh immediately after seizing power in China? What role did Chinese advisers play in Ho Chi Minh's victory over the French? Why did Beijing participate in the Geneva Conference in 1954 and promote a partition of Vietnam? What was China's role in the DRV's efforts to reconstruct the north after 1954? How did China react to Hanoi's decision in 1959 to revive revolutionary war in the south? How did Mao respond to Washington's escalation of the war in Vietnam in the mid-1960s? And how did Mao's desire to reorganize the Chinese state and society influence his decisions on Vietnam?

Further questions emerge from China's interactions with its Soviet and Vietnamese allies. Was there a division of labor between Mao and Stalin during the early years of China's entanglement in Vietnam? How did the Sino-Soviet dispute affect Beijing's policies and influence its relations with Hanoi? How did China and the DRV differ over the approaches to waging war and pursuing peace? How did China's strategic realignment in the early 1970s affect its relations with the DRV? And how did cultural differences, historical distrust, and regional rivalry affect Sino-Vietnamese cooperation?

Both Laos and Cambodia existed in the shadow of the Vietnam wars, and the conflict in Vietnam often spilled over into those two countries. This study also discusses Beijing's response to developments in Laos and Cambodia, especially when they interacted with events in Vietnam. It places Beijing's reaction in the context of both its general foreign policy and its specific consideration of Vietnam.

In a broader sense, what insights about Mao's foreign policy might be gained by a close examination of China's attitudes and conduct toward Vietnam? Further, what conclusions about coalition building and alliance management on the Communist side of the Cold War might be drawn by a detailed investigation of the rise and decline of the Beijing-Hanoi entente?

The chapters that follow identify a complex blend of motives behind Beijing's Indochina policy. The consideration of geopolitical realities constituted one central element in Mao's calculations. Throughout the 1950s and most of the 1960s, Mao considered the United States the primary threat to China's security and revolution. Support for Ho Chi Minh and the Pathet Lao thus served Mao's purpose of weakening American influence in Southeast Asia and rolling back Washington's containment of China. In the late 1960s and early 1970s, when Mao perceived a greater menace from the Soviet Union and a lesser threat from the United States in Vietnam, he began to adjust his policies and encouraged the North Vietnamese to conclude a peace settlement.

The sense of an international obligation and mission to assist a fraternal Communist party and to promote anti-imperialist revolution in Asia was another crucial, often the most decisive, factor in Mao's Vietnam decisions. Beijing's actions in Indochina were often driven by Mao's vision of China's place in the world. When he devoted his life to revolution, Mao aimed at transforming not only the old China but also the old world order. French colonial rule in Indochina constituted part of the corrupt and unjust world order that Mao wished to sweep away. In Mao's mind, without a correspondent change in the existing international system, the recent Communist victory in China would not be secure, consolidated, and legitimized. Just as the old international order had helped cause China's suffering and humiliation, so too would the creation of a new order contribute to the rebirth of a strong and prosperous China. Mao equated security and prosperity at home with the development of anti-imperialist insurgencies and socialist revolutions abroad. A world of like-minded, Communist states would be the best guarantor of Mao's government in China. There was a fusion of security and ideological concerns in Mao's thinking. Mao and his associates identified their revolution with similar national liberation movements in developing countries and considered the Chinese model relevant to those movements. To a large extent, Mao intervened in Indochina to define China's identity or self-image in the world.

Mao, however, did not pursue his revolutionary goals in Southeast Asia with the same intensity throughout the years covered by this study. While sympathetic to anti-imperialist and anticolonial movements in the world, Mao did not desire war with the United States. The Chinese leader was a realist fully capable of making policy adjustments when he faced either domestic economic difficulties or international pressures. He was capable of beating tactical retreats from time to time, but always sticking to his colors. Between 1954 and 1960, for instance, he soft-pedaled Beijing's support for Communist insurgencies in Indochina so that China could concentrate on economic development at home. Mao would not hesitate to recommend moderation and concession if he believed that the reactionary force was too overwhelming for a fledgling revolutionary movement to press on with its struggle. That was why he accepted a divided peace in Vietnam at the 1954 Geneva Conference and discouraged Ho Chi Minh from pursuing Vietnamese unification at the time. Fearful of an American intervention in Vietnam if the war continued, Mao did not want to involve China in another Korea-like conflict, which would divert China from executing its much-needed domestic reconstruction. The apprehension about American intentions also explains Mao's decision to restore neutrality to Laos at the 1961–62 Geneva Conference. Mao endorsed neutralization of Laos at the time not because he wanted to create a permanent neutrality in the country, as the Soviet Union desired, but because he wanted to win time for the Pathet Lao to consolidate and develop its forces for the eventual seizure of power. In Mao's calculation, retraction and moderation did not mean abandonment; revolution went through stages. Mao fully understood Lenin's dictum of "taking one step back in order to make two steps forward" in making revolution. And from his own experience, he concluded that preparation for revolutionary change was a marathon, not a sprint.

Personality was a third important factor in shaping Beijing's attitude toward revolution in Vietnam. In considering aid to the Viet Minh, CCP leaders could not ignore the close personal ties and revolutionary solidarity that they and Ho Chi Minh had forged in the years of common struggle in the past. Sharing identical beliefs and values, they had gone through similar hardships and ordeals. Ho became acquainted with such CCP veterans as Zhou Enlai, Liu Shaoqi, Wang Ruofei, Peng Pai, and Li Fuchun in the 1920s, when he first worked for the French Communist Party in Paris and later served as a Comintern agent in Canton assisting the labor and peasant movements there. During the Chinese civil war in the late 1940s, Ho's government provided sanctuaries for the CCP troops in southern China, who withdrew into Vietnam to avoid attacks by the Nationalist forces. In deciding to assist the Viet Minh in 1950, Mao stressed the importance of reciprocating friendship.

Finally, the intention to use international struggle to promote domestic political agendas often figured prominently in Mao's deliberations on Vietnam. This was clearly the case in 1962 when Mao criticized the so-called revisionist foreign policy proposals made within the party and reemphasized the need to combat imperialism and support national liberation movements, including the struggle in Vietnam. The renewed emphasis on supporting anti-imperialist causes in the world in general, and in Vietnam in particular, gave Mao an effective instrument to mobilize domestic support for his program of "continuous revolution" and to dismantle obstacles within the party leadership, which had been divided by the disasters of the Great Leap Forward. Similarly, between 1965 and 1966 Mao used the need to support Hanoi's war against the United States to launch anti-imperialist campaigns at home, to reinvigorate revolutionary radicalism, and to mobilize the population in the struggle against "revisionist" leaders in the party, who were supposedly following the Soviet example to restore capitalism in China. In sum, Beijing's Indochina policy was the result of a convergence of geopolitical realities, ideological beliefs, personality, and political circumstances.

This book highlights the role of human agency in the making of history.

First there was the all-powerful Mao, whose ideas and visions set the general framework for China's Vietnam policy. He decided whether to assist Ho Chi Minh, to negotiate with Western powers, to confront American pressure, to reject Soviet proposals, or to improve relations with Washington at crucial moments. Then there were Mao's close associates and secondary party functionaries, including Head of State Liu Shaoqi, Premier Zhou Enlai, party secretary-general Deng Xiaoping, Foreign Minister Chen Yi, Ambassador Luo Guibo, and Generals Chen Geng and Wei Guoqing, who faithfully implemented Mao's diplomatic and military decisions concerning Vietnam. The chapters that follow particularly describe and assess the charismatic Mao as a revolutionary visionary, the reticent Liu as a careful organizer of Beijing's aid to the Viet Minh, the skillful Zhou as a shrewd diplomat at international meetings, the blunt Deng as a tough negotiator with the North Vietnamese, the straightforward Chen Yi as Mao's voice on international issues, and the combat-seasoned Chen Geng and Wei Guoqing as efficient military advisers on the Vietnam battlefield. They achieved victories but also made errors. Their voices defined China's policy, and their behaviors left a deep imprint on Sino-Vietnamese relations.

The Beijing-Hanoi relationship was composed of both agreements and contradictions, cooperation and confrontation. This study explores the nature and dynamics of that relationship and places it in its complex historical context. Throughout their history, the Vietnamese had a love/hate attitude toward China. On the one hand, they had a tradition of looking to the Central Kingdom for models and inspiration. Vietnamese rulers had copied and adapted China's methods and institutions for their own use as a legitimizing force. Paying respect to Chinese imperial superiority was the only way to avoid war for Vietnamese, and recognizing Chinese cultural norms became a habit of ruling-class Vietnamese. On the other hand, the Vietnamese were eager to preserve their independence and cultural heritage.

During the 1950s and 1960s, the Vietnamese Communists confronted formidable enemies, the French and the Americans, in their quest for national unification. Ho Chi Minh avidly sought advice and weapons from China. But sentiments of distrust were never far below the surface. The Chinese, for instance, were suspicious of Hanoi's intentions to incorporate Laos and Cambodia in an "Indochinese Federation" while the North Vietnamese guarded closely their "special relationship" with Laos when China increased its aid to the Pathet Lao.

The PRC-DRV relationship included both converging and diverging interests. The two countries shared a common ideological outlook and a common concern about American intervention in Indochina, but leaders in Hanoi wanted to avoid the danger of submitting to a dependent relationship with China. As long as policymakers in Hanoi and Beijing shared the common goal of ending the U.S. presence in the region, such diverging interests could be subordinated to their points of agreement. But the turning point came in 1968, when Sino-Soviet relations took a decisive turn for the worse just as Washington made its first tentative moves toward disengagement from South Vietnam. In the new situation, Beijing's strategic interests began to differ fundamentally from those of Hanoi. Whereas the Chinese now regarded the United States as a potential counterbalance against the Soviet Union, their Vietnamese comrades continued to see Washington as the most dangerous enemy. After the withdrawal of U.S. troops from Vietnam and the unification of the country, Hanoi's bilateral disputes with Beijing over Cambodia, a territorial disagreement in the South China Sea, and the treatment of Chinese nationals in Vietnam came to the fore, resulting in a border war in 1979.

This study utilizes for the first time fresh sources released in China during the last few years. The new materials fall into four categories: archival sources, published documentary collections, memoirs and diaries, and secondary writings based on archival holdings.

ARCHIVAL SOURCES

While such key documentary depositories as the CCP Central Archives and the Foreign Ministry Archives in Beijing are not open to researchers, regional party archives in the provinces are much less restrictive and more cooperative with scholars. Between 1995 and 1996, I made two research trips to the Jiangsu Provincial Archives (JPA) in Nanjing and found very useful materials in the collection of the Foreign Affairs Office of the Jiangsu Provincial People's Government. The collection includes internal memorandums sent by the CCP Central Committee in Beijing to provincial leaders explaining China's position on a wide range of international issues, including those of Indochina. Between 1958 and 1966, the Foreign Affairs Office of the State Council convened annual conferences on foreign affairs in Beijing, during which officials from central party and government organs such as the CCP International Liaison Department, the Foreign Ministry, and the Commission on Overseas Chinese Affairs briefed and explained to provincial officials in charge of foreign affairs recent developments in China's foreign relations. Many of the speeches and internal documents from these conferences are held in the JPA. These papers provide more accurate descriptions of Chinese leaders' perceptions of and reactions to developments in the world in general and Indochina in particular than contemporary Chinese newspaper accounts.

PUBLISHED DOCUMENTARY COLLECTIONS

In recent years Beijing has published many collections of the manuscripts, writings, conversations, and speeches by such leaders as Mao, Liu Shaoqi, and Zhou Enlai. These volumes contain numerous telegrams from these leaders to Chinese advisers in the DRV and record countless conversations between them and their Vietnamese counterparts. The most relevant volumes for this study are *Jianguo yilai Mao Zedong wengao* (Mao Zedong's Manuscripts since the Founding of the Country), 13 vols. (Beijing, 1987–98); *Mao Zedong junshi wenji* (Collection of Mao Zedong's Military Writings), 6 vols. (Beijing, 1993); *Mao Zedong waijiao wenxuan* (Selected Diplomatic Works of Mao Zedong) (Beijing, 1994); *Zhou Enlai nianpu, 1949–1976* (A Chronicle of Zhou Enlai's Life, 1949–1976), 3 vols. (Beijing, 1997); *Zhou Enlai waijiao wenxuan* (Selected Diplomatic Works of Zhou Enlai) (Beijing, 1990); *Zhou Enlai waijiao huodong dashiji, 1949–1975* (A Chronicle of Zhou Enlai's Diplomatic Activities, 1949–1975) (Beijing, 1993); and *Liu Shaoqi nianpu, 1898–1969* (A Chronicle of Liu Shaoqi's Life, 1898–1969), 2 vols. (Beijing, 1996).

MEMOIRS AND DIARIES

Many retired party officials, military commanders, diplomats, secretaries, and translators have published their personal recollections and diaries in the last decade. In some cases, the authors relied on younger assistants, who helped them check documents in the archives. These diaries and memoirs often suggest hidden motives and calculations behind bland policy situations. They provide not only fresh texts of what Mao said, which are not available elsewhere, but also an important window into what he read. As a result, the interactive nature of Mao's activities—with his top colleagues and his secretaries—is open to examination. A sense of the policymaking process, as well as Mao's opinions, emerge from these accounts. The most useful personal journals and reminiscences for this study are those by Bo Yibo, Chen Geng, Hu Zhengqing, Li Yueran, Luo Guibo, Shi Zhe, Tong Xiaopeng, Wang Bingnan, Wu Xiuquan, Xiong Xianghui, Zeng Sheng, and Zhang Dequn.[5]

SECONDARY WRITINGS

Since the mid-1980s, a large number of secondary publications based on archival sources have appeared in China. They include general party, military, and diplomatic histories, biographies, monographs, and articles. Their authors, mostly based in Beijing, are either writing teams organized by the party or individual scholars who enjoyed privileged access to archives. These works often quote illuminating archival documents. But, because of party restrictions, they refer to archival items without identifying their locations.

In approaching the new sources mentioned above, I have tried not to allow my excitement over their discovery to impair my critical attitude and sensitivity to context that are so crucial in examining any body of historical data. In using the published documentary collections, I have been fully aware that they were selected by party editors, often for political purposes, and that they may not constitute the complete documents. I have tried to work critically with these collections, dismissing large amounts of official hyperbole and mystification. I have treated memoirs with similar caution, fully conscious that human memories are fragmentary and fallible and that individual recollections are often self-serving. Whenever possible, I have cross-checked and verified accounts, pointing out discrepancies and contradictions. In dealing with secondary writings based on archival documents, I have been cognizant that I am at the mercy of the judgment of their authors as well as the inadequacies of the sources to which those authors may have been permitted access.

1 RECOGNITION AND ASSISTANCE 1950–1953

EARLY CONTACTS BETWEEN HO CHI MINH AND THE CCP

Ho Chi Minh's connection with the Chinese Communists went back to the early 1920s when Ho was active in the circles of the French Communist Party in Paris. It was in the French capital that he met CCP figures such as Zhou Enlai, Wang Ruofei, Xiao San, and Li Fuchun. In late 1924, the Communist International sent Ho from Moscow to Guangzhou to assist Mikhail Borodin, the Comintern representative to the new Chinese revolutionary government led by the Kuomintang (KMT). At Guangzhou, Ho also engaged in anticolonial activities, running a "special political training class" for Vietnamese youth. He invited Liu Shaoqi, Zhou Enlai, Li Fuchun, and Peng Pai to speak before his class.[1] Zhou Enlai later remarked to a group of Vietnamese visitors: "In 1922, I became acquainted with Chairman Ho. In 1925, Chairman Ho came to Guangzhou to support the Chinese revolution. This was a relationship of blood and flesh."[2]

Ho took an active part in the upsurge of labor and peasant movements in South China in the mid-1920s. During the general strike against the British in Canton and Hong Kong in June 1925, Ho spoke in Chinese before labor rallies, applauding their actions.[3] He also took an active interest in the Peasant Movement Institute established by Sun Yat-sen's government in Canton as a vehicle for mobilizing support in rural regions in southern China. Ho encouraged Peng Pai's attempt to organize revolutionary activities among peasants in Haifeng County and acted as a liaison between the Canton government and the Peasant International (Krestintern) in Moscow.[4]

Chiang Kai-shek's break with the Chinese Communists in 1927 and a shift in the ideological line of the Comintern forced Ho to depart China for Moscow. He returned to Hong Kong in early 1930 to convene a meeting to establish the Vietnamese Communist Party. At Comintern's demand shortly afterward, the name of the organization was changed to the Indochinese Communist Party (ICP).[5] Imprisoned by British police in Hong Kong in June 1931, Ho was set free two years later and traveled to Moscow, where he spent five years studying Lenin's writings. In the fall of 1938, Ho came to Mao's headquarters in Yanan, where he stayed for several weeks. He then traveled south to set up liaison offices in KMT-occupied areas of the country and to restore contact with ICP elements who were operating in the region.[6]

In May 1941, Ho presided over a meeting of the ICP Central Committee at Pac Bo, a village just inside the Vietnamese border. The most important result of the gathering was the emergence of a new national united front called the League for the Independence of Vietnam, commonly known as the Viet Minh. The organization was designed to unite all nationalist groups in the common struggle for national independence. Ho and his fellow Communists who provided leadership for the Viet Minh shrewdly appealed to Vietnamese nationalism, downplaying their commitment to social revolution and advocating a broad platform emphasizing independence and "democratic" reforms. In August 1945, the Viet Minh, taking advantage of the political void left by the surrender of Japan, seized power in Hanoi and established the DRV.[7]

While Ho Chi Minh was celebrating his victory for the moment, the Chinese Communists were bracing for a renewed civil war with the KMT after the defeat of Japan. The small and poorly equipped CCP forces in southern China came under serious threat when Chiang Kai-shek's 46th and 64th Armies moved into the provinces of Guangdong and Guangxi. The CCP's Guangdong District Committee decided to withdraw the First Regiment of the Southern Guangdong People's Force, the main CCP unit in the region, into Vietnam to avoid a KMT attack. The Guangdong Committee sent Pang Zi and Zhu Lanqing, two cadres familiar with Vietnam, to Hanoi to request support. Hoang Van Hoan, who was in charge of liaison with the Chinese Communists, received the CCP envoys and expressed welcome for the First Regiment.[8]

Led by Commander Huang Jingwen and political commissar Tang Caiyou, the First Regiment, with a total force of about 1,000, entered Vietnam in March 1946. Ho Chi Minh not only satisfied the Chinese demand for food and other supplies but also provided medicine to treat the Chinese soldiers who were suffering from malaria and dysentery. In preparation for a war against France, which was determined to reassert its colonial domination over Indochina, Ho asked the CCP unit in Vietnam to help train his troops. To strengthen ties with the Viet Minh, the CCP Hong Kong Sub-Bureau in June 1946 sent Zhou Nan, deputy director of the Organization Department of the CCP Guangdong District Committee, to Hanoi to serve as the CCP's liaison representative. Hoang Van Hoan asked Zhou to organize both the First Regiment and overseas Chinese in Vietnam to contribute to the anti-French war. Specifically, Hoan wanted the CCP to help the Viet Minh army train its officers and create an intelligence system.[9]

After discussing with Huang Jingwen, Tang Caiyou, and Lin Zhong, secretary of the CCP Guangxi-Vietnam Border Interim Working Committee, Zhou Nan worked out a plan to assist the Viet Minh. According to the plan, the First Regiment would send officers to the Vietnamese Advanced Infantry School and the Thai Nguyen Cadre Training Center as advisers and teachers, to the Vietnamese Defense Ministry as intelligence specialists, and to the units of the Viet Minh forces as military trainers or as commanders. The First Regiment would also receive Viet Minh officers for training in its camp. As to the mobilization of overseas Chinese, the plan asked the First Regiment and the CCP's Guangxi-Vietnam Border Interim Working Committee to dispatch cadres to the province of Bac Giang to organize overseas Chinese armed units. The Viet Minh leadership approved the plan. By July 1947, over 830 officers and soldiers from the Viet Minh army had received training in the camp of the First Regiment. An overseas Chinese self-defense force of over 1,000 members had been created, which was later incorporated into the Viet Minh army. The First Regiment returned to southern China to reestablish a revolutionary base area in August 1949 when Mao's main forces in North China were crushing Chiang's troops and marching victoriously southward.[10]

On the whole, the connection between the Chinese and Vietnamese Communist Parties between 1945 and 1949 remained limited. In addition to the mutual assistance between the First Regiment and the Viet Minh troops, the CCP Hong Kong Sub-Bureau had also irregularly provided funds for the Viet Minh.[11] No evidence of substantial technical assistance from the CCP during this period is available. The direct telegram communications between the Chinese and Vietnamese party centers were not established until spring 1947.[12] Mao was preoccupied with the struggle against Chiang Kai-shek in Manchuria and North China. The First Regiment's encounter with the Viet Minh, however, was important because it strengthened the link between the two revolutionary movements and paved the way for their future cooperation.

U.S. intelligence sources had reported in 1946 that the DRV was in direct touch with the Soviet Union and Mao's headquarters and that Russian and Chinese advisers were training Ho Chi Minh's troops.[13] As to the Chinese involvement, the U.S. analysts were inaccurate in stating that the Viet Minh maintained direct contact with the CCP central leadership because there was no direct communications between Ho and Mao at that time. The U.S. intelligence officials were right in pointing out that Chinese advisers were training the Viet Minh forces.

There is no mention, however, in recently available Chinese sources of any Soviet presence in Viet Minh ranks during this period. Stalin, like his counterpart in Washington, was inclined to consider Indochina from a European perspective: endorsement of Ho might jeopardize the prospects of the French Communist Party to assume power in France.[14] Furthermore, Stalin was not certain whether Ho was a bona fide Communist. The Vietnamese leader's united front policy, which gave priority to national independence over social revolution, and his dissolution of the ICP in 1945 caused uneasiness in the Kremlin.[15] (It is interesting to note that the CCP's similar united front approach in organizing the new government in 1949 also caused suspicion in Moscow.) According to the Russian scholar Igor Bukharkin, between September and October 1945, Ho sent two telegrams to Moscow requesting aid but received no reply.[16] Given Stalin's preoccupation with European developments and his caution in supporting Asian revolutionary movements after World War II, it remains highly unlikely that he sent any Soviet advisers to the DRV in 1946.

RECOGNITION OF THE DRV

Mao proclaimed the founding of the PRC on October 1, 1949. Shortly afterward, Ho Chi Minh sent two envoys, Ly Bich Son and Nguyen Duc Thuy, to Beijing to seek China's assistance in his struggle against the French.[17] At the time, Mao was in Moscow negotiating the Sino-Soviet alliance treaty. During his absence from Beijing (between December 16, 1949, and February 17, 1950), Liu Shaoqi, acting chairman of the CCP Central Committee, was in charge of the party's daily work. While maintaining close consultation with Mao in Moscow, Liu was responsible for the actual handling of Beijing's Indochina policy during this period. In later years, he would often be involved in managing relations with fraternal parties.

After receiving the request from Ho's envoys, Liu called a politburo meeting on December 24 to discuss the issue of establishing diplomatic relations with the DRV. The meeting concluded that it would be more beneficial than harmful for China to form diplomatic ties with the DRV before the French recognition of the PRC.[18] Four days later, Liu, on behalf of the CCP Central Committee, sent a cable to Ho Chi Minh, indicating China's agreement to enter into diplomatic relations with his government. The Soviet Union and Eastern European countries might follow suit, Liu said. To facilitate this development, Liu advised Ho to issue a statement on behalf of the DRV expressing willingness to

Luo Guibo, head of the Chinese Political Advisory Group in the DRV, *1951–54; China's ambassador to the* DRV, *1954–57. (Courtesy Xinhua News Agency)*

establish diplomatic relations with foreign countries. Notifying Ho that the CCP would send a representative to Vietnam,[19] Liu also asked the Viet Minh leader to send a high-level delegation to Beijing to discuss the issues concerning the common struggle against imperialism.[20]

To facilitate communications with the Vietnamese Communists, Liu in early January 1950 selected Luo Guibo to serve as the CCP Central Committee's liaison representative to Ho's party. Luo at the time was director of the General Office of the CCP Central Military Commission. Liu instructed Luo to go to Vietnam to establish contact with the ICP, to investigate the conditions there, and to report his findings to Beijing so that the party leadership could make decisions regarding assistance to Ho. Liu expected Luo to stay in Vietnam for three months.[21]

To familiarize Luo with Vietnamese customs, Liu asked Yang Shangkun, director of the General Office of the CCP Central Committee, to introduce Luo to Ly Bich Son and Nguyen Duc Thuy, who were visiting Beijing at the moment. Liu also supervised the selection of the members of Luo's team, including a staff, a telegraph operator, secretaries, and guards. After Luo's departure for Vietnam on January 16, Liu cabled the ICP Central Committee the next day, announcing the appointment of Luo as the CCP's representative.[22] Luo in fact stayed in Vietnam much longer than Liu had anticipated. He later became the head of a Chinese political advisory team and was appointed China's ambassador to the DRV in 1954. He remained in that position until 1957.

Eager to win legitimacy and international recognition, the DRV on January 15, 1950, telegraphed Beijing officially requesting the establishment of diplomatic relations. Mao cabled Liu Shaoqi from Moscow two days later asking him to convey immediately to the DRV China's agreement to establish official ties. In the same telegram, Mao also instructed the Chinese Foreign Ministry to forward the DRV's request for establishing diplomatic relations to the Soviet Union and Eastern European countries.[23]

In Moscow, Mao informed Stalin that China was prepared to recognize the DRV and provide active support for the Indochinese peoples' struggle for national independence. Endorsing Mao's plan, the Soviet leader said that China should recognize the DRV first and the Soviet Union would do so afterward. He also told Mao that Moscow was willing to supply necessary aid to Ho Chi Minh.[24] Stalin procrastinated in recognizing the DRV because of his fears of alienating France since Paris at this time objected to the U.S. plans for rearming West Germany.[25]

On January 18, the PRC became the first country in the world to recognize the DRV. The Soviet Union followed suit on January 30 and was followed shortly after by the Communist governments in Eastern Europe and North

Korea. By taking the lead in recognizing the DRV and urging the other socialist countries to do the same, the CCP was making a clear choice in the emerging revolution in Indochina and was placing solidarity with a fraternal party above possible diplomatic relations with France.[26]

The French were angry at the actions of Moscow and Beijing. Paris blamed the Soviet Union for violating international law: "Vietnam is part of the French Union, and it is to the government of Bao Dai that France has just transferred the sovereignty she possessed in this Union." Until then, France had vacillated over whether or not to follow the British example in recognizing the PRC. Any idea of this sort was now completely dropped.[27]

Anxious to establish personal contact with the CCP leadership, Ho decided to visit Beijing himself. Demonstrating his characteristic tenacity and perseverance, the fragile Viet Minh leader, accompanied by Tran Dang Khoa, a member of the ICP Central Committee, walked on foot for seventeen days in Vietnamese jungles before crossing into Guangxi province.[28] Informed of Ho's arrival, Liu Shaoqi on January 26 instructed party officials in Wuhan to conduct a "warm reception" for the Vietnamese visitor and to "carefully escort him to Beijing."[29]

Upon Ho's arrival in Beijing on January 30, Liu Shaoqi and Zhu De, vice chairman of the Central People's Government and commander in chief of the People's Liberation Army (PLA), hosted a reception in his honor. Ho reported on the situation in Vietnam and requested China's aid. The Chinese leaders immediately agreed to satisfy his demands. Afterward, Liu cabled Mao to inform him of the meeting.[30] He told Mao that the party had formed a committee composed of Zhu De, Nie Rongzhen, acting chief of the General Staff of the PLA, Li Weihan, director of the CCP United Front Department, and Liao Chengzhi, vice chairman of the Overseas Chinese Affairs Commission under the Central People's Government, to deal with the issues Ho raised.[31] Mao and Zhou Enlai sent Liu a telegram from Moscow asking him to pass on their best regards to the Vietnamese leader. They congratulated Ho on the DRV's joining the "big anti-imperialist and democratic family headed by the Soviet Union" and wished Ho an early success in unifying his country.[32]

According to Hoang Van Hoan, the first DRV ambassador to the PRC, Liu told Ho that he expected France to postpone recognition of the PRC as a result of Beijing's solidarity with the Viet Minh. China would not be afraid, Liu continued, because when China became stronger later, the French would have to recognize it.[33] Liu's remarks are important because they make it clear that China was ready to pay a price in supporting the Viet Minh by foregoing French recognition, a fact that displays Beijing's commitment to "proletarian internationalism." They also show French misperceptions of China's inten-

Luo Guibo poses with Vietnamese Communist leaders in front of a guest house, 1950.
Front row, left to right : *Vo Nguyen Giap, Pham Van Dong, Truong Chinh, Luo Guibo,*
Ton Duc Thang. (Courtesy Xinhua News Agency)

tions because some officials in Paris had wanted to trade recognition for Beijing's termination of assistance to Ho.

The Chinese government asked Soviet ambassador N. V. Roshchin to convey to the Kremlin its suggestion that the Soviet Union invite Ho to visit Moscow and talk to Stalin directly. Ho made his trip to the Soviet Union on February 3. In the Soviet capital, Stalin told Ho that assisting the Viet Minh was primarily a Chinese business. Attending the Soviet state banquet in honor of Mao on February 16, Ho said to Stalin—"half jokingly," according to Wu Xiuquan—that the Soviet Union might sign a treaty with the DRV along the same lines as that signed with China. But Stalin refused to do that. Ho left Moscow to return to Beijing together with Mao and Zhou on February 17.[34]

Reaching Beijing on March 3, Ho held further talks with CCP leaders regarding China's assistance to the DRV. After mutual briefings concerning each party's history and current conditions, Liu suggested that in order to facilitate China's aid to Vietnam, the DRV establish consulates in Nanning and Kunming, capitals of Guangxi and Yunnan provinces, respectively. Ho accepted the proposal. During his stay in Beijing, Ho also instructed Hoang Van Hoan that from then on the focus of Vietnamese foreign relations would be on China not

Luo Guibo (sixth from right) and his wife, Li Hanzhen (fifth from left), pose with Ho Chi Minh (eighth from right) and other Vietnamese Communist officials, 1952. (Courtesy Xinhua News Agency)

Thailand. (Between 1948 and 1949, Hoang Van Hoan had been engaged in organizing overseas Vietnamese in Thailand to support the anti-French war.) Ho designated Hoan as the official representative of the Vietnamese party and government to China, asking him to start preparations for the establishment of the Vietnamese embassy in Beijing.[35]

In April, Ho forwarded to Beijing a number of aid requests, including the establishment of a Vietnamese military school in China, the dispatch of Chinese military advisers to Vietnam, and the supply of weapons. Liu Shaoqi supervised the implementation of Beijing's aid. He helped select the site of the Vietnamese military school, insisting that the positions of the school president and department chairmen be occupied by Vietnamese. Ho adopted Liu's proposal, and the school was later built in Yunnan province.[36]

To familiarize the Vietnamese with Mao's military thought, Liu instructed Luo Guibo to introduce to them the ten military principles that Mao had first summarized in December 1947.[37] The principles were: (1) attack dispersed and isolated enemy forces first and attack concentrated, strong enemy forces later; (2) take small and medium cities and extensive rural areas first before occupying larger cities; (3) make the elimination of the enemy's effective strength rather than the holding or seizing a city the main objective; (4) in every battle, concentrate an absolutely superior force to wipe out the enemy forces; (5) fight no battle unprepared; (6) maintain high morale among the soldiers; (7) strive to wipe out the enemy when it is on the move; (8) when attacking cities, resolutely seize all enemy fortified points and cities that are weakly defended; (9) obtain weapons and new recruits from the enemy; (10) make good use of the intervals between campaigns to rest, train, and consolidate troops.[38]

With regard to Ho's request for the dispatch of Chinese military experts to Vietnam to act as advisers at the Viet Minh army command centers and at the division level and as commanders at the regimental and battalion levels, the CCP leaders responded that it would send advisers but not commanders. On April 17, the CCP Central Military Commission ordered the formation of the Chinese Military Advisory Group (CMAG), including advisers capable of assisting the Viet Minh army headquarters, three divisions, and an officers' training school. The military experts would be selected from the PLA's Second, Third, and Fourth Field Armies. The CMAG included seventy-nine advisers and their assistants. The total number of the CMAG was 281.[39] The Vietnamese request for Chinese commanders at the regimental and battalion levels indicates the Viet Minh's serious leadership problems and shows their lack of confidence and experience in maneuvering units above the company size.

To meet Ho's demands for military supplies, Liu Shaoqi told Luo Guibo that the CCP would "do its best to satisfy the Vietnamese requests." As to the Vietnamese needs for nonmilitary goods such as clothes, medicine, and equipment, Liu outlined a generous principle in terms of payment: "If the Vietnamese do not have or lack materials to exchange, those goods can be viewed as military aid for the time being. In the future when mutual trade is possible and when the Vietnamese can offer materials, [we] will ask them to pay for some of our goods. At present since they are unable to pay, we will not mention it. We should now focus our attention on how to help them defeat imperialism effectively and should relegate other issues to a secondary place."[40]

On June 27, 1950, Mao, Liu Shaoqi, and Zhu De received the senior members of the CMAG in Beijing. To prepare them for conditions in Vietnam, the party leadership asked Hong Thuy (Vo Nguyen Bac), a Vietnamese-born general in the PLA, to give a quick course on Vietnamese geography, climate, and military developments. In late July, the CMAG was formally established at Nanning with General Wei Guoqing as chairman and Mei Jiasheng and Deng Yifan as deputy chairmen. In Nanning, Hoang Van Hoan provided the CMAG further information about conditions in Vietnam.[41]

Anxious to formalize diplomatic relations, Ho Chi Minh proposed to exchange ambassadors with the PRC. In a telegram to the Vietnamese leader on July 7, 1950, Zhou Enlai declined Ho's request on the ground that the ongoing fighting in Vietnam made it "inconvenient" for the DRV to receive ambassadors from foreign countries. Zhou stated that it was more appropriate to keep Luo

Guibo as the CCP's liaison envoy and to delay the announcement of him as China's ambassador.[42] Ho made a similar request to Moscow during this period. While agreeing to receive an ambassador from Ho's government, the Soviet Foreign Ministry viewed the appointment of a Soviet ambassador to the DRV as undesirable because the Vietnamese government had not established a permanent residence.[43]

From April to September 1950, China sent to the Viet Minh large quantities of military and nonmilitary supplies, including 14,000 rifles and pistols, 1,700 machine guns and recoilless rifles, 150 mortars, 60 artilleries, and 300 bazookas, as well as munitions, medicine, communications materials, clothes, and 2,800 tons of food.[44] The Viet Minh troops especially prized bazookas and recoilless rifles, calling them "as powerful as elephants."[45] Mao's resolve to assist the Viet Minh is all the more remarkable given the fact that the Korean War forced him to postpone his operations to occupy Taiwan.[46]

MAO'S MOTIVES

Why was Mao so eager to aid Ho Chi Minh in 1950? Mao's decision was motivated by a complex blend of geopolitical, ideological, and historical factors. First of all, Indochina constituted one of the three fronts (the others being Korea and Taiwan) that Mao perceived as vulnerable to an invasion by imperialist countries headed by the United States. The CCP leader viewed developments in Korea, Taiwan, and Vietnam as interrelated. He was concerned not only with possible international hostility emanating from Indochina but also with remnant KMT forces in Vietnam. After the Communist occupation of Guangxi in December 1949, some of Chiang Kai-shek's units had fled to northern Vietnam while others had escaped into the mountains in Guangxi. After the outbreak of the Korean War, these KMT troops, both those in Vietnam and those in the Guangxi mountains, began to harass the newly established Communist authorities in Guangxi. Mao was very apprehensive about this situation. Throughout 1950 and early 1951, he devoted much effort to eliminating these KMT remnants.[47] Viewed in this context, the defeat of the French troops in northern Vietnam would greatly strengthen China's border and consolidate the position of the PRC.

In addition to this immediate security concern, the sense of an international mission to support anti-imperialist revolution in Asia carried greater weight in Mao's determination to lend a hand to Ho Chi Minh. When Mao committed himself to revolution, he was determined to transform not only China but also the world. Just as the old international system had helped bring about China's degradation, so too would the emergence of a new system contribute to the rejuvenation of China. Mao and his comrades perceived a close connection between the Chinese and world revolutions. An international revolution would help consolidate and legitimize the Chinese revolution.[48]

An internal party directive prepared by Liu Shaoqi on March 14, 1950, exemplified the CCP's conception of the linkage between the Chinese and world revolutions. "After the victory of our revolution," the document declared, "to assist in every possible way the Communist parties and people in all oppressed nations in Asia to win their liberation is an international obligation that the CCP and the Chinese people cannot shirk. It is also one of the most important methods to consolidate the victory of the Chinese revolution in the international arena."[49]

In believing that China had a special role to play in the reshaping of a future revolutionary order in the world, Mao was following in the footsteps of messianic forerunners in the French and Russian Revolutions. "Ambitious visions," the historian John Lewis Gaddis has observed, "are probably necessary if revolutions of any kind are to occur: those who would overturn old orders require some basis for suspending belief in the existence of practical difficulties."[50] An ideological vision could encourage people from different backgrounds to work together as comrades and inspire them to take the risks and pay the prices associated with revolution against established authority.[51]

To a significant degree, the CCP leaders intervened in Indochina to define China's identity or self-image in the world. Identifying the Chinese revolution with national liberation movements in underdeveloped countries, Mao and his associates believed that their revolutionary model had international relevance and significance, pointing out a direction for other peoples fighting for national liberation. In his political report to the CCP Seventh Congress in 1945, Liu Shaoqi heaped lavish plaudits on Mao's contribution to the Chinese revolution, asserting enthusiastically that Mao's ideas held relevance for the emancipation of people everywhere, especially "the peoples of the East." As Europeans, Marx and Lenin were mostly concerned with European issues and paid little attention to China or Asia, Liu commented in early 1946, while Mao was an Asian who had transformed Marxism "from a European to an Asian form." Overwhelmed by the euphoria of the recent CCP victory, Liu claimed at the Trade Union Conference of Asian and Australasian Countries held in Beijing in November 1949 that "the path taken by the Chinese people in defeating imperialism and its lackeys and in founding the People's Republic is the path that should be taken by the people of various colonial and semicolonial countries in their fight for national independence and people's democracy."[52] On January 4, 1950, *Pravda* published Liu's address, confirming Stalin's approval.[53]

In June 1951, Lu Dingyi, a leading CCP theorist, published a celebrated article entitled "The World Significance of the Chinese Revolution" in *Shijie zhishi*

(World Knowledge), a journal of international affairs reflecting the views of the Chinese Foreign Ministry. He distinguished between the October Revolution as the "classic example of revolution in the imperialist countries" and the Chinese revolution as its counterpart for the "colonial and semi-colonial countries." "Among the colonial and semi-colonial countries," Lu declared, "the people of Vietnam, Burma, Malaya, and the Philippines have already been waging national liberation war against imperialism and the national liberation movements in such countries as India and Japan are growing. The Chinese model and experience serve to increase the confidence of the people in those countries in winning victory and increase their will to fight." Mao Zedong's thought, Lu concluded, had significance not only in China and Asia but also in the world. "It remains a new contribution to the general treasure-house of Marxism-Leninism."[54]

The Indochina conflict therefore provided both a test and a validation of the adopted PRC national identity as a champion of national liberation struggles in colonial and semicolonial areas. It presented the exogenous trigger for national identity mobilization and confirmed for the national self and "others" that China could stand up for the integrity of its self-image as a supporter of national liberation movements against imperialism and colonialism.[55]

Stalin's endorsement further encouraged Mao to play an active part in promoting revolution in Asia. There was an international division of labor within the Communist world at this time. When Liu Shaoqi visited the Soviet Union in July 1949, Stalin told him that the center of world revolution had moved from the West to the East, to China and East Asia. With this eastward movement of the focus of world revolution, the Kremlin boss wanted the CCP to bear more responsibility in assisting national democratic revolution in colonial and semicolonial countries while the Soviet Union would assume more responsibility in the West.[56]

The CCP leadership's enthusiasm for fostering revolution in Asia was clearly revealed in an instruction sent by Liu Shaoqi in early 1950 to party officials in southern China directing them to be ready to establish contact with Communist parties in Southeast Asia. In a March 3 telegram to Chen Geng, chairman of the Yunnan Provincial Government and commander of the Yunnan Provincial Military District, and Song Renqiong, secretary of the CCP Yunnan Provincial Committee and political commissar of the Yunnan Provincial Military District, Liu Shaoqi wrote that with the liberation of Yunnan and Guangxi, the Communist parties in Southeast Asia, especially those in Vietnam and Burma, would send representatives to China to seek contact with the CCP. "The Vietnamese Communist Party Central Committee has already established relations with us," Liu continued. "The central committees of other Communist parties have not established regular and formal relations with us yet. If they send people to Yunnan and Guangxi provinces to establish such relationships, we should give a warm welcome and assistance to them. In the future, they may dispatch appropriate representatives to station secretly in Yunnan or Guangxi."[57]

Mao's militant approach to Asian revolution also manifested itself in his treatment of the Japanese Communist Party (JCP). On January 6, 1950, the Cominform journal carried an article lashing out at Nosaka Sanzo, a member of the JCP politburo, for his insistence on the peaceful path to power and his contention that American forces in Japan were advantageous to Japanese democratization. The article called on the JCP to oppose with violence the use of its country for U.S. military purposes.[58] Echoing the Cominform's position, Mao on January 14 directed Hu Qiaomu, director of the General News Department of the PRC, to prepare a *Renmin ribao* (People's Daily) commentary urging the JCP to "take appropriate measures to correct Nosaka Sanzo's mistakes."[59]

In providing aid to the DRV, the CCP leaders also considered the close personal ties and revolutionary solidarity that they and Ho Chi Minh had forged in the years of struggle in the past. Sharing identical beliefs and values, they had gone through common hardships and ordeals. Still fresh in the memory of the CCP policymakers was the timely and crucial assistance that Ho had provided for their forces in southern China in 1946 when they faced annihilation by the KMT troops. In his conversation with Luo Guibo on January 13, 1950, Liu Shaoqi mentioned this incident in particular to stress the necessity of helping Ho.[60] There was a parallel in the calculations of the CCP leaders in their decisions to support Kim Il Sung and Ho Chi Minh in 1950. Like Ho, Kim had also provided crucial shelter and supplies to the CCP troops and their families, who were forced to withdraw into northern Korea from Manchuria during the early phase of the Chinese civil war, when the KMT forces were far superior in numbers and weapons. In deciding to enter the Korean War to rescue the crumbling Kim regime in 1950, the CCP leaders stressed the importance of paying back the friendship they had received from the Korean Communists in the past.[61]

In their meeting with the senior members of the CMAG on June 27, 1950, the CCP leadership was unanimous in emphasizing the theme of internationalism. Mao said that "since our revolution has achieved victory, we have an obligation to help others. This is called internationalism." Liu Shaoqi contended that the party had "important reasons" for deciding to assist the Viet Minh. "Vietnam is the area that has attracted most attention in the world today," Liu continued, "and your mission has international significance." Zhu De added that "as internationalists we should regard assistance to Vietnam as an important international task and should spare no effort to help the Vietnamese achieve victory."[62] It is clear that, riding on the crest of their recent victory over the KMT, the CCP leaders were eager to promote revolution beyond the Chinese border. It was likely that Kim Il Sung's initial success in the Korean War encouraged Mao and his comrades at this point.

Finally, Beijing's involvement in Indochina should be viewed in the context of China's traditional relations with neighboring countries. Historically speaking, the Chinese held a Sino-centric view of the world, regarding other countries as inferior. Chinese emperors considered Vietnam as within the orbit of China's influence and kept that country within the tributary system. They would not hesitate to send troops into Vietnam to restore peace and order if the authority of an existing tributary ruler there was endangered by either domestic uprisings or foreign invasion. For instance, between 1788 and 1790, Qing emperor Qianlong dispatched an expeditionary force to Vietnam to restore the Le King, who had been overthrown by a domestic rebellion. About one century later, the Qing government again intervened in Vietnam in 1884–85 to resist a French invasion.[63] These historical parallels would be inescapable to Mao and his lieutenants, who took history seriously.

As for the Vietnamese, they had a tradition of looking to China for models and inspiration. Throughout their history, Vietnamese rulers had copied and adapted China's methods and institutions for their own use as a legitimizing force, despite the Central Kingdom's frequent interference in their affairs. Paying respect to Chinese imperial superiority was the only way to avoid war for the Vietnamese, and recognizing Chinese cultural norms became a habit of ruling-class Vietnamese. It was only the arrival of the French in the nineteenth century that fundamentally disrupted Vietnam's centuries-long cultural connection with China, whereby all educated Vietnamese learned the Chinese language and the cultural and ethical principles embedded in it. The French policy to suspend the use of Chinese and Vietnamese characters among literate Vietnamese resulted in the adoption of a twenty-nine-letter alphabet for writing the Vietnamese language, which by the 1920s and 1930s led to an intellectual revolution that became the basis for the modern nationalist awakening. Vietnamese nationalists turned to Europe rather than China for intellectual ideas.[64] In a sense, by looking to Beijing for assistance, Ho Chi Minh resumed Vietnam's historical link with China. Therefore, Ho's decision to seek Mao's help was determined not solely by ideological reasons. It was consistent with Vietnam's history-long habit of looking to China for models while maintaining independence.

It is important to note that from the very beginning the CCP leaders paid close attention to their relationship with the Viet Minh and instructed the Chinese advisers not to display arrogance in Vietnam. Liu Shaoqi told Luo Guibo on April 8, 1950, that neither Vietnamese Communists nor Chinese cadres knew each other well. Because of this lack of mutual understanding, Liu cautioned the CCP envoy, "unnecessary misunderstandings and excessive vigilance" might occur. Since both parties had gone through long years of revolutionary struggle, Liu concluded, they could establish mutual trust and confidence.[65]

Both Mao and Liu stressed to the CMAG on June 27 the importance of unity and cordial relations between the two parties. They asked the Chinese advisers to avoid the mentality of big-state chauvinism and not to display contempt for the Vietnamese.[66] In a telegram to Luo Guibo in August, Liu instructed Luo not to impose his views on the Vietnamese and not to take offense if they refused to adopt his suggestions.[67]

These statements by Mao and Liu clearly indicate that the two men were sensitive to Vietnamese national pride and were aware of the historical animosities between the two countries as a result of China's interventions in Vietnam. It was also possible that when the CCP leaders urged the Chinese advisers to be modest and respectful in Vietnam, they had in mind the bitter lessons of Soviet advisers in China during the formative years of the Chinese revolution. In the early 1930s, it was the bungling and arrogance of the Comintern advisers that caused great damage to the CCP and the Red Army, forcing them to abandon their base areas in southern China and to embark on the Long March. Despite their professed effort to respect Vietnamese opinions, as later chapters will demonstrate, the Chinese leaders were disappointed and angry when their Vietnamese comrades deviated from the Chinese line.

Ho Chi Minh's "leaning to one side" had major consequences for the conflict in Indochina. By aligning with the socialist camp, he further polarized the Cold War in Asia. Just as Mao sought the Sino-Soviet alliance treaty to balance China against the American threat and to advance the Communist cause, Ho asked for Chinese and Soviet assistance to resist the French and to protect his revolutionary gains. By inviting China to help his endeavor, he increased the likelihood of later American intervention. Through his own choices, Ho hardened Cold War alignments. As a move toward the left, the ICP, theoretically disbanded in the fall of 1945 to appeal to non-Communist nationalists, reappeared at the Second National Congress of the party in February 1951 as the Vietnam Workers' Party (the Lao Dong); a separate organization for Cambodia was created later in 1951, and the Lao People's Party (LPP) was established in 1955. Ho was elected as party chairman, and Truong Chinh, secretary-general. The congress emphasized the importance of studying the Chinese revolutionary experience, and the new party charter pointed out that "the VWP will combine the theories of Marx, Engels, Lenin, Stalin and the Mao Zedong

Thought with the Vietnamese revolutionary practice as the ideological basis and action guide for the party." The portrait of Mao hung alongside those of Marx, Engels, Lenin, and Stalin at the congress hall.[68]

CHEN GENG AND THE BORDER CAMPAIGN

In June 1950, Ho Chi Minh decided to launch a border campaign to clear the line of communications with China. The French at this time controlled a string of outposts along the Chinese border. The elimination of these French positions would help consolidate the Viet Minh's base area in the Viet Bac, remove obstacles to the shipment of supplies from China, and place Ho's troops in a stronger position to launch attacks against the rich rice-producing area of the Red River delta in the future.

Originally, the People's Army of Vietnam (PAVN; the Viet Minh army adopted this name in 1950) planned to employ the four crack regiments that had been undergoing training and organization in China since April 1950 to attack Lao Kay and Cao Bang, two important French outposts located on the RC4 (Route Coloniale 4), parallel to the border with China. After considering logistical difficulties, it modified its plan by concentrating on Cao Bang. In addition to asking China to provide supplies and to send the military advisory group to Vietnam as soon as possible, Ho also requested the dispatch of a senior Chinese military adviser to coordinate the whole border operation.[69]

Upon Ho's request, the CCP leadership selected General Chen Geng as its senior military adviser and representative to the PAVN. Unlike many other PLA generals who were of peasant stock, Chen was an educated man. Handsome and refined, he was known as a "scholar general." He was born in 1903 into a wealthy landowning family in Hunan province; his grandfather had been a military commander in the Qing army. At the age of six, Chen began his Confucian education. In 1919, he joined the army of a Hunan warlord; five years later, he became a Communist. Military history was his favorite subject when he was a student at the Whampoa Military Academy in Guangzhou in the mid-1920s. During that time, he also became acquainted with Ho Chi Minh. During the civil war, he was commander of the Fourth Corps of the Second Field Army of the PLA. His unit occupied Yunnan in early 1950.[70]

In a telegram on June 18, 1950, Liu Shaoqi instructed Chen to prepare a practical and workable plan after taking into account the Vietnamese conditions in military affairs, political development, economy, topography, and transportation as well as China's aid capabilities, particularly in the area of transportation. The party, Liu went on, would use this plan as a basis to implement its various aid programs, including the shipment of supplies, the training of cadres, the reorganization of troops, the recruitment of new sol-

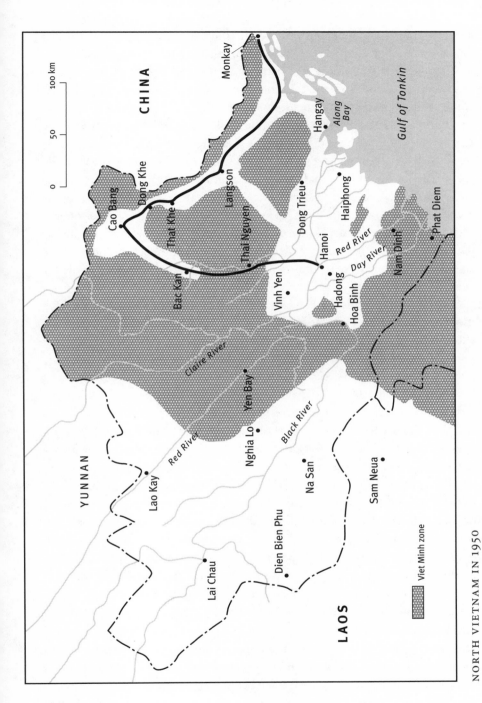

NORTH VIETNAM IN 1950

Source: Jacques Dalloz, *The War in Indo-China, 1945–54* (Dublin: Gill & Macmillan, 1987).

diers, the management of logistics, and the conduct of battles. Liu insisted that the plan should be approved by the Vietnamese party Central Committee.[71]

Chen Geng left Kunming for Vietnam on July 7. Along the way, he made careful investigations into the conditions in Indochina. He first stopped at the Yanshan training camp in Yunnan where the PAVN's 308th Division was receiving training and equipment. General Zhou Xihan, commander of the Chinese 13th Army who was responsible for the training of the Vietnamese troops, reported to Chen on his work. Chen also talked with the commanders of the 308th Division about the situation in their country. Disguised as a PAVN officer after crossing the border, Chen continued investigating the deployment of the French forces in northern Vietnam and the conditions of the PAVN troops.[72] This emphasis on reconnaissance on the part of Chen was in line with China's traditional military teachings on making full investigation before engaging the enemy. Sun Zi (Sun Tzu), an ancient Chinese strategist, advised: "Know the enemy, know yourself; your victory will never be endangered."[73]

As Chen wrote in his diary, he discovered that the Viet Minh neglected the mobilization of women in its struggle against the French. Since women constituted more than half of the Vietnamese population, Chen believed that ignoring them meant wasting more than half of the human resources. He pointed this out to Viet Minh leaders.[74] Clearly, Chen was applying Mao's "people's war" doctrine to Vietnam. During the anti-Japanese war and the civil war, Mao had successfully mobilized women in his cause.

On July 22, Chen reported to the CCP leadership his findings about the PAVN troops: "Some Vietnamese crack units are in high morale after receiving training and equipment in Yunnan and Guangxi, but Vietnamese cadres above the battalion level lack command experience in actual combat." Given this condition, Chen suggested that the principle for the border campaign should be "to destroy the enemy mobile force in field battles and occupy some small and isolated outposts in order to win initial success while gaining experience and boosting the troops' morale. After gaining the complete initiative, we can gradually proceed to large-scale battles." As to the Vietnamese plan to attack Cao Bang, Chen suggested the strategy of "encircling the outpost while attacking the rescue force." Specifically, Chen proposed that the PAVN should first attack some isolated outposts close to Cao Bang while attracting French rescue forces from Lang Son. "If we can annihilate three to five mobile battalions from Lang Son, then it will be easier to occupy Can Bang and some outposts near Lang Son." If that happened, Chen believed, the situation in northeastern and northern Vietnam "will greatly change." In a telegram on July 26, the CCP Central Military Commission consented to Chen's plan for the campaign.[75]

On July 28, Chen arrived at the Viet Minh administrative headquarters at

Thai Nguyen, where he met Ho Chi Minh and Luo Guibo. A beaming Ho embraced Chen with open arms. At his residence, Ho recited a Chinese poem he had composed to welcome Chen.[76] The Chinese envoy stayed at Thai Nguyen for four days, during which he informed Ho of his plan for the border operation. He told the Vietnamese leader that the PAVN was not combat ready for occupying Cao Bang at the moment. The Viet Minh should first attack smaller French outposts in order to train its commanders and troops. Tactically, the PAVN should adopt the approach of surrounding an outpost while wiping out the enemy's rescue forces in mobile battles. Specifically, Chen suggested that the PAVN first assault Dong Khe, a French outpost between Cao Bang and Lang Son, so as to lure the enemy out of the latter two positions and then decimate it in field combat. Ho endorsed Chen's plan.[77] Chen noted in his diary that, after talking with Ho and other Vietnamese officials and listening to Luo's report, he found that the Viet Minh leaders showed "impatience" and "sole emphasis on weapons" in their struggle against the French.[78]

The CMAG, accompanied by Hoang Van Hoan, left Nanning, Guangxi province, on August 9 and reached the PAVN headquarters at Quang Nguyen, a town near Cao Bang, on August 12. The CMAG immediately dispatched its members to the Vietnamese 304th, 308th, and 312th Divisions. Later in the year, it also sent advisers to the 316th Division and the 351st Engineering and Artillery Division (also called the "Heavy Division"). At the same time, General Li Tianyou, deputy commander of the Guangxi Military Region, became the head of a logistics committee responsible for the preparation and transportation of food, ammunition, and medical supplies to Vietnam. Two special field hospitals were set up to treat wounded Vietnamese soldiers.[79]

Two days after the CMAG's arrival, Chen Geng also reached Quang Nguyen, where he met the CMAG led by Wei Guoqing. General Hoang Van Thai, chief of staff of the PAVN, briefed Chen on the French military deployment along the RC4. Chen told Vo Nguyen Giap, general commander of the PAVN, of his plan for the border campaign. Accepting Chen's plan, Giap invited the Chinese adviser to speak at a meeting of the PAVN commanders above the regimental level. Chen talked for four hours, concentrating on the "deficiencies" of the PAVN. The audience paid great attention to his speech; Giap mentioned several times that Chen's address was "very educational." On the eve of the border campaign, Ho visited the PAVN command center, entrusting his troops to Chen's direction.[80]

On September 16, the PAVN launched an assault on Dong Khe and captured the outpost two days later. At Dong Khe, Ho's troops won their first artillery duel.[81] But the demanding Chen Geng was not satisfied with the combat effectiveness of the Viet Minh army. The French garrison at Dong Khe had

Vo Nguyen Giap (right) greets Luo Guibo (left) at the Sino-Vietnamese border, 1950. (Courtesy Xinhua News Agency)

about 260 soldiers, while the Viet Minh force numbered approximately 10,000, with superior artillery power. By the end of the fighting, the PAVN had suffered about 500 casualties and had let more than twenty French troops escape. Chen had first expected the Viet Minh troops to occupy the garrison within one day, but it took them two days and three nights to conclude the battle. Chen discovered several problems with Ho's units. First, they did not follow the attack time as originally planned. The general offensive was supposed to begin at dusk on September 16, but the Viet Minh units did not start the action until the early morning of the next day. When the sun rose, they had to withdraw for fear of a French air strike. Then they had to restart the offensive at dusk on that day. Second, PAVN commanders were afraid of going to the front, thus losing touch with the assault units. Third, there was a lack of communications between command and units. Fourth, some cadres made false combat reports to hide bad news. Chen mentioned these problems to Giap.[82] Clearly these shortcomings were examples of the "deficiencies" that Chen had pointed out before the Dong Khe battle.

The occupation of Dong Khe, however, represented a great victory for the PAVN for it isolated Cao Bang by cutting the RC4. The French sent a column headed by Lieutenant Colonel Lepage from Lang Son via That Khe to recapture Dong Khe. At the same time, another French unit headed toward the Viet Minh headquarters at Thai Nguyen. Chen judged that the French move toward Thai Nguyen was designed to divert the Viet Minh forces from Dong Khe so that the French troops at Cao Bang could escape and join the Lepage column. Therefore, Chen suggested that the PAVN stick to its original plan by staying at Dong Khe.[83]

Chen decided to waylay the enemy coming from That Khe.[84] On September 30, the Lepage column left That Khe for Dong Khe but was ambushed in the mountainous area south of Dong Khe. On October 3, Lieutenant Colonel Charton abandoned Cao Bang and led his force southward. Determined to prevent the meeting of the Lepage and Charton units, the PAVN command, at Chen's suggestion, ordered the 308th Division, the 209th Regiment, and one independent battalion to surround and annihilate the Lepage group first before attacking the Charton unit.[85] On October 8, the Viet Minh army mauled the Lepage column. Two days later, it also destroyed the Charton unit. Both Lepage and Charton were captured. In subsequent operations, Ho's forces occupied Cao Bang and That Khe. The French soon afterward evacuated Lao Kay, Lang Son, and Hoa Binh, leaving behind 11,000 tons of ammunition and abandoning virtually all of Vietnam north of the Red River delta.[86]

The success of the border campaign had great significance for the Viet Minh. At the end of the year, except for the coastal redoubt of Monkay, the Viet Minh had completely cleared the Chinese border of French outposts and there were no longer any obstacles to the passage of men and arms from China. The French evacuation of Hoa Binh also opened up communications between the Viet Bac and the "liberated" area of North Annam, combining Viet Minh territory into one block. The Viet Minh could now raid the Red River delta at will and retreat to its base area in the Viet Bac without fear of French reactions. In the words of the historian William J. Duiker, the Viet Minh was "in a position, for the first time, to seize the initiative in the war."[87] The border victory also relieved Beijing's fear of attacks by the remnant KMT troops in Southeast Asia.

After the conclusion of the border campaign, Mao sent a telegram to Chen expressing "great gratification" at the Viet Minh victory. The CCP leader asked Chen to help Ho's army draw lessons from the campaign.[88] Chen went to the battle sites, showing PAVN commanders how to improve their combat leadership. On October 11, Chen talked with Ho and Giap, making comprehensive suggestions for improving the PAVN. His proposals ranged from the reorganization of Ho's army and the promotion of cadres to the treatment of enemy prisoners of war and the repair of captured artillery pieces and guns. Chen asked the Viet Minh leaders to convene celebration rallies to publicize the border victory, emphasizing the importance of selecting and rewarding role models as a way to maintain high morale among soldiers. According to Chen, there should be different role models for cadres, soldiers, and civilian transporters. In order to encourage "revolutionary heroism," Chen also urged the Vietnamese to conduct memorial meetings for those who had died during the border engagements. As for the treatment of POWs, Chen suggested that the Viet Minh first try to use them to undermine the enemy's morale by asking them to write letters and make speeches, and then recruit as many Vietnamese POWs as possible while releasing Moroccan and French POWs after indoctrinating them with revolutionary ideas. According to Chen's diary, Ho and Giap "happily" accepted his suggestions.[89] Chen's advice about the celebration of victories, the selection of role models, and the treatment of POWs was based on similar Chinese practices during the anti-Japanese war and the civil war. By spreading such Maoist rituals as commemorations and celebrating role models in Vietnam, Chen helped introduce a highly important process, through which the Viet Minh members came to bond together.

From October 27 to 30, the Viet Minh convened summing-up meetings attended by its commanders above the battalion level. On behalf of the Viet Minh leadership, Truong Chinh delivered a report reviewing the border campaign. At Ho's request, Chen addressed the meeting for four successive days. He first analyzed the reasons for the Viet Minh success, praising the courage and tenacity of the soldiers. Warning them not to be conceited with their triumph, Chen asked the Viet Minh to be on guard against American intervention. He then went on to point out the shortcomings of the PAVN, which included commanders' lack of concern for soldiers, physical punishment, delay in implementing orders, laxity in discipline, and a tendency to report only good news.[90]

The Viet Minh leadership was very pleased with the outcome of the border campaign. Ho Chi Minh showed Chen his telegrams to Stalin and the French Communist Party reporting the success of the operation.[91] Commending Chen highly on his military leadership, Ho said that the border campaign achieved a greater victory that he had expected, calling it "a triumph of proletarian internationalism." Giap claimed that the campaign thwarted the French plan to close the Vietnamese border and to isolate the Viet Minh. "The victory shows," the PAVN commander continued, "Mao's military thought was very applicable to Vietnam."[92] Ho asked Chen to stay in Vietnam to direct the next military operation, but Chen received new orders from Beijing and left Vietnam in early November 1950. (On June 8 of the following year, Chen was appointed deputy commander of the Chinese Peoples' Volunteers and went to Korea in August.) After Chen's departure, the CMAG bore the sole responsibility of advising the PAVN.

SETBACKS AND REORGANIZATION IN 1951

Clearly encouraged by the success of the border campaign and emboldened by the Chinese victory in the initial offensives against United Nations (UN) troops in Korea, the CMAG and the PAVN in late 1950 decided to launch a general offensive in the Red River campaign. Some ranking party cadres viewed the border campaign as a "partial offensive" that constituted the gradual transition to the general offensive.[93] Vo Nguyen Giap was a major proponent of the shift to the third and final stage of people's war (the first two stages included strategic defensive and stalemate). He had published a pamphlet entitled "The Military Task in Preparing for the General Counter Offensive" in 1950, in which he declared that the conditions were ripe for the revolutionary forces to move into the general offensive to eliminate enemy forces in large numbers and to occupy cities. Giap mentioned four conditions that would mark the switch to the final stage: (1) the absolute moral superiority of the revolutionary forces and the corresponding collapse of the enemy's determination to fight; (2) the continuing national superiority of the enemy in purely military terms, which would pose difficult but not insuperable problems for the Viet Minh; (3) the growing significance of international factors (referring to China's assistance); and (4) the superior strategic leadership of the revolutionary forces.[94] There were also officials in the party who favored the seizure of the Red River delta in order to relieve the rice shortage in the liberated areas.[95]

In January 1951, Giap started Operation Hoang Hoa Tham I by attacking the provincial capital of Vinh Yen, thirty-seven miles northwest of Hanoi at the western end of the Red River delta.[96] Giap adopted the human wave tactics the Chinese were concurrently employing in Korea.[97] General Jean de Lattre de Tassigny, the new French commander in chief in Indochina,[98] responded by airlifting reserve forces from Cochin China to Vinh Yen and by attacking the enemy with napalm bombs. The Viet Minh failed to occupy the city and lost at least 6,000 soldiers.[99]

But the setback did not change Giap's plan. In late March, he moved his units to the east in an assault against Mao Khe on the northern edge of the delta (Operation Hoang Hoa Tham II). After the initial breakthrough of the first French defensive line, the attackers failed to take the town and had to abandon their offensive after sustaining heavy casualties. The same fate befell Giap's strike in May in the region of Phu Ly and Ninh Binh on the Day River south of Hanoi.[100] This series of reversals convinced the Chinese advisers that it was difficult and premature for the Viet Minh to achieve a decisive victory through big offensives conducted in a region where the colonial army, close to its base, could utilize its superior firepower. They realized that they had to be realistic and cautious in helping the PAVN plan their future operations.[101]

In a telegram to Mao on January 27, 1951, Wei Guoqing complained about the PAVN and proposed to train and reorganize it. In his reply two days later, the CCP leader first endorsed Wei's plan and then asked him to show patience with the Vietnamese and not to arouse their resentment. "Their current shortcomings," Mao continued, "are the ones that the Chinese army also possessed when it was young. There is nothing strange about it. Only through persuasion can we help them make gradual progress over a long period of struggle."[102] Obviously, Mao was referring to the impatience of the PAVN to launch large-scale offensives and occupy cities, comparing this to the similar experience of the Chinese Red Army in its early years. Mao's remarks to Wei Guoqing were not only condescending toward the PAVN but also rather ironic since the CCP leader himself was simultaneously pushing the Chinese offensives in Korea beyond what his own commander Peng Dehuai was recommending. In Korea, Mao was guilty of the same impatience he accused the Viet Minh leaders of displaying.

In early 1951, the CMAG suggested to the PAVN a plan for streamlining its command structure and for training and reorganizing its troops. With Ho's approval, the CMAG helped the PAVN's three general departments (the General Staff, the General Political Department, and the General Supply Department) and divisions to simplify their command structure. Redundant personnel were cut and sent to lower combat units. The CMAG assisted the three general departments to draw up rules and regulations so that each cadre had a clear sense of duty. The Chinese advisers stationed at division levels offered training classes for PAVN company, platoon, and squad leaders. As a result, the PAVN became more professional.[103]

The method of ideological indoctrination introduced by the Chinese advisers to the PAVN was called *chinh huan* in Vietnam. A dictionary published in Hanoi refers to *chinh huan* as "a movement of ideological reform among cadres and people conducted by a political studies organization and by personal self-examination in connection with the course." The reference also indicates *chinh huan*'s genesis in *zheng feng*, the rectification campaign that Mao launched to fortify his position in the CCP in Yanan during the early 1940s. In June 1951, *Quan chinh tap san*, the PAVN's journal of political studies, mentioned a *chinh huan* campaign following the Hoang Hoa Tham battle the previous April and outlined a course for the following summer. *Chinh huan* campaigns would be institutionalized later during the land reform movement in 1953.[104]

By helping the Viet Minh to conduct *chinh huan* campaigns, the Chinese advisers spread to Vietnam the Maoist "mind over matter" approach, a style of inquiry that emphasized the rectified mind over objective factors. The Maoist approach was based on the earlier neo-Confucian stress on the minds of well-trained elites as the self-transforming agents of moral and political cultivation.[105] Given the influence of neo-Confucian ideas in Vietnam, it was not difficult for the Chinese advisers to find a receptive audience to the Maoist doctrine of emphasizing the "correct thought" in political action.

The CMAG's effort to consolidate the PAVN was part of a general campaign by Ho, with the assistance of the Chinese advisers, to consolidate and strengthen the government of the DRV in 1951. At the beginning of the year, at the request of the VWP, the Chinese Political Advisory Group (CPAG) was formed with Luo Guibo as chairman. The group was divided into sections dealing with military affairs, finance and economy, public security, culture and education, united front, party consolidation, and land reform. The group included over one hundred advisers. Throughout the year, the CPAG was busy helping Ho make laws and policies concerning finances, taxation, grain requisition, suppression of counterrevolutionary elements, newspaper and radio management, relations with non-Communist parties and groups, and treatment of minorities.[106]

Deficit and inflation were the two most pressing problems plaguing the DRV economy. To cope with the shortage of food and the lack of commerce, Ho's government had adopted the drastic policy of overissuing the currency at the beginning of 1951. On January 22, Liu Shaoqi asked Luo Guibo to warn the Vietnamese Communists about the danger of such a practice. The correct way to overcome financial difficulties, Liu insisted, was to develop production and trade.[107]

Aside from the economic mismanagement at the top, the Chinese also discovered corruption among lower-level Viet Minh cadres in charge of financial matters as well as negligence and waste of the materials provided by China.

Between April and May, Liu Shaoqi twice sent messages to alert Ho Chi Minh to these problems. In an April 20 cable, Liu stressed to Ho the importance of punishing those officials who had violated financial rules and discipline so that all financial and material resources could be best used for the purpose of fighting the French. In a second message sent on May 2, Liu told Ho that many Chinese materials, including munitions, transmitter-receivers, and X-ray equipment were left unattended either by roadsides or in caves in Vietnam. He asked the Vietnamese leader to correct the problem.[108]

New financial and economic measures were designed primarily to place the VWP in a better economic position to wage the war against the French. To establish a healthy revenue system for the DRV, the Chinese advisers helped the Vietnamese Communists reform their taxation structure by abolishing the old system, including the taxation of wine, salt, and opium, and introducing five new taxes on agriculture, trade, forestry, slaughtering, and import-export. The most important of them was the agricultural one, which was to be paid by landlords and peasants alike. The taxation percentage was to be determined by the officials and the population according to income and family expenditures. Because the new tax system was a Chinese borrowing unfamiliar to the Vietnamese cadres and people, the VWP created a special agricultural tax department to examine the system, operated classes to train tax collectors, and sought to explain the new tax codes to the public. In addition to the new tax system, the government also established the National Bank of Vietnam and issued a new currency, with the new bank notes printed in China. The Vietnamese claimed in 1952 that the tax system of 1951 was successful.[109]

THE NORTHWEST CAMPAIGN

In early 1952, the CMAG proposed to the PAVN the launching of the Northwest campaign. Adjacent to the border of Laos, the Northwest was a region where French defenses were weak. The liberation of this area would relieve the threat from the rear to the Viet Minh–controlled Viet Bac while providing a broader base of support. Luo Guibo, who was directing the CMAG in Wei Guoqing's stead while he was in China for medical treatment, was responsible for planning this operation. On February 16, Luo sent a report to the CCP Central Military Commission outlining his plan for the PAVN in 1952. He suggested that the PAVN rest and train its main forces in the first part of the year while continuing guerrilla warfare and that it attack Nghia Lo and Son Lo in the Northwest during the second part of the year. With the Northwest as a base, Luo continued, the PAVN could send troops into Laos the following year. Approving Luo's plan, the Central Military Commission instructed him to adhere to the principle of "making steady progress and ensuring victory in every battle" during the campaign. Liu Shaoqi told him that "it was crucially important to help Laos achieve liberation." Luo conveyed his plan to Giap, who accepted it. Ho paid much attention to the Northwest campaign, asking the CMAG to provide assistance throughout the operation. In April, the VWP politburo approved the campaign.[110]

On April 14, Luo outlined to Beijing his plan for the Northwest campaign: The PAVN would start the operation in mid-September by first attacking Nghia Lo; they would follow with an assault on Son Lo; occupy most of the Northwest by the end of the year; and then attack Lai Chau the next year. Five days later, the CCP Central Military Commission approved Luo's proposal with the proviso that the PAVN make careful field investigations and logistical preparations before the campaign while paying attention to minority issues in the Northwest. (The Northwest was a region inhabited mostly by ethnic minorities.) On July 11, Luo sent to the Central Military Commission a detailed operational plan for the campaign. The plan also included a Vietnamese request that China send troops into Vietnam from Yunnan to coordinate the operation. On July 22, the Central Military Commission replied that it was an important principle of China not to send troops into Vietnam, but it could deploy some units along the border as a gesture of support. It was the PAVN's own responsibility to eliminate the French in the Northwest. Beijing also suggested modifications for Luo's battle plan.[111]

On July 31, Luo told the Central Military Commission that the PAVN would start minority-issue education among the soldiers in early September before they marched toward the Northwest in the middle of the month. On August 8, the Central Military Commission responded to Luo that it would be premature to begin the operation in mid-September, and that it should be postponed to October or even November so that the VWP would have sufficient time to make political, military, and logistical preparations.[112] Zhou Enlai, during his visit to the Soviet Union between August 17 and September 22 to seek Soviet economic aid, mentioned the Northwest campaign to Stalin. Approving the operation, the Soviet leader also talked about peace negotiations with France. If the Viet Minh surrounded Hanoi, Stalin suggested, Ho Chi Minh could bring up the issue of peace talks with France. If Paris rejected, the Viet Minh could move southward after conquering Hanoi. Zhou agreed with Stalin's assessment.[113] Clearly, Stalin wanted Ho to negotiate with the French from a position of military advantage.

In early September, the VWP convened a politburo meeting and invited Luo to attend. Giap reported on the preparations for the Northwest campaign. He pointed out the difficulties involved, especially with regard to the attack on Son Lo. In late September, Ho made a secret trip to Beijing to discuss with Chinese leaders the Northwest campaign as well as the strategic plan for winning the war against the French. The Chinese leaders suggested that the PAVN first seize the Northwest and northern Laos and then move troops south to capture the Red River delta. Ho accepted this proposal, and in a telegram to Giap and Luo on September 30, he informed them of the decision he had made with the Chinese leaders: the Northwest campaign would only involve Nghia Lo, not Son Lo; after the occupation of the former, the PAVN should build a revolutionary base there.[114]

Ho Chi Minh traveled secretly to Moscow from Beijing on October 6 to attend the Nineteenth Congress of the Communist Party of the Soviet Union.[115] On October 28, Stalin, Liu Shaoqi, and Ho discussed the Viet Minh's current policies.[116] While the details of the talks remain unknown, it is possible that Ho sought Stalin's support.

In early October, the VWP politburo discussed Ho's September 30 instructions and agreed to drop the Son Lo part of the Northwest campaign. At this time, Giap was already at the Northwest front, and Truong Chinh informed him of the politburo's decision. On October 14, the PAVN concentrated eight regiments to attack Nghia Lo and some nearby outposts. On October 16, Wei Guoqing returned to Vietnam to join Luo in directing the Northwest operation. After the PAVN captured Nghia Lo, the French abandoned Son Lo on November 22. By December 10, the PAVN had liberated a vast area of the Northwest region,[117] which provided the PAVN a convenient staging area to conduct operations in Laos.

THE 1953 LAND REFORM

Vietnamese reformers had been calling for land reform since the 1930s, but the French colonial government had consistently disregarded their demand. In the north, poor peasants and agricultural laborers, 60 percent of the population, owned only 11 percent of land.[118] For many years, Ho's party had confined itself to the moderate policy of reducing rents and taxes for fears that a radical land reform would undermine resistance unity by alienating the landlords.[119]

The military conflict with the French, however, proved more difficult than Ho had anticipated, even though, with Chinese assistance, the PAVN's strength had developed rapidly. To conclude the protracted war and to relieve the increasing organizational and economic burden on the party, the VWP leadership decided in late 1952 to mobilize the peasants to support the war effort. The reward would be land for them and the methods would be class struggle not just against the French and their collaborators but also against those members of the party and the government who were from landlord or rich peasant families. The land reform would serve two goals for the party: eliminate the

*Luo Guibo (fourth from left) inspects a Vietnamese factory.
(Courtesy Xinhua News Agency)*

weaknesses in the party and state organs and mobilize peasant support for the war.[120] In January 1953, the Fourth Plenum of the vwp passed a resolution calling for land reform in the liberated areas.[121]

The ccp had rich experiences in land reform, so the Vietnamese sought the suggestions of the Chinese advisers. Mao had realized early in his career that in a peasant country the most effective way to mobilize the population for social change was land reform. Mao had finally seized power in China largely because he was able to appeal to the peasants' need for land. Now the Chinese were eager to transplant their model in Vietnam. In the spring of 1953, Zhang Dequn became the head of the Land Reform and Party Consolidation Section under the cpag. To strengthen Zhang's team, Beijing sent forty-two additional land reform specialists to Vietnam during that year. As a first step in land reform, the Chinese advisers taught Vietnamese cadres how to analyze class conditions in the countryside before sending them there to conduct rent reduction campaigns. They helped the vwp establish peasant associations and youth and women's leagues and reorganize local administrative committees by recruiting and promoting poor peasants. They also recommended to the Vietnamese the "Three Together System" (*san tong* in Chinese): to live, eat, and work together with peasants. The practice was intended to familiarize cadres with the hard-

Luo Guibo poses with Vietnamese factory workers. (Courtesy Xinhua News Agency)

ships and sufferings of the peasants as well as their complaints against the landlords. The cadres, after learning about the miseries of the peasants, encouraged them to "pour out grievances" (*suku*) against French collaborators and despotic landlords at mass rallies designed to arouse peasants' class consciousness. (The mass rally had been an effective method used by Mao during the Chinese revolution.) The property and land of those French collaborators and local tyrants were confiscated and distributed to poor peasants.[122]

The VWP's decision in the winter of 1952–53 to carry out land reform caused uneasiness and complaints among the PAVN officers who were from landlord families. Considering this development, and drawing upon the Chinese revolutionary experience, the CMAG believed that it was necessary for the PAVN to carry out a land reform education campaign among its officers and soldiers to prepare them for the coming land reform movement. During the Chinese land reform in the 1940s, Mao had carried out a campaign of political consolidation of the PLA (*zhengjun*) in order to channel the thought of his officers and soldiers along the party line on land reform. On February 7, 1953, Luo Guibo sent a report to the CCP leadership, proposing that the PAVN conduct a political consolidation campaign to make its officers and soldiers aware of the distinction between the peasant and the landlord. Through such an education campaign, Luo insisted, the VWP could improve the quality and combat effective-

Luo Guibo (fifth from left) and other Chinese advisers in Vietnam, 1950. (Courtesy Xinhua News Agency)

ness of its army and guarantee the successful implementation of the land reform. On March 4, the CCP Central Committee approved Luo's suggestion.[123]

On April 8, the CMAG presented to the PAVN "A Preliminary Proposal Regarding the Political Consolidation of the Army," which outlined the purposes, requirements, and methods of the campaign. In May, the VWP adopted the CMAG's proposal. A wave of political reeducation swept across the units of the PAVN. The method of asking soldiers of poor peasant background to "pour out grievances" against despotic landlords was introduced and proved effective in awakening the class consciousness of the officers and soldiers. The CMAG showed the Chinese movie "The White-Hair Girl," which was about the sufferings of a poor peasant daughter at the hands of a cruel landlord. Many Vietnamese soldiers broke into tears after viewing the sad story of the girl. One soldier was so angry that when the landlord appeared on the screen, he lifted his rifle and shot at him. During the political consolidation campaign, individuals with peasant and worker backgrounds were promoted through the ranks of the PAVN. The campaign increased the morale of Ho's army, preparing them for the coming showdown with the French at Dien Bien Phu.[124]

On the basis of the progress in the campaigns of rent reduction and class-consciousness awakening, the VWP in December 1953 issued the Land Reform Law, which stipulated that in carrying out land reform the party would rely on poor peasants and tenants, unite middle peasants, work with rich peasants, and gradually eliminate the feudal system of exploitation in order to develop production and facilitate the anti-French war. The law included items that protected industry, commerce, and small land renters, and shielded cadres of landlord backgrounds from attack. The law also banned imprisonment, beating, physical torture, and execution. To supervise the implementation of the law, the VWP established the Committee on Land Reform, with Truong Chinh as chairman.[125]

The 1953 land reform measures introduced significant changes both in the existing rural structure and in the VWP. In the implementation of the Land Reform Law in the following two years, not just pro-French or neutral landlords but also those who had been supportive of the Viet Minh, or even had joined the party, were fined, lost property and land, and were occasionally imprisoned or executed.[126] While the land reform was successful in satisfying the need of the poor peasants for land and in rallying them behind the party—as would be demonstrated during the Dien Bien Phu campaign, when over 200,000 peasants carried supplies over mountains and valleys to help the PAVN—it also produced negative consequences for the party. The excessive class struggle and repression during the land reform contradicted the party's united front policy, poisoned the atmosphere, polarized the society, and alienated an important segment of the population. Imbued with Maoist ideological fanaticism, the Chinese advisers were responsible for introducing the drastic method of class struggle into the Vietnamese land reform process. Its negative impact on the Vietnamese land reform was an important reason for the Vietnamese's later criticism of the Chinese model.

By 1953, a close bond had been created between the Chinese and Vietnamese Communist parties. Ho Chi Minh's visit to China and his meetings with Mao and other CCP leaders in 1950 helped establish an intimate relationship between the two revolutionary movements at the highest level. In taking the lead to recognize the DRV, Mao rendered important diplomatic support to Ho's government. By providing advisers and supplies, Beijing greatly improved the Viet Minh's strength in its war against the French.

2 FROM DIEN BIEN PHU TO GENEVA 1953–1954

The Viet Minh advance in the Northwest toward the end of 1952 provided the PAVN a convenient staging area to conduct operations in Laos. In January 1953, Wei Guoqing returned to Beijing to report on his plan for the Laotian campaign. The Chinese adviser intended to help the Pathet Lao create a base area in the northern part of Laos in order to connect that region with Northwest Vietnam. On March 5, Wei went back to Vietnam to help direct the Laotian operation. Between March and April 1953, Giap launched two assaults in northern Laos: one aimed at the royal capital of Luang Prabang, the other directed at the Plain of Jars. In so doing, Giap threatened to take Cambodia from the rear and to torpedo the pacification in South Vietnam. But the PAVN forces encountered strong French resistance. In May, the Viet Minh divisions withdrew due to exhaustion, lack of supplies, and the arrival of the rainy season. They left guerrilla units and political cadres in Laos in anticipation of a future attack and in order to strengthen the Lao Communists.[1]

CONFRONTING THE NAVARRE PLAN

In May, General Henri Navarre assumed command of the French forces in Indochina. To reverse the balance of forces and strengthen the French military position in Indochina, he devised a three-stage strategy: to secure the strategically crucial Red River delta in the fall and winter of 1953–54, to pacify the Communist-controlled areas in central and South Vietnam in the spring of 1954, and to launch a general offensive to pursue and destroy the PAVN main forces in the north. To implement this plan, Navarre requested new units from the French government and expanded the Army of the Republic of Vietnam (ARVN) with U.S. assistance. In September 1953, the Eisenhower administration agreed to provide Paris with an additional $385 million in military aid to help it implement the Navarre plan. (By the time Harry Truman left the White House, the United States was already bearing over 40 percent of the cost of the war.)[2]

The Navarre plan posed a new challenge to the Viet Minh. On August 13, 1953, the VWP sent a cable to the CCP requesting help in "reviewing the situation and working out the direction of the future war effort." In the meantime, the PAVN scrapped its original plan to concentrate on the Northwest and Lai Chau and proposed instead to attack the enemy in the Red River delta. Luo Guibo attended the meeting held by the VWP politburo on August 22, during which Giap talked about operations in the flat area of the delta, ignoring Lai Chau and downplaying the importance of the Laotian campaign. (Wei Guo-qing was back in China at this time.) Luo reported the discussions to Beijing. The CCP leadership sent two telegrams to Luo on August 27 and 29, analyzing the situation in Vietnam since Navarre's arrival and insisting that the PAVN stick to its original plan of focusing on the Northwest and Laos. "By eliminating the enemy in the Lai Chau area, liberating the northern and central parts of Laos, and then expanding the battleground to the southern part of Laos and Cambodia to threaten Saigon," the CCP's August 29 cable pointed out, the VWP could "reduce the supplies of soldiers and money for the puppet army, scatter the French forces . . . expand the PAVN itself, and weaken and annihilate the enemy gradually and separately." If this approach was to be adopted, the leaders in Beijing contended, the Viet Minh could prepare its forces for the later seizure of the Red River delta and the eventual defeat of the French colonial authority in Indochina. For the moment, the Chinese leaders insisted, the Viet Minh should first occupy the Northwest and northern Laos before pushing toward the south.[3]

Accordingly, the Chinese advisers suggested to the PAVN that it select the Northwest as the main theater with the goal of occupying Lai Chau so as to attract French troops and to annihilate them on a terrain favorable to the Viet Minh. The Red River delta, the Chinese advisers insisted, should be a secondary theater, where the Viet Minh could conduct guerrilla assaults to coordinate with operations in the main theater and to lay the foundation for future occupation of Hanoi and Haiphong.[4] Clearly, the Chinese advisers recognized that the Red River delta was not an ideal place for the PAVN to have a major engagement with the French at this time.

In September, the VWP politburo discussed the war plan for the winter of 1953–54. Favoring the Chinese idea, Ho Chi Minh concluded that "the strategic direction remains unchanged," namely, the Viet Minh would concentrate on the Northwest and northern Laos. He vetoed Giap's plan to focus on the Red River delta.[5]

Beijing notified Ho on October 10 that it had appointed Wei Guoqing as general military adviser and Luo Guibo as general political adviser to the Viet Minh.[6] After returning to Vietnam, Wei Guoqing on October 27 reaffirmed Beijing's proposals regarding the Viet Minh's military strategy, handing to Ho Chi Minh a copy of the Navarre plan that China had obtained. After reviewing the French plan, the VWP leader said that the CCP leaders' suggestions were correct and that if the Viet Minh followed them, it could smash the Navarre plan.[7] That Beijing gave a copy of the Navarre plan to Ho indicates the close cooperation in intelligence sharing between the two Communist parties during the First Indochina War.

In mid-November, the PAVN's 316th Division and parts of the 325th and 304th Divisions headed for Lai Chau. In line with the Chinese suggestion of seeking access to South Vietnam via Laos, Ho's government during this time also worked out a road construction plan for 1954. The plan envisioned the building of a number of roads through Laos. But Zhou Enlai found the plan too ambitious. In a telegram to Luo Guibo on December 12, Zhou pointed out that "the number of civilian laborers required by the plan is too large" and that this heavy demand on civilian workers "will increase excessively the burden of the people and undermine production a great deal." Zhou urged the DRV to scale down its plan by concentrating on just the three most important lines, including the one running through Sam Neua.[8]

After receiving intelligence reports about the Viet Minh movement in the direction of Lai Chau, General Navarre decided to occupy Dien Bien Phu, a small valley village in the northwestern highlands of Vietnam, on the road to Luang Prabang. When the news of the French occupation reached Wei Guoqing, he was on his way to the Northwest with the Viet Minh army. After discussing the new situation with other members of the CMAG, Wei proposed to the VWP a campaign to surround and annihilate the French at Dien Bien Phu while continuing the original plan to attack Lai Chau. He also reported his plan to Beijing. Approving Wei's proposal, the CCP Central Military Commission stressed that the Dien Bien Phu campaign would have not only military and political importance but also international consequences. Promising to provide all the weapons that the PAVN required, the Chinese leaders instructed the CMAG to help the VWP leadership "make up its mind" and to assist it in the direction of the campaign.[9]

Clearly, Mao had international diplomacy in mind when he considered military developments in Vietnam. In September 1953, the Communist world had started a peace initiative. On September 28, the Soviet Union had sent a proposal to the United States, France, and Britain, calling for a five-power conference, including China, to examine ways of reducing international tensions. About ten days later, Chinese premier Zhou Enlai had issued a statement supporting the Soviet suggestion. On November 26, Ho Chi Minh had told the Swedish newspaper *Expressen* that he was prepared to negotiate with the French on the Indochina conflict. Mao wanted a victory at Dien Bien Phu in order to strengthen the Communist position at the negotiating table. Accepting the CMAG's proposal, the PAVN command worked out a battle plan for the Dien Bien Phu operation, which was approved by the VWP politburo on December 6. The Dien Bien Phu Campaign Command was subsequently established with Vo Nguyen Giap as commander in chief and Wei Guoqing as general adviser. Ho Chi Minh asked the entire party and the Vietnamese people "to exert all their efforts to ensure the success of the campaign."[10]

In retrospect, the September 1953 meeting of the VWP politburo was a major turning point of the First Indochina War. Given the fact that Navarre's deployment of troops in Dien Bien Phu in November that year was a direct reaction to the Viet Minh push toward Lai Chau and northern Laos, Ho Chi Minh's rejection of Vo Nguyen Giap's plan to concentrate on the Red River delta was crucial. If he had proceeded with Giap's strategy, there would have been no Viet Minh–French showdown at Dien Bien Phu.

SIEGE OF DIEN BIEN PHU

In late November 1953, the Viet Minh 308th Division headed north toward Dien Bien Phu. After occupying Lai Chau on December 13, the 316th Division moved south to complete the encirclement of Dien Bien Phu. In early January 1954, the CMAG decided to launch a swift attack at Dien Bien Phu before the French had firmly established themselves in their positions. At the urging of Chinese advisers, Giap unleashed a "human wave" attack against the French. But the PAVN incurred heavy losses partly because the Viet Minh could not move its artillery pieces to the positions surrounding Dien Bien Phu in time and partly because the French moved more rapidly than expected to increase the size of their force.[11]

In telegrams to Wei Guoqing on January 24 and 27, the CCP Central Military Commission instructed him not to strike the enemy at Dien Bien Phu "from all directions" at the same time but to employ the strategy of "separating and encircling the enemy and then wiping them out bit by bit." "You should strive to eliminate one enemy battalion at a time," the Beijing direction continued. "So long as you can destroy four to five battalions, the enemy at Dien Bien Phu may lose confidence. They may either retreat southward or wait for reinforcements. Either development will be favorable to us." Acting along the line of Beijing's suggestion, the CMAG and the PAVN abandoned the plan for "a quick solution" and opted for "steady progress" by eliminating French perimeter outposts one by one and by wearing down the enemy through attrition and exhaustion.[12]

To break French air superiority and incapacitate the Dien Bien Phu airstrip, China furnished the PAVN with antiaircraft guns. Four Viet Minh battalions that had been undergoing training in China were sent back to the Dien Bien Phu front equipped with 37 mm antiaircraft guns. At Dien Bien Phu, the Chinese applied the sniping and fortification experience they had gained in Korea. They taught the PAVN soldiers how to use snipers to disrupt French troop activity and to undermine the enemy's morale. A dozen Chinese army engineering experts who had fought in Korea were dispatched to Dien Bien Phu to assist in the construction of trenches. The formation of a network of several hundred miles of trenches allowed the Viet Minh assault units to approach the outlying French positions without severe exposure to French firepower. China also supplied large quantities of ammunition to the PAVN for the battle.[13]

While the Viet Minh was tightening up its encirclement of Dien Bien Phu, international preparations were under way for the peace negotiations planned to open at Geneva in early May. In attendance would be diplomats from France, Britain, China, the Soviet Union, the United States, as well as the DRV and the three associated states of Vietnam, Laos, and Cambodia.[14]

While following international events attentively, Mao also watched closely the progress of the Dien Bien Phu campaign. He was keenly aware that Viet Minh victories on the battleground would greatly enhance the Communist bargaining power at the coming peace talks. He was eager to facilitate the Viet Minh progress in military operations. In an April 3 message to Peng Dehuai, deputy chairman of the CCP Central Military Commission, Mao said that the DRV should form two new artillery divisions (including four regiments) and two engineering regiments; these units should complete training and receiving equipment within six months. If there were not enough cannons available, China should transfer artillery pieces from its own troops to equip the Vietnamese units. These new artillery divisions, the CCP leader argued, should be converted from regular Viet Minh infantry divisions rather than drawn from the new recruits. The instructors and advisers for these units should be selected from the Chinese troops that had fought in Korea, and should include division- and army-level cadres. The ideal training site for the proposed Viet Minh units would be in Vietnam, but Guangxi would also be acceptable. Mao asked Peng to discuss the matter with the Chinese General Staff and Artillery Command and to work out plans. With the two new artillery divisions, Mao continued, together with the previously established artillery division and five infantry divisions, the PAVN could attack Hanoi and Haiphong. Mao instructed Peng to make "immediate preparations of *sufficient* ammunition and engineering equipment" (emphasis in the original) for the two new artillery divisions and to increase the supply of antiaircraft guns for the Viet Minh. Regarding the Dien Bien Phu battle, Mao insisted that the fortress "should be conquered resolutely" and that if conditions were ready, the Viet Minh should start a general attack as early as possible.[15]

Mao also made suggestions concerning Viet Minh operations after Dien Bien Phu. In order to make up for the loss of soldiers at Dien Bien Phu, he proposed, the Viet Minh should immediately start mobilizing "at least five to eight thousand new recruits" and train them for three months. After the conclusion of the Dien Bien Phu campaign, the PAVN should rest for one and a half months, two months at most, and then attack Luang Prabang and other locations. "If there are no insurmountable difficulties," Mao asserted, the conquest of those places should be completed during the summer or autumn. After that, the Viet Minh should attack Hanoi in the winter or at the latest in the early spring of next year. Even if the Geneva peace negotiations reached agreement, Mao concluded, his plan for creating new artillery divisions should remain unchanged.[16] Mao's message was important because it demonstrated that he was anxious not only to conquer Dien Bien Phu but also to expand Ho's victory by liberating Hanoi. Like his management of the Korean War, Mao here again displayed his penchant for paying attention not only to the general strategy but also to tactical details in directing military operations.[17]

In a message of April 17 to Huang Kecheng and Su Yu, both deputy chiefs of staff, Mao further ordered: "Given the possibility of a cease-fire in Vietnam, the training for the new artillery divisions should not be conducted within China, and artillery pieces should be shipped to Vietnam as early as possible."[18] It is clear from this message that Mao followed closely international developments when he was considering the military situation in Vietnam. His sensitivity to the political dimensions of warfare stemmed from his experience with the CCP's armed struggle for survival and power during the preceding three decades.

During the final phase of the campaign in April, however, some PAVN officers wavered in their resolve to occupy Dien Bien Phu partly because of the exhaustion of their troops and the coming monsoon season and partly because of the threat of American air intervention made by Admiral Arthur Radford, chairman of the U.S. Joint Chiefs of Staff.[19] The crisis at Dien Bien Phu had made the French desperate for U.S. assistance. During his visit to Washington in late March, General Paul Ely, French chief of staff, had requested the transfer of additional U.S. airplanes to be used by the French for assaults on Viet Minh positions around Dien Bien Phu. Radford had given Ely the impression that the Eisenhower administration would approve the plan originally devised by French and American officers in Saigon, which called for an intervention by American B-29s, possibly employing tactical nuclear bombs, to relieve the encirclement of Dien Bien Phu. In fact, this proposal had received little support in Washington.[20]

The CMAG and the PAVN command were concerned by the lack of resolve among the Viet Minh troops. After analyzing the situation, Wei Guoqing and the Viet Minh leaders felt that the true purpose of Washington's threat was to compel the Viet Minh to withdraw from Dien Bien Phu. If the Viet Minh did so, they reasoned, the French would surely seize the chance to counterattack, which would produce serious consequences. It was agreed that since the Viet Minh army was ready for the final assault at Dien Bien Phu, it should not abandon the effort at the last minute. On April 19, the VWP politburo held a meeting discussing the problem of lack of confidence among some cadres. Pointing out the favorable conditions the previous operations had created for the final conquest of Dien Bien Phu, the VWP leadership urged its troops to keep confidence in the eventual victory over the French. The party decided to launch the general offensive before the arrival of the rainy season.[21]

The looming prospect of the peace conference at Geneva made a decisive Viet Minh success at Dien Bien Phu ever more pressing. In fact, by mid-April, the Viet Minh's approach of "steady attack and steady advance" had proved successful. It increased French casualties and paralyzed the Dien Bien Phu airfield, forcing the French to rely on airlift for supplies and making the garrison of 12,000 men isolated and vulnerable.[22] To facilitate the Viet Minh's final strike, China provided more logistical support. Two Viet Minh battalions equipped with 75 mm recoilless cannons and "Katyusha" multitube rocket launchers arrived at Dien Bien Phu from China on the eve of the final attack. The CCP Central Military Commission instructed the CMAG "not to spare artillery shells" in order to achieve "a total victory."[23] On May 1, the PAVN launched the final offensive, and six days later, on May 7, the last French stronghold at Dien Bien Phu capitulated. After the conclusion of the Dien Bien Phu battle, world attention immediately shifted to Geneva, where the next day the Indochina phase of the conference was scheduled to open.

ZHOU ENLAI AND THE GENEVA CONFERENCE

When Mao established the PRC in October 1949, he had planned to complete several nationalist and revolutionary goals: to unify China's territories, including Taiwan, and to transform the country economically, politically, and socially into a fully developed socialist state. But the Korean War disrupted his plans. The war had a great sobering effect on the Chinese leader, who learned that any violent effort to alter the international balance of power would encounter firm resistance by the United States and its allies. The war inflicted heavy damages on Chinese forces and exposed glaring weaknesses in their military technology and organization. With the conclusion of the Korean conflict in July 1953, Mao was eager to reduce tensions in Asia and to concentrate on the implementation of the First Five-Year Plan at home. The urgent domestic agenda and the realization of the power of the United States combined to force Mao to settle for a peaceful international environment. Accordingly, the Chinese government responded positively to the Soviet proposal of September 28, 1953, that called for an international meeting to settle international disputes.[24]

China attached great importance to the Geneva Conference. Within Mao's framework of reducing tensions in Asia through consultations and negotiations, Zhou Enlai brought his diplomatic skills into full play. Under his direction and supervision, the Chinese Foreign Ministry on March 2, 1954, prepared the "Preliminary Paper on the Estimation of and the Preparation for the Geneva Conference," which contended that China should take advantage of the differences between the United States, France, and Britain over the Indochina issue and try to reach agreements, even temporary ones. After noting that restoring peace in Indochina might require a long-term struggle, the document contended that China should strive to avoid a fruitless conference. A situation of negotiation in the midst of fighting, the document concluded, would increase internal difficulties within France and intensify the French-American conflicts, thus proving beneficial to the development of the liberation struggle of the Indochinese people. The CCP leadership approved the document.[25]

Zhou Enlai assembled a Chinese delegation that included almost all the senior and experienced CCP diplomats. He entrusted Li Kenong, deputy foreign minister, and Wang Bingnan, director of the General Office of the Foreign Ministry, to select participants and to draft principles, regulations, and background reports for the delegation. While organizing cadres to study the history and politics of Korea and Indochina as well as the policies of the United States, France, and Britain, Zhou also recalled Qiao Guanhua and Huang Hua from the Chinese negotiating team at Panmunjom to Beijing in early March so that they could contribute their knowledge and expertise in international negotiations to the Geneva delegation. Huang was appointed spokesman for the Chinese delegation. In order to ensure that Huang would be able to handle different questions that were likely to arise at the conference, a mock press meeting was held to test the appropriateness of his answers.[26]

With the Korean War lesson in mind, Zhou Enlai in early March sent a telegram to the CMAG asking them to organize and win several battles so that the Communist delegates at the Geneva Conference could "obtain diplomatic initiative."[27] In mid-March, Zhou also cabled Ho Chi Minh urging him to begin preparations for the conference and to consider the issue of the demarcation line in case of a cease-fire. "The current international situation and the military development in Vietnam," Zhou remarked, "are advantageous for the DRV to conduct diplomatic struggle. No matter what results will come out of the Geneva Conference, we should actively participate in it just the same." As to the question of the dividing line, the Chinese premier stated that "if a cease-fire is achieved, it is better to have a relatively fixed demarcation line so that [the DRV] can keep a relatively complete area." The site of the demarcation line, Zhou continued, would be determined by two factors: its advantage to the DRV and its acceptability to the enemy. "The farther south the line is drawn, the better," Zhou said. "The sixteenth parallel can be considered as one possible choice." Zhou concluded his message by inviting Ho to come to Beijing for consultation in late March or early April and to travel to Moscow to exchange views with the Soviet leadership.[28]

In March, the VWP politburo held three meetings to discuss the principles and policies to be adopted at the Geneva Conference. The meetings concluded that it would be beneficial to divide Vietnam into the northern and southern parts. Considering the successful siege of Dien Bien Phu, the party leaders concluded that where to draw the dividing line would depend on the development of the military situation and that the farther south the line was drawn, the better. The meeting decided that Pham Van Dong would lead the DRV delegation to the conference.[29]

In late March, Ho Chi Minh and Pham Van Dong visited Beijing to hold discussions with CCP leaders. After analyzing the current international situation and examining the military development in Vietnam, Mao, Liu Shaoqi, and Zhou Enlai urged the Vietnamese visitors to do their utmost to achieve results at Geneva.[30] On March 31, the CCP politburo convened an expanded meeting to hear Zhou's report on China's preparation for the Geneva Conference. Approving the report, the meeting authorized Zhou to travel to Moscow to discuss with Soviet leaders issues concerning the conference.[31]

Zhou Enlai made three visits to Moscow in April. On April 1, Zhou, together with Ho Chi Minh and Pham Van Dong, flew to Moscow, where they conducted discussions with Nikita Khrushchev and Soviet foreign minister Vyacheslav Molotov. The Soviet Union had only limited interest in Indochina and was primarily concerned with wooing France to reject the European Defense Community. To the Soviet leadership, the opportunity to undermine the plan for German rearmament was more important than the continuation of a revolutionary war in Southeast Asia. While the Soviets and the Chinese shared the goal of ending the war in Indochina, they held different expectations about the Geneva Conference. Appearing more pessimistic, Khrushchev contended that people should not place too much hope on the conference because it might not be able to solve any problem and that the outcome of the meeting could hardly be anticipated. Zhou argued that China's, the Democratic People's Republic of Korea's, and the DRV's participation in the international conference was in itself a matter of extraordinary significance. "Although we should not have excessive expectations from the conference," the Chinese premier continued, "we must strive to achieve some results. It is possible to do so. It is not an illusion. We must recognize that imperialist countries are undergoing a hard time." Zhou told the Soviet leaders that China wanted to maintain close contacts with the Soviet Union, which included exchanging of views, intelligence sharing, and policy coordination, because Geneva was the first international conference for the PRC, which lacked knowledge and experience in international politics. He also asked the Soviet Foreign Ministry to inform the Chinese delegation in detail of the origins of the Geneva Conference. The Soviets satisfied Zhou's requests.[32]

After completing the first visit to the Soviet Union, Zhou returned to Beijing to report to the Chinese leadership on his trip. Several days later, he went to Moscow again to hold further talks with Soviet officials regarding conference strategy as well as the composition of the Chinese and Soviet delegations. Molotov informed Zhou how the Soviet Union had selected its delegation, which included experts in various fields. So the Chinese delegation also included people with diverse areas of expertise.[33] Zhou even included two master cooks in the delegation so that at Geneva he could hold Chinese banquets to "make friends."[34]

On April 19, the Chinese delegation was announced, with Zhou Enlai as chief representative and Deputy Foreign Ministers Zhang Wentian, Wang Jiaxiang, and Li Kenong as representatives. The CCP leadership gave the delegation the following instructions: first, exercise active diplomacy at Geneva in order to break the American policy of isolation and embargo against China and to reduce world tensions; and second, try to conclude agreements so as to set a precedent for solving international problems through great-power consultations.[35] In a speech to the Chinese delegation on the same day, Zhou Enlai emphasized the importance of discipline and cooperation at Geneva. He employed the analogy of informal and formal plays to describe the difference between the CCP's negotiation experience in the past and the forthcoming meeting at Geneva. He compared the party's previous negotiations with Chiang Kai-shek and the Americans to an informal play, a "rude performance" not conducted on a formal stage. The Geneva Conference, on the other hand, was a formal international meeting. "We are going to be present on the international stage," Zhou stressed. China must produce "a civilized play," "a formal play" that was performed on the stage.[36] Zhou's use of the metaphor of formal and informal plays reflected his earlier interest in drama when he was a student at Nankai Middle School in Tianjin.

Zhou made his third visit to Moscow on April 21, when he was en route to Geneva, leading the Chinese delegation. In order to familiarize the Chinese with the usual proceedings of an international meeting, Molotov asked Andrei Gromyko, Soviet deputy foreign minister, to talk to the Chinese delegation about Soviet experiences in international gatherings, including the techniques of preventing conversations being bugged by the enemy. Ho Chi Minh and Pham Van Dong, also in Moscow at the time, participated in the Sino-Soviet discussions. After the talks, the Chinese and Soviet delegations left Moscow for Geneva separately. Zhou's arrival at the Geneva airport on April 24 was a media sensation.[37]

The Korean session of the Geneva Conference did not produce any agreement largely because the contending sides had different views about the role of the United Nations in the political settlement of the dispute. The South Koreans, backed by the United States, insisted on using the international organization to supervise the postwar election in Korea. China rejected UN authority over collective security in Korea, stressing the international role of neutral countries. To the Chinese, the United Nations was not an impartial force because it had been used by the United States to condemn China as an "aggressor" in Korea.[38]

It was during the Indochina session that Zhou Enlai found more opportunities to prove himself a skillful diplomat. China's basic objective was to prevent the internationalization of the Indochina conflict, as had happened in Korea. There were both internal and external reasons for this position. Domestically, China needed to concentrate on its plan to rehabilitate the economy, a process that had been disrupted and postponed by the Korean War. According to Khrushchev, Zhou Enlai told him in Moscow before the Geneva Conference that China could not meet Ho Chi Minh's demands to send Chinese troops to Vietnam. The Chinese premier claimed: "We've already lost too many men in Korea—that war cost us dearly. We're in no condition to get involved in another war at this time."[39]

Internationally, the Chinese leaders were apprehensive about the possibility of U.S. intervention in Indochina. They believed that Washington, determined to torpedo the Geneva Conference, was looking for opportunities to move into Southeast Asia.[40] China's concern with American intentions was clearly revealed in Zhou Enlai's conversation with the Indian ambassador to China on April 19, 1954. The Chinese premier contended that Washington's primary goal was to prevent a cease-fire in Indochina because if peace was restored there, the United States would lose an excuse to make war in Asia. At the moment, Zhou went on, the Americans were putting pressure on France not to reach agreement on Indochina. After assailing U.S. secretary of state John Foster Dulles's "united action" proposal, Zhou called the Indian ambassador's attention to U.S. vice president Richard Nixon's statement that if the French troops withdrew from Indochina, U.S. forces must move in. Zhou asserted that the United States wanted to create a colonial empire over the peoples of Southeast Asia, the Middle and Near East, as well as the Far East.[41] Zhou was referring to the speech that Nixon had made on April 16 to a conference of newspaper editors in Washington. Nixon contended that it was crucial to keep Indochina and that if it was necessary to send U.S. troops, Washington "must face up to the situation and dispatch forces."[42] It is clear that Zhou took Dulles's and Nixon's bluster and threats seriously.

Qian Jiadong, an official in the Asian Department of the Foreign Ministry and a member of the Chinese delegation to the Geneva Conference, later recalled that China's major concern in 1954 was that "after the DRV drove the French out, the United States would come in. Therefore, it would be better to stop the war for the moment and rest for a few years before completing unification."[43]

In the course of the conference, the Chinese media repeatedly condemned "the American plot of organizing a Southeast Asian military bloc" in order to "use Asians to fight Asians." A May 20 editorial in *Shijie zhishi* (World Knowledge) contended that "the ruling clique in the United States is carrying out a policy of establishing new colonial authority in Asia" to replace the old imperial powers such as Britain, France, and the Netherlands. Another commentary in the same journal two weeks later asserted that the plan to create a military organization in Southeast Asia was part of Washington's general policy of establishing a new colonial empire, which resembled the "Greater East Asian Co-prosperity Sphere" advocated by Japan during World War II.[44]

Finally, a moderate policy in Indochina was in line with Beijing's new diplomatic emphasis on peaceful coexistence. Zhou Enlai had first mentioned the "Five Principles of Peaceful Coexistence"—mutual respect for territorial integrity and sovereignty, nonaggression, noninterference in each other's internal affairs, equality and mutual benefit, and peaceful coexistence—during the meeting with an Indian delegation on December 31, 1953.[45] Chinese leaders had contended that the Five Principles were applicable not only to Sino-Indian relations but also to international affairs in general. The Geneva Conference provided China a good opportunity to enhance its international prestige and increase influence among the neutral nations in Asia by playing the role of peacemaker. Beijing insistently claimed that it was speaking for all Asia. During the break between sessions of the Geneva Conference, Zhou Enlai visited New Delhi and Rangoon in June, and in the ensuing Sino-Indian and Sino-Burmese agreements, the "Five Principles of Peaceful Coexistence" were officially evoked.[46]

With the strategy of avoiding an extension of the Indochina conflict and denying the United States the chance to intervene, Zhou Enlai engaged in active diplomacy, displaying an unexpected flexibility. His approach was to win over the majority of the participants, including France, and to isolate the United States. His job was made easier by the Viet Minh victory at Dien Bien Phu, which made the French all the more eager to extract themselves from Indochina. As Wang Bingnan later recalled, when the news of Dien Bien Phu came, "we spread it to each other. We were very much encouraged and felt more confident in solving the Indochina issue."[47]

In response to what China perceived as the American strategy of "using Asians to fight Asians," Zhou Enlai employed his "Five Principles of Peaceful Coexistence." At the third plenary session on Indochina on May 12, Zhou stated:

Asian countries must mutually respect each other's independence and sovereignty and not interfere in each other's internal affairs; they must solve their disputes through peaceful negotiation and not through threats and military force; they must establish normal economic and cultural relations on the basis of equality and mutual benefit and disallow discrimination and limitation. Only in this way can the Asian countries avoid the neocolonialist exploitation of the unprecedented catastrophe of Asians fighting Asians and achieve peace and security.[48]

The historian King Chen has summarized Zhou's three contributions to the conclusion of the Geneva Conference: first, he persuaded the DRV to withdraw its troops from Laos and Cambodia; second, he obtained Ho Chi Minh's consent to proceed with the general peace plan at Geneva; and third, he resolved the issue of the composition of the International Supervision Commission.[49] Recently released Chinese sources throw new light on Zhou's role in settling the Laotian and Cambodian questions and in persuading the North Vietnamese to accept the seventeenth parallel as the demarcation line.

Before coming to Geneva, the Chinese officials had had little knowledge about the conditions in Laos and Cambodia, maintaining no contact with the royal governments in Vientiane and Phnom Penh. Beijing had only kept relations with the DRV. At the beginning of the conference, the Chinese delegates were shocked and annoyed when Phoui Sananikone and Tep Phan, the representatives of the Royal Lao and Cambodian delegations, respectively, accused China of practicing imperialism and using the DRV to commit aggression against their countries.[50] Zhou Enlai subsequently asked Shi Zhe and Wang Bingnan to talk with the Laotian and Cambodian delegates to find out the situations in their countries. With the new knowledge, Zhou immediately adjusted China's policy toward Laos and Cambodia.[51]

In an internal meeting with the Chinese delegation on July 12, Zhou pointed out that there were clear national boundaries between the three Indochinese countries. Laos and Cambodia, Zhou continued, were different from Vietnam. While the DRV was a revolutionary state with a Communist party leading the struggle, Laos and Cambodia were basically nationalist countries, where the royal governments were still popular and recognized by several dozens of countries in the world. The anti-French movements in Laos and Cambodia were primarily the creation of the Viet Minh, and the revolutionary forces there were small and occupied little territory.[52] Clearly, Zhou was prepared to treat the kingdoms of Laos and Cambodia as separate and independent from Vietnam. It is possible that he was uneasy with the prospect of Vietnam inheriting the full writ of French imperialism.

The Geneva Conference reached a deadlock in mid-June over the treatment of Laos and Cambodia because the Western delegates insisted that the Viet Minh troops withdraw from those two countries while the DRV representatives denied the presence of their troops there. At this juncture, Zhou Enlai stepped in to remove the obstacle. To prevent American intervention, he was ready to compromise on the Laotian and Cambodian issue. On June 15, the Chinese, DRV, and Soviet delegations held a joint meeting. After pointing out that the key question at the current phase of the negotiations was whether the DRV admitted the presence of its troops in Laos and Cambodia, Zhou argued: "If we do not admit this fact, then there is no way to continue the discussion on the Laotian and Cambodian questions, which in turn will undermine the negotiations on the Vietnam issue. Therefore, we must admit that Vietnamese volunteers once fought in Laos and Cambodia." The advantage of making such a concession, Zhou contended, was that the DRV could later demand a compensation from France when the negotiations moved on to the agenda of the demarcation line in Vietnam. Molotov agreed with Zhou's analysis. After considerable rethinking, Pham Van Dong also accepted Zhou's idea.[53] For Zhou, the term "volunteers" was a euphemism for troops.

In a meeting with British foreign secretary Anthony Eden the following morning, Zhou said that the DRV would respect the independence and sovereignty of Laos and Cambodia and that China could recognize the governments of the Lao and Cambodian kingdoms. In the past, the Chinese premier admitted, Vietnamese volunteers had conducted military operations in those two countries. Some of them had already been pulled back, Zhou continued. If there were still Vietnamese volunteers in Laos and Cambodia, the method of withdrawing all foreign military personnel could be applied to them.[54] Satisfied with Zhou's explanation, Eden later wrote that he obtained the "strong impression that Chou wanted a settlement."[55]

During the restricted session in the afternoon, Zhou presented a formal proposal for the withdrawal of the Viet Minh troops from Laos and Cambodia.[56] The participants from other countries welcomed Zhou's proposal. Walter Bedell Smith, the U.S. delegation head, stated that the Chinese suggestion was worthy of study. The Western media commented positively on Zhou's proposal and viewed it as an advance in the conference. Following Zhou's move, Pham Van Dong for the first time acknowledged the royal governments of Laos and Cambodia and abandoned his earlier demand for the seating at the conference of the two "resistance governments" of Khmer and Pathet Lao. At the restricted session the following day, the DRV chief delegate admitted that the Viet Minh "volunteers army" had fought in Laos and Cambodia but contended that it had already been pulled back. He added, nevertheless, that "if there are still some troops staying there, they should also be withdrawn." On July 19, a cease-fire agreement for Laos and Cambodia was concluded.[57] Zhou's adroit diplomacy helped move the negotiations at Geneva forward. To achieve his primary objective of denying the United States any excuse to establish bases in Laos and Cambodia, Zhou was willing to bargain away the Viet Minh–supported local Communist position in those countries.

With the stalemate over the Laotian and Cambodian questions removed, Zhou concentrated on the Vietnam issue. The recent change of government in Paris provided hope for progress in the negotiation. On June 16, Pierre Mendès-France was elected premier in France. During the election campaign he had promised that he would secure a settlement of the Indochina dispute by July 20 or resign. In a telegram to Mao and Liu Shaoqi on June 19, Zhou said: "If we can put forward a reasonable and detailed proposal in the military talks, we can strive to settle the problem with France rapidly and conclude a cease-fire. In this way, we can encourage the new French government to resist American intervention and delay the issue of the European army [referring to the

European Defense Community]. It will be helpful to both the East and the West." Zhou proposed to talk with the VWP leadership directly in southern China to explain his positions after his visit to India.[58] Beijing approved Zhou's proposal.[59]

According to Shi Zhe, the Chinese initially were not sure of Mendès-France's intentions regarding Indochina, and Zhou decided to visit him. On June 23, the two leaders met in Berne, Switzerland. From this discussion, Zhou learned that France was very tired of the Indochina war and that domestic antiwar sentiment was high. The French government was anxious to withdraw from Indochina, but it wanted to do so "gracefully in appearance." In this way, Mendès-France hoped to consolidate his power at home.[60] According to American documents, Zhou dominated the conversation during his talk with Mendès-France. The French side detected "a considerable advance over Zhou's previous position." By acknowledging the presence of two governments in the territory of Vietnam, the Chinese premier for the first time "recognized the valid existence" of the government of the Republic of Vietnam. Mendès-France told Zhou that negotiations with the Viet Minh had been "at a practical standstill for the past week or ten days" and that he wanted the Chinese leader to talk to the head of the DRV delegation in order to speed up things. Zhou agreed to intervene with the Viet Minh and ask them to make progress in negotiations.[61] In a private talk with Chinese officials regarding his impression of Mendès-France, Zhou commented that the French leader was frank and could be counted as a friend. The Chinese premier believed that peace in Indochina could be realized in the hands of Mendès-France.[62]

Zhou Enlai saw an opportunity in French distress to reach agreement at Geneva. After the meeting with the French prime minister, Zhou reported his findings on the French situation to Pham Van Dong, asking him not to "haggle over" (jijiao) the sixteenth or seventeenth parallel. Giving Mendès-France a way to save face would be a small price to pay for his withdrawal of French troops. Zhou went on, "After French withdrawal, the whole of Vietnam will be yours."[63] Clearly, Zhou considered the acceptance of the seventeenth parallel as a temporary tactical concession on the part of the Viet Minh. In his view, when the French troops were no longer in Vietnam, the DRV would be able to unify the country.

Zhou held discussions with Ho Chi Minh and Vo Nguyen Giap in Liuzhou, a city in southern China, from July 3 to July 5. Giap began the conversation with a description of the military situation in Indochina. When Zhou asked, "If the United States does not intervene and France continues the war by increasing troops, how long will it take us to win the entire Indochina?," the PAVN commander replied that it would take two to three years. Ho added that if the United States stayed away from intervention, it would take "at least three to five years" to defeat the French.[64]

After the initial discussion of the military situation, Zhou Enlai went on to elaborate on the political and international consequences of war and peace in Indochina, especially their effects on Southeast Asia, on U.S. relations with its allies, and on the Bao Dai government. Zhou first admitted that China was ignorant about the conditions in Laos and Cambodia: "Indochina consists of three countries. But in the past we thought there was only one country there. . . . In fact, all three countries are national states. They have remained this way for the past several thousand years. We had not realized this until we arrived in Geneva." He then asserted that Laos and Cambodia could be united through peace and that war could only push them onto the side of the United States. The same was true for Southeast Asia, South Asia, and the western Pacific, Zhou continued. Stressing that the Indochina issue could affect Burma, Thailand, Malaya, Indonesia, Pakistan, India, Australia, New Zealand, Ceylon, and the Philippines, Zhou quoted Mao as saying that if not cautiously handled, the issue could "impact ten countries with a total population of 600 million people." If the Viet Minh maintained a good relationship with Laos, Cambodia, and the other states in Southeast Asia, Zhou explained, countries like India, Burma, and Indonesia would not object to the control of all of Vietnam by the DRV, and conditions would be ripe to unify Vietnam through elections. Speaking of U.S. intentions in Indochina, Zhou asserted that Washington might invade Vietnam rather than China. Therefore, it would be better to win Vietnam through peace. The Dien Bien Phu battle and the international situation made it easy for the Viet Minh to secure the Red River delta.[65]

As to the effects of war and peace on U.S. relations with its allies, Zhou argued that peace could increase conflicts between the United States and France and the United States and Britain and that war could cause the collapse of the Mendès-France government and push Washington and London together to make the Southeast Asian Treaty Organization (SEATO). In terms of the effects of war and peace on the Saigon regime, Zhou contended that peace might divide Emperor Bao Dai and his rival Ngo Dinh Diem by making Bao Dai reluctant to align himself with the United States and pushing him to purge Diem, while war could not achieve the purpose of eliminating Bao Dai and Diem. Zhou insisted that peace was beneficial to all sides and would isolate the United States. Turning to specific proposals to end the war, the Chinese premier said that the sixteenth parallel could be the dividing line, but if this was unacceptable, the RC9 (Route Coloniale 9), which was close to the seventeenth parallel, could be used as the alternative dividing line.[66]

Ho Chi Minh agreed with Zhou's speech: "We must help Mendès-France and prevent him from stepping down. This will be helpful to us. We must have good talks with France to obtain peace before U.S. November elections take place because the United States has misgivings about intervention. After November, we are not certain what its position will be. Vietnam is at a crossroad of peace and war. Our main direction is to win peace and prepare for war." The VWP leader recognized the unpopularity of a divided peace in Vietnam and stressed that the party leadership needed to "change the minds of senior cadres." Anticipating the problems related to the future takeover of Hanoi and Haiphong, Ho mentioned that the party must begin to prepare cadres. In this regard, he also asked the Chinese for assistance.[67] Ho's remarks are important because they demonstrate that he shared China's fears about American intervention in Vietnam.

The VWP politburo informed Pham Van Dong of the conclusions of the Liuzhou meeting in a directive titled "July 5 Document." The document instructed him to adopt an active position at the negotiations by proposing: (1) to end the war with the sixteenth parallel as the dividing line if possible; but considering the fact that France would not compromise on this point because the RC9 north of the sixteenth parallel was a crucial Laotian outlet to the sea, to be prepared to adjust policies regarding the dividing line; (2) to designate Sam Neua and Phong Saly, the two Laotian provinces close to China and Vietnam, as the regroupment zones for the Pathet Lao; and (3) to reach a political solution in Cambodia.[68]

On July 6 Zhou Enlai returned to Beijing and spoke the next day at an enlarged session of the politburo about the Geneva negotiations and his talks with the VWP leaders in Liuzhou. "The principles we have adopted at the [Geneva] Conference," Zhou asserted, "are to unite with France, Britain, Southeast Asian countries, and the three Indochinese states—that is to unite with all the international forces that can be united with—to isolate the United States and to limit and break the American plan for expanding its world hegemony. The key issue is to achieve peace in Indochina." After reviewing the progress at the conference over the previous two months, Zhou claimed that those achievements had helped reduce tensions in the world and "have blocked the U.S. plan to expand its world domination." He predicted that there was a great possibility of realizing a cease-fire in Indochina and concluding an agreement at Geneva. Mao commended Zhou on his work at Geneva.[69]

On his way back to Geneva on July 10, Zhou stopped in Moscow to confer with Georgi Malenkov, chairman of the Council of Ministers, and other Soviet leaders. They shared China's view that it was time to conclude a settlement at Geneva while Mendès-France was still in office. The United States was putting pressure on the French leader, the Soviets believed; if the Viet Minh insisted on

Mendès-France accepting "unacceptable" demands, the Americans would take advantage of this, the prowar faction within France would gain the upper hand, and the Mendès-France government would collapse. This would be detrimental both to the solution of the Indochina conflict and to the welfare of the DRV.[70]

Arriving in Geneva on July 12, Zhou Enlai called a meeting of the Chinese delegation. Li Kenong reported on the Geneva negotiations during Zhou's absence, and Zhang Wentian said that Pham Van Dong, reluctant to follow the VWP "July 5 Document," insisted on the fourteenth or fifteenth parallel as the demarcation line. Commending Li and Zhang for their work, Zhou stated that the United States was isolated on the Indochina issue and wanted to carry out its "global strategy of containing Communism" by expanding the Indochina war. After noting Washington's pressure on Mendès-France not to make concessions at Geneva, Zhou insisted that the Communist side should help the French prime minister resist the United States.[71]

As to Pham Van Dong's reluctance to make compromises at the negotiations, Zhou said that "it is possible to achieve victory by continuing the war but that will take a long and hard struggle. Furthermore, we have to be prepared for the U.S. expansion of the war. Therefore, peace will be more helpful because we can have an opportunity to consolidate and develop our forces in order to make further progress later on." Zhou then went on to criticize Dong for advocating the "Indochina Federation," which, he maintained, was a serious infringement on the sovereignty and independence of Laos and Cambodia. The conditions for revolution in those two countries were not ripe, Zhou concluded, and "revolution cannot be exported." Stressing that the neutrality of Laos and Cambodia should be encouraged, Zhou decided that Dong needed to be persuaded further.[72]

Clearly, the Chinese diplomats were apprehensive about Vietnamese intentions to create a military bloc of all three Indochinese countries after the ouster of the French from the region. They resented the Vietnamese attempt to subordinate the interests of Laos and Cambodia to those of the DRV. Although the ICP had been dissolved in 1951 and separate Communist organizations had been established in Laos and Cambodia, Vietnamese strategic thinking remained unchanged. In devising strategic plans, the Vietnamese continued to consider Indochina as a single critical space. This habit of thinking had a French root. During French colonial rule, Paris treated the region as one strategic unit, always connecting Laos and Cambodia to the defense of Vietnam. The French control of Cambodia in 1863 was intended primarily to safeguard their colony in Cochin China, and Paris's domination of Laos, achieved between 1893 and 1907, was designed similarly to defend their Tonkin and Annamese protectorates.[73]

After the meeting with the Chinese delegation, Zhou Enlai notified Molotov of his plan to talk with Pham Van Dong. He hoped to persuade the DRV leader to make a new proposal at the negotiations that would help Mendès-France and frustrate U.S. secretary of state John Foster Dulles's policy of undermining the Geneva Conference. The Soviet foreign minister fully supported Zhou's idea. During the discussion with Dong on the evening of July 12, Zhou reiterated the conclusions of the Liuzhou meeting, using the Korean War as an example to warn the DRV chief negotiator of the consequences of American intervention. To convince Dong to abandon Viet Minh areas in southern Vietnam, Zhou cited the CCP experience during the anti-Japanese war and the Chinese civil war to highlight the dialectical relationship between retreat and advance.[74] Realizing that Dong still had doubts about the Geneva negotiations, Ho Chi Minh cabled him on July 15, urging him to proceed at Geneva in accordance with the "July 5 Document."[75] Pressured by Zhou and Ho, Dong finally gave up his stiff position.

The Geneva Accords of 1954 reflected the moderating influence of the Chinese and Soviet delegations. Vietnam was to be divided temporarily along the seventeenth parallel to allow the regrouping of military forces from both sides. The country was to be neutralized, and neither side was to enter a military alliance. Elections were to be held in July 1956 under the supervision of an international commission composed of Canadian, Indian, and Polish representatives. The accords also made cease-fire arrangements for Laos and Cambodia. The Viet Minh forces were to leave Laos and Cambodia, and French forces were to vacate all three countries. The Pathet Lao forces were to be regrouped in Sam Neua and Phong Saly. Laos and Cambodia were not to enter military alliances or permit foreign bases on their soil except in cases where their security was clearly threatened.[76]

The Viet Minh accepted the solution reluctantly. As Wang Bingnan admitted, "Some people in the DRV hoped to unify the whole of Vietnam at one stroke."[77] Ho Chi Minh must have realized that without Chinese and Soviet assistance, he could not have defeated the French and achieved the position he now had. He could not afford to resist the pressure of his two Communist allies. On the other hand, the VWP leader no doubt had every reason to believe, as did Zhou Enlai and Molotov, that all Vietnam would be his in two years.

To the surprise and disappointment of the three Communist countries, Diem consolidated his regime in South Vietnam with the assistance of the United States. When the time came for the national election on reunification in accordance with the Geneva Accords, Saigon refused to participate on the ground that a free vote was impossible in North Vietnam. Furthermore, Diem claimed that his government was not bound by the Geneva Accords since it had not signed them.

It is likely that Zhou's pressure at Geneva alienated Pham Van Dong and other DRV negotiators and probably rekindled long-term suspicions among the Vietnamese that China harbored its own ambitions in Indochina. For the Vietnamese Communists, the Geneva Conference served as a lesson about the nature and limits of Communist internationalism. For the moment they suppressed their resentment in order to maintain close relations with their ally, but the seeds of later disputes were sowed at Geneva.[78]

ASSESSING CHINA'S ROLE IN THE FIRST INDOCHINA WAR

Why did the Viet Minh prevail over the French during the First Indochina War? Some historians stress French mistakes and stupidity—the reluctance to give adequate autonomy to moderate political groups, to understand the nature of political and social transformation in a traditional rural society in transition, and to provide sufficient aid to the French military commander in the field.[79] Other scholars point to the importance of the popular support that Ho Chi Minh enjoyed among the Vietnamese people.[80] Still other writers attribute the party's strength to its policy of terrorism and its sophisticated organization.[81]

While Beijing's support for Ho's party has been acknowledged in the past, it has not rested on careful documentary evidence, primarily because of the lack of Chinese sources. The narrative presented here so far has demonstrated that China played an important role in the Viet Minh victory over the French. Between 1950 and 1954, Beijing sent some of its most capable generals to Vietnam as military and political advisers; they helped the DRV professionalize and politicize its army, reorganize its administrative structure, establish a sound financial policy, and mobilize the masses. The Chinese military advisers actually planned and often helped direct Viet Minh operations, and there was a direct transmission of strategy and tactics from China to Vietnam. The CMAG contributed greatly to the success of the border, Northwest, and Dien Bien Phu engagements. Chen Geng's leadership proved indispensable to Ho's triumph, especially during the border operation in 1950, when the Viet Minh force was still poorly organized and its commanders inexperienced.

The CMAG certainly made errors in advising the PAVN. In early 1951, it encouraged Giap to attack French strongholds in the Red River delta, causing heavy casualties for the Viet Minh force. In the initial phase of the Dien Bien Phu campaign, Chinese advisers used poor judgment by asking the Viet Minh to launch an all-out assault against the French. They miscalculated the strength of the enemy. Despite these occasional misjudgments, China's strategy and tactics in general proved successful in Vietnam.

A comparison of the French Indochina War with the British Malayan War further illustrates the importance of China's support. Both Ho Chi Minh's struggle and the Malayan conflict were Communist insurrections waged to destroy colonialism and to realize socialism. Both became entangled in the emerging Cold War. Although the British and the French used similar methods in suppressing the insurgents, London succeeded in crushing the Malayan rebellion. One crucial reason for the British success was that the Malayan rebels were isolated and did not receive massive Chinese assistance as the Viet Minh did.[82] It is true that the Vietnamese won the First Indochina War because, as a French survivor of Dien Bien Phu admitted later on, "they were fighting for an ideal."[83] They were fighting for a just cause: national independence. But it is also true that without China's assistance the Vietnamese could not have defeated the French as soon as they did.

Despite overall CCP–Viet Minh cooperation and solidarity between 1950 and 1954, there were also problems between the two parties. The relationship between Chinese advisers and the Viet Minh troops was not always characterized by cordiality and trust. In his diary, Chen Geng described Giap as "slippery and not very upright and honest." According to Chen, Giap once complained to Chen about Luo Guibo's criticism of him, but in Luo's presence, Giap always showed intimacy and warmth. "The greatest shortcoming of the Vietnamese Communists," Chen wrote, "was their fear of letting other people know their weaknesses. They lacked Bolshevist self-criticism." Giap, Chen felt, was the most notable example of this. Chen said that he had pointed this out to Giap and other Viet Minh comrades but had never received a response.[84] While Giap did not show complete trust in the Chinese, some Chinese advisers demonstrated arrogance and contempt toward the Vietnamese. In his diary, Chen recorded that he once criticized Wang Yanquan, a member of the CMAG, for displaying reluctance to work in Vietnam and for looking down upon the Viet Minh army.[85] The friction between the Chinese advisers and Ho's troops may have been rooted in traditional Vietnamese resentment against China's Han chauvinism. It may also have been inherent in the advisory relationship.

The deepest divergence in the Viet Minh–Chinese relationship must have been over the outcome of the Geneva Conference. Under the pressure of Beijing and Moscow, the Viet Minh had to abandon its effort to unify the whole of Vietnam. In this case, Chinese and Soviet national self-interests overweighed any ideological obligation to assist the struggle of a fellow Communist party.

3 CONSOLIDATION AND UNIFICATION 1954–1961

In the immediate years following the conclusion of the Geneva Conference, China desired a peaceful international environment in order to focus on domestic reconstruction. This policy of moderation was epitomized by Zhou Enlai's performance at the Afro-Asian Conference at Bandung in Indonesia in 1955, where the Chinese premier charmed his audience with his gestures of compromise and reconciliation. In Indochina, Beijing sought to break the U.S. policy of isolation against China by wooing neutralist governments in Laos and Cambodia and by assisting the DRV to consolidate its power and rebuild its economy.

ENDORSING NEUTRALISM IN LAOS AND CAMBODIA

At the 1954 Geneva and the 1955 Bandung conferences, China supported both Laotian and Cambodian neutralism. So long as Vientiane and Phnom Penh stayed away from U.S.-sponsored military blocs, Chinese leaders were willing to maintain friendly relations with them. In 1956, both Laotian prime minister Souvanna Phouma and Prince Norodom Sihanouk visited Beijing, where they conducted cordial conversations with Mao and other Chinese officials.

After Geneva, China began to promote a peaceful settlement of the Pathet Lao issue, namely the participation of the Pathet Lao in a coalition government as the quid pro quo for transferring Phong Saly and Sam Neua provinces to the Royal Lao government authority. Such a solution served China's purpose of keeping Laos from accepting military protection from SEATO or the United

States and of establishing Beijing-Vientiane diplomatic rapport. At the Bandung conference, Zhou helped arrange a meeting between Lao prime minister Katay D. Sasorith and Pham Van Dong, who agreed to develop friendly relations in accordance with the Five Principles of Peaceful Coexistence.[1]

To the disappointment of the Chinese, Katay Sasorith, in the months following Bandung, resumed a hard-line policy toward the Pathet Lao and signed an aid agreement with the United States. Chinese leaders were relieved when Prince Souvanna Phouma became prime minister in March 1956. The new Vientiane leader responded positively to the Chinese policy of peaceful coexistence and reached an agreement with the Lao Patriotic Front (Neo Lao Hak Sat), the political arm of the Pathet Lao, by which a government of national union would be established with the Front's participation.[2]

During Souvanna Phouma's visit to China between August 19 and 28, 1956, Mao applauded his agreement with the Pathet Lao, commending him for having done "an excellent job" in defusing domestic tensions. After reasserting the Chinese principle of treating large and small countries equally, Mao assured the Laotian visitor that "we will not interfere in your internal affairs and will abstain from propagating communism in your place." Souvanna reiterated Vientiane's intention to follow a peaceful and neutral policy and to stay away from military alliances.[3]

On August 21, Zhou Enlai emphasized to Souvanna Phouma the importance of keeping the United States out of Laos. Commenting on foreign military bases in Laos, the Chinese premier said that only "the French bases are permitted by the Geneva Accords." At the time of the Geneva Conference in 1954, Zhou continued, "What worried us was the possibility of the U.S. entry. Now we are very relieved to see that thus far neither Laos nor Cambodia has allowed the United States to enter its territory." He reassured the Laotian leader that China would respect its neighbors and seek friendly relations with them. Mutual support between China and Laos, Zhou stressed, served the interests of peace in Asia and the world. China would respect Laotian independence and sovereignty.[4]

In response to Souvanna Phouma's concern about the presence of North Vietnamese troops in Laos, Zhou in a subsequent meeting on August 25 told the Laotian prime minister: "If there are still Viet Minh personnel in certain parts of Laos, you have every reason to talk with Premier Pham Van Dong and get a solution." Zhou also expressed China's willingness to help Laos build its economy without attaching political conditions.[5]

On August 27, Zhou Enlai sent a letter to Ho Chi Minh informing him of Souvanna Phouma's visit to China and again urging him to normalize relations with the Vientiane government. Zhou wrote that Souvanna had declared

Prince Norodom Sihanouk (center) *accompanies Premier Zhou Enlai* (right) *during his visit to Cambodia, November 1956. Vice Premier He Long is on Sihanouk's left. (Courtesy Xinhua News Agency)*

in Beijing that because of its geographical location, Laos was inclined to follow a policy of peace and neutrality, not to participate in military blocs, and not to permit foreign countries to establish military bases in its territory. "We have expressed our respect and support for such a position," Zhou told Ho. "The current moment is an advantageous period. [You] should take advantage of it to realize gradually the normalization of relations between the DRV and Laos so that the issue of democracy and unity within Laos can be settled under relatively favorable circumstances."[6] Clearly, Zhou wanted the Hanoi leadership to follow a similar policy of reconciliation toward Laos.

At Bandung, Sihanouk established a friendly relationship with Zhou Enlai. The Chinese premier expressed Beijing's willingness to apply the Five Principles of Peaceful Coexistence to its relations with Cambodia, warning the prince about the United States and suggesting that he keep a French military mission to train his troops instead of using American advisers. He invited Sihanouk to visit China. The Cambodian leader told Zhou that he would not join any military bloc and would not provide military bases to the United States.[7]

During Sihanouk's visit to China on February 13–21, 1956, Mao praised Cambodia's peaceful and neutral policy, declaring that such a policy had a great impact in the world. Zhou Enlai stressed the principle of equality between states in international affairs, regardless of their size. In the joint declaration issued at the end of Sihanouk's trip, the two countries endorsed the Five Principles of Peaceful Coexistence as a guideline in Sino-Cambodian relations. In the wake of Sihanouk's trip, China signed several agreements of economic aid with Cambodia. In November 1956, Zhou Enlai paid a state visit to Phnom Penh, where he reaffirmed China's respect for Cambodia's neutrality. The Chinese premier was also careful to lessen Sihanouk's fears that China would seek to dominate Cambodia indirectly through the influence of the country's Chinese population, which numbered about 400,000 and included business leaders and merchants in every community, by urging the Chinese in Cambodia to pledge loyalty to Cambodia rather than China.[8]

Certainly, China's relations with Laos and Cambodia included frictions. Beijing was unhappy with Souvanna Phouma's and Sihanouk's acceptance of American military aid. In turn, Sihanouk, preoccupied with the protection of his country's borders from the irredentist demands of South Vietnam and Thailand, was critical of China's reluctance to make a blanket guarantee of Cambodian territorial integrity.[9]

Despite these differences, Chinese leaders chose to befriend Souvanna Phouma and Sihanouk to advance several goals. First, by encouraging Laos and Cambodia to stay out of alliance with the United States, the Beijing leadership sought to frustrate Washington's containment policy against China. This consideration constituted the primary motive in China's policymaking. To Chinese leaders, who were preoccupied with domestic consolidation and reconstruction at this time, improving relations with the neutralist states in Indochina was preferable to inciting Communist insurgencies there because the latter option ran the risk of triggering American intervention. Second, Chinese policymakers undoubtedly intended to use Souvanna Phouma and Sihanouk, both of whom were proud and ardent nationalists, as instruments to limit Vietnamese influence in Laos and Cambodia.

Chinese leaders' endorsement of neutralism was a significant departure from their previous adherence to the rigid "two camp" theory. In 1949, Mao had lashed out at the "illusion of a third road," while Liu Shaoqi had ridiculed neutral statesmen such as Jawaharlal Nehru, U Nu, and Sukarno as "stooges of imperialism" and urged the Communist groups in those neutral states to launch armed struggle after the Chinese model. By the mid-1950s, however, this radical approach had been replaced by a more pragmatic and moderate policy of peaceful coexistence, with Asian countries having different political systems.[10]

It is unclear how North Vietnamese leaders viewed in private Beijing's improvement of relations with Vientiane and Phnom Penh. In public, Hanoi endorsed Sihanouk's visit to China. In an editorial on February 20, 1956, the *Nhan*

Dan (People's Daily) referred to the establishment of friendly ties between China and Cambodia as beneficial to the implementation of the Geneva Accords.[11] The Vietnamese Communists themselves had been eager to establish diplomatic relations with Cambodia and had approached the Indian leader Jawaharlal Nehru as their intermediary. They had supported Sihanouk's position of neutrality and his refusal to enter into any military alliance. At Bandung, Pham Van Dong had assured Sihanouk of Hanoi's respect for Cambodia's independence and territorial integrity and noninterference in its internal affairs.[12]

MEETING HANOI'S DEMANDS

After the close of the Geneva Conference, the VWP faced two fundamental tasks: to reconstruct the north and to unify the south. In both areas, it sought China's support. On the first issue, Beijing was willing to provide economic aid and to introduce the Chinese model of socialist development to the DRV. On the second issue, Chinese leaders advised caution and patience, urging the Vietnamese to make preparations and wait for opportunities. This moderation in Beijing's position reflected Mao's preoccupation with domestic reconstruction and his intention not to provoke an American retaliation.

In October 1954, Ho Chi Minh returned to Hanoi amid welcoming celebrations and ceremonies. But behind the facade of victory lay a war-ravaged economy: destroyed irrigation facilities, abandoned farm land, shortages of rice in cities, and paralyzed transportation and communications networks.[13] The VWP was confronted with the difficult task of stopping the speculation and inflation triggered by the scarcities and moving the previously French-owned enterprises, especially coal, cement, and textiles, back into production. Almost all French technicians had departed from the DRV, and Vietnamese skilled workers were in short supply. French owners and others had removed production equipment and taken away stocks of raw materials and goods for sale when they moved south, depriving the Communist government of much-needed machinery and capital.[14]

To rebuild the north, the VWP leadership continued to look to China for assistance. Realizing the enormous work of recovery and reconstruction after the war, they had asked the CCP at the Geneva Conference to help them consolidate peace in the north, build the armed forces, continue the land reform program, rectify the party, strengthen diplomatic work, administer cities, and restore the economy.[15]

After the Geneva Conference, China immediately began to offer aid to help the DRV relieve famine, rebuild the transportation systems, revive agriculture, reconstruct the urban economy, and improve the armed forces. To provide economic and financial advice, Beijing sent a team of economic advisers and experts, led by Fang Yi, to North Vietnam.[16]

The treatment of the French-owned enterprises topped the DRV's economic agenda. China offered important advice on this issue. On October 8, 1954, Zhou Enlai sent a telegram to Luo Guibo, China's ambassador to the DRV, Fang Yi, the Chinese general adviser, and Qiao Xiaoguang, the Chinese deputy general adviser, directing them to convey to Ho Chi Minh some principles in dealing with French business interests. "The general guideline," Zhou stated, "is to adhere to the cease-fire agreement as well as its appendices, to maintain independence and sovereignty, and to show consideration for the united front and the future reunification." In making plans, the Chinese premier continued, the DRV should "give overall consideration to such issues as the recovery of the economy, the stability of market prices, and the treatment of war traumas. The new economic relationship should be based on equality and mutual benefits." As to the procedure of recovering sovereignty, Zhou suggested a gradual, step-by-step approach. First of all, Zhou remarked, the DRV should unify the issuance of currency and establish control over export and import and foreign currency, as well as other key aspects of the economy. In implementing these measures, Zhou urged the DRV leadership to give proper consideration to the sentiments of French businessmen.[17] Zhou's suggestions combined principle and flexibility. While respecting the Vietnamese desire to achieve independence and recover sovereignty, he considered a drastic policy by Hanoi toward the French enterprises unwise and disadvantageous to the pressing need of restoring the economy.

Between late 1954 and early 1955, the Hanoi leadership worried that a famine might occur in the DRV because of the October crop failure and the suspension of food supplies from the south. The war had severely diminished the productive forces in agriculture in the north. By July 1954 French bombing had destroyed eight major irrigation systems, covering 252,000 hectares. (The total hectares under irrigation coverage in 1939 was 326,000.) Furthermore, the north had always been a rice-deficit region in the colonial era, depending on imports from the south. Thus, any drop in production while the south remained under hostile forces posed a grim threat.[18]

Beijing agreed to provide rice to North Vietnam. The Chinese rice was transported to the DRV on Soviet ships.[19] A similar arrangement was made between the DRV, the Soviet Union, and Burma. In exchange for rice to Hanoi, Moscow would provide Rangoon with industrial equipment.[20] In December 1954, China dispatched over 2,000 railroad workers to the DRV to repair railway lines, roads, and bridges. Early the next year a group of Chinese irrigation specialists went to North Vietnam to help construct five irrigation projects. Be-

Mao and Ho Chi Minh at Beijing airport, 1955. (Courtesy Xinhua News Agency)

tween June 25 and July 8, 1955, Ho Chi Minh made an official visit to China as head of state of the DRV. During his trip, Beijing agreed to provide the DRV with a grant of 800 million Chinese yuan ($200 million) to be used to build eighteen projects, including the Haiphong cement plant, the Hanoi power station, and the Nam Dinh cotton mill. In addition to agreeing to expand trade relations in the future, the two sides also established a manpower exchange program whereby China would send technical experts to work in the DRV and Vietnamese workers would learn as apprentices in Chinese industrial enterprises.[21]

While providing extensive assistance to the DRV, leaders in Beijing also wanted Hanoi to diversify its sources of international aid. In a message to Ho Chi Minh transmitted through the Chinese advisers on January 18, 1955, Zhou Enlai said that "the material and technological aid to the DRV cannot and should not be all covered by China, although, of course, China will do its best to assist the DRV." The Soviet Union and Eastern European countries, Zhou went on, should also provide help, and the DRV government and the VWP should request aid from those states directly.[22] Clearly, China's own development demands and limited resources handicapped its capacity to satisfy all the financial and technical needs of the DRV.

Mao hosts a banquet in honor of Ho Chi Minh during Ho's visit to China, 1955.
(Courtesy Xinhua News Agency)

During the first five months after the Geneva Conference, the Soviet Union paid little attention to the DRV, except for providing Soviet ships to transport PAVN troops back from the south and sending relief rice to North Vietnam. No long-term plans for assistance were contemplated. This situation did not change until late December 1954, when the Moscow leadership began to offer advice to the DRV on policy toward the regime in South Vietnam.[23]

From July 12 to 18, 1955, on the eve of the deadline for consultations for elections stipulated by the Geneva Accords, Ho Chi Minh visited the Soviet Union as head of the DRV government delegation. Ho's journey had two primary purposes: to obtain economic aid from the Soviet Union and to win Moscow's support for Hanoi's position on consultations. Ho received a Soviet grant of 400 million rubles ($100 million) to be applied toward the construction of twenty-three industrial and public service projects, including engineering and textile factories, and the development of tin and phosphate resources. The two countries also concluded separate technical, trade, and personnel exchange agreements. On the issue of reunification, Moscow wanted Hanoi to follow strictly the terms of the Geneva Accords. The Soviet Union endorsed the DRV proposal for establishing a united front with the French and pro-French elements against the United States in South Vietnam.[24] While sharing a common interest with the Chinese to help the Vietnamese Communists consolidate their power, Moscow at this juncture appeared to expect Beijing to play a larger role in North Vietnam. The fact that Ho Chi Minh visited Beijing before he visited Moscow indicates the priority the DRV gave then to relations with China.

Between 1955 and 1957, assistance from China and the Soviet Union played an important role in the DRV's efforts to reconstruct and develop its economy. Beijing and Moscow provided crucial raw materials, technical know-how, and consumer products, helping lay a foundation for the later development of heavy industry in North Vietnam.[25]

In the area of military cooperation, the CMAG remained in North Vietnam to help the PAVN streamline its organizations, carry out the political indoctrination of its troops, and establish a sound logistical system. In early 1955, the Chinese military advisers suggested that the PAVN reduce its current troop level of 320,000 by 40,000 and reorganize its forces to include infantry, artillery, antiaircraft artillery, engineering, and tank units, as well as air force and navy. They promised that China would help train PAVN officers above the battalion level. In March, Wei Guoqing accompanied Vo Nguyen Giap in an inspection trip of the DRV's coastline from Haiphong to the seventeenth parallel. After the journey, Wei offered advice concerning the deployment of troops and the construction of defense works along the coast.[26]

Noticing defection and laxity of discipline within the PAVN as a result of peace in Vietnam, the Chinese military advisers also urged the Vietnamese leaders to tighten up the political control of their troops. Adopting Chinese advice, the PAVN conducted an education campaign between August 1954 and the spring of 1955 to indoctrinate its soldiers with the party line. The General Political Department of the PAVN operated classes to teach Marxist-Leninist knowledge to middle- and high-ranking officers. About 3,000 officers participated in the classes.[27]

In dealing with logistical matters, the CMAG cautioned the PAVN that excessive military spending could produce an extra burden on the government. They suggested reduction in the PAVN's plans for building military installations and storing supplies. For instance, in its construction plan for 1955, the General Logistical Department of the PAVN had originally intended to build seventeen new hospitals. The Chinese advisers asked them to cut down on the number of new hospitals and to revamp and utilize existing hospitals instead. The Vietnamese accepted the Chinese proposal.[28]

On June 27, 1955, Vo Nguyen Giap, accompanied by Wei Guoqing, led a Vietnamese military delegation in a secret visit to Beijing. The Vietnamese visitors held discussions with Chinese defense minister Peng Dehuai and General Petroshevskii, a senior Soviet military adviser in China, regarding the DRV's reconstruction of its armed forces and war plans for the future. The Vietnamese delegation visited the Chinese North Sea Fleet before returning to Hanoi in mid-July. On October 15, Giap led another secret military delegation to China, where he talked with Peng Dehuai and General Gushev of the Soviet Union again about the DRV's military building and war planning. The Vietnamese inspected Chinese military facilities and academies and watched a Chinese military exercise before traveling back to North Vietnam on December 11. On both of his visits, Giap asked the Chinese to continue dispatching military advisers to the PAVN.[29]

On December 24, the Chinese government decided to withdraw the CMAG from North Vietnam. Considering the repeated requests by Giap for the continued dispatch of Chinese advisers, Beijing agreed to keep a smaller team of military experts, headed by Wang Yanquan, in the DRV. In a letter to Vo Nguyen Giap, Peng Dehuai explained the reason for the withdrawal of the CMAG: after eight years of war against the French, "the PAVN has made great progress in both combat and training and has accumulated a considerable amount of battle experience." Given this situation, the Chinese defense minister stated, the current method of sending Chinese military advisers to the DRV needed to be changed, and if the PAVN still wanted Chinese assistance, Beijing could send a few cadres as experts. Wei Guoqing delivered Peng's message to Giap on December 29. Before the departure of the last members of the CMAG in mid-March 1956, the VWP leadership held a farewell party in honor of Wei Guoqing, with Ho Chi Minh serving as an interpreter.[30]

In the immediate post-Geneva period, Hanoi looked primarily to Beijing for models of development. It borrowed the Maoist idea of New Democracy, according to which the transition to socialism should be postponed until political consolidation and economic development had been realized. It adopted Chinese practices in agricultural methods, administrative organization, cadre training, and social mobilization. And in 1957, it even introduced its own version of China's Hundred Flowers Campaign.[31] But the pitfalls of copying the Chinese model in building socialism soon manifested themselves. The most clear case involved the conduct of the land reform campaign in the DRV.

THE LAND REFORM BACKFIRES

With the help of Chinese advisers, the VWP expanded its land reform campaign in North Vietnam after the Geneva Conference. In mid-1955, the campaign intensified with more emphasis on class struggle against the landlords. One important reason for the intensification was that by the beginning of 1955 the VWP had realized that Ngo Dinh Diem, with the support of Washington, had no intention to implement the Geneva Agreements. Taking seriously Diem's statements about a "march North," leaders in Hanoi feared that if Saigon launched an attack, landlords in the north might serve as a fifth column to support the enemy. They reacted by adding the counterreactionary campaign to the land reform movement, treating the landlords as enemies of the state.[32]

The momentum of the land reform campaign itself was also responsible for the overreaction against the landlords as poor peasants joined with over-enthusiastic cadres to promote their own economic interests. Execution of landlords became a popular method of establishing and increasing the power and prestige of poor peasants. Many rich and middle-class peasants as well as small land renters were also affected. While the land reform law had included elements that sought to limit violent action and preserve the united front, the actual situation often developed beyond the control of the party center.[33]

The extreme methods of the land reform campaign were uncongenial to Ho Chi Minh. After discovering that the campaign had caused extensive popular hostility in early 1956, Ho publicly admitted that mistakes had been made in conducting the program.[34] The VWP convened a Central Committee Plenum in September to rectify the campaign. The meeting lasted for a month, the longest conference of the party since its establishment, according to Hoang Van Hoan. At the meeting, Ho made a self-criticism of his failure to supervise the land reform program while Truong Chinh refused to acknowledge errors, insisting that the program was a victory because it had allowed poor peasants to obtain land. Chinh's recalcitrance was the primary reason for the prolonged meeting. Finally, the party decided to relieve Chinh of his post. Le Duan, a party leader in the south, was promoted to the central leadership in Hanoi. He accused Chinh of applying the Chinese land reform experience in Vietnam without considering the Vietnamese reality.[35]

While the Vietnamese land reform achieved its major goals of rearranging landownership, increasing rice production, and dismantling the control held by rich peasants and landlords over the rural population, it also created a great deal of chaos and unrest.[36] The disruption and instability generated by the land reform indicated the folly of introducing the drastic Maoist formula of class struggle in a small and fragile rural society, where many landlords and rich peasants had identified with the Communist Party in opposing France.

Burned by the land reform experience, Ho Chi Minh and his colleagues would gradually veer from the Maoist model of mass mobilization, class struggle, and continuous revolution toward the Soviet model of centralization and managerial control in the late 1950s. The elimination of the capitalists as a class, for instance, did not involve anything like the Three-Antis and Five-Antis movements organized by Mao between 1951 and 1952. The party center would carefully introduce new measures in the DRV step by step and supervise closely through party and government organs mobilizing actions such as political indoctrination in general and popularizing technological innovation in particular.[37]

Another consequence of the mistakes of the land reform was the official adoption by the VWP leadership of the principle of collective decision making in the late 1950s. Truong Chinh had made key policy decisions regarding land reform without consulting the entire politburo. Learning from the lessons of the land reform campaign and de-Stalinization in the Soviet Union, the party leadership sought to avoid the dangers of major decisions being made without the participation of the whole politburo.[38]

Chinese leaders were disappointed and unhappy with Hanoi's decision to downplay class struggle in the wake of the land reform campaign. During his visit to Hanoi on November 18–22, 1956, Zhou Enlai insisted that the achievements of the land reform should be acknowledged and that mistakes were unavoidable. In the process of rectifying the land reform, he continued, correct policies should not be abandoned; otherwise, the party would be in a passive position and the masses would lose faith in it.[39]

In a 1963 internal report on conditions in North Vietnam, officials in the International Liaison Department of the CCP Central Committee criticized the way Hanoi settled the land reform dispute. After noting Hanoi's decision to reclassify landlords into rich peasants and rich peasants into middle-class peasants in its effort to correct the mistakes of the land reform program, Chinese officials argued that the VWP should have conducted a serious debate to clarify the confusion surrounding the land reform program rather than simply passing a party resolution to close the case. They chastised the Hanoi leadership for stressing unity at the expense of principle.[40]

REUNIFICATION

In addition to the work of consolidating party rule and constructing the north, the vwp faced another important task: reunification of the country. After the Geneva Conference, there was uncertainty in Hanoi regarding whether elections would take place. Some party leaders, reportedly including Ho Chi Minh himself, expected that the elections would be held, although they also realized that they might not. If the elections did take place, leaders in Hanoi were confident that Ho's prestige as the spokesman of the Vietnamese struggle for independence would ensure the party's victory in the elections.[41]

On the approach to reunification, Hanoi consulted with Moscow and Beijing. Neither the Russians nor the Chinese advised the North Vietnamese to abandon the goal of peaceful reunification of Vietnam. The Soviets favored peaceful coexistence between North and South Vietnam, urging Hanoi to "reunify the country through peaceful means on the basis of independence and democracy." The Chinese had less confidence in the prospects of peaceful reunification through elections. They contended that because of imperialist sabotage it was impossible to reunify Vietnam through general elections in accordance with the Geneva Accords and that, consequently, North Vietnam should prepare for a protracted struggle.[42]

Reflecting their lack of optimism about the likelihood of national elections in Vietnam, Chinese leaders registered concern about American intervention in their talks with Ho Chi Minh during his state visit to China between June 25 and July 8, 1955. The two sides condemned the U.S. violations of the Geneva Agreements, reaffirming their commitment to the Geneva settlement.[43] In a conversation with the Burmese ambassador to China on June 30, 1955, Zhou Enlai said that, according to the Geneva Accords, after July 20 leaders in Hanoi and Saigon should begin consultations on elections, but the Diem government, pressured by the United States, was displaying not the slightest intention to hold the meetings. If contacts between the governments of North and South Vietnam could not take place after July 20, the Chinese premier warned, the implementation of the Geneva Agreements would be in danger.[44]

Refusing to hold consultations on elections, Diem launched a "Denounce the Communists" campaign in the summer of 1955 to arrest and imprison antigovernment elements. Hanoi's immediate response to Diem's hostility was cautious. The vwp Central Committee reiterated its existing stand on consolidating power in the north while pursuing a peaceful approach to national reunification with the south. Some of the party's leaders in the south criticized this position, urging a tougher reaction to Saigon.[45]

There were both internal and external reasons behind Hanoi's decision to approach the issue of reunification with great caution at this time. Domestically, economic difficulties created by the war and social instability caused by the extreme actions of the land reform may have greatly hamstrung the DRV leadership. Internationally, neither China nor the Soviet Union encouraged an aggressive policy of armed violence. Preoccupied with economic reconstruction at home and conforming to Soviet policies, Mao soft-pedaled his support for Communist insurgencies abroad between 1954 and 1956 and endorsed the principle of "peaceful coexistence" in dealing with the ruling governments in neighboring countries. In Mao's calculations, however, moderation did not mean abandonment; revolution should go through stages. He was fully aware of the Leninist tradition of calculating revolutionary moves according to circumstances.

At the Twentieth Congress of the Soviet Communist Party in early 1956, Khrushchev advocated "peaceful coexistence" with capitalist countries. Jettisoning Lenin's views on the inevitability of war and the role of war as a midwife of revolution, the Soviet leader announced the possibility of achieving Communism through parliamentary or peaceful means.[46] Khrushchev was loath to see any exacerbation of the situation in Vietnam that could increase international tensions and undermine his emphasis on peaceful coexistence. It was very likely that Anastas Mikoyan, a Soviet politburo member, informed VWP leaders of Moscow's decisions when he visited Hanoi before the opening of the Ninth Central Committee Plenum in April. Mikoyan emphasized publicly in Hanoi the importance of strictly adhering to the Geneva Agreements and the need to achieve the reunification of Vietnam through peaceful means.[47]

The Khrushchev line apparently triggered a heated debate at the Ninth Plenum. While proponents of the policy of peaceful political struggle in the south found ideological justification, skeptics of that policy criticized the thesis of peaceful transition as a dangerous deviations from Marxism-Leninism because it overlooked the possibility that the United States and the Diem government would oppose a peaceful outcome. They implied that North Vietnam should be ready not only to defend itself but also to assist the revolutionary struggle in the south by military means if necessary. Despite doubts about Khrushchev's theme of peaceful transition, the VWP Central Committee agreed to follow the Kremlin's line. In their instruction to party cadres in the south in 1956, the leaders in Hanoi drew upon the authority of the Soviet Party Congress to support the policy of peaceful political struggle.[48] The VWP leadership realized that without Soviet political support and economic aid, it could hardly expect to achieve its major goals whether in the north or in the south.

The economic malaise compounded by the uncertainty and confusion surrounding the uprisings in Poland and Hungary prompted Hanoi to seek consultation with Beijing. In a cable to the CCP on November 12, 1956, the VWP suggested: "Taking the opportunity of Zhou Enlai's forthcoming visit to Hanoi, the VWP's politburo plans to ask his opinion with regard to the following: his view and forecast about the current international situation; the task in the struggle for the implementation of the Geneva Accords; the conditions of the current Vietnamese finance and economy and the task for future financial and economic work."[49]

On November 18–22, 1956, Zhou visited the DRV, where he held talks with Ho Chi Minh and Pham Van Dong on such issues as the current international situation, criticism of Stalin, relations between fraternal parties, bilateral relations between the Chinese and Vietnamese parties, as well as the major projects the CCP had undertaken and the lessons from those works. Speaking of the DRV's domestic developments, Zhou offered suggestions with regard to two primary issues: reunification and economic policy, including the financial deficit, inflation, and market instability. On the question of unification, Zhou advised the North Vietnamese that since reunification of the two zones of Vietnam was a protracted struggle, the VWP should regard the principle of reunification through free elections as a slogan for political struggle rather than as a guideline for daily action. Since the DRV was the base for reunification, the VWP should make every effort to consolidate the north. As to the issue of economic policy, Zhou advised that the key to the financial problem was the increase of production, development of state-controlled commerce, and strengthening of market management. Responding to the Vietnamese request, Zhou agreed to let Chinese financial and economic advisers continue their work in the DRV, but he added that the opinions of the Chinese advisers only served as references for Vietnamese leaders in making their decisions on financial and economic matters.[50]

To win the goodwill of the Vietnamese population, Zhou resorted to diplomatic symbolism during his stay in Hanoi. He presented flowers at the altar of the Nhi Chinh Temple as a gesture of respect for the revolt conducted in A.D. 39 against Chinese rule.[51] He assured the North Vietnamese that China would always follow the Five Principles of Peaceful Coexistence and firmly oppose big-country chauvinism in international relations.[52]

The political scientist Donald Zagoria has argued that between 1957 and 1960, the DRV shifted its loyalties from Beijing to Moscow in order to obtain Soviet assistance for its economic development.[53] It is true that leaders in Hanoi looked to Moscow for economic aid in implementing their Three-Year Plan (1958–60), but it is also true that they had serious doubts about Khrushchev's policy of peaceful coexistence. They were shocked at the Soviet proposal made in January 1957 that the United Nations admit both North and South Vietnam as independent members. In the weeks after they advanced their proposal, the Soviet officials had to defend their position repeatedly to the North Vietnamese and the Chinese. On January 30, M. V. Zimjanin, the Soviet ambassador in Hanoi, told his Chinese counterpart, Luo Guibo, that there were "no inconsistencies" in Soviet policy and that the Soviet Union had always "defended the fundamental interests of the DRV." Between 1957 and 1959, however, Hanoi refrained from informing Moscow of its reunification strategy.[54]

While multiplying its international support, the Hanoi leadership could not afford to ignore Beijing's opinions and assistance. Ho Chi Minh, in fact, followed closely developments in China's international and domestic policies and continued frequent consultations with the CCP on economic consolidation in North Vietnam and revolutionary struggle in South Vietnam. In late August 1958, for instance, tensions in the Taiwan Strait arose as a result of Mao's decision to bombard Quemoy. On September 8, Ho cabled Mao, asking whether there was a possibility of a Sino-American war given the tensions over Taiwan and the recalcitrant attitude of the American imperialists, and what preparations the DRV should make. The CCP leader replied two days later: "The Americans are afraid of war. Currently speaking, there is very little possibility of a large conflict. Your country might as well continue its normal work."[55]

With the completion of its economic recovery in 1958, the VWP began to pay more attention to the issue of reunification. The debate within the upper echelons of the party over the proper approach to the south intensified during that year. The advocates of armed struggle almost succeeded in altering the existing policy.[56] The VWP sought Chinese advice by presenting in the summer of 1958 to the CCP for comment two documents titled "Our View on the Basic Tasks for Vietnam during the New Stage" and "Certain Opinions Concerning the Unification Line and the Revolutionary Line in the South." After a careful study, the Chinese leadership responded with a written reply, which pointed out that "the most fundamental, the most crucial, and the most urgent task" for the Vietnamese revolution was to carry out socialist revolution and socialist construction in the north. As to the south, the Chinese reply continued, Hanoi's task should be to promote "a national and democratic revolution." But since it was impossible to realize such a revolution at the moment, the Chinese concluded, the VWP should "conduct long-term underground work, accumulate strength, establish contact with the masses, and wait for opportunities."[57] According to Hoang Van Hoan, the Chinese advised Hanoi that it was not opportune "to expose its armed forces in south Viet Nam."[58] Clearly, Chinese leaders at this time did not believe that the time was ripe for Hanoi to wage military struggle in the south.

The VWP leadership reaffirmed its existing policy in a directive to its southern branch in late 1958. After admitting that Diem's repression had inflicted great damage on the revolutionary movement and anticipating more of the same in the coming year, the document nonetheless demanded a continuation of peaceful political struggle for everyday economic and political rights as well as for Hanoi's suggestion for normalization of relations with the south.[59]

REVIVAL OF INSURGENCY IN SOUTH VIETNAM

Partly responding to the pressure by southern leaders within the party and partly reflecting its own confidence with the improvement of the economy in the north, the Fifteenth Plenum of the VWP Central Committee in January 1959 authorized the use of armed struggle in the south while the consolidation and development of power in the north continued.[60] Instead of outlining any specific strategy to follow, the plenum merely mentioned that a blend of political and military struggles would be required.[61]

Chinese leaders remained cautious in treating the revival of revolutionary war in South Vietnam. While there had been a general turn to the left in Mao's foreign policy since 1958, the change had not brought an immediate impact on Beijing's attitude toward Communist insurgency in Indochina. By early 1958, a number of foreign policy setbacks and frustrations had caused Mao to become dissatisfied with the "Bandung spirit" of peaceful coexistence, which Zhou Enlai had earnestly promoted since 1955. These setbacks included the continuation of the UN embargo ensuing from the Korean War, the lack of progress in the Sino-American ambassadorial talks, and the hostility to China by the Kishi Nobusuke cabinet in Japan. In all of these cases, U.S. antagonism was a major factor in the frustration of Beijing's objectives.

Inspired by the Soviet launching of the Sputnik satellite and encouraged by his perception of his own standing within the international Communist movement as a result of de-Stalinization, Mao believed that "the East wind was prevailing over the West wind."[62] Domestically, he vetoed the cautious approach by Zhou Enlai and Chen Yun, both of whom preferred balanced economic development,[63] and launched the radical Great Leap Forward. To realize his dream of building socialism with Chinese characteristics, the great helmsman organized Chinese peasants to establish people's communes, leaping directly to communism by dismantling families, abolishing money, and melting household utensils in order to produce "backyard steel." Internationally, he opted for confrontation with the West headed by the United States by supporting national independence movements. In August 1958, Mao launched the bombardment of Quemoy to counter Anglo-American interventions in the Middle East.

From late 1957, Mao began to diverge from Khrushchev in the assessment of the nature of communist-capitalist relations and the role of force in promoting revolution. Abandoning the view that war was not inevitable, the CCP leader now accused the Kremlin of timidity in dealing with Western imperialism. In 1958, China demonstrated more enthusiasm than the Soviet Union for the July revolution in Iraq and the independence movement led by the Front de Liberation Nationale (FLN) in Algeria. In December 1958, the Provisional Government of the Republic of Algeria sent a military delegation to Beijing and obtained China's agreement to provide weapons.[64] In 1959, Beijing granted the Provisional Algerian Government $10 million to purchase weapons and agreed to provide large quantities of American weapons captured in Korea.[65] Between 1958 and 1963, China supplied the FLN with 150,000 guns and cannons, about 30,000 of which were American-made.[66]

Mao's post-1958 efforts to rectify the international revolutionary movement by reemphasizing the role of national liberation movements, however, did not immediately translate into an active support for Hanoi's war efforts in South Vietnam in 1959. This discrepancy in Beijing's policy showed the cautious side of Mao, who did not want to provoke a U.S. retaliation closer to home. This fear of American power also manifested itself during the shelling of Quemoy in 1958, when Mao strictly forbade his generals to engage American warships.[67]

In October 1959, Pham Van Dong visited Beijing, where he asked Zhou Enlai for military aid and the dispatch of a Chinese military technical team to the DRV.[68] There is no indication that China immediately set out to provide weapons to North Vietnam after Pham Van Dong's visit. During the winter of 1959–60, however, Beijing did send a military technical team in a fact-finding mission to the DRV. In November 1959, Luo Ruiqing, chief of staff of the PLA, had ordered the formation of the team, with Xu Shenji, deputy commander of the air force, as head, and Zeng Sheng, first deputy commander of the South Sea Fleet, as deputy head. The task of the team was to inspect North Vietnamese military technology and coordinate with the PAVN in its work on equipment development as well as on border, coastal, and air defense. Before its departure, Zhang Aiping, deputy chief of staff of the PLA, informed the team of China's position on aid to the DRV: China would satisfy whatever requests the North Vietnamese put forward so long as China was in a position to do so. He instructed the team to listen to North Vietnam's requests only and make no commitments. The Chinese group arrived in Hanoi on November 10 and spent over two months in the DRV visiting all of its five military districts, its navy, air force, and artillery units, its military academies, and its airfields, harbors, and factories. On behalf of the politburo of the VWP, Premier Pham Van Dong mentioned three times in his conversation with the Chinese group that the DRV placed great hope on China's assistance. The Chinese visitors received specific lists of request not only from the General Staff of the PAVN but also from each of the military districts they visited. The military academies requested Chinese textbooks and equipment. The Chinese were left with the impression that the DRV was making preparations for war with the United States. For instance, the North Vietnamese wanted storage facilities to be constructed near the Chinese border and inside China. The Chinese envoys felt that the quantity of materials demanded by the North Vietnamese was several times larger than the actual needs of the PAVN at its existing size.[69]

It was not until 1960 that the Chinese leadership became more enthusiastic about Hanoi's strategy of armed struggle in the south. According to Hoang Van Hoan, Beijing acknowledged its earlier miscalculations about the chances for a Communist victory in South Vietnam: "In 1960, after learning more about the new conditions in south Viet Nam, the Chinese comrades expressed explicitly to the Vietnamese that they were not as well-informed as the Vietnamese comrades, for they had considered the time not ripe for revealing the[ir] strength. Now they agreed that the Vietnamese position for armed struggle in the south was correct and that they would fully support it."[70]

In May 1960, North Vietnamese and Chinese leaders held discussions in both Hanoi and Beijing over strategies to pursue in South Vietnam. Zhou Enlai and Deng Xiaoping argued that, in general, political struggle should be combined with armed conflict and that since specific conditions varied between the city and the countryside in South Vietnam, a flexible strategy of struggle should be adopted. In the city, the Chinese advised, political struggle would generally be recommended, but in order to deliver a final blow on the Diem regime, armed force would be necessary. Since there was an extensive mass base in the countryside, military struggle should be conducted there, but military struggle should include political struggle.[71] While approving Hanoi's decision to conduct revolutionary war in South Vietnam, the Chinese leaders did not encourage a rapid escalation of the fighting.

In December 1960, at Hanoi's direction, southern revolutionaries established the National Liberation Front of South Vietnam (NLF), a broad-based united front led by the Communists against the Diem regime. The leadership of the NLF, according to the Vietnam specialist Carlyle Thayer, included "long-time VWP cadres who had been active in the south, members of the sect forces, former non-Party members of the Resistance and non-Communist opponents of the Diem regime. Rank-and-file membership consisted of rural folk long under the influence of the Party's underground or areas under the influence of dissident sect forces."[72] After the establishment of the NLF, China immediately granted recognition.

Apart from the issue of armed struggle in the south, the development of the socialist economy in the north continued to pose a challenge for the DRV leadership. In January 1960, the DRV government approved an economic plan for the year, which emphasized the importance of continuing the transformation of agriculture, private trade, and manufacturing, raising living standards, and preparing for the Five-Year Plan (1961–65). The treatment of the petty bourgeoisie, particularly its mercantile sector, required careful handling. Because the capitalists as a class force had been greatly weakened as a result of the implementation of the Three-Year Plan, the petty bourgeoisie, which remained the most numerous class next to the peasantry and were of considerable significance both in the production of commodities and in retail trade, became the main focus of class struggle.[73] To deal with these thorny issues, the VWP solicited Beijing's opinions.

In March 1960, China sent a delegation of planning specialists to the DRV. Before their departure, Zhou Enlai met with them in Nanning on March 5, instructing them on how to advise the North Vietnamese. On the question of the transformation of the petty bourgeoisie, the premier recommended the North Korean method of organizing small retailers and handicraftsmen, combining production and sale, and educating and managing them through the state-controlled wholesale. As to the Five-Year Plan, Zhou asked the experts to introduce China's experience but not to over peddle it: "Advise them on what they can achieve and seek truth from facts." Turning to the general principle of building an economy, Zhou stressed that a country must develop its own steel, machinery, fuel, power, and hydroelectric industries and establish a production system that fitted the country's politics, manpower, and natural resources. Zhou concluded his remarks by asking the specialists to maintain cordial relations with Soviet advisers in the DRV and to avoid quarrels with them.[74]

During his state visit to the DRV on May 9–14, Zhou continued to offer advice on how to facilitate economic development. He identified two key issues in the construction of North Vietnam: socialist transformation and thought remolding. In these two areas, Zhou said very confidently: "We are very willing to introduce our experience. A rapid socialist transformation can resolve the problem of labor." Turning to the Vietnamese Five-Year Plan, Zhou recommended the principle of "producing more, quicker, better, and more economically" in building socialism, a slogan that Mao had adopted in the Great Leap Forward. Responding to Pham Van Dong's request for a loan of 500 million Chinese yuan to implement the Five-Year Plan, Zhou indicated that China could provide a loan larger than that figure.[75]

Le Duan asked Zhou to explain the people's communes. Defending Mao's experiment, the Chinese premier remarked that the peasants, finding the cooperatives not big enough to accomplish large purposes, spontaneously came up with the idea of establishing communes. After two years of experimentation, Zhou continued, the communes had been consolidated. Stressing the importance of developing heavy industry and agriculture simultaneously, Zhou pointed out: "We are giving priority to the development of heavy industry while making a big effort at agriculture at the same time. In retrospect, our First Five-Year Plan did not pay enough attention to agriculture." Zhou urged the DRV to allocate a higher proportion of attention to agriculture and light industry in its new plan than the Chinese had during its First Five-Year Plan. "In this way, [you] can accumulate capital and improve life. Of course, heavy industry should not be ignored." Commending the VWP on its achievement in agricultural collectivization, Zhou contended that a high percentage of collectivization in the rural areas was beneficial to irrigation construction and manure collection.[76]

Zhou's praise of North Vietnam's collectivization was premature. As developments in the DRV between 1960 and 1965 would demonstrate, the collectivization failed to increase agricultural production. That failure stemmed from the lack of significant technological improvement and the absence of material incentives for peasants to put intensive labor into the collective economy.[77]

While the VWP leaders showed curiosity in Mao's commune experiment, they had no intention of copying it. In fact, when the Great Leap Forward produced disastrous results in China, the Vietnamese Communists, despite their initial attraction to it, asserted in internal party communications that the Chinese commune program was a mistake.[78] Specialists of the North Vietnamese State Planning Board said in 1962: "We are still too unsophisticated politically and economically to be able to judge the merits of the communes policy."[79]

Zhou Enlai's conversations with the VWP leaders in May 1960 also covered international developments. Zhou brought up the issue of the Sino-Indian conflict. Between the two major camps in the world, Zhou asserted, an intermediate zone had emerged. There were three tendencies in this zone: some countries had "turned from being bad to good"; other states had continued their policy of peace and neutrality; and still others had "turned from being good to bad." Zhou placed India in the third category. "Nehru," Zhou maintained, "wants to exploit the Sino-Indian border issue to attack domestic progressive forces and control the Congress Party while at the same time appealing to the United States and the Soviet Union for assistance."[80] Clearly, Zhou desired Hanoi's support in China's conflict with India.

To the disappointment of Chinese leaders, the DRV adopted a neutral policy toward the Sino-Indian feud between 1959 and mid-1962. The North Vietnamese were clearly in a dilemma. They did not want to alienate India because it was a member of the International Control Commission (ICC) on Indochina and played a prominent role in world affairs. It was not until June 1962, when India voted with Canada in an ICC report criticizing Hanoi's role in the subversion of South Vietnam, that the DRV openly sided with the PRC in accusing New Delhi of colluding with the Western imperialists in attacking China.[81] The Sino-DRV alliance clearly threatened to entrap Hanoi into a conflict from which it wished to stay away.

HO AND THE SINO-SOVIET DISPUTE, 1960–1961

Sino-Soviet relations had steadily deteriorated since 1956, when Khrushchev denounced Stalin and preached "peaceful coexistence" at the Soviet party's Twentieth Congress. Mao disagreed with Khrushchev's analysis of Stalin's legacy and opposed the new Soviet line on international politics. The Chinese requested nuclear technology from Moscow, but Khrushchev refused partly because he distrusted Mao and partly because he feared that if he shared nuclear weapons with Beijing, he might encourage Washington to do the same with West Germany. When the Sino-Indian border conflict broke out in 1959, Moscow sympathized with New Delhi. During his visit to China in October that year, Khrushchev asked Mao not to use force to test the stability of capitalism. In April 1960, *Renmin ribao* (People's Daily) published an article titled "Long Live Leninism," indirectly attacking Khrushchev's policy.[82]

In mid-1960, the Sino-Soviet debate escalated from written polemic to verbal slugfest. In June, at the Rumanian Communist Party Congress an argument broke out publicly between Khrushchev and Peng Zhen, head of the CCP delegation. The Soviet leader accused China of being "mad," "resisting peaceful coexistence," "wanting to launch war," and employing "Trotskyite ways" against the Communist Party of the Soviet Union. Many East European Communist parties (except the Albanians) joined the Russians in denouncing Beijing. Peng Zhen returned the attack by charging that Khrushchev was arrogant, patriarchal, arbitrary, and tyrannical in treating fraternal parties.[83] The Chinese now called the Soviets "revisionists," a serious charge in the Marxist-Leninist lexicon.[84]

The increasing animosity between Beijing and Moscow caught the DRV in a dilemma. Ho Chi Minh feared that the Sino-Soviet estrangement would weaken the world Communist movement, undermine international support for the Vietnamese struggle for reunification, and make a U.S. military attack on Vietnam more likely. Among the Communist parties in the world, the DRV perhaps had the greatest stake in preventing a complete split between Beijing and Moscow. At the time of the Bucharest Conference, Ho forwarded a letter to Khrushchev through Soviet chargé d'affaires N. I. Godunov in which the VWP leader voiced his concern about the schism within the Communist camp, contending that the imperialist countries might exploit such a dispute and that the present situation was not in the interest of the Communist cause.[85]

In July, Sino-Soviet relations further deteriorated when Khrushchev moved to withdraw all Soviet specialists from China. Alarmed by the sharp turn in the Beijing-Moscow relationship, Ho decided to talk directly with Chinese and Soviet leaders to appeal for unity. On August 7, Ho Chi Minh came to Beidaihe, a summer resort for Chinese leaders, to promote unity between China and the Soviet Union. He held discussions with Zhou Enlai and Deng Xiaoping on August 8. Mao called a politburo meeting the next day to hear Zhou's report on his talks with Ho and to discuss the North Vietnamese leader's proposal for the Chinese and Soviet parties.[86]

Ho talked with Mao on August 10. After mentioning the "serious differences" between the CCP and the Communist Party of the Soviet Union and the existence of "many prejudices and misunderstandings" on both sides, Ho suggested that Beijing and Moscow suspend polemics and conduct bilateral discussions before calling a meeting of all Communist parties. Mao disagreed with Ho's argument that the Chinese and Soviet parties were equally at fault in the dispute. He told Ho that he supported his proposal for holding Sino-Soviet bilateral talks and a meeting of fraternal parties but that he would not abandon his principle. Mao expressed his indignation at Khrushchev's cooperation with the United States, Britain, France, and India and at Moscow's withdrawal of experts from China. Responding to Ho's question about the likely outcomes if the current Sino-Soviet conflict continued, the CCP leader mentioned five possible Soviet reactions; it might expel China from the international Communist movement; abrogate the Sino-Soviet Friendship Treaty; increase tensions along the border; suspend the transfer of machinery equipment to China; or pass a resolution condemning China and conduct subversion and limited war against China. Mao asked Ho not to be nervous about the Sino-Soviet tensions.[87] Clearly, Mao had no intention to soften his ideological position and was prepared for the worst consequences of a complete breakdown of Sino-Soviet relations.

Mao also told Ho that both the Chinese and the Vietnamese were "poor people." "The people in Asia, Africa, and Latin America are all poor people," the CCP leader continued. "I prefer poor people. When people become rich, trouble begins."[88] Rejected by the West and estranged from the Soviet Union, Mao reaffirmed China's identification with countries in Asia, Africa, and Latin America. The Third World theory that Mao officially pronounced in the early 1970s was now beginning to take shape.

Chen Yi told Ho during the latter's stay in China that the Sino-Soviet dispute had "a long history" with both historical and social roots. China might be a minority in the dispute, the Chinese foreign minister contended, but it was "not afraid of the majority." China would oppose everything that was incorrect and practice correct Marxism-Leninism. After talking with Ho, Chen made this private observation about the North Vietnamese leader: "Ho is a nice person, but he can not stand up to" the Soviet Union.[89] Clearly the Chinese leaders wanted Ho to support them in their dispute with the Soviet Union. The vwp leader, however, tried to avoid being entrapped in the Sino-Soviet quarrel and to remain neutral, which must have displeased Mao and his associates.

After talking with his Chinese colleagues, Ho went to Moscow for discussions with Khrushchev. He returned to Beijing on August 19 to report to Mao his conversations with the Soviet leader. Once again Ho expressed the hope that the Chinese and Soviet parties would resolve their differences, strengthen unity, and save the international Communist movement.[90] Given the later complete breakdown of relations between China and the Soviet Union, Ho's mediation was obviously not successful. Clearly, he had underestimated the ideological gap between Mao and Khrushchev and overestimated his ability to influence policies in Beijing and Moscow.[91]

With the memory of the Sino-Soviet clash at the Bucharest Conference in mind, Ho Chi Minh feared that a similar situation might develop at the vwp's Third National Congress scheduled for September 1960. At a meeting with representatives from the socialist countries in late August prior to the congress, the North Vietnamese presented a four-point text outlining their views on the Sino-Soviet conflict.[92] While the contents of the four-point text are unknown, the Hanoi leaders undoubtedly called again for solidarity between China and the Soviet Union.

Mao refrained from embarrassing the Vietnamese Communists by toning down Sino-Soviet differences at the Third Congress. Leaders in Hanoi had planned the fifteenth anniversary celebration of the founding of the DRV on September 2, immediately preceding the Third Congress. To demonstrate international socialist support for its effort to reunify Vietnam, the DRV had invited China and the Soviet Union to send military delegations to attend the national day gala. For fear of jeopardizing its policy of détente with the United States, the Kremlin replied that it was inconvenient to send a military delegation and that, instead, it would include a military representative in its party delegation to the Third Congress. After learning about the Soviet decision from Ho Chi Minh, Mao told him that China would also include a military figure in the Chinese party delegation instead of sending a separate military mission.[93] This episode demonstrates Mao's sensitivity to Hanoi's delicate position in the emerging Sino-Soviet dispute.

The vwp's Third National Congress was the first such congress since 1951.

About 500 delegates attended the meeting, representing a party membership that had grown to half a million. The congress considered two main issues: the plan for socialist transformation in the north and the strategy in the south. In response to the first issue, the congress passed the Five-Year Plan, which was based on the Soviet model of emphasizing heavy industry over light industry and agriculture.[94] Industry was to receive 49 percent of the investment for the plan, while agriculture was given only 22 percent. The heavy industrial sectors, including electricity, mining, engineering, metallurgy, and chemicals, would receive 80 percent of the investment in industry, whereas consumer goods industries would receive only 20 percent.[95] Clearly, Zhou Enlai's earlier advice of giving equal emphasis to both heavy industry and agriculture was ignored.

The Third Congress downplayed the role of drastic class struggle by stressing the correction of ideological backwardness and feudal thinking rather than the purge of traitors and class enemies.[96] The avoidance of class struggle clearly indicated that the vwp had become very cautious in adopting the Maoist model of building socialism. The problems that were emerging in China as a result of the failure of the Great Leap Forward must have alerted policy planners in Hanoi to the folly of copying Mao's methods blindly.

On the second issue of struggle in the south, the congress made no major recommendations affecting existing strategy but simply stated that disintegration was replacing stability in the south. To take advantage of this new situation, the congress urged the party to carry out both political and military struggles in the south and called for an increase of support from the north. Le Duan, who became officially the party's first secretary—the new designation for the general secretary, following a similar change in the Soviet Union—spoke vaguely about the strategy in the south, merely stating that it would be "a long and arduous struggle, not simple but complex, combining many forms of struggle."[97] Duan's ambiguity about the approach to adopt in the south demonstrated that the party leadership had not reached a consensus on the issue.

Unlike the resolution of 1959, the decision made at the Third Congress had been discussed with the Soviets and the Chinese in advance. In May 1960, the vwp Central Committee had consulted with both Soviet and Chinese officials in Moscow on the theme of the political report to be delivered at the Third Congress. The Soviets had asked the North Vietnamese not to omit the slogan of peaceful reunification of Vietnam in accordance with the Geneva Agreement.[98]

Both the Soviet and the Chinese representatives refrained from harshly criticizing each other at the Third Congress. In his public statement, Nuritdin Mukhitdinov, head of the Soviet delegation, dwelt on the importance of improving socialist unity and commended the North Vietnamese for their success

Zhou Enlai and Ho Chi Minh at Beijing airport, December 6, 1960. Deng Xiaoping is in the background. (Courtesy Xinhua News Agency)

in building their country. In a private report, however, the Soviet embassy complained that in his open speech at the congress, Li Fuchun, head of the Chinese delegation, had failed to credit Soviet assistance to the DRV and completely ignored the resolutions of the Soviet Twentieth and Twenty-first Congresses.[99]

The Sino-Soviet clash over the inevitability of war continued at the Moscow Conference of the Communist and Workers' Parties in November 1960. Mao and Kim Il Sung were the only bloc leaders absent. Liu Shaoqi led the CCP delegation that attended the meeting. Khrushchev's effort to isolate China was abortive because the Albanians backed the Chinese to the hilt while Communist parties from Indonesia, North Korea, and North Vietnam remained mute. The final statement adopted at the conference bore the scars of the dispute, blending divergent views on peaceful versus nonpeaceful ways to socialism. The compromise statement avoided the embarrassment of an open break but did little to strengthen the "unity" to which all delegates pledged support.[100]

Assuming a conciliatory position at the conference, Ho Chi Minh continued to try to patch up the differences between China and the Soviet Union.[101] He organized a meeting of the Japanese, Korean, and Indonesian parties, discussing ways to resolve the Sino-Soviet divergence. Afterward, he informed the Soviets and the Chinese of the discussions.[102] The VWP leader told Khrushchev that "China is a large country and the Chinese Communist Party is a big party. You cannot let a split happen in our movement. You must get the Chinese to sign the declaration together with us. The document will have broad international effects only if it is signed unanimously."[103] Ho worked closely with the Chinese and Soviet delegates to produce the compromise statement, paragraph by paragraph, in order to avoid a public display of disunity.[104] Beijing and Moscow viewed the declaration as a possible foundation to prevent a complete break.

Ho Chi Minh's endeavor to promote unity within the international Communist movement continued in 1961 with his attempts to reconcile the dispute between the Soviet Union and Albania.[105] China, on the other hand, persisted in its efforts to influence Hanoi's position in the Sino-Soviet dispute. On October 12, 1961, Ho and Le Duan made a stopover in Beijing on their way to Moscow to attend the Twenty-second Congress of the Soviet Communist Party. Informing the North Vietnamese visitors that he would lead the CCP delegation to the Soviet meeting, Zhou Enlai discussed the purposes of his forthcoming trip: in addition to conveying congratulations to the conference, he said, "We are prepared to stress unity and anti-imperialism. There are advantages in emphasizing the struggle against the enemy."[106]

At the Soviet congress, Zhou Enlai clashed with Soviet leaders over the evaluation of the Soviet Twentieth Congress, the judgment of Stalin, and the treatment of Tito. He especially disputed Khrushchev's public condemnation of the Albanian Party of Labour at the meeting. To register his protest, Zhou withdrew from the congress to return early to Beijing on October 23.[107] Ho Chi Minh and Le Duan, on their part, abstained from making a public stand at the meeting.[108] Clearly, navigating the rapids of the Sino-Soviet competition required a great deal of skill, caution, and patience.

The North Vietnamese's intention to maintain a neutral position in the Sino-Soviet split was clearly demonstrated in their announcement on March 10, 1962, of the enlargement of both the Soviet and Chinese friendship associations in the DRV.[109] For the moment, Hanoi could not afford to alienate either Moscow or Beijing. But as the Kennedy administration increased its military involvement in South Vietnam and as Khrushchev demonstrated further inclination to avoid a confrontation with the United States after the Geneva Conference on Laos and the Cuban Missile Crisis in 1962, the voices within the VWP calling for a Vietnamese departure from Moscow's line of peaceful coexistence with the West would gain an upper hand and the DRV would move closer to Beijing in its ideological orientation.

THE GENEVA CONFERENCE ON LAOS 1961–1962

In early 1961, the attention of the world focused on Laos, where a civil war raged between a right-wing general, Phoumi Nosavan, the neutralist force headed by Prince Souvanna Phouma, and the left-wing Pathet Lao. The civil war threatened a confrontation between major powers. On May 16, fourteen nations gathered at Geneva to discuss a solution to the Laotian crisis. Beijing sent a large delegation to the conference, the first international East-West meeting at which China had been represented since the 1954 Geneva Conference.

CRISIS IN LAOS

Since Geneva, Washington had been providing economic and military aid to Laos with the hope of influencing its political orientation. At the end of 1954 the Eisenhower administration established a United States Operations Mission (USOM) to administer U.S. economic and military aid to Laos. Vientiane's requirement for American military assistance quickly overwhelmed the U.S. embassy, which was small and understaffed. Officials in Washington considered the introduction into Laos of a U.S. Military Assistance Advisory Group (MAAG), the standard mechanism of implementing a foreign military aid program, which would have been a violation of the 1954 Geneva Accords. The State Department bypassed that obstacle in December 1955 by placing the administration of U.S. military aid to Laos under the control of a newly established Program Evaluation Office (PEO), which was affiliated with the USOM. The PEO staff members were technically civilians, although many of them had recently served in the military. The PEO confined itself to providing military aid to Laos, leaving the training of the Laotian troops to the French Military Mission, an exclusive prerogative of France authorized by the Geneva Accords.[1]

Souvanna Phouma's decision to reach an accommodation with the Pathet Lao insurgents in 1956 irritated the United States and the right-wing group in Laos. Fearful of Communist penetration into Southeast Asia under the cover of aid, peace, and neutrality, American leaders opposed the formation of a coalition government in Laos and disapproved Souvanna Phouma's conciliatory policy toward Asian Communism. U.S. ambassador J. Graham Parsons persistently advised Souvanna not to establish a coalition government with the Pathet Lao.[2]

On June 30, 1958, following left-wing victories in the national elections in May, the U.S. embassy suspended all economic aid to Laos, forcing Souvanna Phouma to resign as prime minister on July 23 and ending the first experiment of building a coalition government in Laos. In August, Phoui Sananikone, a pro-Western diplomat, formed a new cabinet, excluding Souphanouvong and Phoumi Vongvichit, the Pathet Lao representatives. As prime minister, Phoui developed closer ties with the United States and Thailand, which resulted in an increase of Western economic and military aid. He also established relations on a consular level with South Vietnam and Nationalist China on Taiwan. In January 1959, Phoui reshuffled his cabinet to include a number of military figures such as General Phoumi Nosavan. On February 11, Phoui declared that his government regarded the application of the Geneva Agreements as fully accomplished and that, therefore, Laos was no longer bound by their provisions.[3]

Chinese leaders watched these developments in Laos with great apprehension. The U.S.-instigated coup dashed their optimistic expectations formed at Geneva and Bandung about preserving a neutral and integrated Laos and confirmed their worst suspicions of American intentions in the region. They worried that the United States would draw Laos into SEATO. A pro-U.S., pro-Taiwan regime in Laos posed a grave threat to China's southern frontier. There were remnants of Chiang Kai-shek's units operating in the Lao-Burmese border area where they had settled since they were driven out of Yunnan by the Communist forces in 1949. Although the primary engagement of these fugitive Nationalist troops was farming and opium smuggling, they occasionally conducted operations against China in collaboration with Taiwanese and American intelligence agencies.[4]

In a speech at the Second National Conference on Foreign Affairs on March 4, 1959, Vice Foreign Minister Luo Guibo, who had completed his term as China's first ambassador to the DRV in 1957, contended that "with American encouragement, Laos was becoming more and more reactionary. It not only wantonly suppressed democratic forces at home but also publicly declared its freedom from the restrictions of the Geneva Accords in foreign policy." Furthermore, Luo continued, Laos "connived with" Chiang Kai-shek's regime. The events in Laos constituted "part of the American imperialist plot of aggression against Indochina." The United States desired to "sabotage the Geneva agreements, occupy the whole of Indochina, threaten the Democratic Republic of Vietnam and our country, and create tensions." China's task, Luo pointed out, was to concentrate on the "exposure of the American plot and of the reactionary measures of the Lao government." Such action by China, Luo concluded, could not only provide important support for the Pathet Lao but also serve as a "warning" against the anti-Chinese activities of Thailand and Malaya.[5] Luo's remarks clearly showed that he saw domino effects in Laos: the success of the reactionary forces in that country would encourage reactionary regimes in Thailand and Malaya. Chinese officials viewed developments in Southeast Asia as a whole. They related hostile policy in Vientiane to the recent pro-U.S. turn in Thailand, where Sarit Thanarat had in October 1958 proclaimed military rule to replace the constitutional system, committing Thailand to the American alliance and banning trade with the PRC.

On March 20, 1959, *Shijie zhishi* (World Knowledge) carried a commentary attacking the Vientiane government's claim that it was not bound by the Geneva Accords and denouncing the United States for introducing military personnel into Laos and for encouraging fugitive KMT troops to harass the border between Laos and China. The U.S. activities, the commentary asserted, were designed to abolish the Geneva Accords, to establish an American foothold in Southeast Asia, and to bring Laos and South Vietnam into SEATO.[6]

In a conversation with Ho Chi Minh in Beijing on October 3, Zhou Enlai expressed China's apprehension about American intentions in Laos and the necessity of countering the American move. The U.S. plan in Laos, Zhou contended, included three phases. The first phase involved the provision of weapons and equipment and the second phase the dispatch of troops and the establishment of military bases. In the third phase, the United States would draw Laos into SEATO. The United States had already completed the first phase, the Chinese premier continued. "It is possible that we can prevent the United States from realizing its second phase and there is even a greater possibility to forestall the realization of its third phase because countries like India and Burma oppose it."[7]

While displaying serious concern about the Laotian threats to China's security, Chinese officials were also aware of Laos's crucial position in the growing revolution in South Vietnam. In line with the resolution of the Fifteenth Plenum to resume revolutionary war in the south, the VWP in 1959 established special military units to infiltrate men and supplies into South Vietnam via the Ho Chi Minh Trail, which ran through eastern Laos. Hanoi's effective control of the Ho Chi Minh Trail was the key to the success of the revolution in South Vietnam.

The pro-American government under Phoui Sananikone firmly demanded integration of the two Pathet Lao battalions into the Lao national army. In May 1959, one of the two Pathet Lao battalions revolted, and with the help of North Vietnamese advisers, it began pushing Lao government troops out of Sam Neua and Phong Saly. Charging that regular North Vietnamese troops had invaded its northern territory, the Lao government asked the United States and the United Nations for military aid. The Eisenhower administration responded by increasing military assistance by 30 percent and expanding the PEO with the dispatch of 100 Special Forces advisers. A UN investigation team failed to find evidence of the entry of North Vietnamese troops into Laos, but the investigation helped to reduce the tension. Rigid anticommunism resumed in December 1959 as a result of a military coup staged by General Phoumi Nosavan. On August 9, 1960, government policy was changed one more time when Phoumi was toppled by Captain Kong Le, commander of the Second Paratroop Battalion, who had strong reservations about the growing American influence in Laos and viewed the Lao government's departure from international neutrality as the reason for the escalating civil war and corruption at home.[8]

Beijing viewed with relief the overthrow of Phoumi Nosavan by Kong Le and the subsequent reappointment of Souvanna Phouma as prime minister, who pledged to avoid civil war and restore neutrality in Laos. In an internal speech, Chinese foreign minister Chen Yi called Kong Le's action "a revolution by the Lao Bourgeoisie against the United States."[9] A September 5 article in *Shijie zhishi* hailed the program of the Kong Le committee and the Souvanna Phouma cabinet as "reflecting the urgent desires of the Laotian people."[10]

When Kong Le's rebellion took place, Ho Chi Minh was in China to mediate the Sino-Soviet dispute.[11] He asked the Chinese for a joint declaration to support Kong Le. Chen Yi told him that it was better to wait until the situation clarified. Otherwise, the Chinese foreign minister believed, the United States would accuse China and the DRV of "subverting" Laos. Chen insisted that "it was better for us to speak on the sideline" and that "the three-way civil war in Laos is beneficial."[12]

After briefly joining Souvanna Phouma in a national unity cabinet, General Phoumi Nosavan separated to organize his own government at Savannakhet, where he established Prince Boun Oum as the leader. Phoumi quickly gathered assistance for a countercoup from his cousin, Sarit Thanarat in Thailand, and from U.S. Pentagon and CIA advisers. Bangkok imposed an unofficial embargo on food and fuel against Vientiane. To overcome the increasing shortages as a result of Thailand's economic blockade, Souvanna appealed for U.S. rice and oil supplies, but Washington turned a cold shoulder. Out of desperation, Souvanna accepted Moscow's offer of economic aid. On November 16, 1960, realizing that Phoumi's troops were pushing toward Vientiane, Souvanna accused the United States of failing to keep its promise not to allow Phoumi to use American equipment to attack the new Lao government. Souvanna's cabinet also decided to establish friendly relations with China and to dispatch goodwill delegations to Beijing and Hanoi. On December 3, the Soviet Union began an emergency airlift of rice and oil from Hanoi to Vientiane.[13] Beijing facilitated the transportation of Soviet oil and gasoline to Laos. On December 9, Zhou Enlai discussed with the Soviet chargé d'affaires in China the passage through China of Soviet fuel bound for North Vietnam.[14]

On December 16, Phoumi's forces drove Kong Le's troops out of Vientiane. A new Laotian government was established with Boun Oum as prime minister and Phoumi as deputy prime minister and defense minister. The United States, Britain, France, and Thailand immediately recognized the new regime, but the Soviet Union, China, India, and other countries continued to treat Souvanna as the legitimate leader of Laos.[15]

Leaders in Beijing and Hanoi were greatly worried about the advance of the right-wing forces in Laos. On December 12 and 16, Zhou Enlai met with Tran Tu Binh, the DRV ambassador to China, twice to review the situation in Laos.[16] While the details of the talks remain unknown, Zhou and Tran Tu Binh undoubtedly discussed plans to assist the Pathet Lao forces. Taking advantage of the clash between Kong Le's troops and Phoumi's forces, the Pathet Lao strengthened and expanded their ground position in the last months of 1960 and the spring of 1961. According to American intelligence, North Vietnamese army elements infiltrated the ranks of Pathet Lao units to serve as "stiffeners."[17] Marek Thee, the Polish delegate to the ICC, observed that the main decisions and plans of the Pathet Lao were "a joint enterprise" with leaders in Hanoi.[18] In the one year after December 1960, Beijing provided the Pathet Lao forces with weapons and supplies that could equip 20,000 soldiers.[19]

SIHANOUK CALLS FOR A GENEVA CONFERENCE

On January 1, 1961, Prince Sihanouk proposed an expanded Geneva Conference to resolve the Laos crisis. China immediately endorsed the proposal. Leaders in Beijing viewed the meeting as a way to prevent American infiltration into Laos. During a conversation with General Ne Win, chief of staff of the Burmese army, in Rangoon on January 5, Zhou Enlai stated that although the

Soviet Union and North Vietnam had provided indirect assistance to Souvanna Phouma's government, the United States not only had assisted the Boun Oum regime but also had sent U.S. troops to Laos. The United States "had thus lost justification" for its actions and had to consider the possibility of a direct confrontation with the Soviet Union if it decided to dispatch troops on a larger scale. Calling Sihanouk's proposal for an enlarged Geneva Conference on Laos "excellent," Zhou went on to point out that China opposed the presentation of the Laos question to the United Nations and objected to the international organization's intervention.[20] While condemning the dispatch of U.S. troops to Laos, Zhou said nothing about the presence of North Vietnamese soldiers in the Pathet Lao–controlled territory.

Meeting with a DRV Economic Delegation headed by Deputy Premier Nguyen Duy Trinh in Beijing on January 31, Zhou Enlai pointed out that "the Laotian civil war initiated by the Phoumi–Boun Oum clique with the backing of the United States, Thailand, and South Vietnam is threatening the security of Southeast Asia, the DRV, and China. We cannot but pay the greatest attention to the development of the Laotian situation."[21]

In a conversation with U Nu, prime minister of Burma, in Kunming on April 12, Zhou blamed the United States for the civil war in Laos. He observed that the cause of the current problem in Laos was American assistance to Phoumi Nosavan against Souvanna Phouma's government and American attempts to involve Thailand and remnant KMT troops in Laos. As to the prospect of military conflict in Laos, the Chinese premier continued, the war would not develop into a larger confrontation. "Even if the United States initiated a partial war, it would be difficult to fight it due to the lack of open space" in a country "full of forests." If Washington launched a partial war in Laos, Zhou warned, it would encounter a conflict worse than the Korean War.[22] Zhou, however, continued to ignore North Vietnam's involvement in Laos.

In addition to seeing the Geneva Conference as a way to forestall American intervention in Laos, Chinese leaders also calculated that, given the weak conditions of the Pathet Lao, a temporary cease-fire in Laos was necessary so that the Pathet Lao could win time to build base areas, mobilize masses, and develop its armed forces for the eventual success of the revolution in the country. What the Chinese sought at Geneva was "a conditional compromise for a period of time." They did not intend to pursue neutralization as a permanent solution to the Laotian problem.[23]

Furthermore, the severe economic difficulties China was undergoing as a result of the failure of the Great Leap Forward also made Chinese leaders unwilling to confront the United States at this time. By 1960, famine had spread from the countryside to the cities. The food shortage had caused millions of deaths and a drop in the number of births from 21.2 million in 1957 to 12.5 million in 1960. The central government had to adopt food rationing for urban residents. At its Ninth Plenum held in Beijing from January 14 to 18, 1961, the CCP Central Committee formally decided to end the Great Leap by adopting an economic policy of adjustment and consolidation.[24] Finally, China's participation at the Geneva Conference provided the country with an opportunity to augment its influence in Laos.

Zhou Enlai closely supervised the preparations and coordination with the DRV for the conference. On March 29, 1961, he revised "the Chinese Government's Memorandum on the Laotian Question to the Soviet Government," in which he argued that the situation in Laos was still changing and that "if the United States is unwilling to convene an international conference because of the failure to bring about a cease-fire, then the responsibility will fall on the United States."[25] On April 9, Zhou arrived in Pingxiang, Guangxi province, to discuss with Ho Chi Minh, Le Duan, and Pham Van Dong the situation in Laos as well as the Soviet government's April 7 memorandum to the British government regarding the Laotian question. The Chinese and the North Vietnamese reached a basic agreement concerning the Laotian issue.[26]

CHEN YI TAKES CHARGE

The Beijing leadership appointed Foreign Minister Chen Yi to head the Chinese delegation to the Geneva Conference. In selecting Chen as China's chief negotiator, Mao had found a person who was both knowledgeable about international affairs and blunt and outspoken in confronting adversaries. As a youth, Chen had spent three years in France as a work-study student. He had been a loyal supporter of Mao and a prominent military leader during the Communist revolution in the 1930s and 1940s. In 1949, he became mayor of Shanghai, the most international city in China. Five years later, he was appointed a deputy premier to assist Zhou Enlai in foreign affairs. He worked as Zhou's chief associate at the Bandung conference. After Bandung, Chen engaged himself extensively in the work of the Foreign Ministry in preparation to replace Zhou as foreign minister, but poor health delayed that occurrence. In February 1958, Chen officially became foreign minister.[27]

During the preparations for the Geneva Conference, Chen made careful analyses and proposals. He pointed out that the domestic conditions in Laos were helpful for the meeting because the combined forces of the neutral group under Souvanna Phouma and the leftist group represented by Souphanouvong were superior politically and militarily to the right-wing clique headed by Boun Oum and Phoumi Nosavan. China, Chen proposed, should encourage the Pathet Lao to develop its armed forces and to expand the united front with

Souvanna Phouma. The problem, as Chen saw it, was that the Boun Oum–Nosavan group received the support of the United States, which was determined to undermine the Geneva Conference in order to prevent the independence and neutrality of Laos. Chen urged that China keep vigilant against American intentions and prepare for a hard struggle at the meeting. It was possible to make progress at Geneva, according to Chen, because there was international pressure to achieve a cease-fire in Laos. The Western bloc was not a monolith: Britain and France might not follow the United States completely. As members of the ICC, India was neutral, Canada had the same attitude as Britain, and Poland supported the independence and neutrality of Laos. Burma and Cambodia preferred Lao neutrality. Chen insisted that China work on these Western and neutral countries to reach agreement with them, forcing the United States to go along.[28]

As to cooperation with Moscow, Chen argued that although China had developed major differences with the Soviet Union in the last few years, the two countries were still socialist states under Communist leadership. "At this coming international meeting," Chen insisted, "we must make a distinction between enemies and friends. We must have a good relationship with the Soviet Union and Poland and coordinate our actions . . . in dealing with the enemy." While stressing unity, Chen also cautioned that China should be on alert against the Soviet tendency to compromise with the United States. Chen concluded that prior to the conference, China should consult with the Soviet and North Vietnamese delegations to achieve a common position. On the whole, Chen's assessments of the situation demonstrated his grave concern about the possibility of American intervention in Laos. To him, a cease-fire in Laos was necessary to keep the United States out of Laos.

The CCP central leadership approved Chen's analysis and proposals. Mao and Zhou Enlai gave the Chinese delegation the following instructions: adhere to principle, persevere in struggle, adopt flexible tactics, and strive to reach agreement.[29] Mao also cautioned the Chinese participants that because of the possibility of reactionaries undermining the planned agreement after the cease-fire, China should be prepared.[30]

The deputy head of the Chinese delegation to the Geneva Conference was Vice Foreign Minister Zhang Hanfu, a man with a rich international background. His education included graduate work in international politics and economy at Columbia University in the United States. He once worked for the Comintern in the Soviet Union. As editor in chief of the Communist newspaper *Xinhua ribao* during the anti-Japanese war, he wrote numerous commentaries on international affairs. In 1945, he participated as a Communist member in the Chinese delegation to the founding meeting of the United Nations in San Francisco. He was well versed in several Western languages.[31]

Qiao Guanhua was the third member of the Chinese delegation. He studied German philosophy at Qinghua (Tsinghua) University in Beijing before pursuing an advanced philosophy degree in Japan and Germany. Like Zhang Hanfu, Qiao also contributed many commentaries on international affairs to newspapers during the anti-Japanese war. He worked under Zhou Enlai in the foreign relations section of the CCP's Southern Bureau in Chongqing, China's wartime capital. He participated in the armistice negotiations during the Korean War and the 1954 Geneva Conference.[32]

The Chinese delegation also included Wang Bingnan, the ambassador to Poland, a German-educated intellectual and a close associate of Zhou Enlai during the Chongqing days, and Huan Xiang, chargé d'affaires in London and a former student of the London School of Economics. Of all the delegations to the Geneva Conference, China's was the largest. The Chinese government saw the meeting as a training ground for its officials and diplomats.[33] As Brian Crozier has noted, the size of Beijing's diplomatic effort at Geneva was "a legitimate yardstick to measure the importance of the conference in Chinese eyes."[34]

While preparing for the Geneva Conference, Beijing improved relations with Souvanna Phouma's government. Between April 22 and April 25, 1961, Souvanna visited China, where he concluded agreements with Zhou Enlai to establish diplomatic relations beginning with the exchange of economic and cultural missions. Beijing also agreed to assist Laos to construct roads in the northern province of Phong Saly.[35] The joint statement issued by Zhou Enlai and Souvanna on April 25 pointed out that an expanded Geneva Conference represented the only effective way to reach a peaceful settlement of the Laotian problem.[36]

The Soviet Union urged upon the Pathet Lao and their North Vietnamese mentors the acceptance of a cease-fire, despite the Pathet Lao's favorable military conditions.[37] As one scholar has observed, when the United States "publicly threatened to intervene in Laos and then, in March–April 1961, backed this threat with a series of overt military steps including the mobilization of several thousand troops in Asia," Khrushchev began "pressuring the Pathet Lao and the North Vietnamese to halt their military advances in Laos and commence negotiations in Geneva."[38] At Souvanna Phouma's insistence, Khrushchev summoned Souphanouvong to Moscow on April 16 to discuss and agree "to normalize the situation in Laos," with a cease-fire as a "primary measure." After conferring in Beijing and Hanoi, Souphanouvong expressed his willingness on April 25 to go along with a cease-fire.[39] On May 2, Hanoi radio broadcast a cease-fire order for the Pathet Lao, to take effect the following morning.[40]

The Chinese delegation at the Geneva Conference on Laos, May 1961. Foreign Minister Chen Yi is third from left in the front row. (Courtesy Xinhua News Agency)

On May 10, the Chinese delegation led by Chen Yi arrived in Geneva. At the beginning of the conference, the Laotian rightists claimed that they alone should speak for Laos at the meeting. Disputes over this issue delayed the opening of the conference for four days. The issue of Laotian representation at the conference constituted part of the larger problem of establishing in Laos a government of national union that would represent the whole country.[41]

Unlike Zhou Enlai, who in 1954 had made concessions on the Pathet Lao's representation to achieve an Indochinese settlement, Chen Yi in 1961 insisted on the participation of the Pathet Lao delegation. After the British and French delegates had moderated U.S. secretary of state Dean Rusk's objection to the Pathet Lao's participation, the Geneva cochairmen agreed that any Laotian group could be represented at Geneva so long as it was sponsored by a participating country. This enabled China to sponsor the Pathet Lao delegation.[42]

China's strategy at the conference was to seize the moral high ground by presenting the Communist side as victims and identifying the United States as the aggressor. Chen Yi made full use of rhetoric and image making. He insisted on speaking at the very first session of the conference on May 16. After criticizing the United States as the main culprit in the Laotian crisis and demanding the abolition of SEATO and the withdrawal of U.S. and allied military personnel, including the KMT remnant troops in the Laotian-Burmese border region, from Laos, the Chinese foreign minister stated that the Chinese government had consistently followed the foreign policy of peace and "supported South-

Chen Yi meets with Prime Minister Souvanna Phouma (center) and Prince Souphanouvong (left) during the Geneva Conference on Laos, June 1961. (Courtesy Xinhua News Agency)

east Asian countries in their just cause of practicing a policy of peace and neutrality, safeguarding national independence and opposing interference and aggression from outside." He concluded by claiming that China was ready to work together with other participating countries to make contributions to the peaceful settlement of the Laotian question.[43] Chen's remarks displayed his skillful use of the technique of victimization and the method of combining militancy with reasonableness.

In his address on May 24, Chen proposed five principles that would be the basis for dealing with the Laotian question: adherence to the 1954 Geneva Accords; respect for the independence and sovereignty of Laos; strict insurance of Laotian neutrality; clear distinction between Laos's internal problems to be settled by the Laotians themselves and external problems to be addressed at Geneva; and acceptance of the common agreements by all Geneva participants.[44]

Beijing's guideline of seeking agreement while condemning U.S. policy explained some of the seemingly contradictory remarks Chen Yi made at the conference. For instance, in his comments on the Franco-American draft proposal on June 26, Chen first dismissed it as "absolutely impermissible" and irreconcilable with the Soviet proposal, claiming that "any attempt to impose on Laos an international trusteeship, as provided in the draft protocol, will lead to no other result but rekindling war-flames in Laos." Immediately after this statement of strong opposition to the Franco-American draft, Chen went on to say that "our Conference has all the conditions for reaching an international agreement on the peaceful settlement of the Laotian question, acceptable to all."[45]

In conversations outside formal conference sessions, Chen Yi actively promoted a meeting between the three Laotian princes: Souvanna Phouma, Souphanouvong, and Boun Oum. He urged Sihanouk and the French and Indian delegates to bring the three princes together for the meeting.[46] Eventually, the three princes met in Zurich and agreed, on June 22, 1961, to a set of principles for the creation of a government of national union representing the three parties, following a foreign policy of peace and neutrality in accordance with the 1954 Geneva Accords and reinstituting the electoral law and democratic liberties of 1957.[47]

Zhou Enlai welcomed the Zurich communiqué. He told Leng Ngeth, the Cambodian ambassador to China, on July 10, that "the joint statement by the three princes is beneficial to both the independence and neutrality of Laos and the peace in Southeast Asia." At the same time, the Chinese premier realized that the communiqué had not solved all the internal problems in Laos. He pointed out that "it will not be an easy matter to unite the three factions" in a coalition government.[48]

Zhou believed that the combined strength of the neutralist and leftist forces was superior to that of the rightist force and therefore a new coalition government in Laos should reflect this reality. While attending the Twenty-second Congress of the Communist Party of the Soviet Union in Moscow, Zhou told Quinim Pholsena and Phoumi Vongvichit on October 21, 1961, that the Zurich communiqué indicated the existence of three forces in Laos. Of the three forces, Zhou continued, the neutralist force under Souvanna Phouma was the strongest, the force of the Pathet Lao was the second strongest, and the force of Boun Oum was the weakest. Therefore, Zhou concluded, "a coalition government must reflect this condition."[49]

To protect the interests of the Pathet Lao and prevent U.S. intervention in Laos, China at the Geneva Conference sought to detach Laos from SEATO's protection and minimize the role of the International Control Commission in Laos. Beijing's tactic of demanding more than it really expected to achieve was clearly demonstrated in the controversy over SEATO. Chen Yi demanded not only the removal of SEATO's protection over Laos but also the complete abolition of the organization itself. In private, Chinese officials acknowledged that the latter demand was just a bargaining chip to extract U.S. concessions.[50] What China sought was an agreement that would minimize the American role in Laos and preserve the Pathet Lao's strength.

Despite the unresolved issue of SEATO's protection over Laos, the conference was able, in December 1961, to reach provisional agreements on the international aspect of Laos's neutrality. But negotiations among the three Laotian factions arrived at a deadlock, preventing the conference from moving ahead. On December 27, Boun Oum abruptly called his earlier agreements with Souvanna Phouma and Souphanouvong regarding a coalition government invalid and requested the portfolios of defense and interior for his right-wing group. Boun Oum's hardening position reflected his and Phoumi Nosavan's lingering hope of defeating the Pathet Lao–Kong Le forces on the battleground.[51]

Officials in Beijing were fully aware of the connection between the military and political conditions in Laos. Drawing upon their own experience in dealing with the KMT during the Chinese civil war and the lesson of Dien Bien Phu, the Chinese believed that military advance was a precondition for political solution and that military and political instruments should be used simultaneously. They urged the Pathet Lao to negotiate with the rightist group from a position of strength. In a conversation with Souphanouvong in Beijing on January 28, 1962, Zhou Enlai said: "It will be fine if a coalition government can be organized. . . . You must be prepared to carry out struggle within the coalition government. In any case, to increase your own strength is the most important matter. The final settlement will be decided by force."[52]

In March 1962, the Pathet Lao decided to attack Nam Tha, a town fifteen miles south of the Chinese border, where Phoumi had concentrated 5,000 soldiers.[53] For this purpose, Pathet Lao leaders asked China to provide material assistance. Beijing immediately agreed and directed the Kunming Military Region to implement the aid program. The Kunming Military Region dispatched 2,149 soldiers, 1,772 civilian workers, 203 trucks, and 639 horses and mules to collect and transport military supplies to the Pathet Lao.[54] There is no evidence in the available Chinese sources to confirm the allegation that Chinese troops were involved in the Nam Tha attack.[55]

On May 6, the Pathet Lao captured Nam Tha. About 1,000 defending troops surrendered to the Pathet Lao. To deter further Communist advance in Laos and reassure Thailand, the Kennedy administration reacted to the Nam Tha battle by ordering the Seventh Fleet into the Gulf of Siam and sending two American air squadrons, 5,000 American Marines and infantrymen, and contingents from Britain, Australia, and New Zealand to Thailand between May 12 and 15. In the meantime, Washington sent messages to Moscow through multiple channels that the American political objective remained a neutralized Laos but that the Soviet Union must prevent the Communist forces from making further military moves.[56]

The Nam Tha defeat weakened Phoumi's bargaining position with regard to cabinet portfolios.[57] On June 12, the three princes finally signed an agreement that distributed the portfolios in a government of national union. The agreement made Souvanna Phouma the prime minister in charge of the Ministry of Defense and Phoumi and Souphanouvong deputy prime ministers, each having veto power over cabinet decisions and departmental decisions in defense, interior, and foreign affairs. On July 2, a Lao delegation representing the new government of national union appeared in Geneva to work out the Declaration on the Neutrality of Laos. On July 9, the new Lao leadership issued a statement of neutrality, announcing that Laos would not "recognize the protection of any alliance or military coalition, including SEATO." The fourteen nations attending the Geneva Conference on July 23 signed the declaration.[58] The Geneva Agreements reestablished Laos as a neutral state and created a tripartite government representing the Pathet Lao, the neutralists, and the rightists.

China had good reason to be satisfied with the outcome of the Geneva Conference. By actively intervening in the Laotian issue and presenting itself as a spokesperson for the Communist side at Geneva, Beijing increased its influence and prestige in Southeast Asia. With China's help, the Pathet Lao benefited from the Geneva settlement. It won international recognition at the conference, and its members were included in the coalition government after the meeting. The Geneva Agreements called for the withdrawal of U.S. military personnel and deprived SEATO of all pretexts for interfering in Laotian affairs, leaving the Pathet Lao in control of the eastern part of Laos. The role of the International Commission was confined within the framework of cooperation with the Lao government.

SINO-SOVIET INTERACTIONS AT GENEVA

Despite Chen Yi's intention to unite with the Soviet Union at the conference and despite the Sino-Soviet shared goal of keeping the United States out of Laos without provoking direct American intervention, the Chinese found themselves at loggerheads with the Russians regarding the long-term prospect for Laos.[59] Beijing's action was taken in the context of its policy to roll back the U.S. containment shield against China in Southeast Asia, to preserve the Pathet Lao's strength, and to increase China's influence in the region. Moscow's position, in contrast, was determined by its search for a détente with Washington.[60]

In his speech at the opening day of the conference Chen Yi clearly indicated the independent nature of China's stance. That Chen spoke before the Soviet delegate constituted a departure from the usual practice. At the United Nations and at other international meetings, one of the Soviet Union's delegates was always the first speaker among Communist delegations.[61]

In behind-the-scenes comments, Chinese officials criticized the Soviet

Union for attempting to "freeze" Laos and establish a permanent neutrality in the country on the model of Austria and Switzerland.[62] Zhang Yan, a senior associate of Chen Yi, stated in his internal report on the Geneva Conference that, rather than assuming responsibility for the Laotian revolution, the Soviet Union wanted to reach a compromise with the United States in order to demonstrate the success of its policy of peaceful coexistence. During the conference, Zhang went on, the Soviet delegation was in a hurry to conclude agreement without making sure that the Pathet Lao was in a strong military position at the negotiation table. Zhang criticized the Soviet Union for pressuring Souphanouvong to make undue concessions in his negotiations with the rightists. He suspected that in addition to exploiting the Laos issue to create an example of peaceful coexistence, Moscow also desired to limit China's influence through its intervention in Laos.[63] Clearly, the emerging Sino-Soviet dispute colored Chinese officials' perceptions of Soviet intentions.

Chinese leaders' suspicion of Moscow's intention to minimize China's role in Laos was shared by U.S. policymakers. In response to President Kennedy's query as to why the Soviet Union was unwilling to push the Laos crisis to a broader conflict, Secretary of State Rusk said that the Soviets "had an interest in controlling Communist intervention in Laos rather than letting the Chinese Communists take charge."[64] Llewellyn Thompson, the U.S. ambassador to the Soviet Union, believed that Khrushchev's main reason for intervening in Laos was to keep the Chinese out.[65]

Beijing's and Moscow's difference in opinion over Laos was clearly revealed in their attitudes toward the Nam Tha battle. While the Chinese encouraged and supported the Pathet Lao's offensive, the Russians opposed the operation. According to J. M. Addis, the British ambassador to Laos, A. N. Abramov, the Soviet ambassador in Vientiane, failed in his attempt to persuade Souphanouvong to stop the attack at Nam Tha.[66]

The Chinese showed disdain for the Soviet tendency to solve local issues through superpower dialogues. While Soviet foreign minister Andrei Gromyko emphasized the importance of the Kennedy-Khrushchev summit in Vienna in June 1961 to the successful negotiations at Geneva, Chen Yi dismissed the summit.[67] In a conversation with Wu Lengxi, the Chinese foreign minister criticized the two superpowers for treating Laos as a bargaining chip in their negotiations.[68]

At the 1954 Geneva Conference Soviet foreign minister Molotov had intervened in Sino-American relations by bringing up the issue of Chinese students who were unable to return to China in his talks with U.S. officials and had facilitated China's rapprochement with Britain by arranging meetings between Zhou Enlai and British foreign secretary Anthony Eden.[69] But in 1961, Soviet delegates paid little attention to the issues of China's security and KMT troops and showed more interest in preserving smooth communications with the United States.[70]

In public, Chinese officials maintained cooperation and unity with the Soviet delegates at Geneva, but in private they criticized Moscow for subordinating the Laotian issue to its global policy of détente with the United States. The experience of the Geneva Conference reinforced China's distrust of the Kremlin's advocacy of peaceful coexistence with the West.[71]

SINO-VIETNAMESE RELATIONS AT THE CONFERENCE

Hanoi had played a special role in Laos. The VWP had a mentor-pupil relationship with the Pathet Lao, which was organized in Vietnam in 1951. During 1953–54, Ho Chi Minh's troops attacked French forces in northern and central Laos and helped establish the Pathet Lao in the two northern Lao provinces of Sam Neua and Phong Saly.[72] A Vietnamese veteran of the 1953–54 Laotian war subsequently told Mieczyslaw Maneli, a member of the Polish delegation to the ICC in Vietnam, that because of the "very low level of national and cultural awareness" and poor communication facilities in Laos, "the Vietnamese, as their older brothers, must bear the brunt of the fighting, must organize and lead" the Laotians. Maneli's Vietnamese interlocutor claimed: "The political border between Vietnam and Laos is an artificial one. Vietnamese living close to the border can be considered Laotians and Laotians Vietnamese. National differences, in the struggle against colonialism, are unimportant anyhow, and in these regions negligible."[73]

The 1954 Geneva Accords required the Viet Minh to withdraw north of the seventeenth parallel in Vietnam, and the Pathet Lao were regrouped in Sam Neua and Phong Saly pending their negotiated integration into a national unity government and the Royal Lao Army. Between 1954 and 1958, the DRV was preoccupied with economic recovery and state-building in the north. In 1959, Hanoi began to intensify revolutionary war in the south. To infiltrate men and supplies into South Vietnam, the control of eastern Laos was crucial for Hanoi. In July 1959, Pathet Lao forces launched assaults in Sam Neua, which is on the border between Laos and the DRV, to recover control of rural territories in the province as a base for future operations.[74]

The Pathet Lao worked closely with leaders in Hanoi in planning for the Geneva Conference. At this time, North Vietnam had about twenty thousand workers repairing roads in Laos and some one thousand drivers in Laotian service. Seven hundred North Vietnamese soldiers and auxiliary personnel were either killed or injured during the spring of 1961. Policymakers in Hanoi viewed their effort in Laos as a part of the protracted struggle for the liberation of the unified strategic area of Indochina. Suspecting that the United States would employ military force if negotiations failed to disarm the Pathet Lao, the Vietnamese believed that the Pathet Lao should preserve its base area, maintain its alliance with the neutralists, and work for the conditions that would strengthen its influence and appeal. Hanoi's main objective for the negotiations was to achieve an independent and neutral Laos recognized by other countries but not requiring any international guarantees.[75] Clearly, the North Vietnamese shared with the Chinese a similar approach to the Geneva Conference: to use neutralization to help the Pathet Lao gain strength.

At Geneva, Beijing and Hanoi worked closely to prevent American intervention and to preserve the Pathet Lao's position. They coordinated their efforts by focusing on the theme of American aggression in Indochina and stressing the importance that the Laotian problem be resolved by the Laotians themselves. Chen Shuliang, an official in the Asian Department of the Chinese Foreign Ministry and a member of the Chinese delegation to the Geneva Conference, recalled that on average he visited the DRV's delegation twice a week at Geneva to discuss the progress of the conference with Ung Van Khiem and Hoang Van Hoan. According to Chen, both he and Chen Yi got along especially well with Hoan at Geneva. Hoan often came to the residence of the PRC delegation to play Chinese chess with Chen Yi.[76]

Because of the presence of their military personnel in Laos,[77] North Vietnamese delegates frequently found themselves in an awkward position at Geneva. They were often hard-pressed by Western diplomats to acknowledge their military involvement in Laos. Chen Yi helped them out by dwelling on American intervention and the threat of SEATO. In private, Chinese officials noted the inexperience of the North Vietnamese at the conference. When Malcolm MacDonald, the chief British delegate, asked the DRV representatives to give a "yes or no" answer to his question of whether they had troops in Laos, the North Vietnamese replied that they only had Red Cross personnel there. Zhang Yan observed in his internal report on the Geneva Conference that the North Vietnamese had not made an appropriate reply. Instead of answering MacDonald's question directly, Zhang pointed out, the North Vietnamese should have asked the British if the United States was prepared to withdraw its troops from Laos.[78]

Chinese leaders had an ambivalent view of Hanoi's role in Laos. On the one hand, they were fully aware of the historical and special relationship between the VWP and the Pathet Lao. Chen Yi acknowledged at an inner party meeting in August 1962 that North Vietnam had provided greater help to the Pathet Lao than either China or the Soviet Union had. According to Chen Yi, Mao once told Ho Chi Minh that "you must bear more responsibility for Southeast Asia, especially Laos."[79] On the other hand, Mao and his advisers were also jealous of Hanoi's special ties with the Pathet Lao. They were apprehensive about the Vietnamese tendency to establish hegemony over Laos. At the 1954 Geneva Conference, they had criticized the Vietnamese for advocating the "Indochina Federation." They saw the current Geneva meeting as an opportunity to increase China's influence in Laos. According to Chen Shuliang, at Geneva Chen Yi at one point invited the representatives from the three Laotian delegations to a banquet. When the chief Vietnamese adviser to the Pathet Lao delegation learned about the event, he asked the Chinese why he had not received an invitation. Chen Yi replied brusquely, "We have only invited the delegates from the three sides of Laos. We did not invite the Vietnamese delegates."[80]

On the whole, the Chinese found more to agree upon with the North Vietnamese than with the Russians at Geneva. At the 1954 Geneva Conference, China had pressured the DRV to accept the partition of Vietnam at the seventeenth parallel. At the Laos conference, there was little evidence of Beijing putting pressure on Hanoi to do anything. The lack of Soviet support was the primary reason for Hanoi's reliance on Beijing. In comparison with China and the Soviet Union, North Vietnam played a minor role at Geneva, one much less influential than at the 1954 conference, where it had negotiated the cease-fire agreement with the French on behalf of the Pathet Lao. The DRV was not included in the Drafting Committee or the important informal meetings among the major powers.[81]

Peace, however, was a mirage in Laos because neither the Pathet Lao nor the right-wing group was ready to give up its struggle for power and neither the United States nor North Vietnam and China really intended to neutralize Laos. Outside powers continued to intervene in Laos. The United States maintained its instruments of intervention: Air America, the Meo (Hmong) army, and the CIA. A special Requirements Office operated by retired military personnel was created within the American embassy in Vientiane to keep contact with the Royal Lao Army and handle its military aid requests. Seventy members of the former U.S. Military Advisory Assistance Group in Laos were reassigned to the U.S. Military Advisory Group in Thailand, from where they helped deliver military supplies.[82]

The North Vietnamese did not withdraw from Laos either. U.S. intelligence estimates of Hanoi's strength in Laos at the time of the 1962 agreement stood at about five thousand, with the Pathet Lao along with an equal number supporting the neutralist troops under Kong Le. Only forty personnel from North Vietnam were counted departing from the country by the ICC observers.[83] The control of eastern Laos was crucial to Hanoi's strategy in South Vietnam. And in 1964 China would dispatch a secret team of advisers to the headquarters of the LPP and provide military equipment to the Pathet Lao.

So long as Hanoi was determined to use Lao territory to infiltrate men and supplies to South Vietnam and so long as the United States was resolved to stop North Vietnam's action, peace was out of the question for Laos. Neither the North Vietnamese nor the Americans saw any benefit in strict adherence to the Geneva Agreements. Both tried their utmost to manipulate political groups in Laos to advance their own interests. In the words of the Laos specialist Martin Stuart-Fox, "Both the United States and the DRV consistently lied over what each was doing in Laos, and though few were fooled, least of all the Lao themselves, the very deception demeaned the nation's independence and international standing."[84]

While Beijing and Hanoi increased their involvement in Laos, Moscow completely disengaged from the country after the Geneva Conference.[85] During the conference, Soviet deputy foreign minister Georgi Pushkin and U.S. representative Harriman had reached agreement on the desirability of a neutral and independent Laos. According to the Pushkin-Harriman understanding, the Soviet Union would be responsible for compliance by the Communist side, including the DRV and the Pathet Lao, while Britain and the United States would be responsible for the non-Communist side. Moscow would ensure that Hanoi would view Lao neutrality to include preventing North Vietnamese use of Laos as a corridor to South Vietnam.[86] After the conclusion of the Geneva Accords, Harriman called Leonard Unger, U.S. ambassador-designate to Laos, to Geneva to meet with Sergei Afanasseyev, the new Soviet ambassador to Laos. Harriman and Pushkin asked the two Vientiane-bound diplomats to "work together and make it [the Geneva Agreements] work."[87]

After the signing of the Geneva Agreements, the Soviet Union suspended the airlift to the Pathet Lao and the neutralist forces. When China complained about the Kremlin's decision, Soviet deputy foreign minister V. V. Kuznetsov on September 3, 1962, delivered a note to the Chinese embassy emphasizing the credibility of the Soviet commitment to international agreements and linking Laos to the German issue. "Surely you will agree," it read, "that the transport of military material to Laos on Soviet planes with Soviet crews could not go unperceived. . . . [H]ow would socialist proposals to guarantee a free city status for West Berlin look if socialist countries began to violate the only recently signed Geneva agreement?"[88]

North Vietnam's continued presence in Laos after Geneva demonstrated that Moscow had little leverage over Hanoi. Moscow was clearly unable to enforce Pushkin's pledges to prevent North Vietnamese violation of Lao sovereignty. As Khrushchev distanced himself from Indochina, the DRV would move closer to China for support in realizing its goal of national reunification.

ASSESSING CHINA'S ROLE AT THE LAOS CONFERENCE

A combination of geopolitical, ideological, and ethnocentric factors shaped Beijing's approach to the Laotian crisis. From the strategic perspective, leaders in China felt threatened by a hostile regime in Laos closely aligned with the United States. They sought to roll back the American presence in Laos. Ideologically speaking, Chinese officials felt an international obligation to help the Pathet Lao preserve its strength. They wished to see the Pathet Lao's revolution succeed eventually. In 1961, they endorsed the Geneva Conference primarily as a means to win time for the Pathet Lao to consolidate its position and to forestall American intervention. The serious economic problems caused by the Great Leap Forward constrained the Chinese leaders, who found it prudent to negotiate rather than to escalate their commitments in the Laotian civil war. Finally, the crisis in Laos and the convening of the Geneva Conference presented Beijing an opportunity to increase its prestige in the international community and to reassert its traditional influence in Southeast Asia.

While Chinese leaders were aware of the special bond between Vietnam and Laos and expected the VWP to play an active role in supporting the Pathet Lao, China's increasing involvement in Laos unavoidably produced rivalry with Hanoi. The North Vietnamese were caught in a dilemma: on the one hand, they needed China's support in resisting the United States in Indochina; on the other hand, they feared that Beijing's engagement might undermine their privileges and special position in Laos. Sino–North Vietnamese competitions in Laos constituted one of the reasons for the eventual breakdown of Beijing-Hanoi cooperation.

5 DEEPER ENTANGLEMENT 1961–1964

When Kennedy entered the White House in early 1961, the number of American advisers in South Vietnam stood at 685. Brushing aside his predecessor Eisenhower's advice that it was Laos and not South Vietnam that was the key to Indochina, the new president set out to increase U.S. commitment to the Saigon regime. He approved an increase in the MAAG of 100 advisers and sent to South Vietnam 400 Special Forces (soon called Green Berets) to train the ARVN in counterinsurgency techniques. Financial support was provided to Saigon to establish a "strategic hamlet" program and to expand local militia.[1]

Concerned about this escalation of the U.S. military involvement in South Vietnam, Pham Van Dong visited Beijing in June to seek China's assistance. Mao expressed a general support for the armed struggle of the South Vietnamese people, while Zhou Enlai continued to stress flexibility in tactics and the importance of "blending legal and illegal struggle and combining political and military approaches."[2]

Between September and October 1961, the VWP reorganized and strengthened its Central Office for South Vietnam (COSVN); at an expanded meeting shortly afterward the latter passed a resolution advocating intensification of the anti-American struggle. Predicting a "high tide" in the southern insurgency in the near future, it called for equal attention to be paid to the military and political aspects of the struggle. It pointed out that the situation could develop into a "total war" either because of an aggressive action by the United States or because of errors in the application of the party's policy in the south.[3] The new decision was immediately reflected in the sharp increase in the number of NLF operations in the fall of 1961. For a short period of time, the Communist insurgents even captured a provincial capital just fifty-five miles from Saigon. U.S. intelligence officers reported a substantial increase in the size of regular guerrilla units.[4] There were 150 guerrilla incident reports in October in comparison with only 50 in September.[5]

Chinese leaders were uneasy about their Vietnamese comrades' tendency to conduct large-unit operations in the south. They expressed their worry both in their internal statements and in their advice to the North Vietnamese. In a speech to the National Conference on Foreign Affairs in December 1961, Zhang Yan complained that while the situation in South Vietnam was favorable, the Vietnamese Communists "have exposed themselves too much." "It is inappropriate for them to wage large-unit operations," Zhang went on. They should carry out protracted guerrilla warfare to expand their forces for "three to five years, even eight or ten years."[6]

Marshal Ye Jianying, who was leading a Chinese military delegation to visit the DRV between December 15 and 31 in participation of the seventeenth anniversary celebration of the founding of the PAVN, urged caution in his conversations with Hanoi's leaders. A native of Guangdong province, Ye had been acquainted with Ho Chi Minh when the latter returned to southern China from Moscow in the fall of 1938. After 1949, Ye first served as chairman of the Guangdong Provincial People's Government before being appointed director of the PLA Military Inspectorate in 1954. When Ye visited Hanoi in December 1961, he was president of the PLA Military Science Academy. According to PAVN colonel Bui Tin, the Chinese visitors told the North Vietnamese that the correct way to defeat the U.S.-backed regime in the south was to engage in guerrilla warfare in the mountains and not to launch operations at battalion strength. Large-scale battles, the Chinese cautioned, would expose the Vietnamese Communist forces to attack by American airplanes and tanks.[7]

Why did the Chinese advise caution? One explanation seems to be the constraint of the continuing domestic economic problems on the maneuverability of policymakers in Beijing. By the end of 1961, mass starvation had further spread in China. In many provinces, the sick, the elderly, and infants were the first to die. Wives were sold for food and cash. Village cadres signed documents allowing peasants to go begging. In Beijing, per capita annual pork consumption dropped from 13.3 catties in 1958 to 2.1 catties in 1961.[8] Given this grim domestic situation, Chinese leaders were not prepared to risk provoking a confrontation with the Americans. They feared that the Vietnamese Communists' large-scale battles might drag them into an unwanted war with the United States.

The year 1962 saw a major turning point in both the U.S. involvement in

Vietnam and Chinese attitudes toward the Indochina conflict. In February, Washington established in Saigon the Military Assistance Command, Vietnam, to replace the MAAG. The Kennedy administration coupled this move with a drastic increase in the number of American "advisers" and the amount of military hardware it was sending to the Diem regime, marking a new level of U.S. intervention in Vietnam. Kennedy also permitted the employment of defoliants to deprive the guerrillas of cover and secure major roads.[9]

POLICY DEBATE IN ZHONGNANHAI

In the spring of 1962, an important debate broke out within the Chinese leadership over the likelihood of a world war, the possibility of peaceful coexistence with capitalist countries, and the degree to which China should support national liberation movements. The central figure triggering the debate was Wang Jiaxiang, director of the International Liaison Department of the CCP Central Committee.

Wang Jiaxiang had been trained in Moscow in the 1920s. He served as ambassador to the Soviet Union from October 1949 to January 1951, when he became director of the International Liaison Department, which dealt with foreign Communist parties.[10] In the spring of 1960, Wang became seriously concerned with the widespread famine in the countryside as a result of the disaster of the Great Leap Forward. He wanted to reduce tensions with the United States, the Soviet Union, and India so that China could concentrate on domestic recovery and famine relief.[11]

On February 27, 1962, Wang Jiaxiang sent a letter to Zhou Enlai, Deng Xiaoping, and Chen Yi, the three officials in charge of foreign policy. The letter also bore the signature of Liu Ningyi and Wu Xiuquan, deputy directors of the International Liaison Department. In the letter, Wang criticized the tendency to overrate the danger of world war and to underestimate the possibility of peaceful coexistence with imperialism. In terms of support for national liberation movements, Wang emphasized restraint, calling attention to China's own economic problems and limitations in resources. On the issue of Vietnam, he asked the party to "guard against a Korea-style war created by American imperialists" and warned about the danger of "Khrushchev and his associates dragging us into the trap of war." Wang proposed that in order to adjust and restore the economy and win time to get through difficulties, China should adopt a policy of peace and conciliation in foreign affairs, and that in the area of foreign aid China should not do what it could not afford.[12] What Wang demanded was basically a return to the Bandung spirit of "peaceful coexistence" with the international status quo.

Wang Jiaxiang's ideas came under heavy attack by Mao at the Central Work

Conference held at Beidaihe in August 1962. Mao fiercely condemned what he perceived as "revisionist" trends in Chinese domestic and foreign policies during the first half of 1962, when he had voluntarily disengaged himself from daily policymaking. On the domestic front, the CCP chairman criticized the practice of returning to individual farming as a violation of the principle of collectivization in the countryside. In the area of foreign policy, Mao singled out Wang Jiaxiang's proposal, condemning him for promoting a "revisionist" international line of "three appeasements and one reduction" (appeasement to imperialism, revisionism, and international reactionaries, and reduction of assistance to national liberation movements).[13] Wang's suggestion of policy moderation constituted the only known case of an alternative foreign policy line coming from within the bureaucracy that did not reflect the wish of the supreme leader. Mao's condemnation of Wang revealed his limited tolerance for independent opinions.

Why did Mao choose the summer of 1962 to launch a counterattack on his colleagues and to regain control of policymaking? What had happened to inject a new surge of confidence in the CCP leader? The decisive factor, according to Roderick MacFarquhar's study, appears to be the size of the summer harvest. Mao had a track record of taking policy initiatives when he had indications of bumper harvests to come. This was true of his previous two major agricultural initiatives: collectivization in 1955 and the commune drive in 1958, both of which were launched in the summer, presumably after he had been informed of impending good harvests.[14] Encouraged by the promise of a bountiful harvest in the summer of 1962, Mao again became optimistic and bold.

The outcome of the 1962 foreign policy debate had major implications for China's attitude toward Vietnam. If Wang Jiaxiang's moderate suggestions had been adopted, China's role in Indochina would have been limited. But Mao rejected Wang's ideas, preferring confrontation (short of war) with the United States. This militant approach in foreign policy was in line with Mao's heightened emphasis on class struggle and radical politics in Chinese domestic affairs in the second half of 1962. Mao had become increasingly unhappy with the course Liu Shaoqi and Deng Xiaoping were following in the wake of the Great Leap Forward. Convinced that his successors had lost interest in continuing the revolution, Mao felt the need to rekindle class struggle in order to maintain revolutionary momentum. He decided to use the struggle against U.S. imperialism, the conflict with "Soviet revisionism," and support for national liberation movements to give publicity to his political views in China and to overcome domestic obstacles to his program of "continuous revolution." Wang Jiaxiang's proposal came at the right time for Mao to launch his attack on "revisionism." Here was a clear case of the domestic link in Mao's international policy. Similarly, between 1963 and 1964 Mao would use the nine polemics against "Soviet revisionism" to publicize at home what amounted to, in effect, an attack on the policies of his own associates. Mao's criticism of Wang Jiaxiang and his reassertion of his radical views anticipated an active Chinese role in the unfolding crisis in Vietnam. With the rejection of Wang's proposal, Mao gave up the opportunity to avert the later Sino-American hostility over Indochina.

In the summer of 1962, Ho Chi Minh and Nguyen Chi Thanh visited Beijing to discuss with Chinese leaders the serious situation created by U.S. intervention in Vietnam and the possibility of an American attack against North Vietnam. Ho asked the Chinese to provide support for the guerrilla movement in South Vietnam. Beijing satisfied Ho's demand by agreeing to give the DRV, free of charge, 90,000 rifles and guns that could equip 230 infantry battalions. These weapons would be used to support guerrilla warfare in the south.[15]

It is important to note that Ho Chi Minh and Nguyen Chi Thanh came to China at a time when Beijing was confronting pressures from several directions. First, the Chinese military was preparing for war as a result of Chiang Kai-shek's threat to attack the mainland[16] and the rising number of border skirmishes with India. The PLA was facing the danger of a two-front war. Second, the tensions along the Sino-Soviet border were high as a result of an uprising by the Kazakhs in Chinese Central Asia between April and May 1962.[17] In a report to Mao on August 10, the CCP Central Military Commission stated that during the previous three months it had focused on taking emergency measures to prepare for an invasion by the U.S. and Nationalist forces from Taiwan and for a war on the Sino-Indian border. The measures included the early implementation of the 1962 conscription plan and the mobilization of troops.[18] Despite the urgent need to deal with Chiang Kai-shek and India as well as the pressure from the Sino-Soviet border, Mao showed no hesitation in supporting Ho Chi Minh's struggle in Vietnam.

On October 5, Vo Nguyen Giap led a DRV military delegation to Beijing to seek further Chinese aid. Zhou Enlai told the North Vietnamese visitors that the mutual assistance between China and the DRV was all-encompassing, covering not only military cooperation but also political and economic affairs.[19] In a second conversation with the North Vietnamese delegation two days later, the Chinese premier further explained Beijing's position on a series of international issues, including the nuclear question. He criticized Moscow's practice of seeking a monopoly of nuclear secrets by several great powers, asserting that when the Soviet Union proposed a ban on nuclear proliferation, imperialist countries had already spread nuclear information. After criticizing the Kremlin for advocating a nuclear test ban, Zhou turned to a discussion of the relationships between men and weapons in warfare, between the party and the army, and between officers and soldiers. He contended that men were the ulti-mate defining factor in the outcome of war and that weapons only played a supplementary role.[20] Clearly, Zhou wanted to prevent the North Vietnamese from believing in what he viewed as the fallacy of weapons-determinism and overlooking the more crucial factors like party leadership and indoctrination of soldiers.

CHALLENGES AND OPPORTUNITIES

Consultations between Hanoi and Beijing regarding the revolutionary strug-gle in the south stepped up in 1963. China was prepared to make a major commitment to North Vietnam. In March, Luo Ruiqing visited the DRV and discussed with his hosts how China might support Hanoi if the United States attacked North Vietnam.[21] During his official visit to Hanoi as head of state of the PRC in May, Liu Shaoqi assured Ho Chi Minh: "We are standing by your side, and if war breaks out, you can regard China as your rear."[22] Liu also held party-to-party talks with Ho, Le Duan, and other VWP leaders on the issues concerning the international Communist movement.[23]

During the spring and summer of 1963, major events took place in Laos and South Vietnam, presenting both challenges and opportunities for the Com-munist movements there. Active Pathet Lao participation in the coalition government ended in April after the assassination of two neutralist representa-tives and the withdrawal of Souphanouvong to Khang Khay. Between May and June, Buddhist protests and demonstrations against the Diem government broke out, and the self-immolation of a Buddhist monk at an intersection in Saigon shocked the world. In mid-August, an intransigent and enraged Diem declared martial law, suspended all civil liberties, and banned public gather-ings. Madame Ngo Dinh Nhu, Diem's sister-in-law, during a trip to the United States, made highly insensitive remarks about the deaths. These events demon-strated Diem's corruption, repression, and unpopularity.[24] Responding to Ho Chi Minh's call for an international condemnation of the Saigon regime, Mao on August 29 issued a statement strongly denouncing the "atrocities of the U.S.-Diem clique" and resolutely supporting the "just struggle" of the South Vietnamese people.[25]

In view of the rapidly changing situation in Laos and South Vietnam, leaders in Beijing felt the need to review revolutionary strategies and coordi-nate the Communist movements in Southeast Asia. In late September, Zhou Enlai went to Conghua, Guangdong province, to meet with leaders of the VWP, the LPP, and the Indonesian Communist Party (PKI). Present at the meeting were Ho Chi Minh, Le Duan, Muoi Cuc (code name for Nguyen Van Linh), Nguyen Chi Thanh of the VWP, Kaysone Phomvihane of the LPP, and D. N.

Mao meets with Nguyen Thi Binh, August 29, 1963. (Courtesy Xinhua News Agency)

Aidit of the PKI. The conference was held to develop a comprehensive estimate of the existing situations and future developments in Southeast Asia and to work out a regional strategy. After analyzing Washington's tendency to intervene in Vietnam and Laos, Zhou asserted that the United States was overstretched in the world because it had committed troops to too many places. Therefore, if the United States initiated war in Indochina, it would suffer defeat. The countries of Southeast Asia, Zhou said, should establish confidence in their final victory over the Americans. The basic goals for revolution in Southeast Asia, according to Zhou, were anti-imperialism, antifeudalism, and antibureaucratic capitalism. Zhou introduced four methods for realizing these goals: mobilizing masses and expanding the united front; going to the countryside to wage armed struggle and to establish base areas; strengthening party leadership over all fronts; and increasing contact between countries and supporting each other's struggle. Zhou promised that China would serve as a rear area for the revolutionary movements in Southeast Asia and do its utmost to support the anti-imperialist struggle of Southeast Asian countries. In the end, Zhou suggested concrete measures for dealing with American counterinsurgency warfare.[26]

The methods and suggestions that Zhou Enlai outlined for the three Southeast Asian parties were based on the CCP's own experiences during its struggle with the Japanese and the KMT in the 1930s and 1940s. The inclusion of the PKI in the meeting was significant because it indicated Beijing's interest in fostering revolution in a broad area in Southeast Asia.[27] In the early 1960s, Mao and his associates placed great hope on the PKI. While urging the Indonesian Communists to develop their own rural base area, the Chinese also encouraged them to seek a united front with President Sukarno, who was viewed as "progressive" and "anti-imperialist." Mao wanted to exploit Sukarno's confrontation with the Federation of Malaya and Britain to counterbalance the SEATO and to weaken the American influence in Southeast Asia and the Pacific.[28]

In a speech at the 1964 National Conference on Foreign Affairs, Zhang Yan claimed that the PKI had a "mature" leadership.[29] But the events of September 1965 would show that Zhang's judgment was premature and overly optimistic. The PKI's reliance on electoral politics and the "united front from above" and its failure to create an independent armed force and a solid base area made the organization highly vulnerable to the counterattack launched by the right-wing forces.[30]

Zhou Enlai's meeting with the Southeast Asian parties in September 1963 should also be viewed in the context of the widening Sino-Soviet dispute. The meeting took place at a time when the Sino-Soviet feud was bursting into a public exchange of charges and revelations communicated through lengthy, detailed letters and statements issued by both sides, and when Khrushchev was calling for an international conference to expel the Chinese from the international communist movement. Zhou was clearly attempting to win the Southeast Asian parties over to China.[31] In a similar effort to enlist support for China's position, Liu Shaoqi visited North Korea between September 15 and 27 and held talks with Kim Il Sung.[32] (Hanoi's attitude toward the escalating Sino-Soviet dispute will be discussed later in this chapter.)

The internal disturbance and antigovernment demonstrations in South Vietnam in 1963 greatly encouraged policymakers in Beijing and Hanoi, convincing them that it was time to intensify revolutionary war against Diem. U.S. intelligence analysts in October reported an escalation of Communist military assaults in South Vietnam since mid-1963. In his October 22 memorandum to Secretary of State Dean Rusk, Thomas L. Hughes, director of the State Department's Bureau of Intelligence and Research, wrote: "Since July 1963, the trend in Viet Cong casualties, weapons losses, and defections has been downward while the number of Viet Cong armed attacks and other incidents has been upward."[33]

The assassination of Diem by the ARVN's top generals in early November greatly heartened the Communist fighters in South Vietnam, who saw the death of Diem and the consequent political crisis in Saigon as advantageous to their cause. Calling the coups in Saigon "gifts from heaven," Nguyen Huu Tho, president of the NLF, claimed: "Our enemy has been seriously weakened from all points of view, military, political and administrative. Their armed forces have suffered heavy losses on the battlefield and from desertions. The special shock troops which were an essential support for the Diem regime have been eliminated. The military command has been turned upside down and weakened by purges."[34]

In December 1963, General Li Tianyou, deputy chief of staff of the PLA, led a Chinese military inspection mission to North Vietnam. After spending about two months in the DRV visiting various strategic sites, the Chinese delegation presented to the PAVN a war preparation plan, which outlined the way China would assist the DRV in constructing defense works and naval bases in the northeastern part of the country.[35] Confident of support from Beijing and encouraged by the turmoil in South Vietnam in the wake of Diem's assassination, the VWP at its Ninth Plenum held in December 1963 adopted an offensive strategy to intensify its military struggle in the south. The party decided to increase the level of military aid to be provided by the north but not to commit combat units to the fighting in the south.[36] Mao wrote to Ho Chi Minh on December 27, congratulating him on concluding an "excellent" meeting.[37]

THE CCP WORK TEAM IN SAM NEUA

Consultations between the CCP and the Pathet Lao also stepped up in the wake of the Conghua meeting. In October 1963, Kaysone Phomvihane, secretary-general of the LPP, visited Beijing to ask the Chinese to help his party build its bases and wage war against the United States. Zhou Enlai told Kaysone that China was unfamiliar with the conditions in Laos. When the LPP leader suggested that Beijing send a team to Laos to investigate the situation, the CCP agreed to dispatch a secret work team to Sam Neua, where the LPP headquarters were located.[38]

Zhou Enlai was responsible for organizing the work team. He selected General Duan Suquan as the team leader because Duan had administrative, military, and diplomatic experience. After serving as a division political commissar in the Red Army, Duan later participated in the negotiations with the Americans and the Nationalists during the civil war. At the time of his Lao appointment, Duan was deputy provost and director of the Strategic Teaching and Research Section in the PLA's Advanced Military Academy. Zhou praised Duan as "a resourceful man" who could "endure hardships" and was "loyal" to the party.[39]

Duan Suquan and his team arrived in Laos in 1964, instructed by Beijing to do three tasks: investigate the situation of the Pathet Lao, especially in the areas of party, army, and base-area building, report to Beijing its findings, and transmit opinions between the CCP and the LPP. During its four-year stay in Laos, the team provided extensive advice to the Pathet Lao in the areas of military operations and intelligence gathering, the treatment of captured U.S. pilots, policy toward ethnic minorities, and land reform. Zhou Enlai kept in close contact with the team during its sojourn in Laos.[40]

The experiences of the CCP Work Team in Sam Neua revealed the delicate and intriguing relationship between the CCP, the VWP, and the LPP. Upon arriving in Laos, the Chinese advisers immediately felt the strong presence of the North Vietnamese in the Pathet Lao's territory and found their work complicated by the special relationship between the VWP and the LPP. According to Hu Zhengqing's observations, North Vietnam's influence permeated the Pathet Lao's party and government structures. In Sam Neua, Hanoi had stationed an advisory mission headed by Nguyen Trong Vinh, deputy director of the Western Work Committee of the VWP. The mission was divided into two sections: administrative and military. The military section included a command, a political department, and a logistic department. It had dual responsibilities: to advise the Lao People's Army in military planning and implementation, political mobilization of troops, and logistic supplies; and to direct the North Vietnamese army units in Laos. (In the Sam Neua region alone, Hanoi had one infantry battalion, one antiaircraft battery battalion, and one army engineer brigade.) The North Vietnamese administrative advisers were deployed throughout Pathet Lao central government departments as well as provincial and county organizations. The military advisers were sent to all the departments of the Lao People's Army's general command and to each of its battalions and companies. The Kommadam Military School, the Pathet Lao's only military institution for training middle-level and senior officers, used North Vietnamese textbooks for teaching. The North Vietnamese army helped the Pathet Lao's troops fight Vang Pao's forces, who were the allies of the United States in Laos.[41]

The North Vietnamese in general carried more weight with the Pathet Lao than the Chinese. At receptions, Nguyen Trong Vinh usually took the first seat of foreign guests ahead of Duan Suquan. When Vietnamese and Chinese suggestions differed, the Pathet Lao took Vietnamese advice. This was clearly demonstrated by the debate over land reform. In 1964, a joint Pathet Lao–Chinese–North Vietnamese work group on land reform was established to investigate landowning conditions. The Chinese advisers believed that class divisions existed in the Lao countryside and that the existing landowning system was exploitative. They suggested that the Pathet Lao organize mass rallies to denounce and execute big landlords and to confiscate their land and distribute it to landless peasants. The North Vietnamese advisers, however, offered a different approach. They argued that the abolition of the existing landowning system should be conducted through consultation and negotiation rather than class struggle and confiscation. Eventually, the Pathet Lao adopted the Vietnamese position. Kaysone Phomvihane told Duan Suquan that land reform was necessary but at the moment conditions were not ripe for the abolition of the existing landowning system. Thus the LPP rejected the more drastic Chinese methods.[42]

In view of the failure of land reform in the DRV in 1956, the LPP's refusal to adopt China's proposal was a correct decision. A drastic class struggle based on the Chinese model in the areas under the Pathet Lao's control would have created major social and economic problems for the Pathet Lao. Drawing on the bitter lessons of their own land reform, the North Vietnamese were more sensitive to the conditions of Lao rural society. The disagreement over class struggle highlighted Hanoi's main objective in Laos. The VWP was less concerned with Laos as a laboratory of revolution than how the Pathet Lao forces could help keep open the Ho Chi Minh Trail through Laos, which was the lifeline of Hanoi's troops and supplies into South Vietnam.

LEANING TOWARD CHINA IN THE SINO-SOVIET RIFT

Mao's eagerness to support Ho Chi Minh's war effort stood in sharp contrast to Khrushchev's indifference to the Indochina conflict. From 1962 to 1964, Moscow remained primarily an onlooker of events in Vietnam. This role suited Khrushchev's purpose of peaceful coexistence with the United States and the avoidance of clashes similar to the Cuban Missile Crisis of 1962.[43]

While Hanoi wanted to maintain friendly ties with Moscow, the escalation of revolutionary war in the south indicated a growing gap between the views of the Vietnamese and the Soviets. Moscow's refusal to endorse Beijing's position during the 1962 Sino-Indian border conflict and Khrushchev's defense of Yu-goslavia as a socialist state gave credence to the view held by some leaders in the VWP politburo that Khrushchev was a "revisionist," as the Chinese were argu-ing.[44] According to Bui Tin, while Truong Chinh tended to endorse Khru-shchev's policy of peaceful coexistence, Le Duan was inclined to support China and was gradually able to carry the entire politburo along with him. Vo Nguyen Giap attempted to remain neutral in the ideological dispute, but from 1962 onward, he "was edged into a corner" by Le Duan and Le Duc Tho, who dominated the Central Committee and criticized Giap for being "pro-Soviet." There were even endeavors to purge Giap from the politburo and the party, but Ho Chi Minh protected the general.[45] It should be noted that Duan's endorse-ment of China's position did not mean that he was pro-China. Duan was first and foremost a Vietnamese patriot. He echoed Beijing's views because he found them useful in advancing Vietnam's interests at the moment.

Between 1961 and 1963, the Sino-Soviet dispute had rapidly worsened. When the Soviet Communist Party declared at its Twenty-second Congress in Octo-ber 1961 that it was a party of the "whole people," Mao became convinced that Khrushchev had completely betrayed the principle of class struggle and aban-doned the Soviet party's claim to represent the revolutionary interest of the proletarian class. He believed that the consensus politics advocated by Khru-shchev would ineluctably lead to the consolidation of power in the hands of the rulers and the termination of class struggle and social change.

From November 1962 to January 1963, Bulgarian, Hungarian, Czechoslovak, and East German Communist parties held their national congresses, at which Moscow orchestrated harsh invectives against China and Albania. The Chinese refutations were increasingly sharp. At these meetings, the North Vietnamese kept a distance from Moscow by refusing to denounce the Albanians and displaying sympathy for the Chinese (short of open public defense).[46] Accord-ing to Wu Xiuquan, who led the CCP delegation to these congresses, Hoang Van Hoan, the head of the VWP delegation, "expressed friendship" for China and "maintained frequent consultations" with the CCP delegation at the Hungarian Congress in November 1962. Because the congress did not invite the Albanian Party of Labour to attend, Wu and Hoang Van Hoan together visited the Albanian ambassador to Hungary several times, informing him of the events at the congress.[47]

In 1963, Hanoi moved closer to Beijing in the Sino-Soviet dispute. Rejecting the Soviet international line, Le Duan, in a speech at the Nguyen Ai Quoc Party School in March commemorating the eightieth anniversary of Karl Marx's death, stressed the Chinese struggle as the example for the VWP and contended that the revolutionary war in the south promoted, rather than undermined, the defense of world peace because it weakened American imperialism.[48]

During his state visit to the DRV, Liu Shaoqi praised at a Hanoi rally Le Duan's remarks on Marx's anniversary and then launched an attack on Khrushchev's doctrine of peaceful coexistence: "The foreign policy of the socialist countries must not be reduced to the single aspect of peaceful coexistence. Peaceful coexistence refers to relations between socialist countries and capitalist countries. It must not be reinterpreted at will, or extended to apply to relations between the oppressed and oppressor nations. . . . Peaceful coexistence must not be used to abolish the socialist countries' duty of supporting the revolutionary struggles of the oppressed nations and peoples."[49] The Sino-DRV communiqué issued at the end of Liu's visit criticized Tito's revisionism. This constituted an important indication of Hanoi's shift to the Chinese position because Soviet-Yugoslav relations had recently improved after Tito's trip to Moscow in December 1962.[50] In view of Liu Shaoqi's attacks against Soviet revisionism in Hanoi, it is ironic to note that just a few years later he himself would be condemned in China as "China's Khrushchev."

The Soviet demand on the DRV to pay debts in 1963 provided an opportunity for Mao to try to widen the gap between Hanoi and Moscow. He told a VWP delegation in Wuhan on June 4, 1963: "I hear they [the Soviet Union] are pressing you to pay debts. I advise you to borrow less. . . . When you borrow from those countries, they will press for payment of debts and you will find it hard to handle. Don't worry when you borrow from China. You can pay the Chinese debts whenever you are ready and it is all right even if you do not pay. But when you borrow from those countries, you have to pay."[51] Here Mao was sounding sanctimonious. His statement was redolent of the traditional Chinese imperial treatment of tributary envoys: China was more interested in cultural superiority than material gains.

On July 31, Beijing issued a statement rejecting the Partial Nuclear Test Ban Treaty, accusing Moscow of surrendering to U.S. imperialism, and proposing an international conference for the complete and thorough prohibition and destruction of nuclear weapons.[52] Hanoi moved quickly to join Beijing in opposing the treaty on the ground that "socialist countries other than the Soviet Union must not be denied the means of defense."[53] On August 6 and 9, *Nhan Dan* (People's Daily), the party newspaper, carried editorials supporting China in opposing the Test Ban Treaty and in demanding complete and total nuclear disarmament. *Hoc Tap* (Study), the theoretical journal of the VWP, published an article in September denouncing the treaty as "the result of a deal struck by the leaders of nuclear power" and contradicting "the peace-loving peoples of the world."[54] It was likely that the North Vietnamese viewed potential Chinese nuclear capability as a deterrence against future U.S. attack.

In October, Hanoi launched open attacks on Yugoslavia in accordance with Beijing's position. *Nhan Dan* condemned Tito as "a tool of the U.S. imperialists" and assailed the Yugoslav road to socialism as merely "the path of betraying Marxism-Leninism . . . and restoring capitalism in Yugoslavia." In a November editorial, *Hoc Tap*, criticized Moscow's defense of Tito and defended, for the first time, "dogmatism," a term used by the Soviet propagandists in their criticism of China.[55]

The Ninth Plenum of December 1963 completed the vwp's separation from the Kremlin's international line. Dismissing the Soviet strategy for the socialist camp as defensive, Le Duan commended Mao's theory of revolutionary war, applauding his stress on the peasants, his idea of rural areas encircling the cities, and his concept of protracted armed struggle as a "model strategy for many Communists in Asia, Africa, and Latin America," though he fell short of pledging to follow the Maoist model in Vietnam itself.[56] According to Hoang Van Hoan, an early draft of the plenum resolution criticized Khrushchev by name, but at Le Duan's insistence, the final version adopted by the plenum dropped the name.[57] It is clear that although Le Duan disagreed with Moscow's international position, he did not want an open break with the Soviet party.

According to the January 1964 issue of *Hoc Tap*, during the plenum the vwp first refuted Khrushchev's argument that strategic offensives against the imperialists constituted "adventurist policies" leading the world into a major war and then rejected the "defensive" strategy of compromise with the West as "the abandonment of revolution." The party urged the people in the south to "rise up and integrate their political struggle with armed struggle to uphold their right to existence. The road of struggle now taken by the people in South Vietnam is the only correct road to liberation."[58]

These statements clearly suggested that Hanoi had adopted Beijing's strategy of all-out revolution and dismissed Moscow's policies on war and peace. But it is also clear that vwp leaders did not want a permanent break in the Communist camp. None of their criticisms openly attacked Khrushchev or the Soviet party; they confined their attention to only Tito as the principal spokesman of "revisionism." In this regard, Hanoi's statements stood in sharp contrast to the virulent anti-Soviet polemics issued by Beijing during this time. The vwp desired to restore Sino-Soviet solidarity on the basis of an anti-imperialist line. At one point the Ninth Plenum communiqué mentioned "the convening of the conference of representatives of Communist and Workers' Parties," a proposal initially advanced by Khrushchev in September 1963 but later abandoned by the Soviet leader.[59]

Lieutenant General Song Hao published an important lead article in the August 1964 issue of the PAVN's monthly journal, *Tap Chi Quan Doi Nhan Dan*, in an attempt to persuade doubtful people in the army to pluck up their courage and prepare for the war against the United States. Assuring them that they could defeat the United States, even though the Americans possessed atomic weapons, Song Hao criticized a number of the DRV's misjudgments, including overestimating the strength of the Americans and underrating the extent to which the United States was plotting against the DRV. Not expecting Soviet aid, Song Hao asserted that "our revolutionary armed forces . . . resolutely struggle to the end against imperialism and modern revisionism."[60]

The attack on "revisionism" within the VWP produced important personnel repercussions. Foreign minister Ung Van Khiem found himself eased out of office after the Ninth Plenum because he had endorsed peaceful coexistence in a joint statement issued by Ho Chi Minh and President Antonin Novotny of Czechoslovakia in early 1963.[61] Two senior PAVN officers who had opposed the resolutions of the Ninth Plenum requested political asylum in the Soviet Union at the beginning of 1964. As the year went on, *Bao Ve*, the security organization, was interrogating and arresting several dozens of ranking PAVN officers suspected of being "revisionists." Several of these officers were close friends of Vo Nguyen Giap, but he was unable to shield them. The purge also extended into the intellectual circle. An example was Hoang Minh Chinh, who had become head of the Institute of Philosophy in Hanoi in 1962 after studying social science in Moscow. Truong Chinh had asked him to prepare the documents for the Ninth Plenum. The papers were hotly debated and eventually dismissed as revisionist. Consequently, Hoang Minh Chinh was imprisoned for many years. A similar fate befell other Moscow-trained intellectuals during this period.[62]

According to Mieczyslaw Maneli, a member of the Polish delegation to the International Commission for Supervision and Control in Vietnam, Vietnamese officials since 1962 had deliberately turned a cold shoulder to Soviet diplomats in Hanoi and other foreign capitals. He observed during two official receptions in Hanoi in 1963 and 1964 how Pham Van Dong purposely ignored Soviet ambassador Suren A. Tovmassian. In Maneli's vivid description, Tovmassian in those years "was like a caged tiger. He was helpless because he could not 'teach these goddamned Vietnamese' the way his colleagues in the 1940's and 1950's did in Warsaw, Prague, Budapest, and Sofia. He lost his 'freedom' and 'dignity,' because in Hanoi he was a 'paper tiger.' "[63]

The unsuccessful visit of the VWP delegation led by Le Duan to the Soviet Union in February 1964 clearly revealed the widening gap between the two parties.[64] Before its arrival in Moscow, the delegation stopped in Beijing and

Mao greets Le Duan, January 30, 1964. (Courtesy Xinhua News Agency)

held a meeting with Mao on January 30. Duan informed Mao that the purpose of his trip was to explain his party's positions to the Russians and also to find out Soviet policies and that Ho Chi Minh and the politburo had decided not to issue a joint communiqué with the Soviets at the conclusion of the visit.[65] Mao lost no opportunity to disparage the Russians: "It has become a rule that whenever the Soviet Union wants to cut a political deal with the United States, it would put pressure on us in order to let the United States know that they are tough toward China but friendly toward the United States."[66] Le Duan met with Mao at a time when the CCP chairman was directing the full force of his propaganda machine into public condemnations of the Soviet Union. Between September 6, 1963, and July 14, 1964, nine polemics against the Soviets were issued.[67]

In Moscow, Le Duan held extensive discussions with Khrushchev and other high-level Soviet officials on a broad range of issues. In addition to urging unity between China and the Soviet Union, the North Vietnamese visitors criticized the Soviet party for promoting peaceful coexistence with the West, supporting India in its border clash with China, refusing to aid Beijing's nuclear programs, and being unwilling to back national liberation movements. They insisted that a genuine danger of nuclear war existed and that only revolutionary struggle could safeguard peace. The Soviet negotiators on their part wanted Hanoi to support Moscow in its dispute with Beijing. Neither side was able to persuade the other. The Soviet officials received the impression from the talks that Hanoi's views were strongly influenced by China but were more flexible and that the VWP leadership had actually excluded the choice of pursuing a policy of peaceful coexistence. After expressing concern over the resolution of the Ninth Plenum of the VWP, Khrushchev warned the North Vietnamese envoys that close cooperation between the two countries was unlikely unless the VWP changed its position.[68]

The Hanoi press on February 15, 1964, issued what it implied was a joint communiqué but was actually not. This was the first time that the two parties had met officially without producing a joint communiqué. Hanoi's announcement stated that in the course of the discussions "opinions were exchanged, frankly and usefully . . . [because] in spite of the existence of divergences in the international communist movement, exchanges of view between parties are necessary."[69]

By mid-1964, the DRV had so annoyed Khrushchev by its deepening ties with China that he intended to disengage from Indochina by resigning Soviet cochairmanship of the ICC.[70] Moscow's economic assistance and exports to North Vietnam dropped in 1964. Delivery of Soviet heavy machinery and construction materials in 1964 decreased 30 percent from 1963, which had dropped by 20 percent from 1962.[71] In the wake of Le Duan's February visit, the Kremlin confined itself primarily to propaganda support for Hanoi, indicating to the world that the Soviet Union remained an ally of the DRV. In the words of the Russian scholar Ilya Gaiduk, "This vigorous propaganda may have been designed to compensate for Moscow's unwillingness to provide more substantive aid."[72]

While Hanoi's estrangement from Moscow was increasing, its cooperation with Beijing developed steadily. Chinese–North Vietnamese unity on ideological issues, however, did not preclude differences over military tactics. For instance, after the death of the Ngo brothers and President Kennedy, the North Vietnamese in early 1964 were eager to conduct large-unit operations in the south. They had already sent a few companies and even battalions down the Ho Chi Minh Trail to South Vietnam. Now they intended to dispatch whole regiments to the south. The Chinese, however, continued to advocate guerrilla warfare.[73]

It is paradoxical that while the VWP parroted China's international line, it followed the Soviet model of technical-managerial control in building state socialism in the domestic realm. Since 1960, Hanoi had been consolidating this

Soviet pattern of bureaucratic administration and hierarchy and shunning the Maoist model of popular mobilization and the mass line.[74]

Hanoi's emphasis on centralized and bureaucratic management paralleled the policy adopted by Liu Shaoqi and Deng Xiaoping, secretary-general of the CCP, in China in the wake of the Great Leap Forward, when Mao "retired from the front line." Liu and Deng did not share Mao's vision of governance through "uninterrupted revolution."[75] The chaos and instability that would afflict China during the Cultural Revolution as a result of Mao's reassertion of class struggle and mass mobilization would reinforce VWP leaders' belief in the correctness of their earlier choice.

The period between 1961 and 1964 was a crucial one in the evolution of Sino-DRV relations. In Beijing, Mao rejected moderation in China's foreign policy and became more forthcoming in meeting Hanoi's demands in its emerging confrontation with the United States. In North Vietnam, the VWP was moving closer to Mao's position on the issue of war and peace in international politics. Its urgent need to resist American pressure increased its reliance on China's material assistance.

6 CONFRONTING U.S. ESCALATION 1964–1965

THE GULF OF TONKIN INCIDENT AND AFTER

In the first half of 1964, the attention of American officials was shifting increasingly toward Hanoi. This trend reflected a mounting U.S. concern over the infiltration of men and supplies from the north and a growing dissatisfaction with a policy that allowed Hanoi to encourage the insurgency without punishment. In addition to expanding covert operations in North Vietnam, including intelligence overflights, the dropping of propaganda leaflets, and OPLAN 34A commando raids along the North Vietnamese coast, the Johnson administration also conveyed to Pham Van Dong through a Canadian diplomat on June 17 the message that the United States was ready to exert increasingly heavy military pressure on the DRV to force it to reduce or terminate its encouragement of guerrilla activities in South Vietnam. But the North Vietnamese leader refused to yield to the American pressure, claiming that Hanoi would not stop its support for the struggle of liberation in the South.[1]

During this period, tensions were also increasing in Laos. On April 19, a coup took place led by two right-wing generals, Kouprasith Abhay and Siho Lamphouthacoul. Although short-lived, the coup caused chaos in the Lao government. In the wake of the incident, Souvanna Phouma reorganized the government by excluding the Communists. The topsy-turvy nature of Lao politics manifested itself in the fact that the Pathet Lao was now turning against Kong Le. Considering the Geneva Accords irrelevant, the Lao Communists mounted an attack on Kong Le's forces on the Plain of Jars on May 13, which alarmed Washington and Souvanna. The Lao prime minister permitted unarmed U.S. reconnaissance flights over the Plain of Jars. After Communist antiaircraft guns shot one down on June 6, the United States retaliated three days later by using F-100s to strike the Communist antiaircraft battery at Xieng Khouang. Apparently without U.S. authorization, Thai-piloted Royal Lao Air Force T-28s assaulted the Pathet Lao headquarters at Khang Khay and hit the Chinese Economic and Cultural Mission, killing one Chinese and wounding five others.[2]

Chinese leaders watched these developments closely and apprehensively. At a reception hosted by a visiting Tanzanian delegation in Beijing on June 16, a disturbed Zhou Enlai condemned the U.S. bombing of the Pathet Lao head-quarters and the Chinese mission as a violation of the Geneva Accords and an escalation of the conflict in Indochina.[3] He told the Burmese leader Ne Win in Rangoon on July 10 that if the United States wanted to wage a Korean-style war, China must be prepared.[4]

To confront the increasing U.S. pressure in Indochina, Beijing stepped up its coordination with the Vietnamese and Laotian parties. On June 21–24, General Van Tien Dung, chief of staff of the PAVN, visited Beijing, where he discussed with Mao and Zhou Enlai China's military aid to the DRV.[5] Mao told Dung on June 24 that if the United States invaded North Vietnam, China would send troops to the DRV in the form of volunteers.[6] He assured the Vietnamese envoy that "our two parties and two countries must cooperate and fight the enemy together. Your business is my business and my business is your business. In other words, our two sides must deal with the enemy together without conditions."[7]

Between July 5 and 8, Zhou Enlai led a CCP delegation to Hanoi to meet with leaders from the DRV and the Pathet Lao, who described how the United States was using South Vietnam as a base to attack socialism and as a test site for its counterinsurgency warfare. After noting that Southeast Asia was the area in the world where "conficts are most concentrated, struggle most fierce, and revolutionary conditions most ripe," Zhou pointed out two possible military developments in the region: the United States might intensify the counter-insurgency warfare; or it might turn the counterinsurgency warfare into a local war with a direct deployment of American troops in South Vietnam and Laos or with bombing or invasion of North Vietnam. No matter what approach the United States adopted, Zhou pledged, China would surely intervene to support the struggle of the Southeast Asian people. As to concrete measures that the VWP and the Pathet Lao might take, Zhou suggested a combination of political and military struggles: on the political front, to adhere to the two Geneva Accords, exploit Franco-American disagreements, and organize a broad inter-national united front to lay bare the U.S. violations of the two agreements; in the military area, to strengthen armed forces, consolidate base areas, and win battles of annihilation. "Our principle for the struggle," Zhou concluded, "should be to do everything we can to limit the war to the current scale while preparing for the second possibility" of American intervention. Should that second possibility occur, China would match American actions: if the United States sent troops, China would do likewise.[8] Here Zhou reiterated China's willingness to dispatch combat soldiers into North Vietnam if the United States used ground troops to invade it.[9]

On August 2, North Vietnamese patrol boats opened fire on U.S. destroyers in the Gulf of Tonkin. Two days later, the White House claimed that a second assault took place. President Johnson ordered air strikes agains North Vietnamese installations as a reprisal, and then use the alleged attack as a pretext for sending Congress what became the Gulf of Tonkin Resolution, which authorized the president to use military forces as necessary to protect U.S. lives and interests in Southeast Asia.

The Gulf of Tonkin incident prompted Chinese and North Vietnamese leaders into close consultation. Zhou Enlai and Luo Ruiqing cabled Ho Chi Minh, Pham Van Dong, and Van Tien Dung on August 5, asking them to "investigate the situation, work out countermeasures, and be prepared to fight."[10] Le Duan journeyed to Beijing and met with Mao on August 13. He told Mao that the first incident of August 2 was the result of the decisions made by the DRV commander on the spot. The CCP leader informed Le Duan that according to Beijing's intelligence, the second incident of August 4 was "not an intentional attack by the Americans" but caused by "the Americans' mistaken judgment, based on wrong information."[11]

In response to the crisis in Vietnam, China increased military preparations in its southern provinces and stepped up military aid to the DRV. Shortly after the Gulf of Tonkin incident, the leaders in Beijing instructed the Kunming and Guangzhou Military Regions and the air force and naval units stationed in south and southwest China to begin a state of combat readiness. Four air divisions and one antiaircraft division were dispatched into areas adjoining Vietnam and put on a heightened alert status.[12] In August, China also sent approximately fifteen MIG-15 and MIG-17 jets to Hanoi, agreed to train North Vietnamese pilots, and began to build new airfields in areas adjacent to the Vietnamese border, which would serve as sanctuary and repair and maintenance facilities for Hanoi's jet fighters.[13] By moving new air force units to the border area and constructing new airfields there, Beijing intended to deter further U.S. expansion of war in South Vietnam and bombardment against the DRV. Between August and September 1964, the PLA also sent an inspection team to North Vietnam to investigate the situation in case China later needed to dispatch support troops.[14]

On October 5, Mao discussed with Pham Van Dong and Hoang Van Hoan in Beijing the possible expansion of the war by the United States against North Vietnam. The CCP leader asked the Vietnamese Communists to copy the Chinese, who, during the Korean War constructed defensive works along the coast so as to prevent the enemy from pushing into the interior. If the Americans were determined to invade the interior, Mao advised the North Vietnamese not to deploy their main forces in a head-on confrontation in order to preserve strength.[15]

The first months of 1965 witnessed a significant escalation of the American war in Vietnam. On February 7, 9, and 11, U.S. aircraft struck North Vietnamese military installations just across the seventeenth parallel, ostensibly in retaliation for Viet Cong attacks on American barracks near Pleiku and in Qui Nhon. On March 1, the Johnson administration stopped claiming that its air attacks on North Vietnam were reprisals for specific Communist assaults in South Vietnam and began continuous air bombing against the DRV. On March 8, two battalions of marines armed with tanks and eight-inch howitzers landed at Danang.[16]

The U.S. escalation of the war made the DRV desperate for help. Le Duan and Vo Nguyen Giap rushed to Beijing in early April to ask China to increase its aid and send troops to the DRV. Duan told Chinese leaders that Hanoi needed "volunteer pilots, volunteer soldiers, as well as other necessary personnel, including road and bridge engineers." The North Vietnamese envoys expected Chinese volunteer pilots to perform four functions: to limit U.S. bombing to south of the twentieth or nineteenth parallel, to defend Hanoi, to protect several major transportation lines, and to boost morale.[17] On behalf of the Chinese leadership, Liu Shaoqi replied to the North Vietnamese visitors on April 8 that "it is the obligation of the Chinese people and party" to support the Vietnamese struggle against the United States. "Our principle is," Liu continued, "that we will do our best to provide you with whatever you need and whatever we have. If you do not invite us, we will not go to your place. We will send whatever part [of our troops] that you request. You have the complete initiative."[18]

In April, China signed several agreements with the DRV concerning the dispatch of Chinese support troops to North Vietnam.[19] Between April 21 and 22, Giap discussed with Luo Ruiqing and Yang Chengwu, first deputy chief of staff, the arrangements for sending Chinese troops.[20] In May, Ho Chi Minh paid a secret visit to Mao in Changsha, the chairman's home province, where he asked Mao to help the DRV repair and build twelve roads in the area north of

Hanoi. The Chinese leader agreed to Ho's request and instructed Zhou Enlai to see to the matter.[21]

In discussions with Luo Ruiqing and Yang Chengwu, Zhou said: "According to Pham Van Dong, U.S. blockade and bombing has reduced supplies to South Vietnam through sea shipment and road transportation. While trying to resume sea transportation, the DRV is also expanding the corridor in Lower Laos and roads in the south. Their troops would go to the south to build roads. Therefore they need our support to construct roads in the north." Zhou decided that the Chinese military should be responsible for road repair and construction in North Vietnam. Yang suggested that since assistance to the DRV involved many military and government departments, a special leadership group should be created to coordinate the work of various agencies. Approving the proposal, Zhou immediately announced the establishment of the "Central Committee–State Council Aid Vietnam Work Team", with Yang and Li Tianyou as director and vice director, respectively. In the meantime, an "Aid Vietnam Leadership Group" led by Luo Ruiqing was established within the Central Committee to supervise the operations of the work team.[22]

In early June, Van Tien Dung held discussions with Luo Ruiqing in Beijing to flesh out the general Chinese plan to assist North Vietnam. According to their agreement, if the war remained in its current conditions, the DRV would fight the war by itself and China would provide various kinds of support as the North Vietnamese needed. If the United States used its navy and air force to support a South Vietnamese attack on the north, China would also provide naval and air force support to the DRV. If U.S. ground forces were directly used to attack the north, China would use its land forces as strategic reserves for the DRV and conduct military operations whenever necessary. As to the forms of Chinese–North Vietnamese air force cooperation, Dung and Luo agreed that China could (1) send volunteer pilots to Vietnam to operate Vietnamese aircraft; (2) station both pilots and aircraft in North Vietnam airfields; or (3) fly aircraft from bases in China to join combat in Vietnam and to land on North Vietnamese bases only temporarily for refueling. The third option was known as the "Andong model" (a reference to the pattern of Chinese air force operations during the Korean War). In terms of the methods of employing Chinese ground troops, the two military leaders agreed that the Chinese forces would either help to strengthen the defensive position of the North Vietnamese troops to prepare for a counteroffensive or launch an offensive themselves to disrupt the enemy's deployment and win strategic initiatives.[23]

But despite Liu Shaoqi's April promise to Le Duan, and Luo Ruiqing's agreement with Van Tien Dung, China in the end failed to provide pilots to Hanoi. According to the Vietnamese *White Paper*, the Chinese General Staff on

July 16, 1965, notified its North Vietnamese counterpart that "the time was not appropriate" to send Chinese pilots to Vietnam.[24] China's limited air force capacity may have caused leaders in Beijing to have second thoughts. Beijing's intention to avoid a direct confrontation with the United States may also have played a role. Whatever the reasons for China's decision, the failure to satisfy Hanoi's demand must have greatly disappointed the North Vietnamese, since the control of the air was so crucial for the DRV's effort to protect itself from the ferocious U.S. bombing, and must have undoubtedly contributed to North Vietnam's decision to rely more on the Soviet Union for air defense.

Beginning in June 1965, China sent ground-to-air missile, antiaircraft artillery, railroad, engineering, minesweeping, and logistic units into North Vietnam to help Hanoi defend the DRV. The total number of Chinese troops in North Vietnam between June 1965 and March 1968 amounted to over 320,000.[25] The peak year was 1967, when 170,000 Chinese soldiers were present.[26] They operated antiaircraft guns, built and repaired roads, bridges, and rail lines, and constructed factories. They enabled the PAVN to send large numbers of troops to South Vietnam for the fighting. When the last Chinese troops withdrew from Vietnam in August 1973, 1,100 soldiers had lost their lives and 4,200 had been wounded.[27]

One agreement between the PLA's Kunming Military Region and the PAVN's North Western Military Region on June 11, 1967, indicated the magnitude of Beijing's aid to the DRV. According to the agreement, in 1967 China would provide material assistance to the PAVN troops stationed in upper Laos. There were 1,890 North Vietnamese soldiers there, a figure provided by the Vietnamese side. Aside from weapons and other military equipment, China agreed to equip the North Vietnamese troops right down to the articles for daily use, including 5,670 sets of uniforms (three sets per person annually), 5,670 pairs of shoes (three pairs per person annually), 567 tons of rice (0.8 kilogram per person daily), 20.7 tons of salt, 55.2 tons of meat, 20.7 tons of fish, 20.7 tons of sesame and peanuts, 20.7 tons of beans, 20.7 tons of lard, 6.9 tons of soy sauce, 20.7 tons of white sugar, 8,000 toothbrushes, 11,100 tubes of toothpaste, 24,700 bars of regular soap, 10,600 bars of scented soap, and 109,000 cases of cigarettes. In total, the agreement included 687 different items, covering such goods as table tennis balls, volleyballs, harmonicas, playing cards, pins, fountain pen ink, sewing needles, and vegetable seeds.[28]

Both Mao and Zhou Enlai followed events in Vietnam closely and often issued instructions regarding Chinese aid to the DRV. After reading a report about the difficult living conditions of the Vietnamese Communist troops in the mountain regions in the south prepared by a group of Chinese journalists who had visited there in 1965, Mao instructed in November 1965 that China

TABLE 1. *China's Military Aid to the* DRV, *1964–1975*

Items	1964	1965	1966	1967	1968	1969	1970	1971	1972	1973	1974	1975
Guns	80,500	220,767	141,531	146,600	219,899	139,900	101,800	143,100	189,000	233,600	164,500	141,800
Artillery pieces	1,205	4,439	3,362	3,984	7,087	3,906	2,212	7,898	9,238	9,912	6,406	4,880
Bullets (thousands)	25,240	114,010	178,120	147,000	247,920	119,170	29,010	57,190	40,000	40,000	30,000	20,060
Artillery shells (thousands)	335	1,800	1,066	1,363	2,082	1,357	397	1,899	2,210	2,210	1,390	965
Radio transmitters	426	2,779	1,568	2,464	1,854	2,210	950	2,464	4,370	4,335	5,148	2,240
Telephone sets	2,941	9,502	2,235	2,289	3,313	3,453	1,600	4,424	5,905	6,447	4,633	2,150
Tanks	16	—	—	26	18	—	—	80	220	120	80	—
Ships	—	7	14	25	—	—	—	24	71	5	6	—
Aircraft	18	2	—	70	—	—	—	4	14	36	—	20
Vehicles	25	114	96	435	454	162	—	4,011	8,758	1,210	506	—
Uniforms (thousand sets)	—	—	400	800	1,000	1,200	1,200	1,200	1,400	1,400	1,400	—

Source: Li Ke and Hao Shengzhang, *Wenhua dageming zhong de renmin jiefangjun,* 416.

"must give mosquito nets, clothes, canned food, dried meats, medicine, water-proof cloth, hammocks and other materials in large quantities" to the Viet-namese.[29] Zhou Enlai specified that Chinese equipment sent to the south be designed in the way that was "easy to use, easy to carry, and easy to hide." For this purpose, he demanded specifically that each piece of equipment not weigh over thirty kilograms so that Vietnamese women would have no difficulty in carrying it on their heads or on their shoulders.[30]

To supervise the transportation of materials to the DRV, Beijing in 1965 established a special leadership group. Luo Ruiqing was appointed director. Materials provided by China, the Soviet Union, and other socialist countries were shipped by rail to cities near the Vietnamese border (like Ping Xiang, Guangxi province), where they were transported into the DRV either by rail or by trucks. The materials soon overwhelmed the North Vietnamese transpor-tation capacity, and Chinese railway stations and warehouses became over-stocked with supplies. Beginning in 1967, China employed over 500 trucks to help carry supplies into the DRV.[31]

To facilitate moving supplies into South Vietnam, China created a secret coastal transportation line to ship goods to several islands off central Vietnam for transit to the south. A secret harbor on China's Hainan Island was con-structed to serve this transportation route.[32] Beijing also operated a costly transportation line through Cambodia to send weapons, munitions, food, and medical supplies to the National Liberation Front in South Vietnam.[33] Between 1965 and 1967, Chinese weapons for 50,000 soldiers arrived by ship via Siha-noukville.[34] Some of the Chinese arms went to equip the Cambodian army.[35]

Table 1 shows the trend of Beijing's military aid to the DRV. China's ship-ment of military materials to North Vietnam increased rapidly in 1965. In comparison with 1964, the delivery of guns increased 2.8 times, from 80,500 to 220,767; pieces of artillery increased about 3 times, from 1,205 to 4,439; gun bullets increased nearly 5 times, from 25.2 million to 114 million; and artillery shells increased almost 6 times, from 335,000 to 1.8 million. Between 1966 and 1967, China's supply of military goods to the DRV dropped slightly from the 1965 level before reaching its peak in 1968. In 1969–70, a sharp decrease oc-curred at the same time that Beijing withdrew all its support troops from the DRV. Not until 1972 would there be another major increase of China's military shipment to the DRV, but for reasons very different from the ones behind Beijing's rising and falling aid from 1965 to 1969 (see Chapter 8).[36]

The newly available Chinese documents clearly indicate that Beijing pro-vided extensive support (short of volunteer pilots) to Hanoi during the Viet-nam War and in doing so risked war with the United States. As one China specialist has perceptively observed, the deployment of Chinese troops in Vietnam was not carried out under maximum security against detection by Washington. The Chinese troops wore regular uniforms and did not disguise themselves as civilians. The Chinese presence was intentionally communicated to U.S. intelligence through aerial photography and electronic intercepts. The presence of troops, along with the large base complex that China built at Yen Bai in northwest Vietnam, provided credible and successful deterrence against an American invasion of North Vietnam.[37]

While increasing aid to the DRV and making war preparations at home in the first half of 1965, Chinese leaders, determined to avoid war with the United States, also issued clear and repeated warnings to Washington through multiple channels, including the Sino-American ambassadorial talks at Warsaw, third-party leaders, and the British charge in Beijing. The Chinese ambassador to Poland, Wang Guoquan, told John M. Cabot, his American counterpart, that the United States would surely lose in Vietnam and that the "Chinese people will not sit idly by and we know how to deal with your aggression."[38]

Zhou Enlai, during his visit to Pakistan on April 2, asked Pakistani president Ayub Khan, who was scheduled to visit the United States later in the month, to convey to President Johnson a four-point message, which stated that: (1) China would not take the initiative to provoke a war with the United States; (2) it meant what it said and would honor its international commitment; (3) it was prepared; (4) if the United States bombarded China without constraints, China would not sit there waiting to die. If the Americans came from the air, China would fight back on the ground. Bombing would mean war, and the war would have no boundaries.[39]

Ayub Khan, however, did not deliver the Chinese message as Zhou had hoped because just nine days before his scheduled arrival in the United States, President Johnson, dismayed by his flirtation with China, suddenly canceled his invitation.[40] On June 8, Zhou Enlai asked President Julius Nyerere of Tanzania to forward the same message to the United States.[41] A similar signal was sent to the Americans by Foreign Minister Chen Yi during his conversation with the British charge in Beijing a week before, on May 31. Chen declared that "China will not provoke war with the United States" but that "what China says counts." China was prepared for war and that "if the United States bombs China[,] that would mean war and there would be no limits to the war."[42]

These were the most serious warnings issued by the Chinese government to the United States, and there is evidence that American officials took them seriously. Taking note of Chen Yi's May 31 statement, William P. Bundy, assistant secretary of state for Far Eastern affairs, told Secretary of State Dean Rusk on June 5, 1965, that the Chinese foreign minister had drawn a line for the United States. If the United States limited its assaults to the air over North

Vietnam, did not approach China, and did not directly attack China, Beijing would not come into the war. But the PRC would "go all the way if it did come in" to the war. Bundy also informed Rusk that he had told the British the previous day that "they could tell Chen Yi we had received the message."[43]

The specter of Chinese intervention in a manner similar to China's involvement in the Korean War was a major factor in shaping President Johnson's gradual approach to the Vietnam War. He wanted to forestall Chinese intervention by keeping the level of military actions against North Vietnam controlled, exact, and below the threshold that would provoke a direct Chinese entry. He had clearly learned a lesson from the Korean War, when the Truman administration's failure to heed Beijing's warning against crossing the thirty-eighth parallel led to a bloody confrontation between the United States and China. In his discussion with the Joint Chiefs of Staff in July 1965 of whether to send an additional 100,000 soldiers to South Vietnam, for example, the president asked, "If we come in with hundreds of thousands of men and billions of dollars, won't this cause them [China and Russia] to come in?" General Harold Johnson, army chief of staff, replied that he did not think so. When the president then reminded the general that "MacArthur didn't think they would come in [to Korea] either," General Johnson countered that the circumstances were different. But the president persisted that he had to "take into account" that the Chinese would send their troops into the war.[44]

This China-induced U.S. strategy of gradual escalation was a great help for Hanoi, for it gave the Vietnamese Communists time to adjust to U.S. bombing and to develop strategies to frustrate U.S. moves. As the China expert John Garver has aptly noted, "By helping to induce Washington to adopt this particular strategy, Beijing contributed substantially to Hanoi's eventual victory over the United States."[45]

The United States made plain its intention to avoid war with Beijing when it informed China at the Warsaw talks that it had no plan either to destroy North Vietnam or to invade the PRC.[46] Thus through public pronouncements, private messages, and mutual signals, Beijing and Washington came to understand the scope and limits of each other's involvement in the Vietnam War. During the latter part of 1965 and early 1966 they developed a tacit understanding that so long as the United States did not invade North Vietnam or China, nor seek to destroy the DRV as a viable nation, then Beijing would limit its military involvement in the conflict.[47]

MAO'S COMPLEX CALCULATIONS

Mao's decision to aid Hanoi is closely linked to his perception of U.S. threats to China's security, his commitment to national liberation movements, his criticism of Soviet revisionist foreign policy, and his domestic needs to trans-form the Chinese state and society. These four factors were mutually related and reinforcing.

Sense of Insecurity

Between 1964 and 1965, Mao worried about the increasing American in-volvement in Vietnam and perceived the United States as posing a serious threat to China's security. The CCP leader viewed the United States as "the most ferocious enemy of the people of the world," committing neocolonialist aggres-sion against Asian, African, and Latin American countries and seeking "peace-ful evolution" against socialist states. In Asia, Mao contended, the United States was occupying Taiwan, turning South Korea and South Vietnam into its colo-nies, exercising actual control and partial military occupation of Japan, under-mining Laotian neutrality and independence, plotting subversion of the Cam-bodian government, and likewise interfering with other Asian countries. Mao believed that American escalation of war in Vietnam constituted a link in Washington's chain of encirclement of China. For him, support for North Vietnam was a way of countering the U.S. containment of China. The Commu-nist success in South Vietnam would prevent the United States from moving closer to the Chinese southern border.[48]

On several occasions in the first part of 1964, Mao talked about U.S. threats to China and the need for China to prepare for war. During a party conference held between May 15 and June 17, the chairman contended that "so long as imperialism exists, the danger of war is there. We are not the chief of staff for imperialism and have no idea when it will launch a war. It is the conventional weapon, not the atomic bomb, that will determine the final victory of the war."[49] On June 16, Mao delivered a speech to a conference at the Ming Tombs (Shisanling) Reservoir on the outskirts of Beijing, asking the party to prepare for war. Mao's address was later known as "the Ming Tombs Speech."[50] Defense Minister Lin Biao talked with Yang Chengwu twice, on July 10 and 12, stressing the importance of reorienting the PLA's strategy and military planning in accordance with the "carefully considered" speech made by Mao at the Ming Tombs Reservoir.[51]

At first Mao did not expect that the United States would attack North Vietnam directly.[52] The Gulf of Tonkin incident came as a surprise to him. Mao had originally planned to take a horse ride to inspect the Yellow River in the second part of 1964. On August 6, he told Wang Dongxing, head of the Guard Bureau of the CCP Central Committee, that "war is coming and I have to reconsider my activities."[53] The crisis in Vietnam caused Mao to cancel his planned trip to the Yellow River, and on October 22, he again pointed out that

China must base its work on war and make active preparations for an early, large-scale, and nuclear war.[54]

To deal with what he perceived as U.S. military threats, Mao took several domestic measures in 1964, the most important of which was the launching of the massive Third Front project, a major strategic action designed to provide an alternative industrial base that would enable China to continue production in the event of an attack on its large urban centers. This program called for heavy investment in the remote provinces of southwestern and western China and envisaged the creation of a huge self-sustaining industrial base area to serve as a strategic reserve. The project had a strong military orientation and was directly triggered by the U.S. escalation of war in Vietnam.[55]

On April 25, 1964, the War Department of the PLA General Staff drafted a report for Yang Chengwu on how to prevent an enemy surprise attack on China's economic system. The report listed four factors that made China vulnerable to such an attack: (1) China's industry was over concentrated. About 60 percent of the civil machinery industry, 50 percent of the chemical industry, and 52 percent of the national defense industry were concentrated in fourteen major cities with over one million inhabitants. (2) Too many people lived in cities. According to the 1962 census, fourteen cities each had a population over one million, and twenty cities a population between 500,000 and one million. Most of these cities were located in the coastal areas and very vulnerable to air strikes. No effective mechanisms existed at the moment to organize anti-air works, to evacuate urban populations, to continue production, and to eliminate the damages of an air strike, especially a nuclear strike. (3) Principal railroad junctions, bridges, and harbors were situated near large and medium-size cities and could easily be destroyed when the enemy attacked the cities. No measures had been taken to protect these transportation points against an enemy attack. In the early stage of war, they could become paralyzed. (4) All of China's reservoirs had a limited capacity to release water in an emergency. Among the country's 232 large reservoirs, 52 were located near major transportation lines, and 17 were close to important cities. In its conclusion, the report made it clear that "the problems mentioned above are directly related to the whole armed forces, to the whole people, and to the process of a national defense war." It asked the state council "to organize a special committee to study and adopt, in accordance with the possible conditions of the national economy, practical and effective measures to guard against an enemy surprise attack."[56]

Yang Chengwu presented the report to Mao, who returned it to Luo Ruiqing and Yang on August 12 with the comment: "It is an excellent report. It should be carefully studied and gradually implemented." Mao urged the newly established state council's special committee in charge of the Third Front to begin its work immediately.[57] Mao's approval of the report marked the beginning of the Third Front project to relocate China's industrial resources to the interior. It is important to note the timing of Mao's reaction to the report—right after the Gulf of Tonkin incident. The U.S. expansion of the war to North Vietnam had confirmed Mao's worst suspicions about American intentions.

Deputy Premier Li Fuchun became director and Deputy Premier Bo Yibo and Luo Ruiqing became vice directors of the special committee. On August 19, they submitted to Mao a detailed proposal on how to implement the Third Front ideas.[58] In the meantime, the CCP secretariat met to discuss the issue. Mao made two speeches at the meetings on August 17 and 20. He asserted that China should be on guard against an aggressive war launched by imperialism. At present, he continued, factories were concentrated around big cities and coastal regions, a situation deleterious to war preparation. Factories should be broken into two parts. One part should be relocated to interior areas as early as possible. Every province should establish its own strategic rear base. Departments of industry and transportation should move, as should schools, science academies, and Beijing University. The three railroad lines between Chengdu and Kunming, Sichuan and Yunnan, and Yunnan and Guizhou should be completed as quickly as possible. If there was a shortage of rails, the chairman insisted, rails on other lines could be dismantled. To implement Mao's instructions, it was decided at the meetings to concentrate China's financial, material, and human resources on the construction of the Third Front.[59]

While emphasizing the "big Third Front" plan on the national level, Mao also ordered provinces to proceed with their "small Third Front" projects. The chairman wanted each province to develop its own light armament industry capable of producing rifles, machine guns, cannons, and munitions.[60] The Third Five-Year Plan was revised to meet the strategic contingency of war preparation. In the modified plan, a total of three billion yuan was appropriated for small Third Front projects. This was a substantial figure, but less than 5 percent of the amount that was set aside for the big Third Front in this period.[61]

In addition to his apprehension about a strike on China's urban and coastal areas, Mao also feared that the enemy might deploy paratroop assault forces deep inside China. In a meeting with He Long, deputy chairman of the Central Military Commission, Luo Ruiqing, and Yang Chengwu on April 28, 1965, Mao called their attention to such a danger. He ordered them to prepare for the landing of enemy paratroopers in every interior region. The enemy might use paratroops, Mao contended, "to disrupt our rear areas, and to coordinate with a frontal assault. The number of paratroops may not be many. It may involve one or two divisions in each region, or it may involve a smaller unit. In all interior regions, we should build caves in mountains. If no mountain is around, hills should be created to construct defense works. We should be on guard against enemy paratroops deep inside our country and prevent the enemy from marching unstopped into China."[62]

It appears that Mao's attitudes toward the United States hardened between January and April 1965. On January 9, Mao had an interview with Edgar Snow, an American journalist whom he had first met in the 1930s. Mao expressed confidence that Washington would not expand the war to North Vietnam because Secretary of State Rusk had said so. He told Snow that there would be no war between China and the United States if Washington did not send troops to attack China.[63] Two days later, the CCP Central Military Commission issued the "Six-Point Directive on the Struggle against U.S. Ships and Aircraft in the South China Sea," in which it instructed the military not to attack American airplanes that intruded into Chinese airspace in order to avoid a direct military clash with the United States.[64]

In April, however, Mao rescinded the "Six-Point Directive." Between April 8 and 9, U.S. aircraft flew into China's airspace over Hainan Island. On April 9, Yang Chengwu reported the incidents to Mao, suggesting that the order not to attack invading U.S. airplanes be lifted and that the air force command take control of the naval air units stationed on Hainan Island. Approving both of Yang's requests, Mao said that China "should resolutely strike American aircraft that overfly Hainan Island."[65] It is quite possible that the further U.S. escalation of war in Vietnam in the intervening months caused Mao to abandon his earlier restrictions against engaging U.S. aircraft. On April 12, the Chinese air force command prepared the "Combat Plan for Dealing with the Provocation of American Aircraft," which stated that the air force should "not only be ready to engage U.S. aircraft in aerial battles and intercept U.S. bombers in the border region but also be prepared to fight U.S. fighter planes and bombers on a larger and more protracted scale in interior regions."[66]

On the same day, Liu Shaoqi chaired an expanded meeting of the politburo to discuss the situation in Vietnam and war preparation at home, and a directive on strengthening the work of war preparation was passed.[67] Mao approved the directive the next day, and the CCP Central Committee on April 14 distributed the document throughout the party structure above the county level. The instruction alerted party cadres to the grave danger posed by the American escalation of the war in Vietnam and stressed the urgency of war preparation. The U.S. expansion of the war in Indochina and the direct attack on the DRV, the directive pointed out, "are seriously threatening the security of our country. We have already indicated to the whole world our solemn and just position that we cannot ignore this threat and that we are ready at any time to fight together with the Vietnamese people. We must also be prepared to deal with the spread of the war by U.S. imperialism to our territory." The directive asked the party cadres to monitor closely the development of the war in Vietnam and take seriously the possibility of enemy aggressions.[68]

It is important to point out that the entire Chinese leadership, not just Mao, took the strategic threat from the United States very seriously during this period. Zhou Enlai told Spiro Koleka, first deputy chairman of the Council of Ministers of Albania, on May 9, 1965, in Beijing that China was mobilizing its population for war. Although it seemed that the United States had not made up its mind to expand the war to China, the Chinese premier continued, war had its own law of development, usually in a way contrary to the wishes of people. Therefore China had to be prepared.[69] Zhou's remarks indicated that he was familiar with a common pattern in warfare: accidents and miscalculations rather than deliberate planning often lead to war between reluctant opponents.

In an address to a Central Military Commission war planning meeting on May 19, 1965, Liu Shaoqi called for the development of the Third Front as well as the atomic bomb, the hydrogen bomb, and long-range missiles. With these preparations, Liu claimed:

> Even if the United States has bases in Japan, Taiwan, and the Philippines, its ships are big targets out on the sea and it is easy for us to strike them. . . . The enemy's strength is in its navy, air force, atomic bombs, and missiles, but the strength in navy and air force has its limits. If the enemy sends ground troops to invade China, we are not afraid. Therefore, on the one hand we should be prepared for the enemy to come from all directions, including a joint invasion against China by many countries. On the other, we should realize that the enemy lacks justification in sending troops. . . . This will decide the difference between a just and an unjust war.[70]

Zhu De remarked at the same meeting that "so long as we have made good preparations on every front, the enemy may not dare to come. We must defend our offshore islands. With these islands in our hands, the enemy will find it difficult to land. If the enemy should launch an attack, we will lure them inside China and then wipe them out completely."[71]

Scholars have argued over Beijing's reaction to the threat posed by U.S. intervention in Vietnam. Much of this argument focuses on the supposed "strategic debate" that took place in 1965 between Luo Ruiqing and Lin Biao. Various interpretations of this "debate" exist, but most contend that Luo was more sensitive to American actions in Indochina than either Lin or Mao and that Luo demanded greater military preparations to deal with the threat, including accepting the Soviet proposal of a "united front."[72]

There is nothing in the recently available Chinese materials to confirm the existence of the "strategic debate" in 1965.[73] The often cited evidence to support the hypothesis consists of Luo Ruiqing's May 1965 article celebrating the defeat of Germany in World War II and Lin Biao's September piece, "Long Live the Victory of People's War."[74] In fact, although published in Lin's name, the latter article was prepared primarily by the writing group organized by Luo in the General Staff. The final version of the "People's War" article also incorporated opinions from the writing team led by Kang Sheng. (Operating in the Diaoyutai National Guest House, Kang's team was famous for writing the nine polemics against Soviet revisionism.) Although the article included some of Lin Biao's previous statements, Lin himself was not involved in its writing. When Luo asked Lin for his instructions about the composition of the article, the defense minister said nothing. Zhou Enlai and other standing politburo members read the piece before its publication.[75] The article was approved by the Chinese leadership as a whole and was merely published in Lin's name. Luo was purged in December 1965 primarily because of his dispute with Lin over domestic military organization and petty personal squabbles rather than over foreign policy issues.[76]

Luo Ruiqing did not oppose Mao on Vietnam policy. In fact he carried out loyally every Vietnam-related order issued by the chairman. Mao completely dominated the decision making. In the authoritarian Chinese political culture, Mao's power was absolute. Once the "great leader" spoke, the party obeyed. Whatever private opinions were held, the only viable option was to follow the course dictated by Mao. Petty individual hatreds and jealousies rather than disputes over large policy issues characterized political life in China around the time of the Cultural Revolution.[77] The origins of the "People's War" article point to the danger of relying on public pronouncements to gauge inner-party calculations and cast doubts on the utility of the faction model in explaining Chinese foreign policymaking.[78]

It is possible that the two articles published in Luo Ruiqing's and Lin Biao's names were written primarily in response to the Soviet argument on war and peace. On January 30, 1965, Mao asked Yang Chengwu and Lei Yingfu, deputy director of the Combat Department of the General Staff, to find a person well versed in political and military issues to prepare a commentary on the book *Military Strategy*, edited by Soviet chief of staff V. D. Sokolovsky and published by the Soviet Defense Ministry's Military Press in 1962.[79]

The "People's War" article may have been designed mainly to counter Soviet views on war and peace, but its call for the surrounding of the world cities (industrialized nations) by the world rural areas (developing countries) through militant local revolutions greatly alarmed American policymakers, who viewed the article as a Chinese *Mein Kampf*, committing Beijing to undermine vulnerable colonial and newly independent nations.[80] U.S. defense secretary Robert McNamara later recalled: "The Johnson administration—including me— interpreted the speech as bellicose and aggressive, signaling an expansionist China's readiness to nourish 'local' forces across the world and to give a helping pushing when the time came. Lin's remarks seemed to us a clear expression of the basis for the domino theory."[81]

Commitment to National Liberation Movements

The second factor that shaped Mao's decision to support the DRV was his need to form a broad international united front against both the United States and the Soviet Union. To Mao, national liberation movements in the Third World were the most important potential allies in the coalition that he wanted to establish.[82] Between 1963 and 1964, the CCP chairman developed the concept of "Two Intermediate Zones." The first zone referred to developed countries, including capitalist states in Europe, Canada, Japan, Australia, and New Zealand. The second zone referred to underdeveloped nations in Asia, Africa, and Latin America. These two zones existed between the two superpowers. Mao believed that countries in these two zones had conflicts with the United States and the Soviet Union and that China should make friends with them to create an international united front against Washington and Moscow.[83]

Mao initially developed the idea of the intermediate zone during the early years of the Cold War. The CCP leader first broached the idea in a discussion with Anna Louise Strong, an American journalist, in 1946. He claimed that the United States and the Soviet Union were "separated by a vast zone including many capitalist, colonial and semi-colonial countries in Europe, Asia, and Africa" and that it was difficult for "the U.S. reactionaries to attack the Soviet Union before they could subjugate these countries."[84] In the late 1940s and throughout the greater part of the 1950s, Mao leaned to the side of the Soviet Union to balance China against the perceived American threat. But beginning in the late 1950s, with the emergence of Sino-Soviet differences, Mao came to revise his characterization of the international situation. He saw China confronting two opponents: the United States and the Soviet Union. To oppose these two foes and break China's international isolation, Mao proposed the formation of an international united front.

Operating from the principle of making friends with countries in the "Two Intermediate Zones," Mao promoted such anti-American tendencies as French president De Gaulle's break with the United States in the first zone and championed national liberation movements in the second zone. For Mao, the Vietnam conflict constituted a part of a broader movement across Asia, Africa, and Latin America, which represented a challenge to imperialism as a whole. China reached out to anticolonial guerrillas in Angola and Mozambique, to the "progressive" Sihanouk in Cambodia, to the leftist regime under Sukarno in Indonesia, and to the anti-U.S. Castro in Cuba.[85] In the former socialist camp dominated by the Soviet Union, Mao encouraged Albania to persuade other East European countries to separate from Moscow.[86]

During this increasingly radical period of Chinese foreign policy, Mao singled out three anti-imperialist heroes for emulation by Third World liberation movements: Ho Chi Minh, Castro, and Ben Bella. In a speech to a delegation of Chilean journalists on June 23, 1964, Mao remarked: "We oppose war, but we support the anti-imperialist war waged by oppressed peoples. We support the revolutionary war in Cuba and Algeria. We also support the anti-U.S.-imperialist war conducted by the South Vietnamese people."[87] In another address to a group of visitors from Asia, Africa, and Oceania on July 9, Mao again mentioned the names of Ho Chi Minh, Castro, and Ben Bella as models for anticolonial and anti-imperialist struggle.[88]

Envisioning China as a spokesperson for the Third World independence cause, Mao continued to believe that the Chinese revolutionary experience provided a model for the struggle of liberation movements in Asia, Africa, and Latin America. By firmly backing the Vietnamese struggle against the United States, he wanted to demonstrate to Third World countries that China was their true friend. A victorious, China-supported North Vietnam in its war of national unification would demonstrate Beijing's revolutionary credentials and show the political wisdom of Mao's more militant strategy for coping with U.S. imperialism and the incorrectness of Khrushchev's policy of peaceful coexistence.[89]

A number of Chinese anti-imperialist initiatives, however, ended in a debacle in 1965. First Ben Bella was overthrown in Algeria in June, which led the Afro-Asian movement to lean in a more pro-Soviet direction due to the influence of Jawaharlal Nehru in India and Josip Broz Tito in Yugoslavia. The fall of Ben Bella frustrated Mao's bid for leadership in the Third World by setting the agenda at the Algiers conference of Afro-Asian leaders. In September, war broke out between India and Pakistan, a Chinese ally, over the territory of Kashmir. China's effort to deter India's advance failed, and New Delhi won the conflict. The net result, strategically, was a gain for Moscow and a loss for Beijing. On September 30, Sukarno was toppled in a right-wing countercoup, derailing Mao's plan to maintain a militant "Beijing-Jakarta" axis.[90]

Chinese behavior, nevertheless, did convince leaders in Washington that

Beijing was a dangerous gambler in international politics and that American intervention in Vietnam was necessary to undermine a Chinese plot of global subversion by proxy. Robert McNamara wrote in his memoirs: "In retrospect, one can see the events of autumn 1965 as clear setbacks for China. . . . But, blinded by our assumptions and preoccupied with a rapidly growing war, we—like most other Western leaders—continued to view China as a serious threat in Southeast Asia and the rest of the world."[91] That misperception, in turn, may have constituted a missed opportunity for the U.S. to re-evaluate its prior assumptions about the consequences of a U.S. defeat in Vietnam for the rest of Southeast Asia and thus to reconsider the American commitment to "pay any price" to assure the survival of a non-Communist South Vietnam.

Criticism of Soviet Revisionism

Mao's firm commitment to Vietnam also needs to be considered in the context of the unfolding Sino-Soviet split. By 1963, Beijing and Moscow had completely parted ways after three years of increasingly abusive polemics. The conclusion of the Partial Nuclear Test Ban Treaty in July 1963 was a major turning point in Sino-Soviet relations. Thereafter the Beijing leadership publicly denounced any suggestion that China was subject to any degree of Soviet protection and directly criticized Moscow for collaborating with Washington against China. The effect of the Sino-Soviet split on Vietnam soon manifested itself as Beijing and Moscow wooed Hanoi to take sides in their ideological dispute.

After the ouster of Khrushchev in October 1964, the new leadership in the Kremlin invited the CCP to send a delegation to the October Revolution celebrations. Beijing dispatched Zhou Enlai and Marshal He Long to Moscow for the primary purpose of sounding out Leonid Brezhnev and Alexei Kosygin on the many issues in dispute, namely, Khrushchev's long-postponed plan to convene an international Communist meeting, China's support for revolutionary movements, the Soviet Union's desire for peaceful coexistence with the United States, the two countries' attitudes toward Tito, and "revisionist" domestic policies within the Soviet Union. The Chinese discovered during their tour between November 5 and 13 that nothing basic had changed in the Soviet position: the new leaders in Moscow desired an improvement in Sino-Soviet relations with the condition that Beijing stop its criticisms and limit competition in foreign policy, probably in return for the resumption of Soviet economic aid.[92]

Instead of finding an opportunity to improve mutual understanding, the Chinese visitors found their stay in Moscow unpleasant and China's relationship with the Soviet Union even worse. During a Soviet reception, Marshal

Rodion Malinovsky suggested to Zhou Enlai and He Long that just as the Russians had ousted Khrushchev, the Chinese should overthrow Mao. The Chinese indignantly rejected this proposal. Zhou registered a strong protest with the Soviet leadership, referring to Malinovsky's remarks as "a serious political incident."[93] Zhou told the Cuban Communist delegation during a breakfast meeting in the Chinese embassy on November 9 that Malinovsky "insulted Comrade Mao Zedong, the Chinese people, the Chinese Party, and myself" and that the current leadership in the Kremlin inherited "Khrushchev's working style and way of thinking."[94]

Before Zhou's journey to Moscow, the Chinese leadership had suggested to the Vietnamese Communists that they also send people to travel with Zhou to Moscow to see whether there were changes in the new Soviet leaders' policies. Zhou told Ho Chi Minh and Le Duan later in Hanoi on March 1, 1965, that he was "disappointed" with what he had seen in Moscow and that "the new Soviet leaders are following nothing but Khrushchevism."[95] Clearly, Zhou wanted the Hanoi leadership to side with China in the continuing Sino-Soviet dispute. Beijing's extensive aid to the DRV was designed to keep Hanoi within China's orbit.

The collective leadership that succeeded Khrushchev was more forthcoming in support of the DRV. During his visit to Hanoi on February 7–10, Soviet premier Alexei Kosygin called for a total U.S. withdrawal from South Vietnam and promised Soviet material aid for Ho Chi Minh's struggle. The fact that a group of missile experts accompanied Kosygin indicates that the Kremlin was providing support in that crucial area. The two sides concluded formal military and economic agreements on February 10.[96] Clearly, the Soviets were competing with the Chinese to win the allegiance of the Vietnamese Communists. Through its new gestures to Hanoi, Moscow wanted to offset Chinese influence and demonstrate its ideological rectitude on issues of national liberation. The new solidarity with Hanoi, however, complicated Soviet relations with the United States, and after 1965, the Soviet Union found itself at loggerheads with Washington. While Moscow gained greater influence in Hanoi because of the North Vietnamese need for Soviet material assistance against U.S. bombing, it at the same time lost flexibility because of the impossibility of retreat from the commitment to a brother Communist state under attack by imperialism.

Before late 1964, Hanoi was virtually on China's side in the bifurcated international Communist movement. After the fall of Khrushchev and the appearance of a more interventionist position under Kosygin and Brezhnev, however, Hanoi adopted a more balanced stand. Leaders in Beijing were nervous about the increase of Soviet influence in Vietnam. According to a Vietnamese source, Deng Xiaoping, secretary-general of the CCP, paid a secret visit to Hanoi after the Gulf of Tonkin incident with the promise of one billion Chinese yuan in aid if the DRV refused all aid from the Soviet Union.[97]

China's strategy to discredit the Soviet Union was to emphasize the "plot" of Soviet-American collaborations at the expense of Vietnam. During his visit to Beijing on February 11, 1965, Kosygin asked the Chinese to help the United States to "find a way out of Vietnam." Chinese leaders warned the Russians not to use the Vietnam issue to bargain with the Americans.[98] Immediately after his return to Moscow, Kosygin on February 16 proposed to Beijing and Hanoi that an international conference on Indochina be called without preconditions. The Chinese condemned the Soviet move, asserting that the Russians wanted negotiation rather than continued struggle in Vietnam and were conspiring with the Americans to sell out Vietnam.[99] The Chinese criticism of the Soviet peace initiative must have confirmed the American image of China as a warmonger.

In the spring of 1965, Moscow asked Beijing to grant an "air corridor" through which a Soviet airlift could be conducted in defense of the DRV and to cede a base in Yunnan, where hundreds of Soviet military personnel could be stationed to assist Hanoi's war effort. Accusing the Russians of taking advantage of the war in Vietnam to violate Chinese sovereignty, the Chinese turned down the Soviet request. While rejecting this kind of coordination, Beijing did allow the Soviet Union to transport its aid to the DRV through the Chinese rail corridor, which remained a major supply route for the Vietnamese war effort between 1965 and 1968.[100] According to one Chinese account, by the end of 1965 China helped the Soviet Union transport 43,000 tons of military supplies to North Vietnam.[101]

Beijing would spurn any proposal that would grant Moscow access to China. It consented to the transshipment of Soviet military goods through China by rail precisely because it could control it. This situation soon led to Soviet accusations of Chinese tampering and deliberate delays. During 1966–67, Beijing and Moscow exchanged charges regarding whether China had hampered the shipment of Soviet military aid to the DRV.[102] Whether Beijing intentionally blocked the transportation of Soviet military supplies to North Vietnam remains a question. What is certain is that during the Cultural Revolution those supply trains were often attacked and robbed of weapons and munitions by feuding factions. The attacks occurred most frequently in Guangxi province, where the Cultural Revolution seriously divided mass organizations. Between 1967 and 1968, Zhou Enlai held numerous meetings in Beijing with representatives from the feuding factions in Guangxi, urging them to stop fighting, to return the arms they had seized, and not to block the transportation of aid materials to North Vietnam. He also ordered the PLA to take over the control of the railway system.[103] Clearly, the politics of the Cultural Revolution at the mass level affected China's dealings with North Vietnam.

The Sino-Soviet rivalry over Vietnam certainly provided leaders in Hanoi an opportunity to obtain maximum support from their two Communist allies, but one should not overstate the case. Sometimes the benefits of the Sino-Soviet split for the DRV could be limited. For example, the Hanoi leadership wanted Moscow and Beijing to agree on common support actions, particularly on a single integrated logistical system. They failed to achieve this objective, however, primarily because of China's objection.[104]

Domestic Need to Transform the Chinese State and Society

Beginning in the late 1950s, Mao became increasingly apprehensive about the potential development of the Chinese revolution. He feared that his life's work had created a political structure that would eventually betray his principles and values and become as exploitative as the one it had replaced. His worry about the future of China's development was closely related to his diagnosis of the degeneration of the Soviet political system and to his fear about the effects of U.S. secretary of state John Foster Dulles's strategy of "peaceful evolution." Mao took Dulles's statements about encouraging liberalization in socialist countries seriously. He believed that Dulles's plan to induce a peaceful evolution within the socialist world through cultural infiltration was taking effect in the Soviet Union, given Khrushchev's fascination with peaceful coexistence with the capitalist West. Mao wanted to prevent that from happening in China.[105]

The problem of succession preoccupied Mao throughout the first half of the 1960s. His acute awareness of impending death contributed to his sense of urgency. He perceived the emergence of a new ruling elite in China, who, through its centralized control of the economic system, provided little scope for popular participation in the process of development. Mao disliked the economic retrenchment policy followed by Liu Shaoqi and Deng Xiaoping after the Great Leap Forward, viewing them as "taking the capitalist road." While learning from the Great Leap that mass mobilization was not the key to rapid economic growth, Mao retained faith in popular participation as a tool of ideological renewal, social transformation, and rectification.[106]

The U.S. escalation of war in Vietnam made Mao all the more eager to put his own house in order. He was afraid that if he did not nip what he perceived to be revisionist tendencies in the bud and if he did not choose a proper successor, after his death China would be in the hands of Soviet-like revisionists, who would "change the color" of China, abandon support for national liberation struggles, and appease U.S. imperialism. Mao was a man who believed in dialectics. Negative things could be turned into positive matters. The American presence in Indochina was a threat to the Chinese revolution. But on the other hand, Mao found that he could turn the U.S. threat into an advantage by using it to intensify domestic anti-imperialist feelings and mobilize the population against revisionists. Mao had successfully employed that strategy against Chiang Kai-shek during the civil war. Now he could apply it again to prepare the masses for the Great Cultural Revolution that he was going to launch. Accordingly, in the wake of the Gulf of Tonkin incident, Mao unleashed a massive "Aid Vietnam and Resist America" campaign across China.[107]

In sum, aiding Vietnam served four primary purposes for Mao: it countered U.S. threats to China's security, demonstrated Beijing's credibility as a true supporter of Third World nationalist liberation movements, allowed China to compete with the Soviet Union for leadership in the international Communist camp and for influence in Indochina, and drummed up domestic support for Mao's fundamental reshaping of the Chinese state and society.

SINO-VIETNAMESE DISCORDS

Signs of Sino-Vietnamese differences emerged in the early days of China's intervention in the Second Vietnam War. Vietnamese historical pride and cultural sensitivity was one major factor that complicated Beijing-Hanoi interactions. When Chinese troops went to North Vietnam in 1965, they found themselves in an awkward position. On the one hand, the Hanoi leadership wanted their service in fighting U.S. aircraft and in building and repairing roads, bridges, and rail lines. On the other hand, the Vietnamese authorities tried to minimize their influence by restricting their contact with the local population. For instance, Vietnamese officials blocked Chinese medical teams' efforts to treat Vietnamese civilian patients.[108] They objected to the Chinese practice of distributing among Vietnamese villagers materials (written in Vietnamese) on achievements of China's economic construction.[109] They also prohibited their people from accepting and wearing Mao badges.[110] Informed of such incidents, Mao urged Chinese troops in the DRV to "refrain from being too eager" to help the Vietnamese.[111] While Chinese soldiers were in North Vietnam, the Vietnamese media reminded the public that in history China had invaded Vietnam. The journal *Historical Studies* published articles in 1965 describing Vietnamese resistance against Chinese imperial dynasties in the past.[112]

The increasing Vietnamese resentment against the Chinese presence in the DRV prompted Deng Xiaoping to confront Le Duan directly on this issue at a meeting in Beijing on April 13, 1966. The barely five-foot-tall Deng was famous for a temperament as peppery as the cuisine of his native Sichuan province. With characteristic bluntness, he told Duan that Mao had criticized Chinese officials for showing "too much enthusiasm" on the Vietnam question. After mentioning the presence of 130,000 Chinese troops in the DRV, the stationing of Chinese soldiers along the Vietnamese border, and the Sino-DRV discussions about joint fighting if the United States invaded North Vietnam, the CCP secretary-general posed straightforwardly the question of distrust before his North Vietnamese counterpart: "Are you suspicious of us because we have so much enthusiasm? Do the Chinese want to take control over Vietnam? We would like to tell you frankly that we don't have any such intention. . . . If we have made a mistake thus making you suspicious, it means that Comrade Mao is really farsighted." Deng also brought up the incident of a Chinese ship that requested entry to a Vietnamese port during U.S. bombing but was refused. Duan, claiming to be unaware of the ship incident, reassured the Chinese that Hanoi had always appreciated their assistance and that "the more enthusiasm you have, the more beneficial it is for us. Your enthusiastic assistance can help us to save the lives of 2 or 3 million people."[113]

The increasing rivalry between Beijing and Moscow also hampered Sino-DRV cooperation. The Chinese and Soviet efforts to win Hanoi's allegiance put the North Vietnamese in a dilemma. On the one hand, the change of Russia's attitude of reluctance toward Vietnam to active assistance in late 1964 and early 1965 made the North Vietnamese more unwilling to echo China's criticisms of revisionism. On the other hand, they still needed China's assistance and deterrence. But Mao's rejection of the Soviet proposal of a "united action" on Vietnam ruled out the possibility of a closer coordination within the international Communist camp in support of the DRV.

During Kosygin's visit to Beijing in February 1965, he proposed to Mao and Zhou that China and the Soviet Union end their mutual criticisms and cooperate on the issue of Vietnam. But Mao dismissed Kosygin's suggestion, asserting that China's argument with the Soviet Union would continue for another 9,000 years.[114] On April 3, Moscow proposed to Beijing a DRV-Chinese-Soviet summit meeting, but China rejected the suggestion. In a further reply to the Soviet Communist Party on July 10, the CCP Central Committee, with Mao's approval, retorted that on the Vietnam issue the Soviet Union had adopted appeasement toward the United States. Moscow's proposal for a "united action" on Vietnam, the committee continued, was designed to subordinate fraternal parties to the Soviet party and to turn those parties into Russian tools in the USSR's plot to dominate the world with the United States.[115] Mao's arrogance and strongly held ideological convictions eliminated any possibility of reconciliation between Beijing and Moscow. His veto of a joint action with the Soviet Union in support of the DRV made the Vietnamese Communists realize that China's conflict with Moscow was more important to Mao than assisting Hanoi in its fight against the United States.

During February and March 1966, a Japanese Communist Party delegation led by Secretary-General Miyamoto Kenji visited China, the DRV, and North Korea to encourage a "joint action" between China and the Soviet Union to support North Vietnam. Miyamoto first broached the idea with the CCP delegation led by Liu Shaoqi, Zhou Enlai, Deng Xiaoping, and Peng Zhen in Beijing. The two sides worked out a communiqué that included only points of agreement between the two delegations. The communiqué condemned U.S. aggression in Vietnam and pledged support for the Vietnamese people. On the issue of attitudes toward the Soviet Union, the communiqué emphasized the importance of the struggle against modern revisionism in waging the struggle against U.S. imperialism but failed to mention the USSR by name. When Miyamoto came to see Mao in Shanghai on March 28, the chairman burst into a rage, insisting that the communiqué mention the Soviet Union by name in its condemnation of modern revisionism. Miyamoto disagreed, so the Beijing communiqué was torn up.[116] Clearly, by this time Mao had connected the criticism of Soviet revisionism with the domestic struggle against top party leaders headed by Liu, Deng, and Peng. It was no wonder that these officials soon became leading targets for attack when the Cultural Revolution swept across China a few months later.

In the meantime the Vietnamese Communists made clear their different attitude toward Moscow by deciding to send a delegation to attend the Twenty-third Congress of the Communist Party of the Soviet Union, which was to be held between March 29 and April 8. The Chinese had chosen not to participate in the congress. The North Vietnamese were walking on a tightrope at this time. On the one hand, they relied on the vital support of Soviet weapons; on the other hand, they did not want to break their ties with China. Thus Hanoi at this time made a special point of refuting Moscow's accusations that Beijing was blocking Soviet weapons shipment to the DRV. Pham Van Dong, speaking before the North Vietnamese National Assembly, praised China for its "devoted help in the transit of the aid from the Soviet Union and other fraternal East European countries according to schedule."[117] In February 1967, Hanoi again denounced Western "slanders" based on Soviet broadcasts that Beijing had hijacked missiles sent by Moscow to the DRV.[118]

By carefully navigating among the shoals of Sino-Soviet rivalry, Hanoi eventually succeeded in early 1967 in getting Beijing and Moscow to agree on a new arrangement for transporting Soviet arms through China to the DRV. The agreement provided for the North Vietnamese to receive the shipments at the Sino-Soviet border before escorting them through Chinese territory. This arrangement had the advantage of minimizing chances of Chinese-Russian quarrels over weapons transportation and was undoubtedly meant by both powers as a gesture of support for Hanoi's war endeavor rather than as a prelude to a Sino-Soviet rapprochement.[119]

WAS CHINA BLUFFING DURING THE VIETNAM WAR?

The fact that Beijing did not openly acknowledge its sizable presence in North Vietnam raised questions about the justification for Washington's restraint in its conduct of war, both at the time and in later years. Harry G. Summers, the most prominent of revisionist critics of President Johnson's Vietnam policy, asserts that the United States learned the wrong lesson from the Korean War: "Instead of seeing that it was possible to fight and win a limited war in Asia regardless of Chinese intervention, we . . . took counsel of our fears and accepted as an article of faith the proposition that we should never again become involved in a land war in Asia. In so doing we allowed our fears to become a kind of self-imposed deterrent and surrendered the initiative to our enemies." Summers contends that "whether the Soviets or the Chinese ever intended intervention is a matter of conjecture" and that the United States allowed itself "to be bluffed by China throughout most of the war." He cites Mao's rejection of the 1965 Soviet proposal for a joint action to support Vietnam and Mao's suspicions of Moscow's plot to draw China into a war with the United States as evidence for the conclusion that Mao was more fearful of Moscow than Washington and, by implication, he was not serious about China's threats to intervene to help Hanoi.[120]

Was China not serious in its threats to go to war with the United States in Indochina? As the preceding discussion has shown, Beijing had substantial security and ideological interests in Vietnam. From the security perspective, Mao and his associates were genuinely concerned about the American threat from Vietnam (although they did not realize that their own actions, like the supply of weapons to Hanoi in 1962, had helped to precipitate the U.S. escalation of war in Indochina) and adopted significant measures in war preparations at home. China's assistance to the DRV, to use John Garver's words, "was Mao's way of rolling back US containment in Asia."[121] From the viewpoint of ideology, China's support for Vietnam served Mao's purposes of demonstrating to the Third World that Beijing was a spokesperson for national liberation struggles and of competing with Moscow for leadership in the international Communist movement.

If the actions recommended by Summers had been taken by Washington in Vietnam, there would have been a real danger of a Sino-American war with dire consequences for the world. In retrospect, it appears that Johnson had drawn the correct lesson from the Korean War and had been prudent in his approach to the Vietnam conflict.

VIETNAM PEACE TALKS 1965–1968

The Johnson administration's escalation of the war in Vietnam in 1965 triggered strong domestic criticism. Responding to public pressure, President Johnson made a number of peace overtures to Hanoi. The escalating conflict in Indochina also drew serious attention around the world, and various countries initiated steps toward a peaceful settlement. Thus, the war in Vietnam was intertwined with a series of peace initiatives made not only by Washington but also by Moscow, London, Paris, and a number of British Commonwealth capitals.

CHINA'S OBJECTION TO PEACE NEGOTIATIONS

Between 1965 and 1968, Beijing strongly opposed peace talks between Hanoi and Washington and rejected a number of international initiatives designed to promote a peaceful solution to the Vietnam conflict. Some of these initiatives are well-known events such as the Soviet proposal for an international conference on Vietnam, the British call for an international meeting on Cambodia that would provide an opportunity for "corridor contact" between the United States and the Communist powers on the Vietnam question, and the Indian suggestion for a cease-fire along the seventeenth parallel, supervised by an "Afro-Asian Force." Others have remained largely secret, including the Ghanaian mission to mediate between Hanoi and Washington, the French "neutralization of Indochina" plan, and the Polish initiatives to bring the DRV and the United States to the negotiating table.

President Johnson's escalation of the war in Vietnam created a dilemma for the Soviet Union. On the one hand, Soviet leaders felt obliged to stand behind

Hanoi to preserve Moscow's credibility as the leader of the Communist camp. On the other hand, they wished to avoid a direct confrontation with the United States over Vietnam and to continue détente in Europe. As a result, while providing moral, political, and military support for the DRV, the Kremlin actively promoted a peaceful settlement.[1] During his visit to China on February 11, 1965, Soviet premier Kosygin sought a peaceful solution to the Vietnam problem.[2] After returning to Moscow, Kosygin on February 16 proposed to the DRV and China an international conference on Indochina. The Chinese rejected the Soviet proposal.[3]

In the wake of Johnson's escalation of U.S. military involvement in Vietnam, protest against the war increased in the United States. The antiwar campaign built on and merged with both the civil rights and student movements in late 1964 and early 1965. On March 25, 1965, responding to domestic anxiety about Vietnam, Johnson declared his willingness to "go anywhere at any time, and meet with anyone whenever there is promise of progress toward an honorable peace." In fact, the president's statement was pure rhetoric, for none of his close aides had seriously considered either the form or the substance of the talks Johnson claimed to be prepared to conduct.[4]

By contrast, the British Labour government was eager to encourage peace talks on Vietnam. Three days after Johnson made his remarks, Prime Minister Harold Wilson sent Patrick Gordon Walker, a former foreign secretary, as his personal emissary to Southeast Asia to promote discussion of the Vietnam problem among the countries concerned. Both Beijing and Hanoi refused to receive Walker.[5] In a meeting with Algerian president Ben Bella in Algiers on March 30, Zhou Enlai blamed the United States for the fighting in Vietnam and criticized the British effort at peacemaking. Zhou claimed that "the American invasion has prevented the realization of the peaceful unification of South and North Vietnam. At present the United States intends to intimidate Vietnam through expanding the war and to use bombing to force Vietnam to submit and agree to conduct 'peace negotiations.' The United States is promoting peace talks through such countries as the Soviet Union, Britain, and France. The United States wants to gain through peace talks what it has failed to gain on the battleground." The British peacemaking activities, Zhou concluded, were "either directly or indirectly instigated by the United States."[6]

On April 1 and 2, the British office of the chargé d'affaires presented diplomatic notes to the Chinese Foreign Ministry, suggesting that London send a special representative to Beijing to discuss the Vietnam issue. Ten days later, the Chinese Foreign Ministry replied that it was "inappropriate and unwelcome" for the British government to send such an envoy. The British government, the

Chinese continued, had not condemned U.S. aggression in Vietnam and thus had betrayed its obligations as a co-chair of the 1954 Geneva Conference.[7]

Despite Beijing's and Hanoi's refusal to see him,[8] Gordon Walker began his journey in mid-April with hopes of promoting an international conference on Cambodia. Prince Norodom Sihanouk had first shown interest in such a meeting in March 1965 after sponsoring the Indochinese Peoples' Conference in Phnom Penh. He had proposed reconvening the Geneva Conference to allow the participants to reaffirm their guarantee of Cambodian neutrality and territorial integrity. The Soviets endorsed Sihanouk's proposal in early April, as did the British, who viewed it as a possible channel to promote informal discussions on Vietnam. U.S. officials were more reluctant to be too closely linked with Gordon Walker's initiatives for fear of alienating the Thai government, which had a border dispute with Cambodia. Despite their reservations, they expressed support for the conference, partly to avoid pushing Cambodia further into the arms of China and North Vietnam and partly to demonstrate Washington's commitment to peace in Indochina. Beijing supported an international conference on Cambodia but rejected any discussions on Vietnam. Sihanouk met with Zhou Enlai and Pham Van Dong in Indonesia between April 17 and 18 during the celebration of the Bandung conference anniversary. There he announced that he would not participate in a gathering that dealt with more than Cambodia. Gordon Walker's visit to Cambodia between April 26 and 27 was fruitless.[9]

At a banquet in Beijing on April 29 in honor of a Ghanaian government delegation led by Foreign Minister Kojo Botsio, Zhou Enlai praised Sihanouk for his "wisdom in seeing through the American plot regarding an international conference on Cambodia." The Chinese premier pointed out that the real reason for "the Johnson administration's great interest in convening such a conference lies not in really guaranteeing the neutrality and territorial integrity of Cambodia but in continuing the plot of inducing the Vietnamese people into submission."[10]

To silence domestic and international criticism of U.S. escalation of the war, President Johnson had delivered a speech at Johns Hopkins University on April 7 in which he emphasized U.S. resolve to prevail in Vietnam, although he added that he was ready to conduct "unconditional discussions" with Hanoi. Premier Pham Van Dong responded with his Four Points peace formula on April 8. This demanded that the United States withdraw its forces from Vietnam and cease its acts of war; called for the neutralization of both Vietnams pending unification; proposed a settlement of the internal affairs of South Vietnam in accordance with the program of the National Liberation Front;

and insisted that reunification be arranged by the Vietnamese people without outside interference.[11]

Johnson's Johns Hopkins speech triggered renewed efforts at peacemaking by the United Nations and India. In early April, UN secretary-general U Thant stated that he wanted to visit China and the DRV to "explore the possibility of realizing a negotiated settlement in Vietnam."[12] In an editorial on April 12, the *Renmin ribao* (People's Daily) pointed out that the 1954 Geneva Agreement had been concluded outside the UN framework. The United Nations, the Chinese newspaper went on, had never taken a just stand on Vietnam, had never condemned U.S. aggression, and thus had no authority to intervene in Indochina affairs.[13] On April 24, Indian president Sarvepalli Radhakrishnan called for a termination of the bombing of North Vietnam, a cessation of the fighting in South Vietnam, and the deployment of an Afro-Asian police force along the border and at critical points in South Vietnam to supervise the cease-fire. While the United States considered the proposal favorably, China denounced it as a "plot."[14]

The Johns Hopkins address silenced Johnson's critics temporarily, but the president soon realized that some additional conciliation was necessary. In May, he decided to suspend the bombing of North Vietnam for a brief period both as a feeler to see if Hanoi had any interest in negotiations and as a gesture to his domestic and international critics. The bombing pause, which lasted from May 13 to 17, was code-named "MAYFLOWER."[15] The Chinese proclaimed the pause a "hoax" to lure the North Vietnamese into "unconditional discussions" with the United States, the first step in getting Hanoi to recognize the U.S. occupation of South Vietnam.[16]

The failure of the Gordon Walker mission did not dampen Prime Minister Wilson's enthusiasm for a resolution of the Vietnam conflict. At the June 1965 Commonwealth conference, the prime minister, after consulting with President Johnson, proposed a Commonwealth peace mission to include the leaders of Britain, Nigeria, Ghana, and Trinidad; President Julius Nyerere of Tanzania refused to participate. The mission's goal was to bring an end to U.S. bombing of North Vietnam, to persuade Hanoi to stop sending men and materials to South Vietnam, and to work out a cease-fire in the south to pave the way for an international conference that would secure the withdrawal of all foreign troops from Vietnam and establish an international force to maintain peace. Washington supported the British initiative because it embodied most of the objectives the United States had been pursuing.[17]

On June 22, Xiong Xianghui, Chinese chargé d'affaires to Britain, met in London with President Kwame Nkrumah of Ghana, who was selected to participate in the Commonwealth mission because of his good relationship with both Hanoi and Beijing. In accordance with the Chinese government's general policy of opposing peace talks, Xiong told Nkrumah that the British Commonwealth peace mission would only be "beneficial to U.S. imperialism" and that China would not welcome it. Two days later the Chinese Foreign Ministry approved Xiong's position.[18] In a message to the British government on June 25, Beijing officially rejected the Commonwealth mission, claiming that the U.S. violation of the Geneva Agreement lay at the root of the Vietnam problem.[19]

Nkrumah nevertheless did not give up. He sought to visit the DRV personally to promote peace. The North Vietnamese insisted that Nkrumah come to Hanoi as president of Ghana only, not as a member of the Commonwealth mission. Preoccupied with domestic economic problems, Nkrumah immediately dispatched a delegation to Hanoi headed by Kwesi Armah, minister of overseas trade, to try to prepare the way for negotiations.[20] Chinese leaders opposed this mission as well, believing it still represented "the old plot of unconditional peace negotiations advanced several times in the past by the imperialists, revisionists, and reactionaries." They felt that the idea of using Afro-Asian countries as mediators was intended to bypass the Geneva Accords and facilitate a direct negotiation between the United States and North Vietnam. The Chinese government notified the North Vietnamese of Beijing's objection to the Ghanaian mission before its arrival in Hanoi.[21]

In Hanoi the Ghanaian visitors told North Vietnamese officials that Ghana supported Hanoi's Four Points as well as the Five Points peace formula pronounced by the NLF on March 22, 1965. They claimed that the current moment was the best time for peace negotiations because the U.S. position was close to that of North and South Vietnam, and they proposed that Afro-Asian countries serve as mediators in American-Vietnamese talks. The North Vietnamese leaders contended that they had a better understanding of their enemy than Ghana did and that they "would not be taken in by Johnson's carrot." The struggle of the Vietnamese people, they went on, constituted part of the anti-imperialist struggle waged by the Afro-Asian peoples, who should unite against imperialism. Ghana should mobilize Afro-Asian nations to force the United States to accept the demands made by the NLF rather than promote a conference between the United States and Vietnam.[22] Ho Chi Minh told the delegation that negotiations were both irrelevant and undesirable because victory might arrive before the end of the rainy season, but that he would be pleased to receive Nkrumah. Ho then added that he worried about the safety of the Ghanaian president because of the American bombing of North Vietnam.[23] Ho's last point may be interpreted as a polite and indirect rejection of a visit by Nkrumah.

On July 10, *Shijie zhishi* (World Knowledge) condemned Britain's peace initiatives on Vietnam: "An old colonial power is collaborating with a new colonial power. The Labour Party is backing the United States' Vietnam policy in order to win American support for Malaysia, a neocolonial product created by Britain." The journal attributed Wilson's peacemaking effort to his desire to win support before the British election and to please the Americans because London depended on Washington economically.[24] While condemning the British role, officials in the Chinese Foreign Ministry also stressed that Washington was the real instigator behind the African peace initiatives. They believed that the Americans had two goals in their "peace hoax": first, to take advantage of the ignorance of African countries about the Vietnam issue and their fear of an expansion of war to drive a wedge into their relationship with China; and second, to divide China and the DRV by emphasizing Beijing as the barrier to peace negotiations.[25]

On July 19 French minister of state Andre Malraux arrived in Beijing as a special envoy of President Charles de Gaulle. Among other topics, Malraux discussed Vietnam with Mao, Liu Shaoqi, and Zhou Enlai. He proposed a "neutralization of Indochina" plan that would redraw the boundaries of Vietnam. According to the plan, Vietnam would be divided along the Truong Son Ra mountain. The area east of the mountain, including Saigon, would belong to the DRV or the NLF; the area west of the mountain, as well as Laos, Cambodia, and Thailand, would be "neutralized." Malraux also asked the Chinese whether it would be possible to conduct negotiations if the United States "promised" to withdraw troops from Vietnam. Zhou immediately rejected Malraux's "neutralization" plan, claiming that the boundaries in Indochinese countries were long established; furthermore, he asserted, the independence and neutrality of Cambodia and Laos should be respected on the basis of the Geneva Agreement. As to the intentions of Washington, the Chinese premier believed that the United States did not want to leave Vietnam. He told the French visitor that China would firmly support the Vietnamese struggle against the United States.[26]

At the Vietnamese National Day reception given by Tran Tu Binh, the North Vietnamese ambassador to China, on September 2, Zhou Enlai condemned what he viewed as the U.S. "peace talks hoax": "The very aim of the peace talks plot hatched by the United States is to bring about negotiations by cajolery so as to consolidate its position in South Vietnam. As long as the United States does not withdraw its troops, it can carry on endless talks with you so that it may hang on there indefinitely."[27]

During the Twenty-first General Assembly of the United Nations in late September 1965, U.S. and Soviet officials discussed the Vietnam question with

U Thant. The Chinese media immediately denounced this activity. *Renmin ribao* contended that the peace talk proposals by the United States and the Soviet Union at the United Nations meeting demonstrated that Washington and Moscow had gone "a step further in their collusion over Vietnam." In another slap at China's rival, the paper asserted that "the Soviet revisionist leading group" had taken "another step . . . in becoming an accomplice of U.S. imperialism."[28]

While condemning what they perceived as the Soviet-American "peace talks deceit," Chinese officials applauded the actions of those countries that refused to serve as peace brokers in the Indochina conflict. This was clearly demonstrated in Beijing's attitude toward Sihanouk. On September 22, 1965, the Cambodian leader came to China to attend the October 1 National Day celebration. He first arrived in Chengdu, where Vice Premier Chen Yi accompanied him in sightseeing. Two days later, Zhou Enlai flew to Chongqing to meet Sihanouk, with whom he traveled on the Yangtze River to Wuhan. On board the ship, Sihanouk told the Chinese premier that if the United States expanded the war to Cambodia, his people would evacuate the cities and go to the countryside and forests to wage a guerrilla war. He also told Zhou that he had received a letter from Tito of Yugoslavia, who, together with Indian prime minister Lal Bahadur Shastri and Egyptian president Gamal Abdul Nasser, urged him to promote negotiations between the United States and North Vietnam and that he had rejected their proposal. Sihanouk criticized Washington's rigid position on Vietnam: "De Gaulle has shown the foresight of a statesman on the Algerian question, and he has advised the United States not to follow the old path of France, but Johnson would not listen to him." The Chinese hosts were very impressed by Sihanouk's resolute position on Vietnam. When Sihanouk reached Beijing, both Mao and Liu Shaoqi met with him. Calling Cambodia "an anti-American country," Mao told Sihanouk: "You have not only rejected American aid and separated relations with the United States but also opposed American imperialism openly, not covertly. I once worried that after you had rejected American assistance you might not be able to pass the test." Sihanouk replied: "We rejected American aid the way we ended drug addiction. Just as Chairman Liu Shaoqi has put it, 'American aid is like opium. When you have developed an addiction, it is very difficult to stop using it at first. But after a few months of nonuse, you are gradually back to normal conditions.' We have already gradually returned to normal conditions." Mao said: "That is very good. That is not an easy thing to do."[29]

President Johnson initiated another bombing pause over the 1965 Christmas holiday. He also launched a well-publicized "peace offensive" by sending top aides such as W. Averell Harriman, Vice President Hubert Humphrey, and

Assistant Secretary of State G. Mennen Williams across the globe to spread the message that the United States was ready to negotiate without conditions. He likewise dispatched personal letters to numerous heads of state and to U Thant expressing his desire for peace.[30]

In Warsaw, Harriman delivered to the Poles a fourteen-point peace plan that included immediate face-to-face negotiations and requested that Warsaw forward it to Hanoi. Jerzy Michalowski, a high-ranking official in the Polish Foreign Ministry, set off for the DRV. On his way to Hanoi, he stopped in Moscow and Beijing. In the Soviet Union, Foreign Minister Andrei Gromyko voiced support for the mission but warned against China's objection. In Beijing, Michalowski met with Deputy Foreign Minister Wang Bingnan, who denounced the notion of peace negotiations and insisted that the United States be kept deeply involved in the war and that any attempt to prevent Ho Chi Minh from achieving victory would be a betrayal of the Vietnamese cause.[31] Michalowski later revealed in his memoirs that the Chinese delayed his travel for an entire day in Nanning under the pretext that the United States was bombing the DRV. He believed that the Chinese had undermined his efforts to persuade the North Vietnamese to enter into peace talks by delaying him en route to Hanoi so that a Chinese message could precede him.[32]

In Hanoi, Michalowski held separate talks with Pham Van Dong and Ho Chi Minh. He found the former more sympathetic toward the prospects for peace talks than the latter. But in general both DRV leaders contended that they were doing well on the battlefield and that the time had not yet come to exploit these successes at the negotiating table. Ho, in particular, stressed emphatically that it was too early to consider a peaceful settlement and that it was necessary to fight the Americans. Claiming that victory was on Vietnam's side, Ho saw only one basis for peace: the total withdrawal of U.S. troops from South Vietnam.[33] It is possible that the North Vietnamese leaders' own calculations of the military situation made them reject the suggestion of negotiation, but Beijing's pressure may have tipped the balance.[34]

To coordinate the American peace initiative, Soviet politburo member Alexander Shelepin visited Hanoi in January 1966 and discussed with North Vietnamese officials the question of negotiations with the United States. Like Michalowski, Shelepin failed (if he indeed tried) to persuade the North Vietnamese.[35] Suspicious of Soviet intentions, Chinese commentators referred to Shelepin's visit to Hanoi as "a new proof of the Soviet guilt in colluding with the Americans" and called the trip "not an accident," since it came right after the announcement of the U.S. Fourteen Point Plan.[36]

When Shelepin visited Beijing after his Hanoi tour, Mao sent only Li Xiannian, a deputy premier, to talk with him, despite Shelepin's high position within the Soviet politburo. Mao intentionally gave Shelepin a cold reception to show his displeasure with the Soviet policy toward the United States.[37] When Shelepin again proposed a Sino-Soviet united action to assist the DRV, Li rejected the idea and asked the Soviet Union to put military pressure on the United States in Berlin and West Germany. Shelepin called the Chinese idea unrealistic.[38]

That Moscow needed to turn up the heat on the Americans in Europe in order to support the struggle in Vietnam was a consistent theme in Chinese statements during this period. In discussions with the Japanese Communist Party delegation in March, Liu Shaoqi and Deng Xiaoping urged the Soviet Union to "resort to brinkmanship" and create "greater tension in the West" to counter Washington's expansion of the Vietnam War. Peng Zhen, mayor of Beijing, added: "If the Soviet Union were really desiring to support Vietnam in the struggle, it would create a tenser situation in West Berlin, to stop the United States boldly withdrawing its troops from West Germany to send them to Vietnam. This would be more effective than missiles."[39] At a Beijing mass rally on July 10 to condemn the U.S. bombing of Hanoi-Haiphong oil depots, Chen Yi accused the Soviet Union of seeking a relaxation of tensions in Europe so that the United States could "draw away forces to cope with the Vietnamese people."[40]

At the end of January 1966, Nkrumah decided to travel to Hanoi and Beijing to promote peace. He was determined to make the trip primarily to improve his sagging prestige at home.[41] Before Nkrumah's departure for Asia, Zhou Enlai asked the Chinese Foreign Ministry to instruct Huang Hua, the Chinese chargé d'affaires in Ghana, to notify Nkrumah that "any peace proposal can only help the United States reach its goal of continuing its occupation of South Vietnam and dividing Vietnam permanently and deprive the rights of Vietnamese people to oppose American aggression."[42] Nkrumah arrived in Beijing on February 24 only to learn that his army back at home had overthrown him.[43]

Throughout the summer and fall of 1966, third parties continued to search for common ground for Vietnam peace talks. After shuttling between Hanoi and Saigon, the Polish diplomat Januscz Lewandowski put forward a ten-point proposal to settle the war. Although the Johnson administration had serious reservations with some points in Lewandowski's draft, it decided to accept the plan as a basis for negotiations in order not to appear intransigent. At Lewandowski's request, Washington also drafted a two-track formula to respond to Hanoi's opposition to mutual de-escalation. The United States would terminate its air assaults in return for a confidential promise that the DRV would stop infiltrating into key areas of South Vietnam within a reasonable period. Once

North Vietnam had moved, the United States would stop increasing its combat forces and peace negotiations could open. The Polish initiative was code-named MARIGOLD.[44] The initiative was a failure because several days before the planned opening of the negotiations, American aircraft bombed railway yards near Hanoi, inflicting heavy damages to civilian lives and properties. Insisting that they would not negotiate under pressure, the North Vietnamese quickly ended the contact.[45]

China's vehement hostility to peace talks sometimes inhibited potential third parties from even proposing new peace initiatives. In conversations with Michalowski, who at this time was the Polish ambassador to the United States, on December 13 and 14, 1967, Walter J. Stoessel Jr., acting assistant secretary of state for European affairs, noted that "there might possibly be some attractiveness to considering negotiations in the framework of a renewed Geneva Conference." Michalowski expressed doubt about the idea, asserting that "this could only be feasible if agreement had been reached in advance by the United States and the principal interested parties. If this were not the case, a reconvened Geneva Conference would simply be a shambles in which the intransigent views of the Chinese would predominate."[46]

China persistently opposed peace talks in Vietnam for several reasons. In part, the policy reflected Mao's complex calculations of preserving China's international position and mobilizing internal support for his radical social and economic programs at home. Above all, Mao and his associates wanted the North Vietnamese to wage a protracted war to tie down the United States in Vietnam. According to their calculations, the continued conflict in Vietnam could both serve as a model war of national liberation that, if successful, would prove the correctness of Beijing's militant approach, and bog down the United States and drain American resources, making it difficult for Washington to send troops to suppress liberation movements elsewhere. In a conversation with Tanzanian president Nyerere on June 4, 1965, Zhou Enlai contended that "the more U.S. forces were tied down in Vietnam, the more beneficial it would be for national independence movements. China is willing to do its utmost to assist Vietnam on every front. The U.S. distraction in Vietnam is beneficial to the people of the world. Although the American power is great, it loses its strength when it is divided."[47]

In addition to keeping the United States mired in Vietnam, Mao also desired to limit the influence of the Soviet Union in Southeast Asia. He reasoned that any peace meeting on Vietnam would be dominated by the two superpowers, isolating China. Thus a compromise settlement in Vietnam would constitute a victory for Moscow. He feared that if Moscow and Washington succeeded in working together to achieve a settlement of the Vietnam conflict, they might cooperate on other thorny issues in Asia, further diminishing China's influence in the region. The prospect of a joint Soviet-American rule of the world was Mao's strategic nightmare. To preserve China's international position and to forestall what he perceived as Soviet-American "collusion" against China might well have been Mao's overriding objectives in opposing Vietnam peace talks.[48]

By 1965 the Sino-Soviet split had reached the point of no return. Mao believed that Khrushchev's successors in the Kremlin had no intention of changing the policy of peaceful coexistence with the United States. By downplaying Soviet assistance to Hanoi and portraying the Soviet Union as opportunistically seeking a bargain with the Americans at the expense of Vietnam, Mao hoped to discredit Moscow and strengthen Beijing's anti-imperialist credentials both within the international Communist movement and among other Third World countries. Mao rejected a negotiated settlement because he believed that the present course of the war validated his ideological position on "armed revolutionary struggle." In this regard, *Hongqi* (Red Flag), the theoretical journal of the Chinese Communist Party, published a commentary on February 11, 1966, denouncing the Soviet motives in Vietnam. It portrayed Soviet leaders' gesture of support for the DRV as a means "to get more of a say for themselves on the Vietnam question, sow dissension in Sino-Vietnamese relations, and help the United States to realize its 'peace talks' plot. In the final analysis, they want to find a way out for U.S. imperialism on the Vietnam question, enable it to occupy South Vietnam permanently, and strike a political deal with it."[49]

Throughout 1966 and 1967, Chinese leaders would seize every opportunity, whether in talks with foreign visitors or on the platforms of international meetings, to condemn Moscow's cooperation with the U.S. scheme for "peace talks" on Vietnam. At a mass rally welcoming an Albanian delegation in Beijing on April 30, 1966, Zhou Enlai assailed the "counterrevolutionary dual tactics" of the Kremlin, which was following "Khrushchevism without Khrushchev" in its efforts to endorse a peace solution in Vietnam.[50] In 1967, the Chinese government accused the Permanent Secretariat of the Afro-Asian People's Solidarity Organization of surrendering to Soviet revisionism and of failing to criticize Soviet-American collaboration in Vietnam.[51]

Finally, Mao found the continued confrontation in Indochina useful to reinstill ideological commitment in the population at home and to mobilize domestic Chinese support for his grand ideological enterprise: the Great Cultural Revolution. By branding American and Soviet peace proposals as "hoax" and "collusion" and by emphasizing the danger of compromise with the enemy, Mao reminded the Chinese people that they should not slacken in the class struggle and that the Cultural Revolution was necessary to prevent China from turning revisionist.

SINO-VIETNAMESE DIFFERENCES OVER PEACE TALKS

Chinese leaders opposed Hanoi's strategy of negotiating while fighting, even while China provided extensive assistance to the DRV in terms of weapons, equipment, and support troops. A clear gap developed between Beijing and Hanoi regarding the role of negotiations in the war.

The DRV was a small and underdeveloped country facing an industrialized foreign power and could not expect a total military victory over its enemy. Most leaders in Hanoi realized that they had to accept negotiations with the enemy as an integral component of their struggle for national reunification. DRV forces needed periods of peace in which to consolidate military and political strength. In this sense, negotiations were an extension of warfare rather than an alternative to it. North Vietnam's leaders sought direct negotiations with Washington as a way to improve their chance of winning the war, not a way of preventing or ending it. Hanoi often employed the lure of negotiations as a means to win friends in the international arena, to disrupt support for the war in the United States, and to drive a wedge between Washington and Saigon.[52]

Hanoi sometimes expressed an interest in peace talks merely to trick Washington into halting its bombing. For example, at the VWP's Twelfth Plenum in December 1965, Le Duan proposed that the DRV dangle tantalizing diplomatic leads before the United States to keep the Johnson administration off balance, while at the same time using the bombing pauses to rush men and supplies south. By taking advantage of the bombing pauses, Le Duan continued, revolutionary forces could eliminate the bulk of ARVN units while inflicting heavy damages on U.S. troops to compel the United States to withdraw. After much debate, the VWP adopted a resolution (Resolution 12) based on Le Duan's dual strategy of increasing military action in the south while preparing to open negotiations with the United States.[53]

At other times, especially before launching a major military operation, Hanoi offered to negotiate simply to conceal its military preparations and to enmesh the United States in a negotiating trap. DRV foreign minister Nguyen Duy Trinh's declaration of Hanoi's willingness to hold discussions with the Americans on the eve of the Tet Offensive was a case in point. Speaking at the Mongolian embassy in Hanoi on December 29, 1967, Trinh announced that the DRV would open negotiations after the unconditional cessation of U.S. bombing. Hanoi radio broadcast the Trinh announcement in English over its international shortwave facilities. As Hanoi expected, its declaration put the

Johnson administration on the spot, since U.S. officials had been saying for many months that they were waiting for an indication of North Vietnam's readiness to hold negotiations.[54] Similarly, in 1971 Le Duc Tho, the North Vietnamese negotiator, used negotiations with Henry Kissinger to cloak Hanoi's preparations for the 1972 Spring Offensive.[55]

Chinese leaders, however, disregarded the importance of negotiations in Hanoi's strategy. In private communications, Chinese Foreign Ministry officials recognized the difference between Beijing's and Hanoi's approaches to peace talks. In an internal circular prepared on August 19, 1965, they lamented that "the Vietnamese practice on peace talks is different from ours. The DRV has never completely closed the door on peace negotiations, thus creating an opportunity for the imperialists, the revisionists, and the reactionaries and increasing their illusions about pressing the DRV into peace talks."[56]

Beijing continued to urge the North Vietnamese to wage a protracted war against the United States. In a conversation with the DRV party and government delegation led by Pham Van Dong on October 20, 1965, Mao clearly expressed both his disapproval of negotiations and his conviction that the North Vietnamese should continue their struggle against the Americans until the final victory:

I have not noticed what issues you have negotiated with the United States. I only pay attention to how you fight the Americans and how you drive the Americans out. You can have negotiations at certain times, but you should not lower your tones. You should raise your tones a little higher. Be prepared that the enemy may deceive you. We will support you until your final victory. The confidence in victory comes from the struggle you have made. For instance, one experience we have had is that the Americans can be fought. We obtained this experience only after fighting the Americans. The Americans can be fought and can be defeated.[57]

The North Vietnamese leadership was divided on the issue of negotiations with the United States. According to the Vietnam specialist Robert Brigham, the hard-liners within the VWP leadership included Nguyen Chi Thanh, a cadre from the south, and almost everyone in the NLF supported his anti-negotiations position in 1965.[58] The Chinese were aware of the differences within the politburo of the VWP. During a conversation with the Japanese Communist Party delegation led by Miyamoto Kenji on March 6, 1966, Liu Shaoqi, vice chairman of the CCP Central Committee, noted that the Central Committee of the VWP was divided into prowar and propeace groups and that the Soviet Union supported the latter. China, Liu went on, had made its position clear to comrades in Hanoi: "You may wage the boldest struggle against U.S. imperialism. You need not be afraid of the expansion of the war, its expansion into China. If the war expands to China, we will fight shoulder to shoulder with you."[59]

There are indications that China sought to exploit the disagreement between the prowar and propeace groups within the VWP to pressure Hanoi not to enter into negotiations with the United States. On December 18 and 19, 1965, for example, Nguyen Duy Trinh traveled to Beijing to hold talks with Zhou Enlai and Chen Yi.[60] It is possible that Trinh informed the Chinese leaders of the VWP's Resolution 12; in any case, Zhou reiterated China's opposition to negotiations, insisting that the time was not ripe. He admonished the North Vietnamese not to put forward new stipulations such as unconditional cessation of bombing of the DRV as a basis for negotiations. Such conditions, he warned, would "cause difficulties for ourselves, for our internal solidarity, and for the struggle." They would, he continued, confuse people both in Vietnam and around the world into thinking that Hanoi wanted to solve the issues of the North and the South separately. Reminding Trinh that "the North and the South are united as one" and that the VWP "is leading the whole Vietnamese nation in the anti-U.S. resistance," Zhou asked Hanoi not to allow its new terms for negotiations to undermine the unity between the North and the South. He concluded his remarks by warning North Vietnam not to "fall into the trap" set by the U.S. imperialists and the Soviet revisionists.[61]

Between October and November 1966, during the MARIGOLD initiative, Le Duan visited Beijing and talked with Chinese leaders. Zhou Enlai urged North Vietnam to continue the war, at least until 1968. Although Le Duan made no promises, he told Zhou that Hanoi intended to end the conflict with "maximum advantages for itself."[62]

Reacting to international and, in the case of Washington, domestic pressures, both the DRV and the United States in 1967 modified their earlier rigid stances. Hanoi dropped as a precondition for talks its demand for acceptance of its Four Points, including a total withdrawal of U.S. forces, insisting merely that the bombing be stopped without condition. North Vietnam also softened its terms for a settlement, pointing out, among other things, that reunification could happen over a long span of time. Likewise, the United States no longer insisted that Hanoi withdraw its forces from South Vietnam in return for ending the bombing, demanding only a halt to additional infiltration into the south.[63]

At this point, the Chinese leadership was deeply concerned with the recent conciliatory moves made by Hanoi. During talks with Pham Van Dong and Vo Nguyen Giap in Beijing between April 7 and 11, 1967, Zhou Enlai put a premium on continuing the war. Giap opened the first meeting on April 7 by describing the military situation in Vietnam and then explaining the DRV's strategic principle. Dong followed by observing that some of the methods Hanoi was employing on the battleground in South Vietnam were based on Chinese advice and that both the Vietnamese and Chinese military policies were correct. North Vietnam, the DRV premier added, had also developed its own "new methods." Zhou commended the Vietnamese on their innovations, stating that "the latecomers have surpassed the old-timers."[64]

The available Chinese sources that mention this meeting do not specify what Vo Nguyen Giap said about Hanoi's strategic principle or what Pham Van Dong meant by "new methods." Perhaps the DRV officials were referring to the principle of a general offensive and uprising, which had dominated Hanoi's strategic calculations since the early 1960s. The Tet Offensive launched by the Vietnamese Communists in 1968 embodied this principle, but a general offensive differed in several respects from Mao's theory of people's war. It is not clear whether Zhou was being sincere or simply diplomatic when he praised the North Vietnamese for their different approach. According to a captured North Vietnamese document written in 1967, however, China disapproved of the DRV's strategy of seeking a relatively quick victory. Beijing, according to the document, "is determined to help us fight until the generation of our sons and grandsons."[65]

The Sino–North Vietnamese discussion on April 10, 1967, was devoted to evaluating the prospects of the war and the possibility of its further expansion by the United States. Zhou mentioned three possible courses the war might follow: the continuation and expansion of the war; a blockade of the Vietnamese coast by the United States; and the launching of an attack by the DRV during the dry season of 1968 to defeat the United States, forcing it to admit failure and to withdraw from Vietnam. Speaking of the conduct of political struggle, Zhou encouraged the North Vietnamese to strengthen international propaganda, win world sympathy, and exploit disagreements among the enemy. But he gave not the slightest encouragement to a negotiated settlement.[66]

In their last conversation on April 11, Zhou urged the North Vietnamese not to stop halfway in their struggle against the Americans. Expressing full confidence in Hanoi's ability to win the war, Zhou promised that China would "mobilize the people of the whole world to support you to achieve victory." He concluded his remarks by launching a bitter verbal attack against the Soviet Union, reminding his North Vietnamese colleagues how Moscow had failed to support the Chinese revolution in the 1940s.[67] The emphasis on Soviet unreliability remained a familiar theme in the Chinese criticisms during this period. According to a letter written by the Soviet embassy in the DRV in

August 1967, Pham Van Dong and Vo Nguyen Giap in their Beijing talks made a "solemn promise" to continue the war.[68]

In a televised speech on March 31, 1968, President Johnson announced a halt in U.S. bombing above the twentieth parallel in order to facilitate peace talks. He concluded his address with the stunning announcement that he would not run for reelection.[69] In response, Hanoi announced on April 3 its readiness to discuss with the Americans the unconditional end to the bombing.[70] According to Hoang Van Hoan, after hearing Hanoi's announcement, Zhou Enlai immediately asked Ho Chi Minh, who was in Beijing for medical treatment, about the VWP's decision. Amazed, Ho said that he knew nothing about it.[71] Clearly, in making the decision to begin negotiations with the United States, the VWP politburo under Le Duan's leadership had neither reported to Ho in Beijing nor consulted with the Chinese.

The strains in Sino-DRV relations as a result of Hanoi's decision to open negotiations with Washington were clearly revealed in the discussions between Zhou Enlai and Pham Van Dong in Beijing during the week of April 13–20. The Chinese premier criticized the Vietnamese party for making two major compromises: accepting Johnson's partial bombing halt instead of adhering to its previous position of demanding a complete and unconditional end to the bombing before entering into any negotiations; and agreeing to Paris as the location for talks and abandoning its own proposed sites of Phnom Penh or Warsaw. By making these concessions, Zhou continued, the DRV was helping Johnson solve his difficulties. Zhou listed Johnson's poor showing in the primary elections, Congress's refusal to approve General William Westmoreland's request for additional troops, and the dollar crisis as indications of the president's problems. He even drew a strange connection between Hanoi's April 3 announcement and the assassination of Martin Luther King on April 4, claiming that "had your statement been issued one or two days later, the murder might have been stopped."[72]

In his May 7 discussion with Xuan Thuy, the minister of international liaison of the VWP, Zhou again complained about Hanoi's decision to begin peace talks with the United States. He said: "We feel that you have responded too quickly and too impatiently, perhaps giving the Americans a misperception that you are eager to negotiate. Comrade Mao Zedong has told Comrade Pham Van Dong that negotiation is all right but you must assume a high posture." Contending that what counted most was victory on the battleground, Zhou advised the North Vietnamese envoy that Hanoi not let the Americans obtain through negotiations what they had failed to obtain on the battlefield.[73]

The Paris negotiations began on May 13 and quickly ran into a deadlock. So long as the balance of forces on the battlefield remained unfavorable, Hanoi had no intention of engaging in substantive talks. It used the Paris negotiations primarily to advance the goals of securing the cessation of U.S. bombing, encouraging antiwar sentiments in the United States, and widening the gap between Washington and Saigon.[74]

Beijing, however, remained unenthusiastic about the Paris talks. Between May and October 1968, Chinese leaders continued to criticize Hanoi for conducting negotiations with Washington. In his June 29 discussion in Beijing with Pham Hung, secretary of the COSVN, Zhou Enlai launched another attack on the DRV's decision to hold talks with the Americans, accusing the North Vietnamese of falling into the Soviet trap and yielding the initiative to the Johnson administration.[75]

In October 1968, the United States indicated to the North Vietnamese that it would stop the bombing unilaterally. Hanoi responded by informally agreeing to serious peace negotiations that would begin within four days after the bombing had been halted. It also consented to the Nguyen Van Thieu government's participation in the peace talks.[76] Chinese leaders disapproved of this latest concession. During his meeting with Le Duc Tho in Beijing on October 17, Chen Yi censured Hanoi for accepting quadripartite negotiations. Hanoi's decision, the Chinese foreign minister claimed, had accorded the Saigon regime "legal recognition" and eliminated the NLF's status as the sole legal representative of the people of South Vietnam. Chen closed his remarks by accusing North Vietnam of accepting the "compromising and surrendering proposals put forward by the Soviet revisionists."[77]

Between May and October 1968, the Chinese media remained silent about the North Vietnam–U.S. negotiations. Beijing refrained from sending any correspondents to cover them in Paris, but Chinese newspapers criticized France for providing a site for the talks.[78] Only reluctantly did Mao approve the talks in November 1968. He told Pham Van Dong in Beijing on November 17 that he favored Hanoi's policy of fighting while negotiating. But he cautioned the North Vietnamese that it would be difficult to get the United States to withdraw from Vietnam through negotiations and that the Americans did not keep their word.[79] Around the same time, the Chinese press carried in full and without comment both President Johnson's November 1 declaration of the complete cessation of American bombing of the DRV and Hanoi's agreement to expand the talks in Paris. For the first time, the Chinese government publicly informed its population of the existence of the peace negotiations. *Renmin ribao* published a statement made by Mao in March 1949 that endorsed negotiations with the enemy.[80]

Why did Beijing change its attitude toward the Vietnam peace talks? A primary reason was its increasing fear of the Soviet threat in late 1968. By this time, developments in Soviet and American policies had caused Mao and his associates to reassess their "dual enemy" approach in world affairs. Considering Mao's policy a threat to socialism, Moscow had increased its pressure on Beijing in 1968. In addition to seeking to isolate China within the Communist movement, Soviet leaders also launched a diplomatic offensive among countries on China's periphery.[81] In July Brezhnev announced the doctrine of "limited sovereignty," arrogating to the USSR the right to intervene in any socialist countries when socialism was deemed "in danger." One month later, Soviet tanks rolled into Czechoslovakia to crush the "Prague Spring," an action that triggered fierce condemnation from Beijing.[82]

While Soviet pressure on China was growing, American actions indicated a reduced threat to Beijing. The suspension of U.S. bombing and the pullback of American troops from Vietnam revealed Washington's intention to disengage from Indochina. If the Soviet Union now posed a greater threat to China's security, it was in Beijing's interest to seek an accommodation with the United States and to encourage progress in the Paris talks so as to give Washington "a way out."[83]

Although no longer censoring the news about the Paris peace talks, Beijing refrained from intervening in the negotiations between 1968 and 1971. Moscow's active involvement influenced China's stance of indifference. In a meeting with Ion Gheorghe Maurer, chairman of the Council of Ministers of Romania, in Beijing on September 7, 1969, Zhou Enlai made clear China's abhorrence of the Soviet involvement in the Vietnam peace process and sought to drive a wedge between Moscow and Hanoi: "With regard to the Paris talks, we have never intervened partly because the DRV makes its own decisions and partly because the Soviet Union has intervened. The Soviet Union is using the Vietnam issue . . . in its bargaining with the United States."[84]

Hanoi's unilateral decision to proceed with negotiations with the Americans demonstrated the decline of China's influence over the DRV. Clearly, the opening of the Paris peace talks strained Beijing's relations with the DRV. Hanoi was moving closer to the Soviet Union in waging war against the United States and the Saigon regime. The death of Ho Chi Minh in September 1969 removed a figure from the VWP politburo who might have kept the DRV in a more even-handed neutrality in the Sino-Soviet dispute.

EFFECTS OF CHINA'S ACTIONS

Between 1965 and 1968, China did its utmost to sabotage the peace process and to force North Vietnam to follow its lead. Without access to Vietnamese archives, it is difficult to judge the actual effects of Chinese policy on Hanoi's attitude toward peace talks. Given the existence of prowar and propeace groups within the VWP's politburo, however, it is plausible that Beijing's opposition to peace negotiations strengthened the hand of the prowar group and alienated the propeace group.[85] According to Soviet sources, after the DRV opened talks with Washington in 1968, Beijing began to bypass Hanoi and increase contacts with the NLF, encouraging it to continue protracted guerrilla war. China also tried to organize units of the local Chinese population in South Vietnam to intensify military actions there.[86] Increasingly, China's objection to peace talks complicated its relations with Hanoi. That the North Vietnamese had greater confidence in Moscow than in Beijing was suggested by Henry Kissinger, who wrote in his memoirs that the Soviets "often flaunted their knowledge" of the secret talks between him and Le Duc Tho, while Zhou Enlai "professed to be unaware of them."[87]

China's uncompromising position on Vietnam peace talks contributed to the distrust of its foreign policy by countries in the "Two Intermediate Zones" that China hoped to unite. Countries like Britain, France, India, Yugoslavia, Ghana, and Poland wanted to bring about a peaceful solution to the Vietnam conflict but found China's opposition heavy-handed, frustrating, and objectionable. In a speech before Parliament on February 8, 1966, Harold Wilson vented his anger at China: "I should like to have seen 'Peace in Vietnam' outside the Chinese Embassy. . . . I should have liked to have seen the peace lobby outside the Chinese Embassy demanding that the Chinese Government should use their influence . . . on Hanoi . . . to make peace."[88] Beijing's rejection of the role of the United Nations in Indochinese affairs likewise alienated small neutral countries that viewed the international organization as an important platform. The contradictions and rigidity in Chinese foreign policy served to undermine Mao's united front strategy, leaving China isolated throughout the second half of the 1960s.

China's rejection of the Soviet call for "joint action" in supporting Vietnam and its unrelenting attacks on Soviet revisionism confirmed the Kremlin's worst assumptions about the intentions of Chinese leaders and the impossibility of reviving their past friendship. In 1966, Moscow began to increase its troop deployment along the Chinese border. The crack in the Sino-Soviet relationship eventually resulted in a direct military confrontation in 1969.

Beijing's support for Hanoi's war against the United States and its denunciation of various peace proposals reinforced the American image of China as an irresponsible, aggressive, and dangerous player in international politics. To overcome Beijing's hostility, Washington sought Moscow's cooperation in managing the conflict in Vietnam. American and Soviet leaders shared a common interest in limiting China's influence in Indochina.

8 FROM TET TO CAMBODIA 1968–1970

In 1968, China's strategic environment changed drastically, and Sino-Soviet relations took a decisive turn for the worse. In the meantime Washington made its first tentative moves toward disengagement from South Vietnam. In the new situation, Beijing's strategic interests began to differ fundamentally from those of Hanoi. Whereas the Chinese now regarded the United States as a potential counterbalance against the Soviet Union, their North Vietnamese comrades continued to see Washington as the most dangerous enemy.

THE TET OFFENSIVE

The year began with the Tet offensive launched by Hanoi. VWP leaders hoped that the general offensive and uprising would set in motion a train of developments that could bring about the complete withdrawal of American troops and the creation of a coalition government under the control of the NLF. The operation highlighted the crucial importance the VWP had attached to the role of cities in fashioning its strategy for victory. The party's calculations about the role of the urban sector were based not only on its careful consideration of the class nature and problems in the cities and of the steady weakening of the Saigon regime but also on its historical memory of the August 1945 revolution, when it seized power swiftly by combining urban and rural resistance. Ever since the early 1960s, the idea of the general offensive and uprising had preoccupied the thinking of party strategists as they concentrated on the struggle in the south. Throughout 1965–67, the party had persisted in viewing the urban role as both decisive and promising.[1]

The Tet offensive, however, contradicted Mao Zedong's theory of protracted people's war in several respects. Mao's doctrine envisioned three stages in conducting people's war. In the first stage, the revolutionary forces would assume a strategic defensive against the strategic offensive launched by the reactionary forces. In the second stage, a strategic parity or equilibrium would exist, which would be the period of the enemy's strategic consolidation and the revolutionary forces' preparation for the counteroffensive. In the third stage, the revolutionary forces would wage a strategic offensive against the enemy. During the first and second stages, the revolutionary forces would leave the cities in the hands of superior enemy forces and conduct extensive guerrilla warfare in the countryside against the increasingly dispersed and static enemy forces. In the course of the long and difficult second stage of strategic stalemate, the revolutionary forces would consolidate and expand their control of the countryside while the enemy would try to protect the cities. Mobile warfare would be introduced progressively to supplement guerrilla operations. During this phase the balance between the revolutionary and reactionary forces would gradually change. Political mobilization of the rural population was crucial in facilitating this change and was the principal strategic aim of the revolutionary forces during the first and second stages. Rural organizations of all kinds, under party leadership, were to be established to supply manpower and to support the front. As larger and larger guerrilla units were formed, they would be hardened by combat against dispersed enemy outposts or by supporting mobile operations against enemy forces. The strength of the reactionary forces would be gradually depleted by this continuous attrition and by psychological weariness stemming from factors like homesickness and antiwar sentiments. Eventually, the strength of the revolutionary forces would exceed that of the reactionary forces and accordingly the war would proceed to the third stage, in which mobile war supplemented by positional and guerrilla war would become the primary method and the revolutionary forces would carry out a general offensive to capture the cities.[2]

The Tet offensive shifted the focus of revolutionary struggle from the rural to urban areas well before the third stage and committed the revolutionary forces to positional war prematurely. It involved a large-scale strategic offensive by the revolutionary forces before the strategic balance between the revolutionary and counterrevolutionary forces had changed in favor of the former. It exposed the underground infrastructure of the revolutionary forces to the enemy, which still held military advantage. In the process it undermined the mass base of the revolutionary forces, the single most important condition for revolutionary victory.[3]

In its criticism of China's policy toward Vietnam made in the 1979 *White*

Paper, Hanoi accused Beijing of asking the DRV to wage "protracted war, guerrilla warfare, [and] small battles," and of providing North Vietnam with only "light weapons, ammunition and logistic supplies." Chinese leaders, Hanoi's charge continued, "did not want an early end to the Viet Nam war, because they wanted not only to weaken the Vietnamese revolutionary forces, but also to avail, the longer the better, of the publicity obtained by 'aiding Viet Nam' to hold high the banner of 'thorough revolution,' to muster forces in Asia, Africa, and Latin America and to intensify their anti-Soviet campaign."[4]

The Vietnamese statement is partly true and partly inaccurate. It is true that CCP leaders, especially between 1965 and 1967, consistently advocated a protracted war or "a war of attrition," to use Mao's words, in Vietnam.[5] Hanoi's complaint about the Chinese provision of light weapons, however, is unjustified because, given the underdeveloped weapons system of the PLA, China had few choices.

Not until 1968 did policymakers in Beijing begin to talk about large-unit operations in Vietnam. Mao advised Ho Chi Minh that year that the DRV organize large formations to carry out battles of annihilation in the south.[6] On February 7 of the same year, Zhou recommended to Ho Chi Minh a similar approach of employing large units in mobile warfare:

> Given the development of the Vietnam War to the current moment, why not consider the organization of one to two or three field corps, each including thirty to forty thousand troops. Try to annihilate in each battle the enemy's complete unit of four to five thousand soldiers. These corps should be able to operate far from the home base and to fight from this theater to another theater. Engage isolated enemy units. Adopt the methods of digging trenches to get close to the enemy and conducting nighttime and close-range combat so as to render ineffective the firepower of the enemy's aircraft and artillery. Construct trenches in three to four directions. These trenches are different from tunnels. They should be capable of facilitating the movement of troops and the transportation of ammunition. Employ also some forces to intercept the enemy's reinforcement units.[7]

Despite Mao and Zhou's willingness to encourage the use of large units in mobile operations, they stopped short of urging Ho Chi Minh to launch a general offensive against cities, as the North Vietnamese were undertaking during the Tet offensive.

In general, Chinese leaders preferred a low- to mid-intensity war in Vietnam. They perceived several advantages in emphasizing a limited and protracted war: it would keep the United States bogged down in the war and would maintain the importance of China's aid to the DRV; it would reduce the incentive for the United States to expand the war, thus avoiding a potential Sino-American confrontation; and it would help China opt out of a hopeless competition with Moscow to provide large amounts of advanced military hardware. When the VWP adopted General Vo Nguyen Giap's strategy of general offensive and positional warfare, which relied on the employment of modern heavy weaponry, however, the importance of Russian weapons shipments increased.[8]

The Tet offensive was highly costly to the North Vietnamese. They misjudged the reaction of the local populace in South Vietnam and failed to trigger the disintegration of the Saigon regime. The NLF bore the brunt of the assault. Its regular units were destroyed and would never totally recover, and its political infrastructure incurred heavy losses. To the degree that Hanoi intended the Tet offensive to influence the United States, however, it triumphed. Televised coverage of the fierce fighting in South Vietnam discredited the Johnson administration's optimistic year-end reports and emboldened antiwar protesters. Defense secretary Clark Clifford, who had replaced Robert McNamara, now believed that the United States could not win the war at reasonable cost, and he urged Johnson to seek a negotiated settlement. After consulting with a group of senior advisers, popularly known as "the wise men," who voiced serious reservations about any further escalation in the war, the president made the famous March 31 speech, limiting the U.S. bombing of North Vietnam to the area just north of the demilitarized zone and indicating America's readiness to discuss peace.[9]

The VWP's decision to launch the Tet offensive in contradiction to Mao's military doctrine revealed the independent nature of the decision making in the DRV. Hanoi's move toward negotiations with the United States in April 1968 further demonstrated the limitations of China's influence over the DRV. After the opening of the Paris peace talks and the Johnson administration's suspension of the American bombing of the DRVE in November 1968, China began to pull back its support troops from the DRV. It completed the withdrawal of its antiaircraft artillery units in March 1969. By July 1970 all the rest of the Chinese support troops had returned home.[10]

In the meantime, Beijing began to reduce its military aid to the DRV, reemphasizing to the Vietnamese the importance of self-dependence. In a review of international situations with Pham Hung, secretary of the southern bureau of the VWP, and Hoang Van Thai, deputy defense minister of the DRV, in Beijing on April 21, 1969, Zhou Enlai stressed the principle of independence and self-reliance.[11] In 1969 China's supply of military equipment to North Vietnam sharply declined. According to one Chinese account, in 1969 Beijing provided Hanoi with 139,900 rifles, 3,906 pieces of artillery, 119.2 million bul-

FROM TET TO CAMBODIA [179

lets, and 1.36 million artillery shells, as compared to 219,899 rifles, 7,087 pieces of artillery, 247.9 million bullets, and 2 million artillery shells in 1968.[12] Hanoi's preference for more sophisticated Soviet weapons may be partly responsible for the reduction of the Chinese aid.

CHINESE ROAD-BUILDING IN NORTHERN LAOS

At the time that the Vietnamese Communists were engaged in the Tet offensive, Beijing signed an agreement with the Pathet Lao on February 28, 1968, whereby China would construct a road from Mohan, Yunnan province, to Muong Sai in northern Laos. The Chinese road-building contingent included PLA engineering troops and civilian construction workers, as well as antiaircraft, guard, and logistical units, totaling about 20,000 workers. They began to enter Laos in mid-September and completed the road in December 1969. Between 1970 and 1978, China also helped the Pathet Lao build several other roads in northern Laos.[13] The completion of these roads provided the Pathet Lao with greater mobility in countering the guerrilla attacks of the Lao and tribal anti-Communist forces. China used the roads to continue supplying arms to the Pathet Lao.

When the building of the Yunnan–Muong Sai road was under way, U.S. officials speculated about Beijing's intentions. In an intelligence memorandum addressed to National Security Adviser Walt Rostow on January 13, 1969, William L. Lemnitzer, a National Security Council analyst, wrote that the construction of the Yunnan–Muong Sai road was intended, for the short term, "to improve Chinese support of Pathet Lao and communist-leaning neutralist forces in northern Laos." Determining Beijing's long-term motives, Lemnitzer continued, depended on the next move China would make, including whether it planned to extend the road from Muong Sai to the southwest along an existing trail to the Mekong River and Thailand.[14] Clearly, U.S. officials were concerned about potential Chinese threats to northern Thailand, where the Thai insurgents were active.

There is no indication in the currently available Chinese sources that Beijing intended to extend the roads in northern Laos southwestward to the Mekong River and Thailand. Beijing's primary motives appear to have been to strengthen China's ties with the Pathet Lao and to gain leverage over Hanoi by extending its influence into northern Laos. By building roads and providing assistance to the Pathet Lao, China was able to develop some influence within the Lao party, particularly in the northern province of Phong Saly.

China's road-building and the presence of the CCP Work Team at Sam Neua caused friction and rivalry between the Chinese and the North Vietnamese. In September 1968, apparently under pressure from Hanoi, Kaysone Phomvihane asked Li Wenzheng, the director of the Chinese team at the time, to take a vacation in China. Beijing interpreted the proposal as a sign that its advisory team was no longer needed and therefore ordered its withdrawal. The incident deepened the suspicion and competition between Beijing and Hanoi.[15] The conflict between the pro-Chinese members within the Pathet Lao and their Vietnamese allies in the Laotian war became so sharp and irreconcilable that in 1971 several battalions and a special elite company of Pathet Lao forces, together with their commanders, defected to Vientiane in response to what they believed to have been the assassination by the Vietnamese of General Phomma, the anti-Hanoi Pathet Lao leader for southern Laos.[16]

MAO'S STRATEGIC READJUSTMENT

In 1969, Sino-Soviet relations continued to deteriorate. Serious fighting flared up in March when Chinese troops ambushed a Russian patrol unit on the island of Zhenbao (Damansky) in the Ussuri River, which was claimed by both China and the Soviet Union. Over the rest of the year, about 400 border clashes occurred between Chinese and Soviet forces. After these border collisions, Chinese leaders were keenly aware of the technological and strategic superiority of the Russian forces deployed in Siberia and Outer Mongolia. Mao's fear of a Soviet encirclement of China would seriously color his perceptions of developments in Indochina during the remainder of the Vietnam War.

While the Kremlin was intensifying its pressure on China, the new Republican administration in Washington seemed ready to modify America's hostile policy toward Beijing. Shortly after his inauguration, President Richard Nixon announced U.S. intentions to withdraw from Indochina and to retrench throughout Asia. After talking with South Vietnamese president Nguyen Van Thieu on Midway Island in June 1969, Nixon announced the immediate withdrawal of 25,000 American combat troops.[17] (U.S. forces in Vietnam peaked at about 535,000 in early 1968.) While limiting American involvement in Vietnam, Nixon expected the South Vietnamese soldiers to do more of the fighting, with the United States supplying weapons, advisers, and financing. So began the painful process of Vietnamization.

In July 1969, Nixon showed his desire to end the breach with China by lifting travel and trade restrictions that had existed since the Korean War. The patrols of the Seventh Fleet in the Taiwan Straits ended. Through Pakistani and Rumanian leaders, the American president informed Beijing that the United States would not support the Soviet proposal to establish a collective security system in Asia and was interested in opening dialogues with China.[18]

Although Beijing's public statements still emphasized the alleged "collaboration" between the United States and the Soviet Union in seeking domination of the world, Chinese leaders realized that Moscow posed a much more serious threat to China than Washington. Within the changed strategic environment, they began to consider the possibility of playing off the United States against the Soviet Union. In 1969, a group of four marshals, Chen Yi, Ye Jianying, Xu Xiangqian, and Nie Rongzhen, proposed to unfreeze relations with the United States in order to achieve "strategic effects." After analyzing Moscow's aggressive intention toward China and the competition between the two superpowers, the marshals, in their September 17 report, pointed out that there were opportunities for Beijing to capitalize on the American-Soviet contention. They proposed to resume the Sino-American ambassadorial talks.[19]

Through public gestures and private communications, Beijing signaled Washington that it was willing to improve relations. In December 1969, the Chinese government released two American yachtsmen who had been under China's custody for several months after straying into Chinese waters.[20] On January 20, 1970, Beijing and Washington resumed their ambassadorial talks in Warsaw. Lei Yang, the Chinese negotiator, told Ambassador Walter Stoessel that Beijing accepted the U.S. proposal to send a high-level emissary to China to discuss issues in the bilateral relationship.[21] Through these gestures and dialogues, the two sides had taken significant steps to indicate to each other their interest in ameliorating tension and improving relations.

CRISIS OVER CAMBODIA

The overthrow of Prince Sihanouk in March and the U.S. invasion of Cambodia in May, however, disrupted the tentative process of Sino-American rapprochement. The American incursion into Cambodia hurt Mao's personal pride and aroused his lingering suspicions of the United States, for Washington appeared to be taking his interest in reconciliation for granted and disregarding Chinese interests in Indochina.[22] The Cambodian crisis also deepened the strains in the Sino-DRV relationship.

The tensions in Cambodia exploded in early 1967 with the outbreak of an antigovernment uprising in the vicinity of Samlaut in western Battambang. The upheaval greatly disturbed Chinese leaders, who found themselves in a dilemma on the Cambodian issue. On the one hand, they preferred Sihanouk's neutral policy because it had served their purposes of preventing the expansion of the war in Indochina and keeping Hanoi's influence limited. The overthrow of Sihanouk threatened to escalate the war and increase Hanoi's profile within the Cambodian revolutionary movement. And given the DRV's heavy dependence on sophisticated Soviet weapons, Moscow's influence in the region would also increase. On the other hand, they found it difficult and embarrassing to oppose the Samlaut rebellion because they believed that it was organized by the Communist Party of Kampuchea (CPK). A failure to endorse the revolt would compromise China's revolutionary image.[23]

To resolve this dilemma, Zhou Enlai devised the theory of "revolution through stages" in attempting to persuade the Cambodian Communists not to carry out revolution against Sihanouk. According to Zhou's formula, the anti-Thieu struggle in South Vietnam should have the priority over the development of revolutionary forces in Cambodia. The Chinese premier explained this theory to Pham Van Dong and Vo Nguyen Giap during their conversations in Beijing between April 7 and 12, 1967.

In the April 10 discussion, Zhou brought up the question of Cambodia, emphasizing the importance of "winning Sihanouk's sympathy" because he had been helpful in transporting materials to the NLF. When Pham Van Dong asked the Chinese for their opinions about Lon Nol, Zhou replied that the Cambodian general was "not trustworthy" while Chen Yi claimed that he was "pro-American." Zhou, nevertheless, believed that Lon Nol could be used in support of the war in South Vietnam: "Lon Nol once visited China, and he made some impression. If we spend money on him, he can be exploited for some time."[24]

Zhou Enlai continued to stress the necessity of working with Sihanouk and Lon Nol in the meeting with Pham Van Dong the next day. Expressing his disapproval of the Samlaut revolt, Zhou reaffirmed China's preference for concentrating on the war in South Vietnam and seeking a united front with the Cambodian government. "At this moment," Zhou asserted, "Vietnam's victory is the first priority. If the Vietnam-Cambodian border areas are blockaded, armed forces in South Vietnam will be facing difficulties, [and] then the Cambodian revolutionary forces will not proceed. The struggle of Vietnam is in the common interest of the Indochinese and Southeast Asian peoples, and the victory of this struggle is of a decisive nature. In this situation, the Cambodian struggle . . . has limited objectives. . . . One has to know how to place the overall interest above the limited ones." Zhou urged the North Vietnamese to explain this "logic" to the Cambodian Communists. Dong admitted that Hanoi had instructed the COSVN to contact the "people's faction" in Cambodia.[25] Zhou's remarks indicated that Beijing did not have direct contacts with the CPK at this time. His assumption that the CPK controlled the situation in Battambang suggests his ignorance about the actual circumstances in rural Cambodia.

Hanoi had also attached great strategic importance to Cambodia when the revolutionary war in South Vietnam intensified. Appreciating Sihanouk's acquiescence in the presence of the Vietnamese sanctuaries in Cambodia and the shipments of weapons across Cambodia from Sihanoukville, the VWP leadership had urged the Cambodian Communists not to conduct armed resistance to the government. In summer 1965, Pol Pot visited Hanoi for discussions with Vietnamese Communist leaders, but the latter turned down his request to carry out military struggle in Cambodia.[26] From 1967 on, the fear of a U.S. invasion of the North Vietnamese bases in Cambodia preoccupied policy-makers in Hanoi. Sihanouk's importance to them was closely connected with his highly publicized objection to any American incursion into Cambodia. Any change in Sihanouk's attitude would have constituted a serious setback to Hanoi's war effort.[27]

China and the DRV thus adopted parallel approaches to Cambodia, but their similar policies were based on divergent motives and goals. Beijing wanted to encourage the emergence of a group of independent states in postwar Indo-china and to forestall Vietnamese domination in the region. Hanoi sought to establish an Indochinese strategic unity to confront the American pressure and to create a sphere of influence in Indochina in order to guarantee Vietnam's postwar security. The shared interest between Beijing and Hanoi in Indochi-nese solidarity against the United States, as one scholar has rightly observed, "masked an emergent rivalry that stemmed from their divergent visions of an acceptable regional postwar pattern of power."[28]

The CPK decided to wage armed struggle in January 1968.[29] This decision coincided with Hanoi's buildup in eastern Cambodia for the Tet offensive. The increased Communist pressure triggered Sihanouk's harsh reactions. In late January, the Cambodian government arrested several young Communists in Phnom Penh for distributing pamphlets criticizing the Yugoslavian head of state, Tito, who was scheduled to visit Cambodia shortly. In March, Sihanouk sent the air force to attack suspected areas of CPK influence across Cambodia.[30]

Chinese leaders' uneasiness with the developments in Cambodia was clearly reflected in Zhou Enlai's meeting with Pham Hung, secretary of the COSVN, in Beijing on June 19, 1968. After mentioning the military operations conducted by the CPK in eastern Cambodia, Zhou asked Hung whether North Vietnam-ese troops in Cambodia had distributed Chinese weapons to the Cambodian Communists. (The transcript does not supply Hung's reply.) Insisting that China maintained no direct ties with the CPK, Zhou said that Beijing did not want its embassy in Cambodia to establish relations with the Cambodian Communists because of the complicated situation in that country. Zhou also brought up the issue of Vietnamese chauvinism toward the Cambodians. Cit-ing reports about North Vietnamese cadres' "improper attitudes in dealing with Khmer comrades," Zhou asked Hung to urge his officers at lower levels to "show attitudes of equality" toward the Cambodian Communists.[31]

Zhou then stressed again the importance of concentrating on the defeat of the United States in Vietnam first before developing revolution in Cambodia:

"The Cambodian comrades wish to develop the armed struggle. Sihanouk will oppress them, and you can no longer go through Cambodia. . . . If the whole of Indochina joins the efforts to drive the U.S. out of Vietnam, then the Lao and Cambodian revolutions will be successful, although not as fast as expected." Zhou asked Hung to discuss with the Khmer Communists "how to join efforts to fight the Americans first and then fight the reactionary forces in Cambodia." As to the North Vietnamese troops in Cambodia, Zhou urged Hung to remind them of "the overall context" of the Indochina struggle: "You should make them understand the international approach and understand that one cannot fight many enemies at the same time." At the close of the conversation, Zhou asked Hung about the background of Pol Pot: "I heard from Comrade Pham Van Dong that the present General Secretary of the Khmer Communist Party graduated from France and used to travel to Hanoi."[32] This last statement suggests that China had limited knowledge of Pol Pot.[33]

The Communist insurrection in Cambodia during 1968–69 pushed Sihanouk to the right. In December 1968, he ordered his army to tighten its control of the Vietnamese Communists operating in Cambodia and in early 1969 restored dialogue with Washington.[34] According to Henry Kissinger, the prince privately permitted the Nixon administration to bomb secretly the North Vietnamese sanctuaries in Cambodia.[35] In April, Washington agreed to respect Cambodian "sovereignty and neutrality."[36] On June 11, diplomatic relations between the United States and Cambodia were reestablished. While making diplomatic overtures to the United States, Sihanouk also elevated the NLF trade mission in Phnom Penh to the status of an embassy. These moves reflected the prince's typical balancing act. Still wishing to steer his country out of the war, Sihanouk declared in April 1969 that he would change attitudes toward Vietnam only when the Communists' pressure grew too strong for Cambodia's forces to resist.[37]

Sihanouk's improvement of relations with the United States disturbed Chinese leaders. In his meeting with Pham Van Dong in Beijing on April 20, 1969, Zhou Enlai expressed a pessimistic assessment of the Cambodian situation but, noting the Nixon administration's recognition of Cambodia's borders, the Chinese premier said that Nixon's Cambodian policy "is more intelligent than" Johnson's. Zhou also displayed his distrust in Sihanouk, when he referred to the Cambodian leader's policy as "double-dealing" and "tilting to the right."[38]

In late 1969, Pol Pot led a delegation to Hanoi to hold discussions with Vietnamese leaders. Predicting that Lon Nol would take over power in Cambodia with American backing, the CPK leader contended that this would create a favorable condition for the Cambodian revolution because Sihanouk would then join with the Communists against the right and the United States. Not ready to concede that Sihanouk would be overthrown, the Vietnamese continued to subordinate the interests of the Cambodian revolution to those of the Vietnamese revolution. Le Duan asked the CPK delegation to avoid armed struggle and "wait until Vietnam wins victory. At that moment, we will strike one single blow and we will liberate Phnom Penh."[39]

Pol Pot's determination to press on with armed struggle in Cambodia demonstrated that he was not the tool of either Hanoi or Beijing. The Khmer Rouge's local view and priorities contradicted the regional perspective and concerns of North Vietnam and China. The CPK's parochial outlook and localized interests made the party better tuned to the threats and opportunities in its immediate environment than the Chinese and Vietnamese Communists, whose regional range of interests impeded full and lasting attention to specific local issues. To Pol Pot and his cohorts, local events were an absolute, whereas to policymakers in Beijing and Hanoi, they constituted one of many problems competing for attention and resources. The Khmer Rouge took advantage of the Vietnamese Communists' presence in their country to advance their cause.

In early January 1970, Sihanouk traveled to Paris, ostensibly for his annual medical examination. Actually he wanted to use his absence from Cambodia to outmaneuver his domestic opponent Sirik Matak and to employ his diplomatic skills with Moscow and Beijing, which he expected to visit on the way home, to ease the Vietnamese pressure on his country. While the prince was abroad, Prime Minister Lon Nol stepped up anti-Vietnamese activities, including attacking North Vietnamese and NLF positions inside Cambodia. On March 11, massive protests took place outside the DRV and NLF diplomatic missions in Phnom Penh. Demonstrators broke into the two installations, burning their contents and manhandling Vietnamese diplomats.[40]

Chinese leaders watched with great apprehension the sharp turn to the right in Cambodia. Zhou Enlai told the Cambodian ambassador to China, Nay Valentin, on March 14 that "the Chinese government is disturbed by the recent events in Phnom Penh." After expressing regret at the sacking of the DRV and NLF diplomatic buildings in Phnom Penh, the Chinese premier called the ambassador's attention to the appearance of anti-Chinese slogans among the rioters and the rumors of similar actions to be taken against the Chinese embassy. Zhou also voiced concern about Sihanouk's safety: "It is reported that Prince Sihanouk plans to leave Moscow on the 16th and arrive in Beijing on the 17th. Therefore, it is all the more necessary for us to take measures to protect the prince's safety. We support the prince's policy of peace, neutrality, and independence."[41]

In anticipation of possible anti-Chinese riots in Cambodia, Zhou Enlai told the North Korean ambassador to China on March 16 that if the Chinese embassy in Cambodia was destroyed and telegram communications were disrupted, Beijing wanted to maintain contacts with Cambodia through Pyongyang via the North Korean embassy in Phnom Penh.[42]

Sihanouk prolonged his stay in the Soviet Union for more discussions with Russian leaders. In his memoirs, Sihanouk reveals that the Kremlin was prepared to provide military assistance to Cambodia.[43] On March 18, when the prince was still in Moscow, Lon Nol staged a coup, deposing him as head of state. The new regime demanded the withdrawal of all Vietnamese revolutionary forces from Cambodia.[44] On the way to the Moscow airport, Soviet premier Kosygin informed Sihanouk that he had been voted out of office by the National Assembly. The prince called the move unconstitutional and immoral, claiming that he would fight imperialism with all his strength.[45]

To sow discord between Sihanouk and China, Kosygin told the prince: "You can have absolute confidence in the Soviet Union's backing of your struggle. . . . You will see how it will be with the Chinese. They helped you while you were in power in Phnom Penh but now that you are no longer in power, you will see what they will do!" Still confident of China's endorsement, Sihanouk replied: "I will continue on to Peking and get the support of my old friend, Chou En Lai."[46] Moscow's willingness to offer military aid to Cambodia and Kosygin's attempt to drive a wedge between Sihanouk and Beijing indicate that the Soviets were competing with the Chinese for influence over Cambodia.

Zhou Enlai received the shaken Sihanouk at the Beijing airport on March 19. In the meeting that followed shortly afterward, Zhou told the prince that China still recognized him as the Cambodian chief of state. "After the occurrence of the incident," the Chinese premier went on, "you declared that you would return to Cambodia right away. Later you did not do that. We feel that it is better for you not to return." Sihanouk said that in the present situation, he could not return and wished to stay in China for a period of time.[47]

After the discussion with Sihanouk, Zhou Enlai called a politburo meeting to discuss the Cambodian situation and the prince's requests to meet international reporters and to distribute a written statement. At the meeting, it was decided that the politburo would assist Sihanouk in his activities in Beijing and would be prepared for the eventualities of the Chinese embassy in Phnom Penh being smashed and overseas Chinese in Cambodia being arrested. The next day, Zhou reported the conclusions of the meeting to Mao, who approved them.[48] In the meantime, Zhou signed a foreign ministry telegram to the Chinese ambassador to the DRV, Wang Youping, directing him to convey to Vietnamese leaders the results of his meeting with Sihanouk, to indicate China's support for the prince, and to solicit Hanoi's views on the Cambodian crisis.[49]

The coup in Cambodia clearly caught Chinese leaders by surprise. Although

Zhou Enlai (left) greets Sihanouk at Beijing airport, March 19, 1970, shortly after the coup that deposed Sihanouk as the Cambodian head of state. (Courtesy Xinhua News Agency)

they chose to support Sihanouk (mainly to strengthen their position vis-à-vis the Soviets and the Vietnamese), they were unsure about the long-term plans of the erratic and mercurial prince. At the same time, they had not totally given up hope on Lon Nol, who had visited Beijing the previous year to attend the October 1 celebration commemorating the twentieth anniversary of the PRC. This ambivalent attitude was clearly demonstrated in Zhou Enlai's conversation with Pham Van Dong in Beijing on March 21. After noting the French interest in the continuation of Cambodia's neutral policy and the Lon Nol regime's cautious behavior toward Moscow and Beijing in the last two days, including taking security measures to protect the Chinese and Soviet embassies in Phnom Penh, Zhou told Dong: "We should support Sihanouk for the time being and see how he will act. We should support him because he supports the anti-American struggle in Vietnam. . . . We will also see whether he really wants to establish a united front to oppose the U.S. before we support him. But because of the circumstances he may change his position. However, the more we can win his sympathy, the better." The Chinese premier asked his DRV counterpart for his views about negotiations with the Lon Nol–Sirik Matak regime. Dong replied that before his trip to Beijing, the Hanoi leadership had already discussed the issue and had concluded that "negotiations would not bring about any results, because they would eventually fight us."[50] Clearly, the North Vietnamese had no illusions about Lon Nol and Sirik Matak.

According to Nay Valentin, Pham Van Dong assured Princess Monique that North Vietnam's forces could help Sihanouk regain power within twenty-four hours.[51] Sihanouk himself later recalled that Dong requested to see him in Beijing. During their meeting on the morning of March 22, Sihanouk claimed that he had defined the conditions for cooperation, including Chinese assistance to the Khmer resistance, a summit conference of Indochinese peoples, and military training in Vietnam for his followers.[52] Clearly, the prince did not wish to depend solely on Hanoi's aid.

In the afternoon, Zhou Enlai met with Pham Van Dong, undoubtedly to hear the latter's report on his negotiation with Sihanouk.[53] That evening, Zhou held a discussion with Sihanouk, reaffirming China's support for his struggle. Commenting on the broadcast statement that the prince was to deliver the next day, the Chinese premier remarked that it would greatly inspire the Cambodian people.[54]

On March 23, Sihanouk issued his first "Message to the Nation," calling for arms against the Lon Nol regime and urging Cambodians to defy the orders issued from Phnom Penh. He proposed a National Union Government, a National Liberation Army, and a National United Front of Kampuchea (NUFK), which would govern Cambodia according to the principles of "social justice, equality and fraternity."[55] Sihanouk's decision sealed his alliance with the Khmer Rouge, who would exploit his appeal and popularity among the Cambodian peasants for propaganda purposes. The ground for the eventual victory of the Khmer Rouge was laid.[56]

The contrast between Hanoi and Beijing's reactions to the Cambodian situation in the immediate period following Sihanouk's downfall is revealing. Between March 25 and 27, Hanoi released a formal statement in support of Sihanouk and withdrew its diplomats from Phnom Penh. While publicizing Sihanouk's statements, the Chinese media as well as officials in Beijing refrained from commenting on the Cambodian affairs. Chinese ambassador Kang Maozhao remained in Phnom Penh after DRV and NLF representatives had left. China lagged behind the DRV and the Pathet Lao in accusing Washington of plotting Sihanouk's overthrow.[57] It was not until April 5 that Zhou Enlai spoke openly against the United States for engineering Sihanouk's ouster.[58]

In April, Ambassador Kang Maozhao informed Lon Nol that if he permitted the transportation of weapons through Cambodia, maintained sanctuaries for the Vietnamese Communist forces, and helped them in their war propaganda, China would recognize his government. But Lon Nol rejected Beijing's offer. On May 5, the Chinese government finally broke relations with the Lon

Nol regime and withdrew its diplomats from Phnom Penh.[59] Beijing's effort to restore the status quo in Cambodia, whether under Sihanouk or someone else, ended in failure.

Chinese leaders must have perceived that the events in Cambodia were connected with the recent escalation of war in Laos. Beginning on February 12, 1970, the combined forces of the PAVN and the Pathet Lao had launched an offensive to drive the government forces out of the Plain of Jars. An additional 13,000 North Vietnamese soldiers were deployed to reinforce the 50,000 troops already there, and they were in a position to threaten Vang Pao's headquarters at Long Cheng. At Souvanna Phouma's request, U.S. B-52 bombers attacked northern Laos for the first time, halting the Communist advance.[60] Although the Chinese media denounced the American action,[61] leaders in Beijing must have been disturbed by North Vietnam's new initiative in Laos, which threatened not only to expand the war but also, given the DRV's dependence on Soviet weapons, to extend Moscow's influence together with that of Hanoi.[62] While embracing the prospects of a U.S. disengagement from Vietnam, Chinese policymakers were now concerned about the postwar domination of Indochina by Hanoi in alliance with the Soviet Union.

Primarily to compete with the Soviet Union and North Vietnam for influence in Cambodia, Beijing, in the weeks immediately after the coup, adopted a two-track approach: it would support Sihanouk and explore the possibility of cooperation with the Lon Nol regime. It tried to keep its options open, and it sought to drive a wedge between Sihanouk and Moscow. When Sihanouk, during his March 28 talk with Zhou Enlai, expressed his concern that the Soviet Union had been treating him very cautiously and that other socialist countries in Europe were following the Soviet example, the Chinese premier missed no opportunity to discredit the Kremlin. The Russians, Zhou asserted, had always acted that way; they "have not only treated Cambodia in this manner, but have also treated the DRV similarly." When the three Indochinese states issued a statement later, Zhou continued, the Soviet Union "will be embarrassed."[63]

Moscow, driven by its rivalry with Beijing, had been unwilling to break diplomatic relations with the Lon Nol regime. To extend its influence in Cambodia, the Soviet Union suggested on April 17 the holding of another Geneva conference. The Summit Meeting of the Indochinese Peoples, sponsored by China in late April, however, preempted the Soviet move. Beijing denounced the Soviet proposal on the day the summit opened.[64]

The summit meeting was held at the Conghua hot spring resort near Guangzhou on April 24–25.[65] Present at the conference were Sihanouk, Souphanouvong of Laos, Pham Van Dong of the DRV, and Nguyen Huu Tho of the

Provisional Revolutionary Government (PRG) of the Republic of South Vietnam. (As a diplomatic guise for the NLF, the PRG was established by Hanoi in June 1969 for the purpose of presenting a formal alternative to the Nguyen Van Thieu regime.) At the meeting, the delegates developed disputes. On the evening of April 24, Zhou Enlai flew to Guangzhou to help move the conference forward. He talked with Pham Van Dong and Sihanouk to resolve their differences and to work out the details of a joint statement.[66]

On April 25, the summit meeting concluded with the announcement of the joint statement, which called on the Indochinese people to join the common struggle against the United States and its lackeys. China, for its part, pledged to provide a "rear area" and "powerful backing" for the struggle against U.S. aggression.[67] Sihanouk also issued a declaration condemning the United States and granting Hanoi and the NLF formal permission to use Cambodian territory.[68]

Zhou Enlai hosted a banquet in honor of the four Indochinese delegations. Congratulating them on the success of the meeting, the Chinese premier announced the successful launching of China's first satellite the previous day.[69] Clearly, Zhou wanted to impress his listeners with China's latest achievement. By sheltering Sihanouk and sponsoring the summit meeting, Beijing had stolen a diplomatic show from the Soviet Union. China's influence in Indochina had been reasserted for the moment.

Nixon's decision to invade Cambodia in early May prompted a strong reaction from China. On May 11, Mao met with Le Duan in Beijing. According to Lu Huixiang, who served as a note-taker in the Mao-Duan conversation, the CCP chairman said that the main tendency in the world was revolution and that small countries should not be afraid of U.S. imperialism.[70] On May 18, the Chinese government announced the cancellation of the Warsaw talks scheduled to open two days later. At a mass rally on Tiananmen Square on May 20, Mao issued a statement expressing support for Sihanouk and denouncing U.S. aggression.[71] It is important to note that Mao's statement, despite its rhetorical shrillness, lacked substance. It did not make any concrete commitments to the struggle in Indochina.[72] The address was primarily a propaganda gesture designed to serve three purposes: to remind Third World countries that China remained their friend; to embarrass the Russians by highlighting that nearly twenty countries had recognized the Royal Government of National Union of Kampuchea (RGNUK) led by Sihanouk, which the Soviet Union had not done; and to send a message to Nixon that Sino-U.S. rapprochement must be based on a reduction of American involvement in Indochina.

When Mao was delivering his speech, Chai Chengwen, deputy head of the Chinese delegation to the Sino-Soviet negotiations, and Vasilu V. Kuznetsov, head of the Soviet delegation to the negotiations, were also on the reviewing stand. Chai quipped at the Soviet diplomat: "You are always talking about 'united action.' Don't you think that the Soviet Union is lagging too far behind" in supporting Sihanouk?[73] Chai was referring to the past Soviet request for joint action in support of North Vietnam. Clearly, Chai felt that China had scored diplomatically over the Soviet Union on the Cambodian issue.

In sum, the Cambodian crisis had presented both danger and opportunity to Beijing. On the one hand, the American invasion of Cambodia seemed to suggest to Chinese leaders a reversal of the Nixon doctrine. For the first time in the Vietnam conflict, Washington employed ground combat forces outside South Vietnam. The hesitant moves toward Sino-American accommodation came to an abrupt end after the invasion. On the other hand, by hosting the Summit Meeting of the Indochinese Peoples and facilitating the formation of the RGNUK, Beijing increased its influence in Indochina.

Beijing-Hanoi competition in Cambodia unfolded chiefly within the resistance movement. Geographical separation handicapped China's ability to maneuver within the NUFK. As a result, Beijing concentrated its efforts on Sihanouk and the RGNUK. Through cooperation with Sihanouk, China hoped to maintain some leverage over Hanoi on the Cambodian issue. Beijing did not establish contacts with the resistance on the ground in Cambodia until Ieng Sary came to the Chinese capital as a special liaison in late 1971. The DRV relied on its military presence in Cambodia to maintain closer ties with the NUFK, hoping that the Hanoi-trained Khmer returnees would establish domination over the resistance movement. Between 1970 and 1972, Hanoi's forces bore the main burden of fighting Lon Nol's troops. Distrustful of the North Vietnamese presence in Cambodia, however, the Pol Pot group began to purge the returnees in late 1971.[74]

9 SINO-U.S. RAPPROCHEMENT AND VIETNAM 1970–1975

RESUMPTION OF THE SINO-U.S. DIALOGUE

China did not resume negotiations with the United States until Washington completely withdrew from Cambodia in June 1970 and initiated renewed contacts. Mao invited Edgar Snow, his old friend from Yanan, to appear on the high balcony at Tiananmen for the National Day celebration on October 1. For the first time, the Chinese leader was publicly identified with the still tentative opening to the United States. Through the Pakistani channel, Nixon conveyed to the Chinese government that he was prepared to send a high-ranking envoy to Beijing. In November, Zhou Enlai replied that China would welcome a presidential emissary in Beijing. Before the end of the year, Mao told Snow that he would be delighted to meet with Nixon.[1]

While reopening dialogue with the Americans during the second half of 1970, Chinese leaders also encouraged Hanoi to make progress in its negotiations with Washington. During his meeting with Pham Van Dong in Beijing on September 19, Zhou Enlai praised the North Vietnamese negotiator, Xuan Thuy, for his performance at the Paris talks.[2] Mao, in his talk with the DRV premier four days later, dwelled on the restraint demonstrated by the United States during the Vietnam War and expressed satisfaction with Hanoi's diplomatic strategy. "Negotiations have been going on for two years," the CCP leader said. "At first we were a little worried that you were trapped. We are no longer worried. . . . You are fighting very well on the battlefield. Your policy for the diplomatic struggle is correct."[3]

In February 1971, the United States directed and supported a South Vietnamese invasion of Laos, code-named Operation Lam Son 719. The purpose was the same as for Cambodia: to buy time for Vietnamization by destroying the Viet Cong's supply lines. The 1970 Cambodian invasion had driven Vietnamese Communist units either deeper into Cambodia or back up the Ho Chi Minh Trail into southern Laos. The Lon Nol coup and the close of the port of Sihanoukville had increased the importance of the Ho Chi Minh Trail as the only remaining logistical route for Communist troops in South Vietnam. As Hanoi attempted to compensate for the loss of supply lines in Cambodia by increasing shipments through Laos, Washington had intensified its air bombardment of southern Laos. During Operation Lam Son 719, South Vietnamese troops fought on their own, with only American air support. The operation was a quick military failure.[4]

To reassure China, Nixon announced in a news conference on February 17 that the Laotian operation "is not directed against Communist China. It is directed against the North Vietnamese who are pointed toward South Vietnam and toward Cambodia. Consequently, I do not believe that the Communist Chinese have any reason to interpret this as a threat against them or any reason therefore to react to it."[5] Beijing strongly condemned the invasion but at the same time indicated that it would do nothing more. Deputy Foreign Minister Qiao Guanhua told Ole Aalgard, the Norwegian ambassador in Beijing, that China was conscious of a new trend in U.S. policy and that it was just putting off, not canceling, talks with Washington. He asked the Norwegian diplomat to inform the Americans of their conversation.[6]

On March 5–8, Zhou Enlai traveled to the DRV to reaffirm China's support for the Vietnamese struggle.[7] In his talk with Le Duan and Pham Van Dong on March 7, Zhou spoke about the danger of a united action with the Soviet Union because the country had a tendency to subordinate the interests of other countries to the needs of its foreign policy.[8] While Zhou was trying to drive a wedge between Hanoi and Moscow, Le Duan applied the same tactic to forestall a Sino-U.S. rapprochement. He proposed the formation of an international front, with China as the leader, to oppose the Nixon doctrine and the American-Japanese alliance. Zhou equivocated by replying that China needed time to consider the issue and that the DRV was sometimes "in a more advantageous position" than China in the struggle against the American and Japanese reactionaries.[9]

It is important to note that Zhou, in his conversations with the North Vietnamese leaders, dwelled on the Soviet menace rather than the American threat. Clearly, the limited U.S. involvement in the Laotian invasion had indicated to the Chinese that Nixon did not intend to reverse his policy of disengagement from Vietnam. And North Vietnam's success in defeating Nguyen

Van Thieu's troops had again alerted Beijing to the danger of future Moscow-backed Vietnamese hegemony in Indochina. Both Moscow and Hanoi viewed China's response to the invasion of Laos as much less forceful than its reaction to the incursion into Cambodia a year before, when it was less certain about U.S. intentions.[10]

To demonstrate China's commitment to the improvement of Sino-American relations, Mao in early April decided to invite a U.S. national table tennis team to visit China. Meeting with the American Ping-Pong players on April 14, Zhou Enlai said: "Your trip to China has opened the gate for friendly visits by people of the two countries." The U.S. table tennis team's visit speeded up the process of Sino-American rapprochement. Between April and May, the two countries agreed that Henry Kissinger, Nixon's national security adviser, would visit Beijing in July.[11]

China's seeking rapprochement with the United States while North Vietnam was still locked in a desperate struggle with the Americans, however, created serious implications for Sino-DRV relations. China's détente with the United States might push Hanoi further into the arms of the Soviet Union, a development that would run counter to the very objective that underlay Beijing's opening to America. Improving relations with the United States required difficult adjustments in China's relations with the DRV. How would Hanoi react to China's new policy toward America? Chinese leaders fully considered the possibilities. There were officials within the party who believed that a rapprochement with Washington would undermine the war in Vietnam and the Paris peace negotiations.[12]

To clarify thoughts within the party on the eve of Kissinger's visit, the politburo convened a meeting on May 26, discussing the implications of the forthcoming Sino-U.S. negotiations. Among the issues discussed was the Vietnam War. The meeting concluded that while the Sino-American negotiations might cause a short-term "ripple" to the Indochina war and the Paris peace talks, the progress in the Sino-U.S. discussions would eventually benefit the struggle of the Indochinese people. The talks, it was agreed, would facilitate the withdrawal of American troops from Vietnam and promote the peace negotiations in Paris because Nixon had realized that the focus of Soviet-American contention was in Europe and the Middle East rather than in the Far East. The report of the May 26 politburo meeting became a major policy guideline underlying China's approach to the coming Sino-American negotiations.[13]

To convince the North Vietnamese that China's opening to America would not undermine their war effort, the Chinese leadership in 1971 substantially increased weapons shipments to the DRV, which had declined between 1969 and 1970. On July 4, 1971, Beijing concluded a protocol on the provision of supplementary military equipment and materials to Hanoi in 1971. (China's aid would reach record levels in 1972–73. See Table 1.)[14] The North Vietnamese, however, later called this action as an attempt by Chinese leaders "to cover up their betrayal and to appease the Vietnamese people's indignation."[15]

Vietnam was one of the issues that Kissinger raised during his secret talks with Zhou Enlai on July 9–11. In addition to using China to offset Soviet power, the Nixon administration wanted Beijing to make Hanoi more amenable to U.S. suggestions for ending the war. In his talk with Zhou Enlai on July 9, Kissinger attempted to wed China's interest in resolving the Taiwan issue to Washington's interest in closing the Vietnam War. After informing Zhou that the United States sought to end the war in Vietnam through negotiations and was preparing a timetable for the withdrawal of U.S. forces from Vietnam and Indochina, Kissinger stressed that Washington hoped to find an honorable solution that would preserve U.S. prestige. As to the Taiwan issue, Nixon's envoy stated that the United States planned to withdraw two-thirds of its troops from the island within a brief period after the conclusion of the war in Indochina. In response to Kissinger's emphasis on protecting American honor in Indochina, Zhou Enlai pointed out that the Americans always liked to stress their prestige and honor. It would be the greatest honor and glory for the United States, the Chinese premier concluded, if it completely withdrew its forces from Indochina.[16]

After talking with Kissinger, Zhou immediately went to brief Mao. Informed of the U.S. intention to withdraw its forces from Indochina, the CCP chairman noted that "the United States should make a new start and . . . let the domino fall. The United States must withdraw from Vietnam. We are in no hurry on the Taiwan issue because there is no fighting on Taiwan. But there is a war in Vietnam and people are dying there. We should not invite Nixon to come just for our own purposes."[17] In the end, the Chinese leaders ignored Kissinger's request that they pressure Hanoi to change its policy toward the Paris peace talks.[18]

Immediately after Kissinger left China, Zhou Enlai rushed to Hanoi on July 13 to inform Le Duan and Pham Van Dong of his meetings with Kissinger.[19] After mentioning Kissinger's principle of linking the settlement of the Taiwan issue with the resolution of the Indochina problem, Zhou assured the North Vietnamese that China had pointed out to the American negotiator that the withdrawal of American troops from South Vietnam had a priority over the question of Chinese representation in the United Nations.[20] Clearly, the Chinese wanted to dispel doubts in the minds of their North Vietnamese comrades that China had abandoned its commitment to their cause. Mao did not want to alienate Hanoi in the Sino-Soviet competition within the Communist world. He was also nervous that his opening to the United States might tarnish China's self-image as a vanguard in the anti-imperialist struggle in the world.

Despite Beijing's reassurances, the North Vietnamese had drawn the inescapable conclusion that China valued its relationship with the United States more than its revolutionary unity with the DRV. They believed that Beijing's opening to the United States undermined their interests and objectives. Specifically, they felt that the July 15 announcement of Kissinger's secret trip to China and Nixon's planned visit to Beijing significantly undercut their new peace offensive. On July 1, 1971, Madam Nguyen Thi Binh, foreign minister of the PRG, had just pronounced the Seven-Point Proposal, which demanded that the United States set a date for the complete withdrawal of its troops from South Vietnam and the release of prisoners. It also insisted that the United States respect the South Vietnamese people's right to self-determination by ending its support for the Nguyen Van Thieu government and by allowing the South Vietnamese people to establish an administration favorably disposed to peace and democracy and with which the PRG would be willing to negotiate. Leaders in Hanoi and the PRG concluded that, in view of Nixon's continuing unilateral withdrawal of U.S. troops from South Vietnam amid the ongoing antiwar campaign in the United States, and in view of the defeats of Thieu's troops, Washington might be receptive to a political change in South Vietnam that could prepare the ground for settling the conflict through negotiations. They expected that when they made their terms known, the American public would exert pressure on the White House to get negotiations under way. But the spotlight on the sudden and dramatic change in Chinese-American relations seriously weakened the impact of the Seven-Point Proposal on the American public and made it easier for Nixon to ignore the strong public support initially elicited by the publication of the proposal.[21]

Xuan Thuy, Hanoi's chief negotiator at the Paris talks, called Nixon's forthcoming trip to Beijing a "perfidious maneuver" and a "false peace offensive" designed to split the socialist world.[22] The Hanoi media remained silent about the July 15 announcement until late in 1971, when it informed its people of the American president's impending visit to Beijing.[23]

In line with the change in their perception of threats to China's security, Chinese leaders were now keen to see an early conclusion of the Vietnam War in order to preserve American power and contain Soviet influence. Their eagerness to encourage a negotiated settlement of the war, however, further strained Sino-Vietnamese relations. The dispute over Beijing's proposal for a Geneva conference on Indochina highlighted the incipient disagreement over the execution of the war. After returning home from China on July 14, 1971, Australian Labor Party leader Gough Whitlam announced that Beijing now favored a Geneva conference on Indochina that would include non-Asian countries.[24] While in April 1970 China had spurned the Soviet proposal to convene another Geneva conference on Vietnam, it now advocated the holding of such a meeting. Whereas it once served Beijing's purpose to weaken the United States globally by keeping it mired in Vietnam, it was now in China's interest to preserve American strength as a counterbalance against the Soviet Union.

Nhan Dan (People's Daily) responded immediately to Beijing's suggestion, reminding the world that Hanoi's long-standing opposition to a new conference on Indochina remained unchanged. The party organ contended that "decisive voices belong only to those who are defeating" U.S. aggression and that the "most important cause of our victories is our correct and creative independent and sovereign line."[25] The Hanoi media's reaction clearly revealed the gap between the DRV and China.

In the wake of Kissinger's visit to Beijing, *Nhan Dan* carried an editorial titled " 'The Nixon Doctrine' Is Bound to Failure." After reading the piece, Zhou Enlai on July 20 wrote to Zhang Chunqiao and Yao Wenyuan, two party officials in charge of propaganda, that "the editorial reveals the apprehension and estimation of the Vietnamese comrades. I think the whole text can be published. Do not just excerpt passages from it." In this way, Zhou continued, China could demonstrate its "attitude of being open and aboveboard. The progress of the events will prove that China under Chairman Mao's leadership has always supported the resistance war of the people of the three Indochinese countries to the end." Zhang Chunqiao, however, opposed the idea of publishing the Vietnamese commentary in China, so the *Nhan Dan* editorial was not made available to the Chinese population.[26] Evidently Zhang was afraid of the negative impact the Vietnamese article might have on the Chinese public. Zhang's veto of Zhou's proposal clearly demonstrated the power of the ultra-leftist officials, who controlled ideological matters.

In November 1971, after Kissinger's second trip to China, Pham Van Dong, who had turned down an earlier invitation issued shortly after Kissinger's first visit, visited Beijing. During his stay in Beijing on November 20–25, the DRV premier held one meeting with Mao and three formal talks with Zhou Enlai. In his conversation with Mao on November 22, Pham Van Dong ask the Chinese government to cancel the planned Nixon journey to China. Mao refused Dong's request.[27]

In his talks with Zhou Enlai, Pham Van Dong informed the Chinese of the developments in the Paris peace negotiations and requested China's continued support for the DRV's war against the United States, especially in the area of transportation. Zhou explained the basic principles of the United States toward negotiations with the DRV as described by Kissinger.[28] Clearly, Chinese leaders were eager to see progress in the Paris talks.

According to Wang Youping, China's ambassador to the DRV between 1969 and 1974, at the close of their first formal talk on November 21, Pham Van Dong reminded Zhou that North Vietnam had made a contribution to the recent return of the PRC to the United Nations. The DRV premier was referring to the official statement released by the DRV Foreign Ministry back in August of that year in support of the admission of the PRC into the United Nations. Embarrassed by his omission of this subject during the meeting, Zhou hurried to express his thanks for Hanoi's effort.[29] The message Dong was trying to deliver was that the DRV had supported the PRC on the international front but that Beijing had betrayed Hanoi by its attempt to improve relations with the United States.

Washington was persistent in trying to use Beijing to turn up the heat on Hanoi. Preparations for the Nixon visit to China provided another opportunity for U.S. officials to seek Beijing's help in ending the war in Vietnam. But the Chinese again resisted the efforts. Beijing had objected to Ambassador David Bruce's inclusion in Kissinger's October 1971 delegation to China on the ground that Bruce, as American ambassador to France, had been involved in the Vietnamese-American peace talks in Paris. This episode demonstrated the sensitivity of the Chinese to even the appearance of involvement in the Vietnam peace process. When, in the course of preparing for the Beijing summit in January 1972, General Vernon Walters, U.S. military attaché in France, asked Chinese diplomats in Paris to use their influence to moderate Hanoi's negotiating position, the Chinese turned down his request. When Walters asked whether China would arrange a meeting between Nixon and the DRV official Le Duc Tho in Beijing, the reply was again negative.[30]

General Alexander Haig, Kissinger's deputy on the National Security Council staff, encountered similar Chinese reluctance to become involved in the Vietnam peace process when he led the U.S. advance team to Beijing in January 1972 for the summit. Unwilling to discuss the Vietnam peace negotiations, Zhou Enlai defended Hanoi's position in the war. Responding to Haig's charge that the DRV had "insulted" the United States by its recent attack on American forces, Zhou said that North Vietnam was a victim of the latest U.S. bombing and that China had no choice but to support the DRV. If the United States really wanted to end the war and completely withdraw its forces from Vietnam, Zhou went on, it had no reason to reject the reasonable demands of the DRV.[31] The Chinese premier, nevertheless, also showed displeasure with Soviet–North Vietnamese cooperation, adding that China's assistance to Hanoi was the minimum required to avoid a deterioration of Sino-Vietnamese relations.[32]

There were indications that China was prepared to face the negative outcome of a worsening of Sino–North Vietnamese relations and warming of Moscow-Hanoi ties as a result of the Sino-American rapprochement. When Haig told Zhou Enlai on January 4 that the continuation of the war in Southeast Asia could only provide the Soviet Union an opportunity to increase its influence in Hanoi and to implement its plan to encircle the PRC, the Chinese premier replied that the Soviet intervention in Indochina was an "inevitable reaction" by Moscow to the improvement of Sino-American relations and that China was prepared to "bear the consequences of the Sino-American accommodation."[33]

The Sino-U.S. summit in Beijing on February 21–28, 1972, rekindled Hanoi's bitter memories of the 1954 Geneva Conference. When the Chinese informed the North Vietnamese that Vietnam would be discussed during the Nixon visit, they responded: "Viet Nam is our country, you have no right to discuss with the United States the question of Viet Nam. You have already admitted your 1954 mistake, so you should not commit another one."[34] In early February, the Soviet embassy in Hanoi reported to Moscow that the Chinese had pressed the DRV for approval of their plan to discuss the issue of Indochina with Nixon. Moscow was relieved when Hanoi resisted the Chinese pressure.[35]

Indochina was one of the topics Nixon brought up in his discussions with Zhou Enlai in Beijing. Nixon said that while the United States wanted to end the war through negotiations, it would react strongly if Hanoi launched a major offensive in 1972. After noting that the only correct solution to the Indochina problem was U.S. withdrawal from Vietnam, Zhou asserted that "so long as you continue your practice of Vietnamization, Laotianization, and Cambodianization, and so long as the Vietnamese, the Laos, and Cambodians continue to fight, we will not stop supporting them for a single day."[36] Zhou's remarks were clearly made for the North Vietnamese's benefit (a copy of the discussion might be sent to Hanoi) given the fact that Beijing seemed to have agreed with Washington that the war in Indochina no longer should come between them. Nixon and Kissinger drew the impression from the talks that the Chinese gave highest priority to advancing their relations with Washington. In the words of Kissinger, "We indeed understood each other; the war in Vietnam would not affect the improvement of our relations."[37] Nixon concluded his visit to China with the signing of the Shanghai Communiqué on February 27. The communiqué's clause opposing "efforts by any other country or group of countries to establish . . . hegemony" in the Asia-Pacific region constituted an implicit expression of objection to Soviet (or Soviet–North Vietnamese) intentions.[38]

On March 4, within days of Nixon's departure from China, Zhou Enlai flew to Hanoi to brief the North Vietnamese on the Beijing summit and to reassure them of China's continued support. To smooth Hanoi's ruffled feathers, Zhou first apologized for Beijing's failure to endorse the DRV's decision to begin negotiations with the United States in May 1968. He admitted that China had made a misjudgment at the time in insisting that the conditions were not ripe for negotiations.[39] Zhou then reassured the North Vietnamese that in talking with the Americans China had consistently placed the settlement of the Vietnam problem above the resolution of the Taiwan issue.[40]

The North Vietnamese, however, remained unconvinced by Beijing's repeated reassurances. They drew a bitter lesson from Nixon's handshake with Mao that China's foreign policy was concerned less with international Communist unity than with the pursuit of China's national interest. They responded to the Nixon journey with indignation. One high-ranking official in Hanoi said that "while Nixon gets his 21 gun salute in Peking, we'll be giving him a different kind of salute in South Vietnam. There will be more than 21 guns. And they won't be firing blanks."[41] Hoang Quoc Viet, president of the Presidium of the Central Committee of the Viet Nam Fatherland Front and president of the Viet Nam–China Friendship Association, told a Japanese journalist in 1973 that China's invitation to Nixon to visit the country was like "throwing a lifebelt to the drowning Nixon" and that "sometimes dealings between big nations may be made at the expense of a small nation and crush it."[42]

Hanoi interpreted the Shanghai Communiqué's statement that the United States "will progressively reduce its forces and military installations on Taiwan as the tension in the area diminishes" as meaning that China was invited to exert pressure on the Vietnamese to settle the war on American terms as the price for a Taiwan settlement.[43] The Vietnamese *White Paper* later charged that China "at heart wants to make use of the Viet Nam question for the settlement of the Taiwan issue first."[44]

The Chinese embassy in Hanoi immediately felt the cool attitudes of the North Vietnamese. On February 21, 1972, the embassy hosted a party to celebrate the Spring Festival, a holiday for both the Chinese and the Vietnamese. As it had done for many years in the past, the embassy invited North Vietnamese guests to attend. But to the surprise of the Chinese diplomats, not a single Vietnamese showed up this time. They soon discovered the reason: that was the day that President Nixon arrived in Beijing.[45]

Nixon's decision to normalize relations with Beijing nullified the hitherto basic rationale of the Vietnam War, namely to contain and isolate Communist China. The emergence of friendly ties between Beijing and Washington suddenly marginalized and trivialized the Vietnam conflict, which had been the central focus of international politics. The new great power triangle of Beijing, Washington, and Moscow replaced the Vietnam War in dominating the international system. Although Hanoi was unhappy with both Beijing and Moscow for their subordination of its interests to their improvement of relations with Washington, "China's betrayal," in the words of the historian William Duiker, "must have been particularly hard to swallow since it provided additional evidence of Beijing's long-term intentions in Southeast Asia."[46]

THE SPRING OFFENSIVE OF 1972

Since the Tet offensive of 1968, the Hanoi leadership had been preparing for a general offensive in the early 1970s. Vo Nguyen Giap contended in late 1971 that the only effective means to conquer the United States was to return to the strategy of main force warfare and general uprising. In his calculation, a decisive military victory would convince Nixon and the American public that there were only two alternatives to a negotiated withdrawal: further escalation or defeat.[47]

Conscious of the approaching presidential elections in the United States in the fall of 1972, the VWP leaders intended to take the military initiative to extract concessions from Washington. At a PRG cabinet meeting in early January 1972, Nguyen Van Linh, the COSVN secretary in charge of propaganda and training, declared that "to modify the balance of power even further and put us in a position of strength in the negotiations . . . we must ruin the credibility of Nixon and his protégé Thieu, just as we did for Johnson in 1968. We intend to drive the Americans into a corner and force concessions from them before the presidential elections. If possible we mean to destroy Nixon's chances for reelection."[48]

International pressures were also a factor in Hanoi's decision. DRV leaders watched nervously the progress of Washington's relations with both Moscow and Beijing. Their need for a showdown was urgent because they were uncertain just how the emerging U.S. détente with Moscow and Beijing would affect them. Given the interest of China and the Soviet Union in improving relations with the United States, policymakers in Hanoi had reason to worry that their two allies were susceptible to American pressures on Vietnam and that their support for the DRV might diminish if the war dragged on much longer.[49] Therefore, a general offensive in 1972 offered perhaps the last opportunity for the DRV to force a settlement on its own terms. Clearly, the Sino-American rapprochement and the Soviet-American détente were affecting decision making in Hanoi.

In late March 1972, North Vietnam launched the Spring Offensive against the south. At that moment, only 95,000 U.S. troops remained there, 6,000 of them combat soldiers. North Vietnamese troops numbering 120,000 attacked across the demilitarized zone, in the Central Highlands, and across the Cambodia border northwest of Saigon, challenging the United States' policy of Vietnamization. Nixon reacted to Hanoi's attack by authorizing an extensive bombing of military targets across North Vietnam and the mining of the DRV's harbors. For the first time in the war, U.S. troops employed high-tech "smart bombs" to hit their targets with accuracy. Certainly U.S. détente with Beijing and Moscow had made Nixon less worried about the reactions of the two major Communist powers.[50]

Zhou Enlai on April 14 reiterated China's support for Hanoi to carry the war to the end in a meeting with Nguyen Tien, DRV chargé d'affaires in Beijing.[51] On May 9, the day when the United States began to lay mines in North Vietnam's harbors, the DRV ambassador met with Zhou Enlai, requesting China's assistance in mine-clearing. The Chinese premier immediately summoned navy commanders that night, asking them to prepare for the task. The next day, he conducted further discussions with Pan Yan and Lai Guangzu, chief and deputy chief of staff of the navy, respectively, regarding plans for discovering and clearing mines.[52] In the meantime, the Chinese government issued a statement on May 12 condemning the U.S. mining of Haiphong and other North Vietnamese ports and promising Chinese support of the Vietnamese until "final victory" was achieved.[53]

In late May, a Chinese Mine Investigation Team arrived in Haiphong. With the help of the North Vietnamese, the Chinese team collected information regarding the types and characters of the American mines. Two months later, Chinese minesweeping vessels began to operate in the DRV. Between July 1972 and August 1973, Beijing sent twelve minesweepers and four support vessels to North Vietnam. In total, they cleared forty-six mines.[54] To meet Hanoi's petroleum needs after the closure of its ports by the American mine operations, China, beginning in May 1972, constructed five four-inch-wide pipelines from south China to the DRV.[55] By helping Hanoi clear mines and building oil pipelines, the Chinese leadership wanted to reassure the North Vietnamese that despite the improvement in Sino-U.S. relations, China had not wavered in its support for the DRV.

On April 18, 1972, Nixon met with a visiting Chinese table tennis team in the White House, demonstrating that rapprochement was on track despite Hanoi's offensive and Washington's bombing retaliation.[56] Clearly, China was in a serious dilemma. On the one hand, it had to continue its support for the DRV to avoid pushing the latter completely to the side of the Soviet Union and to maintain its self-image as a staunch supporter of national liberation movements. On the other hand, it wanted to preserve the emerging rapprochement with the United States.

The Soviet leadership strongly suspected that China and the DRV had cooperated in launching the Spring Offensive in order to sabotage the upcoming American-Soviet summit in Moscow. Leonid Brezhnev informed Kissinger in April that the Soviet Union was not behind the North Vietnamese offensive and that Beijing and Hanoi were trying their best to undermine détente between the USSR and the United States. Brezhnev also told Kissinger that Hanoi had requested the cancellation of the Moscow summit.[57]

To maintain its influence in the DRV and to drive a wedge between China and North Vietnam, the Kremlin in the spring of 1972 proposed to bypass the U.S. bombing of Haiphong by increasing weapons supplies to the DRV overland through China, including unloading Soviet ship cargoes in Chinese ports. While Hanoi approved the proposal, Beijing turned it down, creating an opportunity for Moscow to reproach China.[58]

The results of the Spring Offensive were disappointing to the Hanoi leadership, which had miscalculated the ability of Washington to react. The North Vietnamese lost about 100,000 soldiers, and the DRV received the most sustained bombing of the war. Although the Saigon regime suffered a loss of 25,000 men, it remained in power. Furthermore, Nixon refused to give in.[59]

The grim outcome of the Spring Offensive, along with the realization that Nixon was likely to be reelected, convinced the North Vietnamese that it was necessary to find a negotiated solution quickly. In late August, Le Duc Tho offered a new proposal in Paris, calling for the establishment of a coalition government that would include elements of both the PRG and the Thieu regime, as well as neutral representatives chosen by each side. For the first time, the DRV had proposed a settlement that left Thieu in power. When the United States rejected the notion of a coalition government in any form, in October Hanoi made a further concession by abandoning the demand for a coalition and agreeing to a cease-fire instead, followed by the complete withdrawal of U.S. troops and the exchange of prisoners of war. The DRV had dropped its refusal to consider a military cease-fire in advance of a full political solution.[60] According to the October draft agreement, within sixty days following a cease-fire, Washington would withdraw its remaining troops, and Hanoi would send back the American POWs. A political solution would then be arranged by the tripartite National Council of Reconciliation and Concord, which would supervise elections and be responsible for implementing the agreement.[61]

Hanoi's concession on the treatment of the Thieu regime came primarily as a result of intense American military pressure and the realization that there might be four more years of war if an agreement was not concluded before the U.S. presidential election. China had also advised the DRV to compromise on this issue. According to Vietnamese sources, in his talk with Pham Van Dong on November 22, 1971, Mao urged the North Vietnamese to postpone the liberation of South Vietnam: "As our broom is too short to sweep the Americans out of Taiwan, so yours is too short to do the same in South Vietnam."[62] Mao told French foreign minister Maurice Schumann in July 1972 that he had advised Nguyen Thi Binh to stop insisting on Thieu's removal as a precondition for a settlement with the United States.[63]

In his meeting with Le Duc Tho in Beijing on July 12, Zhou Enlai used the CCP's experience in negotiating with Chiang Kai-shek during the Chinese civil war and with the Eisenhower administration during the Korean War to underscore the importance of dealing with chief figures in the enemy camp. No results would have been achieved, Zhou continued, if the CCP had insisted on talking with Chiang's ministers rather than with Chiang himself. He urged the North Vietnamese to recognize Nguyen Van Thieu as a representative of one of the three forces in the coalition government. The recognition of Thieu, the Chinese premier concluded, would make it easier for the United States to accept a political solution.[64]

Despite the North Vietnamese claim that they had not been affected by the changes in Sino-American and Soviet-American relations, the unfolding U.S. rapprochement with China and the Soviet Union undermined Hanoi's interests. The limitations of both Chinese and Soviet aid seriously constrained Hanoi's approach to Washington. As one Cold War specialist has observed perceptively, "At the very least, neither the Soviet nor the Chinese leaders had been prepared to subordinate or sacrifice their own interests in improving relations with the United States to support socialist North Vietnam in a crucial struggle with the leading imperialist and interventionist power."[65]

Enraged by Washington's decision to negotiate over his head with the Communists, Nguyen Van Thieu vehemently opposed the October agreement. He contended that he would not agree to a settlement that allowed North Vietnamese troops to stay in the south and accorded the NLF sovereignty. He objected to the phraseology in the text that accorded the tripartite council the status of a coalition government. He insisted on the establishment of the demilitarized zone as a boundary between two sovereign states.[66]

Saigon's opposition and Nixon's support of Thieu caused the breakdown of the October agreement. When the negotiations reopened in November, the American side introduced for reconsideration sixty-nine Saigon government objections. Kissinger demanded at least a symbolic withdrawal of North Vietnamese soldiers from the south and asked for changes in the text that would have reduced the political status of the NLF, limited the powers of the tripartite council, and established the demilitarized zone as a virtual boundary. Feeling betrayed, Le Duc Tho bitterly spurned Kissinger's suggestions. The NLF was no happier with the agreement than Thieu, angrily protesting that it gave Saigon a veto over negotiations and did not guarantee the release of political prisoners held by the Thieu regime. Under heavy pressure from their southern comrades, North Vietnamese negotiators brought up many demands of their own, even reviving their previous insistence on the removal of Thieu. For weeks, the negotiations were in a deadlock. To reassure Thieu and to force Hanoi to conclude an agreement, Nixon ordered another massive bombing operation against the DRV on December 17. The so-called Christmas bombing was the most intensive and destructive attack of the war. In less than two weeks, the United States dropped over 36,000 tons of bombs, exceeding the tonnage dropped during the entire period of 1969–71.[67]

While holding Washington responsible for Thieu's recalcitrance and expressing outrage at the Christmas bombing,[68] the Beijing leadership was eager to see the Paris negotiations succeed. Mao and Zhou Enlai reminded North Vietnamese leaders in the winter of 1972–73 that because the United States had made up its mind to withdraw, Hanoi should conduct serious negotiations with the Americans. Mao told Nguyen Thi Binh on December 29, 1972, that if the Paris talks were successful, not only the PRG but also the DRV could "achieve a certain degree of normalization with the Americans."[69] Zhou said to VWP politburo member Truong Chinh on December 31 that because "Nixon does intend to disengage," the DRV "ought to approach the negotiations seriously in order to produce results."[70] The Chinese premier, in a conversation with Le Duc Tho in Beijing on January 3, 1973, reiterated his belief that Nixon wanted to withdraw from Vietnam: "The U.S. effort to exert pressure through bombing has failed. Nixon was facing many international and domestic problems. It seems that he intends to retreat from Vietnam and Indochina. During the negotiations, you should both adhere to principles and show necessary flexibility. Let the Americans leave as quickly as possible. In half a year or one year the situation will change."[71]

The North Vietnamese–American negotiations resumed in Paris on January 8, 1973, in an icy atmosphere. Both sides were now committed to a settlement. After compromise by both sides, Kissinger and Le Duc Tho settled their differences. The final treaty, signed on January 23, followed basically the October agreement. On the major controversial point of December, the demilitarized zone, Hanoi's negotiators agreed to make explicit reference to it in the treaty, but the United States described it as a "provisional and not a political and territorial boundary," keeping the substance of the North Vietnamese position.[72]

Mao and Zhou Enlai viewed with satisfaction the conclusion of the Paris Peace Agreement. Zhou told Sihanouk on January 24 that it was good that "the cease-fire in Vietnam was not related to Cambodia and Laos." He stressed the principle that the problems of the three Indochinese countries should be resolved by the three countries themselves without outside interference.[73] Clearly, Zhou did not want Hanoi to dictate the terms of settlement in Cambodia and Laos. In a conversation with Penn Nouth, prime minister of the RGNUK, on February 2, Zhou quoted Mao as saying that the Paris agreement was a "successful" one because it brought the departure of the American troops.[74]

The Chinese leaders' reaction to the Paris Peace Agreement indicates that they were pleased with the U.S. disengagement from Vietnam and expected a Communist victory over Saigon. Beijing disagreed with Hanoi not over strategies but over tactics. The Chinese policymakers wished to see the United States out of Vietnam and supported Hanoi's plan to unify the south, but they preferred concessions permitting the Americans to withdraw and allowing a period of several years before a renewed effort was made to defeat Thieu's regime. This position was clearly indicated in Zhou Enlai's conversation with Hoang Van Hoan in May 1973. The Chinese premier compared the situation in Vietnam with that in China after the surrender of Japan in 1945. For about two years the CCP negotiated with the KMT and retreated before starting a counteroffensive and defeating Chiang Kai-shek's forces "without a halt." The DRV, Zhou went on, should also "win a spell of time to get prepared and, when it begins to fight, should eliminate the Nguyen Van Thieu administration without a halt. For after a period of armistice, it would be difficult for the United States to barge in."[75]

In his meetings with Le Duan in Beijing on June 5–6, 1973, Zhou Enlai again urged the North Vietnamese to "relax" and stop fighting in the south for five or ten years. During that period, Zhou said, "South Vietnam, Laos, and Cambodia should build peace, independence, and neutrality." Duan asked China to help the DRV build an oil refinery system, but Zhou turned down the request on the ground that China was unable to solve the waste disposal problem. In the end, however, the Chinese premier did promise to provide aid to the DRV at the 1973 level for the next five years.[76]

In discussions with the North Vietnamese about the settlement of the Vietnam conflict, Chinese leaders adopted a subtle approach. While they advised Hanoi to give the Americans face-saving concessions, they shied away from twisting the arms of the North Vietnamese to achieve that purpose. As John W. Garver has observed, Beijing "apparently distinguished between urging Hanoi to compromise with the United States and actively applying pressure to achieve this. While such a distinction might seem sophistic, it can also be seen as an attempt to synchronize the contradictory objectives of minimizing the influence of *both* superpowers in Indochina while creating optimal conditions for using U.S. power to check Soviet moves elsewhere in the world."[77] The Chinese leaders refrained from actively exerting pressure on the North Vietnamese because they wanted to minimize the opportunities for the Russians to exploit the Sino-Vietnamese differences and to preserve China's self-image as a loyal friend of national liberation movements.

CEASE-FIRE IN LAOS

During the American–North Vietnamese talks in Paris, both sides had agreed that a settlement should include corresponding cease-fire arrangements in Laos and Cambodia. Confident of Hanoi's sway over the Pathet Lao, Le Duc Tho promised to bring about a cease-fire in Laos within thirty days of the Vietnam cease-fire and to sign an understanding to that effect. As to Cambodia, the DRV diplomat was less certain, claiming that Hanoi had less influence over the Cambodian Communists.[78]

Hanoi's influence over the Pathet Lao enabled it to deliver quickly the promised cease-fire and political settlement. On October 17, 1972, formal negotiations began in Vientiane, and a cease-fire agreement was concluded within thirty days of the Paris agreement on February 21, 1973. Reaffirming the 1962 Geneva Accord on Laotian independence and neutrality, the Vientiane agreement declared a cease-fire, called for the withdrawal of all foreign troops, and prohibited foreign countries from using Laos to intervene in the internal affairs of another country. The settlement acknowledged the existence of two zones with separate administrations under a central coalition government.[79]

Hanoi's predominant role in the Laotian peace process must have unsettled Chinese leaders. However, Beijing reported the draft Vientiane agreement without comment. It continued its road-building operations in northern Laos, hoping to preserve some influence within the Pathet Lao.[80]

DRIFTING FURTHER APART

Relations between Beijing and Hanoi continued to worsen during the remaining years of the war. After the signing of the Paris agreement, the DRV began to focus its attention on postwar economic reconstruction. On December 26, 1973, it informed China of its intention to prospect for oil in the Tonkin Gulf and proposed negotiations to resolve disagreements over territorial rights. The Sino-DRV talks opened at the deputy foreign ministers level in Beijing in August 1974. But the negotiations quickly ran aground. The Vietnamese side insisted on the acceptance of the offshore boundary established by the 1887 Sino-French convention. The Chinese delegation rejected this position, contending that a division of the territorial waters in the gulf had never existed in the Sino-French agreement and that acceptance of the Vietnamese claim would yield two-thirds of the area of the gulf to the DRV. With the two sides unable to come to an agreement, the talks were suspended in November.[81]

The controversy over the Paracels (Xisha) and the Spratleys (Nansha) was another source of contention between Beijing and Hanoi. The Paracel and Stratley archipelagoes in the South China Sea consist of 150 largely uninhabited specks of land, coral reef, and sandbanks. The Paracels are about 150 miles southeast of China's Hainan Island in the north; the Spratleys lie about 550 miles to the south, off the coast of Vietnam. For centuries, Chinese, Vietnamese, and Filipino fishermen have ventured to the region for guano (used as fertilizer) and bird's nest (a Chinese gourmet ingredient). The issue of these islands' ownership had been a controversial affair, with China's claiming all of them on the ground of archaeological evidence and occasional visits. Neither China nor Vietnam nor the Philippines had effectively occupied them for any extended period of time.[82]

On September 4, 1958, the Chinese government declared that the territory of the PRC "includes the Chinese mainland and its coastal islands, as well as Taiwan and its surrounding islands, the Penghu Islands, the Dongsha Islands, the Xisha Islands, the Zhongsha Islands, the Nansha Islands and all other islands belonging to China which are separated from the mainland and its coastal islands by the high seas." In a note to Zhou Enlai on September 14, Pham Van Dong stated that the DRV "recognizes and supports" Beijing's September 4 declaration on China's territorial sea and "respects this decision."[83] As a recipient of Chinese aid, Hanoi considered it only practical not to contest Beijing's claims.

In January 1974, however, China clashed with South Vietnam over the Paracels. The Thieu government had established small garrisons on some islets of the Paracel group, and Beijing was determined to wrest control of these islands from Saigon. Zhou Enlai played the key role in organizing the Chinese operation. On January 18, 1974, he chaired a politburo meeting during which it was decided that a five-man group, including Ye Jianying, Wang Hongwen, Zhang Chunqiao, Deng Xiaoping, and Chen Xilian, would be established to take charge of major operations of the Central Military Commission as well as urgent war matters. Ye would serve as the director. Mao approved the decision. On January 19, Zhou Enlai asked Ye to summon a meeting of the five-man group to discuss plans for the Paracels operation. Su Zhenhua, first political commissar of the navy, also participated in the discussion. (Later, he became a member of the enlarged five-man group.)[84] The next day, the Chinese forces launched an attack and seized several islands in the Paracels that for several years had been occupied by the Saigon regime. In the evening, Zhou Enlai, who was the major leader and coordinator of China's actions, chaired another politburo meeting to hear reports on the Paracels operation. After the session, he informed Mao of the battle results.[85]

Hanoi reacted to the Paracels conflict by simply remarking that complex disputes over territories between neighbors frequently required careful examination and that "countries involved should settle such disputes by negotiation and in a spirit of equality, mutual respect, and good-neighborliness."[86] At a time when Hanoi still needed Chinese economic and military aid in waging the war in the south, it refrained from protesting against the Chinese action. Now, however, the DRV ambassador to France, Mai Van Bo, said that the 1974 Paracels war was China's "first act of armed aggression against Vietnam."[87]

In April 1975, on the eve of liberating Saigon, the DRV occupied six islands in the Spratleys, prompting a Chinese Foreign Ministry protest to the DRV embassy the following month.[88] With the war drawing to a close, Hanoi was no longer reluctant to press their territorial claims against China. Beijing's uncompromising stand on the Paracels and the Spratleys, as the China specialist Lucian Pye has observed, "checkmated Hanoi's hopes for a foreign exchange bonanza based on being able to lease clear titles for offshore drilling in the South China Sea."[89]

Since 1973, armed clashes had also begun to take place along the Sino-Vietnamese border. Each side later charged the other of provoking border skirmishes, which numbered 179 in 1974, according to Hanoi, and 121, according to Beijing. On March 18, 1975, Beijing suggested that the two countries negotiate to settle the issue, but Hanoi, pleading preoccupation with the liberation of the south, replied on April 12 that the issue would have to be resolved by local authorities on the two sides.[90] China apparently wanted to reach a settlement before the end of the war, while the DRV was still at a disadvantage.[91]

While its relations with Hanoi were deteriorating between 1973 and 1975, Beijing befriended the PRG during this time, displaying its preference for a political settlement and gradual unification of Vietnam. In November 1973, PRG president Nguyen Huu Tho visited China, where he received a warm welcome and met with Mao. At the conclusion of his trip, Beijing granted his government free economic aid for 1974.[92]

Representatives from the PRG clearly felt that Beijing was treating their government and the DRV differently during this period. According to Truong Nhu Tang, who served as the PRG's roving ambassador in the mid-1970s, he met Yao Wenyuan, an adviser to Mao on ideological matters, at a reception in Albania in late 1974. Yao at first did not know that Tang was representing the PRG, and he showed a cool attitude. Later, however, Yao found out that there was also a delegation from the DRV, "on which he could more appropriately vent his distaste for Vietnamese ingratitude."[93]

Chinese leaders' calculations about their future relations with Hanoi and their intention to preserve their ability to maneuver in Vietnam manifested themselves again in an incident in April 1975. With both DRV and PRG representatives present in Beijing, Vice Premier Li Xiannian deliberately hosted a reception in honor of the PRG, announcing that China had a cargo ship loaded with foodstuff, medicine, and other necessities ready to be dispatched to Danang or Saigon as soon as it was liberated. Truong Nhu Tang, who headed the PRG delegation, recalls: "The implicit meaning of this announcement was not lost on any of those present, from North or South. Throughout our stay the Chinese had treated us with a good deal more cordiality than they had the DRV delegation. They were plainly using this opportunity to express their feelings about Hanoi's already serious romance with the Soviets. At the same time, they were signaling to the PRG that they were open to independent contacts." Tang points out, however, that Beijing "misjudged both our ability and our readiness to respond to overtures of this sort."[94] In their desperation to keep options open, the Chinese clearly exaggerated the difference between the PRG and the DRV.

The new fissures that opened up in Sino–North Vietnamese relations over maritime and land boundaries would have been manageable in the absence of deeper geopolitical differences over the Hanoi-Moscow ties and the competition over influence in Southeast Asia. The rivalry over Cambodia during the final years of the war exemplified the emerging Sino-Vietnamese conflict over the future of the postwar Indochina. After the signing of the Paris agreement, Chinese leaders began to promote a cease-fire and a political settlement in Cambodia, which would remove North Vietnamese forces from that country and prevent what they suspected to be Soviet plans to fill the vacuum. In discussions with Kissinger, Nixon's national security adviser, in Beijing in February 1973, Zhou Enlai expressed China's concern about Moscow's intentions in Cambodia and urged Kissinger to negotiate with Sihanouk. Kissinger responded that it was "out of the question" for the United States to conduct a direct negotiation with Sihanouk while recognizing the Lon Nol government at the same time.[95] Beijing also supported France's efforts in late 1973 to return Sihanouk to Phnom Penh.[96]

Primarily because of the Khmer Rouge's opposition, a negotiated Cambodian solution did not materialize. The continuing war in Cambodia had provided the CPK under Pol Pot's leadership an opportunity to extend its influence within the resistance movement. With the withdrawal of three of the four North Vietnamese divisions fighting in Cambodia into Vietnam in late 1972, the CPK had been able to engineer anti-Vietnamese demonstrations, purge Sihanouk's supporters, and eliminate returnees from North Vietnam.[97]

Abandoning its previous reluctance to support the Khmer Rouge to seize power, China became eager to back its cause in the spring of 1974. In April, Khieu Samphan, deputy prime minister of the RGNUK and commander in chief of the Cambodian People's National Liberation Army, visited Beijing and met with Mao. He was the first Khmer Communist to be granted such an honor.[98] In an agreement with the RGNUK on May 26, China pledged to provide free military equipment and supplies. Beijing's decision to offer material aid to the Khmer Rouge may have been triggered by evidence that Hanoi was trying to strengthen its position in Cambodia, despite Pol Pot's efforts to eliminate pro-Vietnamese members from his party.[99] Beijing's warm reception of Khieu Samphan marked a clear shift in its policy away from a political settlement toward a military solution to the Cambodian problem. Realizing the determination and strength of the Khmer Rouge, Chinese leaders had apparently taken the position that if they wanted to maintain their influence over the Vietnamese and the Russians in Cambodia, they must back Pol Pot.

In November 1974, the Khmer Rouge closed in on Phnom Penh and blocked all overland routes to the capital, leaving only the Mekong River. They launched their 1975 dry-season offensive by showering Phnom Penh with a rocket and artillery barrage on New Year's Day. Government positions north of the capital collapsed immediately, and artillery pieces were abandoned.[100] To choke off the Mekong supply line, through which food, fuel, and military supplies were shipped by barge to Phnom Penh, Ieng Sary asked China to help mine the river in order to accelerate the defeat of the Lon Nol regime. Beijing immediately agreed, and the first batch of Chinese mines reached Cambodia via the DRV in January. The Khmer Rouge began to lay mines in the Mekong in February, shutting down traffic on the river and forcing Phnom Penh to rely on American airlifts for survival.[101]

On April 17, 1975, the Khmer Rouge seized Phnom Penh. With the war over, the Cambodians were no longer hesitant to assert their territorial claims against Vietnam, just as the Vietnamese were no longer inhibited to press theirs against China. Shortly after capturing the capital, the Khmer Rouge sent units to secure their land and sea border, occupying the islands in the Gulf of Thailand that the old regime had controlled or claimed. In June, Vietnamese troops subjugated the Cambodian garrison on Wai Island (Puolo Wai) and raised their flag over the island.[102] China expressed regret at Hanoi's action, urging the two sides to settle the issue through negotiations.[103]

On June 21, Pol Pot visited Beijing and received a hero's welcome from his ideological mentor, Mao. Excited by the victory of the Cambodian party, Mao told Pol Pot: "You have achieved in one stroke what we failed with all our masses."[104] Just as Stalin had felt reinvigorated by the success of the young Chinese Communists in 1949, the aging Mao now saw in Pol Pot's triumph a return to his own revolutionary youth.[105] Assuming the role of an elder brother, Mao told his Cambodian disciple that realizing communism was a tortuous process. Although Khrushchev and Leonid Brezhnev had deviated from Leninism, the Chinese leader continued, the Soviet Union would eventually return to Lenin's principles. The same was true for China: it might turn to revisionism in the future, but it would eventually return to the path of Marx and Lenin.[106] Mao fully approved Pol Pot's radical plans for Cambodia and his policy of seeking independence from Vietnam. He saw Cambodia as a counterbalance against Vietnamese ambitions in Indochina.

In 1975, Beijing reduced aid to the DRV while increasing assistance to Cambodia. In April, North Vietnamese troops occupied Saigon, and the last American helicopter, carrying Ambassador Graham Martin, left the roof of the U.S. embassy, ending an inglorious chapter in American history. Four months later, Le Thanh Nghi, chairman of DRV Planning Commission, scurried to Beijing to seek China's aid for Vietnam's postwar reconstruction. On August 16, Zhou Enlai informed Nghi of Beijing's inability to do so, noting that the corrupt Nguyen Van Thieu regime had left "large quantities of weapons, warehouses, air force, and naval facilities" for Hanoi.[107] In the meantime, however, China hosted a warm welcome to the Cambodian deputy premiers Khieu Samphan and Ieng Sary and promised them $1 billion of assistance over a five-year period. About $20 million of this aid was to be an outright grant.[108]

Tensions between the Chinese and Vietnamese parties were fully revealed during Le Duan's visit to Beijing in September 1975. This was Duan's first visit to China as leader of a unified and independent Vietnam. Mao told the Vietnamese visitor on September 24 that "today, you are not the poorest under the heaven. We are the poorest. We have a population of 800 million."[109] Mao's message was clear: Hanoi should stop looking to China for assistance.

Deputy Premier Deng Xiaoping was the chief Chinese negotiator in talks with Le Duan. The seventy-one-year-old Deng, once pilloried by the Red Guards as the "No. 2 top capitalist roader" during the Cultural Revolution, had been rehabilitated by Mao in 1973. With the now-ailing Zhou Enlai bedridden with cancer, Deng was in charge of daily government affairs. He presented Le Duan with Mao's "Three Worlds" theory, which divided the world into three categories of states: the superpowers, the weaker capitalist nations in the West and Japan, and the developing countries, including China. The doctrine called on the unity of the second and third worlds against the two superpowers, especially the most dangerous superpower, the Soviet Union. The Vietnamese perceived the "Three Worlds" theory as an indication that China had ceased to be a socialist state and was replacing the Marxist-Leninist view that the main contradiction in the world was between capitalism and socialism with the belief that the principal contradiction was between nationalism and socialism.[110] In Hanoi, the Vietnamese media's report on the speeches left out all of Deng's references to superpower hegemony.[111]

In a meeting with Le Duan on September 29, Deng expressed his anger at the appearance of anti-Chinese statements in the Vietnamese media: "We are not at ease when we get to read Vietnamese newspapers and know [Vietnamese] public opinion. In fact, you stress the threat from the North. The threat from the North for us is the existence of Soviet troops at our northern borders, but for you, it means China." Le Duan denied that Vietnam had made such remarks.[112] Clearly, by this time Deng had developed a hatred against what he saw as Hanoi's ingratitude. In 1966, he had already confronted Le Duan directly over the issue of anti-Chinese incidents in the DRV. Unlike Zhou Enlai and Chen Yi, who maintained close personal relationships with such Vietnamese leaders as Ho Chi Minh and Hoang Van Hoan, Deng lacked any deep individual attachment to the Vietnamese. This absence of emotional ties to the Vietnamese and a visceral bitterness about what he perceived as Hanoi's ungratefulness and arrogance help explain why he had no qualms about launching a war in 1979 "to teach Vietnam a lesson."

Le Duan concluded his visit to China without issuing the customary joint communiqué, which indicated the ever-increasing gap between the two parties. He even scrapped the usual return banquet for his hosts, a move that a Chinese official later called "an extraordinary act for a fraternal party leader."[113] Postwar Vietnam had displayed its first open defiance against China.

Acknowledging that Hanoi would not follow their policy of opposing Soviet hegemony, the Chinese notified the Vietnamese that Beijing would not be able to continue providing grants-in-aid at the 1973 level, as Zhou Enlai had pledged. China later told Hanoi that grant aid would stop after 1976 and that it would only be able to offer half of the estimated $600 million annually that the Vietnamese had hoped to receive for their 1976–80 Five-Year Plan in long-term, interest free loans. In October, Le Duan visited Moscow, where Soviet leaders reportedly promised more than $3 billion to Vietnam's Five-Year Plan, $1 billion of which would be in grants. Duan also signed a joint communiqué endorsing Soviet international positions.[114]

As the American threat faded away, Hanoi's bilateral disputes and regional rivalries with China began to come to the fore, pitting the two former comrades as adversaries. The time had arrived for the Vietnamese to follow their own separate nationalist path uninhibited by the wartime considerations of solidarity with China. The long historical conflict between China and Vietnam, previously overshadowed by the French and American interventions and now intensified by different assessments of Moscow's intentions and divergent views of an acceptable regional order in Indochina, had returned to life.

CONCLUSION
THE DUALITY OF CHINA'S POLICY

There were two strands in China's policy toward Vietnam during the two Indochina wars: cooperation and containment. Beijing cooperated with Ho Chi Minh's party in its struggle against France and the United States by investing enormous amounts of energy and resources. This cooperation served China's geopolitical and ideological interests of eliminating a hostile imperialist presence from its southern border and spreading revolution in Indochina. While supporting the vwp's efforts to preserve independence and achieve reunification, Chinese leaders also sought to contain its tendency to establish domination over Laos and Cambodia. These conflicting strands in China's policy made the prc and the drv both comrades and adversaries.

From the 1950s to 1968, the cooperation side of China's policy was predominant. During this period, Chinese leaders were more concerned with the threats from the United States than with the prospects of a Vietnam-controlled Indochina. They found great value in their revolutionary solidarity with the Vietnamese Communists in the common struggle against Western capitalist countries. But they would not hesitate to check Vietnam's aspirations for domination in Cambodia and Laos when they detected such tendencies, as happened at the 1954 Geneva Conference. While Beijing's accommodation of Sihanouk and Souvanna Phouma was primarily designed to keep them from falling into the American orbit, it also reflected a calculation to use these nationalist leaders as potential buffers against future Vietnamese attempts to dominate Indochina.

From the late 1960s, particularly between 1972 and 1975, the containment side of China's policy became more prominent. With the intensification of the Sino-Soviet conflict and the deepening of the ties between Hanoi and Moscow in the late 1960s, policymakers in Beijing became increasingly concerned with the prospects of a postwar Indochina dominated by Vietnam in alliance with the Soviet Union. The U.S. disengagement from Vietnam and the suspicion of Moscow's plan to fill the void made Chinese leaders far more worried about how the Vietnam War would end than about whether the war would become a Sino-American confrontation. Between 1968 and 1969, Beijing urged Hanoi not to encourage revolution in Cambodia. During the Cambodian crisis of 1970, Beijing pursued a two-track policy of backing Sihanouk and exploring possible cooperation with Lon Nol in hopes of preserving China's influence in the country. In the last two years of the war, while continuing to assist the DRV in its final drive to unify Vietnam, Beijing also increased aid to the anti-Vietnamese Khmer Rouge in order to contain the expansion of Hanoi's influence in Cambodia.

THE DYNAMICS OF THE SINO-DRV ALLIANCE

During the Second Indochina War, the DRV was a small power caught in the fight of three giants. It had to confront not only the military might of the United States but also the political and ideological pressure from China and the Soviet Union. While Washington wanted Hanoi to stop its efforts to unify the south, the Chinese and the Russians pressed the Vietnamese Communists to follow their respective international policies. Both Beijing and Moscow approached the Vietnam conflict to advance their own self-interests.

The political scientist Glenn Snyder's description of the alliance security dilemma can be usefully applied to illuminate the problems in the alliance between China and the DRV. According to Snyder, the alliance security dilemma involves a choice between support or nonsupport of allies and tension between fear of entrapment and fear of abandonment.[1] In the late 1950s and early 1960s, Ho Chi Minh was afraid of being entrapped by China in the Sino-Indian conflict and the Sino-Soviet dispute. He did not want to be dragged into conflicts over interests that he did not share with China. Therefore, he visited Beijing and Moscow in 1960 in an attempt to heal the breach between Mao and Khrushchev and to promote unity in the international Communist movement. In the late 1960s and early 1970s, the Vietnamese Communists began to fear that China would abandon the DRV in its search for rapprochement with the United States. Thus Pham Van Dong went to Beijing in November 1971 asking Mao not to invite President Nixon to China.

While policymakers in Hanoi constantly feared being betrayed by their big allies, they were not submissive puppets of Beijing or Moscow. In fact, they were highly self-willed and independent actors who were able to make their own strategic choices, particularly during the Second Vietnam War, often without consulting China or the Soviet Union. They were weak but not meek. They displayed remarkable patience and skill in navigating the shoals of the Sino-Soviet feud. The successive changes and adjustments in their attitudes toward either Beijing or Moscow between 1954 and 1975 depended primarily on the two capitals' policies toward Hanoi's objective of national reunification.

The Sino-DRV alliance was one of mutual needs. While Hanoi wanted China's aid in its struggle against France and the United States, Beijing also needed the DRV's support for its foreign policy goals. Chinese leaders' apprehension of a U.S.-sponsored encirclement made them prize the geopolitical value of Vietnam. As their ideological dispute with the Soviet Union and their border conflict with India escalated in the late 1950s and early 1960s, they sought Hanoi's endorsement of their position.[2]

Mao and his associates, however, often ignored the interests, priorities, and needs of the VWP. Their advice to the DRV not to rely on Soviet support and their disapproval of Hanoi's strategy of fighting while negotiating clearly demonstrated this tendency. For the North Vietnamese, the Russian connection was crucial. Moscow provided not only advanced weaponry but also international contact for the DRV. The Soviet Union was a member of the UN Security Council, it maintained diplomatic relations with the United States, and it enjoyed a wider contact with the global community. Especially in the early stage of the war between 1965 and 1967, the USSR played the role of Hanoi's envoy in its dialogue with the West. Soviet officials and diplomats informed their counterparts in Washington, Paris, London, and other Western capitals of Hanoi's stance on various issues regarding the settlement of the war. They also supplied the North Vietnamese with information on Western views.[3] Chinese leaders, however, were jealous of this Soviet role in Vietnam. They treated Vietnam as a pawn in their strategy against Moscow.

A CLASH OF TWO VISIONS

In a deeper historical sense, the Sino-Vietnamese conflict was caused by the clash of the competing visions held by the leaders of the two countries regarding their respective roles in Indochina. These visions or self-images were informed by historical memory as well as concerns for national prestige and destiny. What Mao and his comrades sought in their commitment to revolutionary struggle was not just the rescue of China from the clutches of perennial poverty, warlord rule, and imperialist penetration but also the rejuvenation of the Chinese nation and the restoration of its historical greatness in East Asia. Historically speaking, the Chinese held a Sino-centric view of the world, regarding other countries as inferior. The Celestial Emperor in the Forbidden City considered small nations on China's periphery, including Vietnam, as within the orbit of China's influence and kept those countries within the tributary system.

Despite his claims of adherence to Marxism and Leninism, Mao fully inherited China's historical legacy. His strong belief in the absolute correctness and universal relevance of his revolutionary practice and theory for the oppressed peoples of the world against colonialism and imperialism was reminiscent of the claims of Chinese imperial rulers about the superiority of Chinese models and institutions.[4] He felt perplexed and indignant when the Vietnamese Communists refused to echo the Chinese line in the Sino-Soviet quarrel after 1965 or when Hanoi defied his wish that it not enter into negotiations with the United States in 1968.

Ho Chi Minh and his associates were also conscientious students of history. What they sought in their struggle against the French and the Americans was not just the end of Vietnam's suffering under colonialism but also the reconstruction of their motherland and the reestablishment of its leading role in Indochina. Since the restoration of independence from Chinese control in the tenth century, Vietnamese imperial rulers exercised hegemony over their neighbors to the west and introduced a tributary system in mainland Southeast Asia. After the establishment of the Indochinese Communist Party in 1930,[5] party strategists saw Indochina as a single strategic space and assumed a leading role for Vietnam in guiding the revolutionary struggle in Laos and Cambodia. Although the Indochinese Communist Party was dissolved in 1951 and separate Communist organizations were established in Laos and Cambodia, Vietnamese strategic thinking remained unchanged.

The CCP's attempt to assert China's influence over Indochina was contradictory to the VWP's effort to maintain its "special relationship" with Laos and Cambodia. In the mid-1960s, when Beijing dispatched an advisory team to Pathet Lao territory, the North Vietnamese advisers there defended their superior position by minimizing the role of their Chinese competitors.

In the end, it was not just the United States that lost the Vietnam War. China also failed in Vietnam. It had shed blood and spent enormous amounts of material resources in Vietnam but had not secured the gratitude and goodwill of the Vietnamese. Instead of having strengthened security along its southern frontier, China found itself at the end of the war highly insecure and vulnerable as Hanoi moved closer to the Soviet Union. Rather than enhancing its influence in Vietnam, Beijing discovered that after the withdrawal of the American forces, Moscow had greatly increased its presence there. China's post-1975 predicament and vulnerability in Indochina was primarily a self-inflicted wound, the result of Chinese leaders' ethnocentrism and paternalism in dealing with the Vietnamese. The Chinese-Vietnamese dispute was determined not only by the contemporary conflict of the two countries' national interests but also by the historically rooted mutual distrust and suspicion.

BROADER IMPLICATIONS

What does this study of the Sino-DRV relationship inform us of the general characteristics of Chinese foreign policy? First, it highlights the centrality of Mao's ideas, visions, and aspirations. Mao was an extremely self-willed and self-confident man. He strongly believed that history was on his side and that his theory provided the key to the problems created by the global trend of national liberation and revolution. His ideology was a unique mixture, including both clearly defined and neatly packaged formal formulations of Marxism-Leninism and poorly articulated informal beliefs and assumptions.[6] Mao carried to his dealings with world affairs sets of values, presuppositions, preferences, and expectations that stemmed from three principal sources: his socialization into a specific culture at a particular period of time; his formative experiences and career path; his conscious choices as a thinking political actor from the menu of systems of thought available to him.[7]

What motivated Mao's foreign policy was his vision of China's place in the world. This vision was shaped not only by Mao's reading of Marxism-Leninism but also by his awareness of China's traditional images of itself and other countries. Determined to end his country's humiliation at the hands of imperialism, Mao intended to transform it from a backward nation to a modern state and reestablish its central position in the world. To Mao, the consolidation and legitimization of his regime in China required a correspondent transformation of the existing Western-dominated international system. In Mao's calculations, security interests and ideological beliefs were closely linked. Defining security concerns in ideological terms, Mao saw an intimate relationship between security and prosperity at home and the spread of anti-imperialist revolutions abroad.

For a long time, the realist paradigm has dominated the literature on international relations, consigning the role of ideas to a marginal position. This study has tried to demonstrate that realpolitik was not the only language spoken by the Chinese leaders. Mao and his comrades were motivated not only by self-preservation and self-aggrandizement but also by a desire to see entitlements fulfilled or respected.[8] They certainly responded to international events and adjusted their policies accordingly. (Their policy turnaround vis-à-vis the United States in the early 1970s was a clear example.) But they were also men of firm beliefs and convictions. They were driven above all by pictures of what they wanted China to become, and it was these visions that determined foreign policy.[9]

This study also reveals the close linkage between Mao's domestic politics and international policy. Mao was a master in manipulating international tensions to secure internal advantages. Just like his exploitation of the crisis in the Taiwan Strait in 1958 to marshal popular support for the Great Leap Forward,[10] Mao skillfully used the conflict in Indochina in the 1960s to break down opposition within the party to his agenda of "continuous revolution," to reinstill ideological commitment among the Chinese population, and to mobilize its enthusiasm for the Great Cultural Revolution.

Finally, this study of the tumultuous relationship between Beijing and Hanoi demonstrates Mao's preoccupation with the Soviet factor in the making of China's foreign policy. Mao and his associates were obsessed by their paranoid fear of anyone engaged in close relations with Moscow. From the late 1950s, when the quenchless feud between Beijing and Moscow erupted, Mao had habitually judged the vwp with the yardstick of anti-Soviet revisionism that distorted far more than it illuminated. This tendency to evaluate fraternal parties through the prism of anti-Soviet revisionism also manifested itself in Mao's attitudes toward Cuba in the 1960s. Just like the deterioration of Beijing-Hanoi relations, the worsening of Chinese-Cuban ties in the mid-1960s derived primarily from Mao's dissatisfaction with Castro's flirtations with Moscow.[11] Mao and his lieutenants were too much prisoners of their competition with the Soviets. Their fixation with Soviet intentions and activities resulted in a distorted understanding of the basic forces at work in Indochina.[12]

What does this account of the waxing and waning of Beijing-Hanoi cooperation tell us about the maintenance of alliances on the Communist side during the Cold War? The Sino-DRV coalition, a product of the Cold War, failed to survive the end of that conflict. Why? Just as in the fragile Sino-Soviet alliance, there was a lack of spontaneous economic or political integration in Sino-Vietnamese relations. In contrast to the sound structure of the American–West European–Japanese alliance, where a close economic integration existed as a result of the globalization of the market and investments, the Communist camp carried out, in the phrase of one Cold War historian, "a raw deal," donating or bartering goods, services, and technology within the confines of its rather limited resources.[13]

In addition to this structural defect, Mao's authoritarian instinct was in no way helpful to the smooth functioning of the Sino-DRV relationship. Mao was, by habit and history, autocratic in his approach to politics. He was not used to accommodating independent thinking. The "bargaining and deal-making, the coercion and conciliation," to use John Lewis Gaddis's words, which characterized the democratic system, were foreign to the Chinese dictator.[14] His insistence on the wisdom and centrality of the Chinese model and experience was easily perceived by the Vietnamese as arrogance, bigotry, and prejudice.

NOTES

ABBREVIATIONS

Black Paper	*Black Paper: Facts and Evidences of the Acts of Aggression and Annexation of Vietnam against Kampuchea* (Phnom Penh: Department of Press and Information of the Ministry of Foreign Affairs of Democratic Kampuchea, September 1978).
FRUS	U.S. Department of State. *Foreign Relations of the United States, 1950–1968*. Washington, D.C.: Government Printing Office, 1976–98.
J	Juanhao (File).
JPA	Jiangsu Provincial Archives.
Liu nianpu	The CCP Central Documentary Research Department, ed., *Liu Shaoqi nianpu, 1898–1969* (A Chronicle of Liu Shaoqi's Life, 1898–1969), 2 vols. (Beijing: Zhongyang wenxian chubanshe, 1996).
Mao junshi wenji	The CCP Central Documentary Research Department and the PLA Military Science Academy, eds., *Mao Zedong junshi wenji* (Collection of Mao Zedong's Military Writings), 6 vols. (Beijing: Junshi kexue chubanshe and Zhongyang wenxian chubanshe, 1993).
Mao waijiao wenxuan	The PRC Foreign Ministry and the CCP Central Documentary Research Department, eds., *Mao Zedong waijiao wenxuan* (Selected Diplomatic Works of Mao Zedong) (Beijing: Zhongyang wenxian chubanshe and Shijie zhishi chubanshe, 1994).
Mao wengao	The CCP Central Documentary Research Department, ed., *Jianguo yilai Mao Zedong wengao* (Mao Zedong's Manuscripts since the Founding of the Country), 13 vols. (Beijing: Zhongyang wenxian chubanshe, 1987–98).
"77 Conversations"	Odd Arne Westad, Chen Jian, Stein Tonnesson, Nguyen Vu Tung, and James G. Hershberg, eds., "77 Conversations between Chinese and Foreign Leaders on the Wars in Indochina, 1964–1977," Cold War International History Project Working Paper No. 22 (Washington, D.C.: Woodrow Wilson International Center for Scholars, 1998).

Q	Quanzhonghao (Record Group).
White Paper	Ministry of Foreign Affairs of the Socialist Republic of Viet Nam, *The Truth about Vietnam-China Relations over the Last Thirty Years* (Hanoi: 1979).
Zhongguo junshi guwentuan	The Editorial Team on the History of the CMAG, ed., *Zhongguo junshi guwentuan yuanYue kangFa douzheng shishi* (Historical Facts about the Role of the Chinese Military Advisory Group in the Struggle of Aiding Vietnam and Resisting France) (Beijing: Jiefangjun chubanshe, 1990).
Zhou nianpu	The CCP Central Documentary Research Department, ed., *Zhou Enlai nianpu, 1949–1976* (A Chronicle of Zhou Enlai's Life, 1949–1976), 3 vols. (Beijing: Zhongyang wenxian chubanshe, 1997).
Zhou waijiao dashiji	The Diplomatic History Research Office of the PRC Foreign Ministry, ed., *Zhou Enlai waijiao huodong dashiji, 1949–1975* (A Chronicle of Zhou Enlai's Diplomatic Activities, 1949–1975) (Beijing: Shijie zhishi chubanshe, 1993).

INTRODUCTION

1 Although there was no formal alliance treaty between them, China and North Vietnam functioned as a close partnership during the 1950s and 1960s.

2 For criticism of a similar tendency to ignore or downgrade China's role in the 1940–45 Vietnam story see Marr, *Vietnam 1945*, 6.

3 Vo Nguyen Giap, *People's War, People's Army*.

4 Before the 1990s, a limited scholarship existed on China's involvement in the Indochina conflicts. King Chen's *Vietnam and China* has long remained the standard account of Beijing's role in the First Vietnam War. While strong in its coverage of Ho Chi Minh's interactions with the Chinese Nationalists, it is weak in its discussion of the CCP's role in Vietnam. Based primarily upon Chinese newspapers and other public sources, Chen's discussion of the performance of Mao's military advisers in assisting the Viet Minh army is sometimes inaccurate. Melvin Gurtov's *First Vietnam Crisis* discusses briefly China's commitment to the Viet Minh.

Beijing's policy toward the Second Vietnam War has attracted relatively more attention from scholars. Some writers have examined China's decisions regarding Indochina in the context of its worldwide competition with the United States and the Soviet Union. For example, see Zagoria, *Vietnam Triangle*, and Papp, *Vietnam*. Some authors have explored the linkage between Beijing's Vietnam policy and interparty politics. See, for example, Gurtov and Hwang, *China under Threat*. The Kremlinologist method adopted in the volume, however, sometimes leads the authors to erroneous conclusions. For instance, Gurtov and Hwang try to establish a causal link between such internal party disputes as the purge of Luo Ruiqing, chief of staff of the PLA, in 1965 and the so-called dispute over China's response to the American escalation in Vietnam. But new sources from China make it clear that Luo's dismissal from office had nothing to do with China's Vietnam policy. The so-called strategic debate in 1965 was nonexistent.

Other scholars have used Vietnam as an example of Beijing's employment of force and practice of deterrence. See, for example, Whiting, *Chinese Calculus of Deterrence*. Still others have explored the roots of conflict between China and the DRV. See in particular Lawson, *Sino-Vietnamese Conflict*; Duiker, *China and Vietnam*; and Gilks, *Breakdown of the Sino-Vietnamese Alliance*. Finally, R. B. Smith's multivolume *International History of the Vietnam War* addresses the international dimensions of the conflict, including the Chinese perspective. None of these authors has benefited, however, from Chinese archival sources.

Since 1992 a number of articles have been written, including four by this author, that use newly released Chinese archival materials to reconstruct Beijing's role in the First and Second Indochina Wars. See Zhai, "China and the Geneva Conference of 1954"; Zhai, "Transplanting the Chinese Model"; Zhai, "Beijing and the Vietnam Conflict; Zhai, "Opposing Negotiations"; Chen Jian, "China and the First Indo-China War"; Chen Jian, "China's Involvement in the Vietnam War"; and Xiaoming Zhang, "Vietnam War." Ang Cheng Guan, *Vietnamese Communists' Relations with China and the Second Indochina Conflict*, makes some use of recently available Chinese sources to reconstruct the evolution of Sino-DRV relations from 1956 to 1962.

5 The titles of their books and articles can be found in the bibliography.

CHAPTER ONE

1 Huang Zheng, *Hu Zhiming yu Zhongguo*, 6–9, 17–39; He Yanhong, "Qingyi shensihai," 5–12.
2 Hong Zuojun, "Fengyu qianzaiqing," 25.
3 Huang Zheng, *Hu Zhiming yu Zhongguo*, 32–34.
4 Duiker, "Seeds of the Dragon," 316; Quinn-Fudge, "Ho Chi Minh," 63.
5 According to Huynh Kim Khanh, *Vietnamese Communism*, 123–29, the designation of the Indochinese Communist Party was imposed by a Comintern instruction in late 1929 and adopted reluctantly in 1930 by the Vietnamese Communists. See also Brown, "Indochinese Federation Idea," 85–86.
6 Huang Zheng, *Hu Zhiming yu Zhongguo*, 53–65; Duiker, "Seeds of the Dragon," 317–18.
7 Huang Zheng, *Hu Zhiming yu Zhongguo*, 77–80, 111–13; Herring, *America's Longest War*, 5–6; Duiker, "Seeds of the Dragon," 318–20.
8 Wu Jilin, "Yiduan xianwei renzhi de yuanYue kangFa lishi," 23–26.
9 Ibid. According to Huang Zheng, *Hu Zhiming yu Zhongguo*, 123, the total number of the First Regiment was about 600.
10 Wu Jilin, "Yiduan xianwei renzhi de yuanYue kangFa lishi," 23–26.
11 Gao Hongdi, "Jiefang zhanzheng shiqi Zhongguo gongchandang zai Xianggang de caijing gongzuo," 92–101. This source does not mention the amount of the money provided by the CCP Hong Kong Sub-Bureau to the Viet Minh.
12 Huang Zheng, *Hu Zhiming yu Zhongguo*, 123; Qu Xing, "Shilun Mao Zedong guanyu ZhongFa guanxi de zhanlue sixiang," 247.
13 Duiker, *Sacred War*, 60.
14 Zagoria, *Vietnam Triangle*, 36–38; Kahin, *Intervention*, 21–22.
15 Duiker, *Communist Road to Power in Vietnam*, 142. According to Vietnamese historians Pham Xanh and Do Quang Hung, Stalin's suspicion of Ho Chi Minh's revolutionary credentials greatly reduced his interest in Indochina. After the adoption of the ultra-

leftist policy by the Sixth World Congress of the Comintern in 1928, Stalin began to criticize Ho's emphasis on national liberation rather than proletarian social revolution and remained distrustful of his objectives for Vietnam until Mao effected a rapprochement between Stalin and Ho in 1950. Cited in Bradley, "Improbable Opportunity," 19.

16 Bukharkin, "Moscow and Ho Chi Minh," 3–7. For a plausible explanation, without the benefit of Soviet archives, of Soviet policy toward insurgent movements in Southeast Asia in the late 1940s, see Duiker, *U.S. Containment Policy and the Conflict in Indochina*, 62–65.

17 Luo Guibo, "Lishi de huigu," 152–53.

18 Ibid., 153.

19 Liu to Ho, Dec. 28, 1949, in *Liu nianpu*, 2:236.

20 Luo Guibo, "Lishi de huigu," 153.

21 Ibid., 152.

22 Luo Guibo, "Shaoqi tongzhi paiwo chushi Yuenan," 235.

23 Mao to Liu, Jan. 17, 1950, in *Mao wengao*, 1:238.

24 Pei Jianzhang, *Zhonghua renmin gongheguo waijiaoshi*, 32.

25 Goncharov, Lewis, and Xue Litai, *Uncertain Partners*, 107. For the French apprehension about the American intention to enlarge the North Atlantic Treaty Organization by admitting a rearmed West Germany, see Leffler, *Preponderance of Power*, 277–86, 317–23.

26 Scholars have debated about the implications of the so-called four-day delay in Beijing's recognition of the DRV. Robert Simmons in his 1975 study of the Korean War noted that there was a lag of four days between the DRV's request on January 14 and China's granting of recognition on January 18. This four-day delay, Simmons argued, indicated that Beijing was not eager to establish formal relations with the DRV that would undermine China's future ties with the West. He contended that "the PRC delayed its recognition of the Ho Chi Minh government until its probable effect of alienating the French vote in the United Nations Security Council no longer had a bearing upon its admission." Simmons concluded that Beijing's reaction, together with its increasingly militant policy toward Washington, "rather than being irrational or impulsive actions generated by ideological machismo, were in fact calculated moves by the PRC, which were assessed in terms of probable costs and benefits" (*Strained Alliance*, 96–97). New Chinese sources suggest that there was no deliberate delay in China's response. Mao demonstrated not the slightest hesitation in recognizing the DRV. He appears to have been motivated primarily by ideological solidarity with the Vietnamese Communists.

27 Dalloz, *War in Indo-China*, 129; Gardner, *Approaching Vietnam*, 83–84.

28 Luo Guibo, "Lishi de huigu," 160; Luo Guibo, "Shaoqi tongzhi paiwo chushi Yuenan," 236.

29 Liu to the CCP Central South Bureau, Jan. 26, 1950, *Liu nianpu*, 2:241.

30 Liu to Mao, Jan. 30, 1950, ibid.

31 Luo Guibo, "Shaoqi tongzhi paiwo chushi Yuenan," 235–36.

32 Mao and Zhou to Liu, Feb. 1, 1950, *Mao wengao*, 1:254.

33 Hoang Van Hoan, *Canghai yisu*, 255–56. Hoan was mistaken when he wrote that Mao hosted a banquet in the Zhongnanhai compound in honor of Ho. In fact, Mao was in Moscow at this time.

34 Hoang Van Hoan, *Canghai yisu*, 256; Wu Xiuquan, *Zai waijiaobu banian de jingli*, 13. A member of the Chinese delegation, Wu Xiuquan participated in the Sino-Soviet treaty negotiations as director of the Department of Soviet and East European Affairs of the

Chinese Foreign Ministry. He was present at the banquet honoring Mao. According to Khrushchev, Stalin was indifferent to Ho in Moscow. See Khrushchev, *Khrushchev Remembers: The Glasnost Tapes*, 154–56.

35 Luo Guibo, "Lishi de huigu," 161–62.

36 Luo Guibo, "Shaoqi tongzhi paiwo chushi Yuenan," 241.

37 Liu to Luo, April 13, 1950, *Liu nianpu*, 2:247.

38 For Mao's ten military principles, see Mao, "The Present Situation and Our Task," Dec. 25, 1947, in Mao, *Selected Military Writings of Mao Tse*, 349–50.

39 Han Huaizhi and Tan Jingqiao, *Dangdai Zhongguo jundui de junshi gongzuo*, 1:518–20; *Zhongguo junshi guwentuan*, 3.

40 Liu to Luo, May 19, 1950, *Liu nianpu*, 2:251.

41 *Zhongguo junshi guwentuan*, 3–4. Born in Hanoi in 1906, Hong Thuy participated in the Long March and the anti-Japanese war in China. He returned to Vietnam at the end of World War II. In October 1950, Hong Thuy came back to China and worked in the PLA until he died of cancer in 1956. For a biographical sketch of Hong Thuy, see Xu Zhongliang, "Renmin jiefangjun lishi shang de waiji jiangjun," 17–18.

According to Li Haiwen, a researcher at the CCP Central Documentary Research Department, after returning to Vietnam in 1945, Hong Thuy got into a serious dispute with Vo Nguyen Giap and had to leave Vietnam in 1950 (author interview with Li Haiwen, January 9, 1996). Giap's distrust of Hong Thuy may have reflected the inherent Vietnamese suspicion of China because, in the eyes of Giap, Hong Thuy carried too much Chinese influence. The Giap–Hong Thuy dispute is reminiscent of the Mao–Wang Ming animosity in the 1940s. Wang returned to China after spending many years in the Soviet Union, and Mao distrusted him for following Moscow's line blindly.

42 Zhou to Ho, July 7, 1950, in *Zhou nianpu*, 1:53.

43 Bukharkin, "Moscow and Ho Chi Minh," 8–9.

44 *Zhongguo junshi guwentuan*, 44.

45 Lockhart, *Nation in Arms*, 226.

46 On the effects of the Korean fighting on Mao's Taiwan plan, see Zhai, *Dragon, the Lion, and the Eagle*, 96–98, and He Di, " 'Last Campaign to Unify China.' "

47 In late 1950 and early 1951, Mao sent many telegrams to PLA commanders in South China asking them to step up their campaigns of "bandit" elimination. These telegrams are included in *Mao wengao*, vols. 1–2.

48 On the linkage between the revival of China and the reorganization of the global system in the Chinese Communist conception, see Hunt, *Genesis of Chinese Communist Foreign Policy*, 213.

49 Party directive, Mar. 14, 1950, *Liu nianpu*, 2:245.

50 Gaddis, *We Now Know*, 160. For a useful description of Mao's "messianic revolutionary nationalism," see Meisner, *Mao's China and After*, 41–45.

51 On the role of a utopian vision in revolutionary movements, see Skocpol, *States and Social Revolutions*, 169–71, and Garver, "Polemics," 13–14.

52 Dittmer, *Sino-Soviet Normalization and Its International Implications*, 121. See also Gurtov, *First Vietnam Crisis*, 7–8.

53 Goncharov, Lewis, and Xue Litai, *Uncertain Partners*, 105.

54 Lu Dingyi, "Zhongguo geming de shijie yiyi" (The World Significance of the Chinese Revolution), June 30, 1951, in Lu Dingyi, *Lu Dingyi wenji*, 432–39. Lu Dingyi's article was

also published in the Cominform journal, *For a Lasting Peace, for a People's Democracy* (June 29, 1951). See Post, *Revolution, Socialism and Nationalism in Viet Nam*, 1:210.

55 For an excellent discussion of foreign policy and China's national identity, see Dittmer and Kim, *China's Quest for National Identity*.

56 Shi Zhe, *Zai lishi juren shenbian*, 412. Shi Zhe went to the Soviet Union as Liu's Russian-language interpreter. For Liu's Soviet trip, see Zhai, *Dragon, the Lion, and the Eagle*, 21–23, and Zhu Yuanshi, "Liu Shaoqi 1949 nian mimi fangSu," 74–89.

57 Liu to Chen and Song, Mar. 3, 1950, *Liu nianpu*, 2:244.

58 Goncharov, Lewis, and Xue Litai, *Uncertain Partners*, 106.

59 Mao to Hu, Jan. 14, 1950, *Mao wengao*, 1:237.

60 Luo Guibo, "Lishi de huigu," 157.

61 On this point, see Chai Chengwen and Zhao Yongtian, *Banmendian tanpan*, 39–40, and Chen Jian, *China's Road to the Korean War*, 107–9.

62 *Zhongguo junshi guwentuan*, 5–6.

63 The fullest treatment of traditional Chinese views of the world can be found in Fairbank, *Chinese World Order*; Mancall, *China at the Center*, 13–39; and Hunt, "Chinese Foreign Relations in Historical Perspective," 1–42. For the episode of Qianlong's intervention in Vietnam between 1788 and 1790, see Truong Buu Lam, "Intervention versus Tribute in Sino-Vietnamese Relations," 165–79.

64 Woodside, *Vietnam and the Chinese Model*; Keith Taylor, "China and Vietnam," 271–85.

65 Liu to Luo, May 8, 1950, *Liu nianpu*, 2:250.

66 *Zhongguo junshi guwentuan*, 6.

67 Luo Guibo, "Shaoqi tongzhi paiwo chushi Yuenan," 238.

68 Hoang Van Hoan, *Canghai yisu*, 274–78. William Duiker stresses the pragmatic consideration of the Viet Minh leadership in their open praise for the Chinese model during this period. He writes that "stroking the egos of Chinese leaders may have been a major reason for the new public deference to China" (*Communist Road to Power in Vietnam*, 148).

69 Han Huaizhi and Tan Jingqiao, *Dangdai Zhongguo jundui de junshi gongzuo*, 1:520; Luo, "Shaoqi tongzhi paiwo chushi Yuenan," 240.

70 For Chen Geng's career, see Xu Peilan and Zheng Pengfei, *Chen Geng jiangjun zhuan*.

71 Liu to Chen, June 18, 1950, *Liu nianpu*, 2:255.

72 Mu Xin, *Ji Chen Geng jiangjun*, 245; *Jiefangjun jiangling zhuan*, 3:252–53.

73 Sun Tzu, *Art of War*, 129.

74 Chen diary entry, July 22, 1950, *Chen Geng riji (xu)*, 11.

75 Chen to the CCP leadership, July 22, 1950, and the CCP Central Military Commission to Chen, July 26, 1950, quoted in Han Huaizhi and Tan Jingqiao, *Dangdai Zhongguo jundui de junshi gongzuo*, 1:522–23.

76 *Jiefangjun jiangling zhuan*, 3:253.

77 Ibid., 253–54; Mu Xin, *Ji Chen Geng jiangjun*, 246.

78 Chen diary entry, July 29, 1950, *Chen Geng riji (xu)*, 13.

79 Han Huaizhi and Tan Jingqiao, *Dangdai Zhongguo jundui de junshi gongzuo*, 1:520; *Zhongguo junshi guwentuan*, 4.

80 Chen diary entries, Aug. 14, 15, 24, and Sept. 10, 11, 1950, *Chen Geng riji (xu)*, 17–19, 24; Han Huaizhi and Tan Jingqiao, *Dangdai Zhongguo jundui de junshi gongzuo*, 1:523–24. King Chen (*Vietnam and China*, 262) made an error in his account of Chen Geng's

activities during this period. He referred to a meeting in Nanning in August 1950 attended by Chen Geng and Viet Minh generals. Actually, Chen Geng was in Vietnam at this time.

81 Specialist Viet Minh artillery operators had received training on gunnery ranges at Jingxi and Longzhou in Guangxi province. Lockhart, *Nation in Arms*, 227.

82 Chen diary entries, Sept. 17, 18, 19, 29, 1950, *Chen Geng riji (xu)*, 26–27, 29.

83 Han Huaizhi and Tan Jingqiao, *Dangdai Zhongguo jundui de junshi gongzuo*, 1:525.

84 Chen diary entries, Sept. 19, 20, 1950, *Chen Geng riji (xu)*, 26–27.

85 Chen diary entries, Oct. 2, 3, 4, 5, 6, 7, 1950, ibid., 30–33.

86 Duiker, *Communist Road to Power in Vietnam*, 152–53.

87 Ibid., 153.

88 Mao to Chen (undated), quoted in Han Huaizhi and Tan Jingqiao, *Dangdai Zhongguo jundui de junshi gongzuo*, 1:526.

89 Chen diary entry, Oct. 11, 1950, *Chen Geng riji (xu)*, 34.

90 Chen diary entries, Oct. 27, 28–30, 1950, ibid., 38–39; Han Huaizhi and Tan Jingqiao, *Dangdai Zhongguo jundui de junshi gongzuo*, 1:526–27. According to Zhang Dequn, a Chinese political adviser in Vietnam, during the border campaign Viet Minh officers showed reluctance to lead the charge against the enemy. As a result, Chinese advisers had to perform that role. In the end, over twenty Chinese advisers were wounded in the battle, which caused resentment among them. See Zhang Dequn, "YuanYue guwentuan gongzuo suoyi," 72.

91 Chen diary entry, Oct. 13, 1950, *Chen Geng riji (xu)*, 34.

92 Chen diary entry, Oct. 25, 1950, ibid., 38; Mu Xin, *Ji Chen Geng jiangjun*, 248–49; Hoang Van Hoan, *Canghai yisu*, 273–74.

93 Duiker, *Communist Road to Power in Vietnam*, 155.

94 Giap's statement was quoted in ibid., 150–51.

95 Ibid., 155.

96 *Zhongguo junshi guwentuan*, 26–28.

97 Both Edgar O'Ballance and King Chen argued that in launching the offensive in early 1951, Vo Nguyen Giap acted independently of the Chinese advisers. O'Ballance wrote that the "Chinese advisers had seen that Giap was too anxious to run before he could walk, and cautioned against impetuous action, but the Viet Minh were rather reluctant to take such advice" (*Indo-China War*, 141). King Chen contended that in ordering the Operation Hoang Hoa Tham I, Giap "dismissed" the cautious Chinese advice (*Vietnam and China*, 267). In fact, recent Chinese evidence indicates that the CMAG fully agreed with Giap's plan. Drawing upon French sources, Lockhart has also taken issue with Chen's argument (*Nation in Arms*, 238).

98 The shifts in command of the French Expeditionary Corps between 1949 and June 1954 were: 1949–Dec. 1950, General Marcel Carpentier; Dec. 1950–Jan. 1952, General Jean de Lattre de Tassigny; Apr. 1952–May 1953, General Raoul Salan; May 1953–June 1954, General Henri-Eugene Navarre.

99 O'Ballance, *Indo-China War*, 127.

100 *Zhongguo junshi guwentuan*, 28–29. King Chen wrote that in starting the third offensive against the French in late May in Ninh Binh province, Giap was "anxious to be independent of the Chinese" (*Vietnam and China*, 267). Actually, as recently released Chinese sources suggest, the CMAG helped Giap plan and direct the campaign in May.

101 *Zhongguo junshi guwentuan*, 29–30.

102 Mao to Wei, Jan. 29, 1951, *Mao wengao*, 2:90. Mao mentioned Wei's telegram in his reply.

103 Han Huaizhi and Tan Jingqiao, *Dangdai Zhongguo jundui de junshi gongzuo*, 1:535.

104 Boudarel, "Influences and Idiosyncracies in the Line and Practice of the Vietnam Communist Party," 162.

105 For a critique of the Maoist "mind over matter" approach in the Yanan rectification campaign, see Munro, *Imperial Style of Inquiry in Twentieth-Century China*.

106 Zhang Dequn, "YuanYue guwentuan gongzuo suoyi," 71–73.

107 Liu to Luo, Jan. 22, 1951, *Liu nianpu*, 2:268.

108 Liu to Ho Chi Minh, Apr. 20 and May 2, 1951, ibid., 276.

109 King Chen, *Vietnam and China*, 253–54. According to Ken Post, "The reform of May 1951 standardized the previous heterogeneous levies into seven different taxes, the most important of which was a consolidated agricultural tax" (*Revolution, Socialism and Nationalism in Viet Nam*, 1:181).

110 Han Huaizhi and Tan Jingqiao, *Dangdai Zhongguo jundui de junshi gongzuo*, 1:528; *Zhongguo junshi guwentuan*, 55–57.

111 *Zhongguo junshi guwentuan*, 57–58.

112 Ibid., 58.

113 Pei Jianzhang, *Zhonghua renmin gongheguo waijiaoshi, 1949–1956*, 32.

114 *Zhongguo junshi guwentuan*, 59.

115 Mao to Liu, Oct. 4, 1952, *Mao wengao*, 3:577. In his telegram, Mao informed Liu, who was in Moscow attending the Soviet Nineteenth Congress, of Ho's journey to the Soviet Union.

116 Shi Zhe, *Zai lishi juren shenbian*, 530–31; Huang Zheng, *Liu Shaoqi yisheng*, 296.

117 *Zhongguo junshi guwentuan*, 59–62.

118 Marilyn Young, *Vietnam Wars*, 50.

119 Lockhart, *Nation in Arms*, 256.

120 Kolko, *Anatomy of a War*, 57–61.

121 *Zhongguo junshi guwentuan*, 82; King Chen, *Vietnam and China*, 259.

122 Zhang Dequn, "YuanYue guwentuan gongzuo suoyi," 74–75; King Chen, *Vietnam and China*, 259.

123 *Zhongguo junshi guwentuan*, 82–83.

124 Ibid., 83–86. "The White-Hair Girl" was adapted from a play of the same title first staged during the Chinese land reform in the early 1940s. Greg Lockhart writes that the propaganda effect of the preparations for land reform in late 1953 "helps to explain why thousands of soldiers would soon die at the culminating battle at Dien Bien Phu in the belief that they were fighting for their land" (*Nation in Arms*, 256–57).

125 Kolko, *Anatomy of a War*, 57–61; Hoang Van Hoan, *Canghai yisu*, 279–81.

126 Kolko, *Anatomy of a War*, 60–61; Hoang Van Hoan, *Canghai yisu*, 280.

CHAPTER TWO

1 *Zhongguo junshi guwentuan*, 63–65.

2 Ibid., 86–87; Duiker, *Communist Road to Power in Vietnam*, 162–68; Herring, *America's Longest War*, 25, 29.

3 *Zhongguo junshi guwentuan*, 87–88.

4 Han Huaizhi and Tan Jingqiao, *Dangdai Zhongguo jundui de junshi gongzuo*, 1:529.

5 Ibid.; *Zhongguo junshi guwentuan*, 88–89.

6 *Zhongguo junshi guwentuan*, 89.

7 Ibid. This source does not explain how China acquired a copy of the Navarre plan.

8 Zhou to Luo, Dec. 12, 1953, *Zhou nianpu*, 1:339.

9 *Zhongguo junshi guwentuan*, 90; Han Huaizhi and Tan Jingqiao, *Dangdai Zhongguo jundui de junshi gongzuo*, 1:530.

10 Han Huaizhi and Tan Jingqiao, *Dangdai Zhongguo jundui de junshi gongzuo*, 1:530–31; *Zhongguo junshi guwentuan*, 90.

11 *Zhongguo junshi guwentuan*, 93–94; Han Huaizhi and Tan Jingqiao, *Dangdai Zhongguo jundui de junshi gongzuo*, 1:531; Karnow, *Vietnam*, 195–96.

12 *Zhongguo junshi guwentuan*, 97–98.

13 Han Huaizhi and Tan Jingqiao, *Dangdai Zhongguo jundui de junshi gongzuo*, 1:532.

14 Duiker, *Sacred War*, 88.

15 Mao to Peng, Apr. 3, 1954, *Mao wengao*, 4:474–75.

16 Ibid.

17 On Mao's hands-on management of the Korean War, see Hunt, "Beijing and the Korean Crisis," 453–78, and Shu Guang Zhang, *Mao's Military Romanticism*.

18 Mao to Huang and Su, Apr. 17, 1954, *Mao wengao*, 4:480.

19 *Zhongguo junshi guwentuan*, 102–3; Han Huaizhi and Tan Jingqiao, *Dangdai Zhongguo jundui de junshi gongzuo*, 1:533.

20 Herring, *America's Longest War*, 32–33.

21 *Zhongguo junshi guwentuan*, 102–3; Han Huaizhi and Tan Jingqiao, *Dangdai Zhongguo jundui de junshi gongzuo*, 1:533.

22 Duiker, *Sacred War*, 88.

23 Han Huaizhi and Tan Jingqiao, *Dangdai Zhongguo jundui de junshi gongzuo*, 1:533–34.

24 Xue Mouhong and Pei Jianzhang, *Dangdai Zhongguo waijiao*, 56.

25 Ibid., 64–65; Li Lianqing, *Da waijiaojia Zhou Enlai*, 8–11; *Zhou nianpu*, 1:356.

26 Li Lianqing, *Da waijiaojia Zhou Enlai*, 7–8; Wang Bingnan, *ZhongMei huitan jiunian huigu*, 5–7.

27 Zhou to the CMAG, early March 1954, *Zhou nianpu*, 1:358.

28 Zhou to Ho, mid-March 1954, ibid.

29 Li Haiwen, "Zhou Enlai zai Rineiwa huiyi qijian wei huifu Induzhina heping jinxing de nuli," 57.

30 Ibid., 57–58.

31 *Zhou nianpu*, 1:359.

32 Li Haiwen, "Zhou Enlai zai Rineiwa huiyi qijian wei huifu Induzhina heping jinxing de nuli," 58; Shi Zhe, *Zai lishi juren shenbian*, 539–41; Shi Zhe, "Rineiwa huiyi sanyi," 37. Shi Zhe was a political adviser to the Chinese delegation.

33 Shi Zhe, "Rineiwa huiyi sanyi," 38.

34 Wang Bingnan, *ZhongMei huitan jiunian huigu*, 7.

35 Ibid., 5–6; *Zhou waijiao dashiji*, 58.

36 *Zhou nianpu*, 1:361.

37 Shi Zhe, *Zai lishi juren shenbian*, 543–44; Shi Zhe, "Rineiwa huiyi sanyi," 38.

38 Xue Mouhong and Pei Jianzhang, *Dangdai Zhongguo waijiao*, 51–52; Keith, *Diplomacy of Zhou Enlai*, 61.

39 Khrushchev, *Khrushchev Remembers*, 482.

40 Wang Bingnan, *ZhongMei huitan jiunian huigu*, 7; Xue Mouhong and Pei Jianzhang, *Dangdai Zhongguo waijiao*, 67.

41 Zhou's talk with the Indian ambassador, Apr. 19, 1954, *Zhou waijiao dashiji*, 58–59.

42 King Chen, *Vietnam and China*, 303–4.

43 For Qian's testimony, see Cheng Hua, *Zhou Enlai he tade mishumen*, 244.

44 "Shixian Yazhou heping he anquan de genben daolu"; "Yazhou renmin de yuanwang shi juedui burong hushi de."

45 *Zhou waijiao dashiji*, 55; Pei Jianzhang, *Zhonghua renmin gongheguo waijiaoshi*, 99.

46 Xue Mouhong and Pei Jianzhang, *Dangdai Zhongguo waijiao*, 79–81.

47 Ibid., 65–66; Wang Bingnan, *ZhongMei huitan jiunian huigu*, 12.

48 *Renmin ribao* (People's Daily), May 14, 1954.

49 King Chen, *Vietnam and China*, 309.

50 Shi Zhe, *Zai lishi juren shenbian*, 556; Li Haiwen, "Zhou Enlai zai Rineiwa huiyi qijian wei huifu Induzhina heping jinxing de nuli," 58.

51 Shi Zhe, *Zai lishi juren shenbian*, 556–57.

52 Li Lianqing, *Da waijiaojia Zhou Enlai*, 351–52.

53 *Zhou nianpu*, 1:383–84; Qu Xing, "Shilun 1954 nian Rineiwa huiyi shang de Zhou Enlai waijiao," 257; Li Lianqing, *Da waijiaojia Zhou Enlai*, 276.

54 Zhou's talk with Eden, June 16, 1954, *Zhou waijiao dashiji*, 65–66, and *Zhou nianpu*, 1:385.

55 Eden, *Full Circle*, 145.

56 Xue Mouhong and Pei Jianzhang, *Dangdai Zhongguo waijiao*, 60.

57 King Chen, *Vietnam and China*, 311–12.

58 Zhou to Mao and Liu Shaoqi, June 19, 1954, *Zhou nianpu*, 1:386.

59 Ibid., 388; Li Haiwen, "Zhou Enlai zai Rineiwa huiyi qijian wei huifu Induzhina heping jinxing de nuli," 59.

60 Shi Zhe, *Zai lishi juren shenbian*, 556; Shi Zhe, "Rineiwa huiyi sanyi," 42.

61 Dillon (U.S. ambassador to France) to State Department, June 24, 1954, *FRUS, 1952–1954*, 16:1240–41.

62 Li Lianqing, *Da waijiaojia Zhou Enlai*, 349.

63 Shi Zhe, "Rineiwa huiyi sanyi," 43.

64 Li Haiwen, "Zhou Enlai zai Rineiwa huiyi qijian wei huifu Induzhina heping jinxing de nuli," 59–61.

65 Ibid.

66 Ibid.

67 Ibid.

68 Li Lianqing, *Da waijiaojia Zhou Enlai*, 335; Qu Xing, "Shilun 1954 nian Rineiwa huiyi shang de Zhou Enlai waijiao," 257.

69 *Zhou nianpu*, 1:395; Li Lianqing, *Da waijiaojia Zhou Enlai*, 336.

70 Xue Mouhong and Pei Jianzhang, *Dangdai Zhongguo waijiao*, 66–67; Li Lianqing, *Da waijiaojia Zhou Enlai*, 337.

71 Li Lianqing, *Da waijiaojia Zhou Enlai*, 347–52.

72 Ibid.

73 For the idea of the "Indochinese strategic space" and its French origin, see Engelbert and Goscha, *Falling out of Touch*, 42.

74 Li Lianqing, *Da waijiaojia Zhou Enlai*, 352–58; Qu Xing, "Shilun 1954 nian Rineiwa huiyi shang de Zhou Enlai waijiao," 258; Xu Yan, "Ximie Induzhina zhanhuo de zhuoyue lishi," 24.

75 Li Haiwen, "Restoring Peace in Indochina at the Geneva Conference," 9.

76 For a complete text of the Geneva Accords, see King Chen, *Vietnam and China*, appendix iv, 375–405.

77 Wang Bingnan, *ZhongMei huitan jiunian huigu*, 13.

78 In 1979, Hanoi issued a *White Paper* on Sino-Vietnamese relations, charging that "the Chinese leaders betrayed the revolutionary struggle of the peoples of Viet Nam, Laos and Kampuchea" (*White Paper*, 23).

The historian Gabriel Kolko argued that at Geneva, China and the Soviet Union "dunned the DRV with the dangers of U.S. intervention to force them to make concessions and avoid allegedly risking the peace of the world" and that when "the Chinese realized there was slight risk of an American intervention, they sought through direct talks with the French to exchange constraints on the DRV for greater diplomatic recognition and prestige and commercial openings to the West for themselves" (*Anatomy of a War*, 64). Kolko implied that China's fears about U.S. intervention were not genuine and that Beijing used the American threat to frighten the Viet Minh and to achieve its own purposes. In fact, as Zhou Enlai's statements during his meeting with the Chinese delegation on July 12 indicate, even to the last days of the conference, he still worried about the American expansion of the Indochina war. It is important to note that Zhou's remarks were made to his colleagues in a closed-door discussion rather than to foreign visitors or to the public. It is quite clear that Beijing's apprehensions about American intervention were genuine and that the Chinese leaders sincerely desired to avoid a Korea-like situation in Vietnam. Certainly China's relations with Britain improved at Geneva, but to prevent the internationalization of the Indochina war remained the primary goal of China's diplomacy at the Geneva Conference.

Kolko also asserted that at the time of the Geneva Conference, "the United States almost certainly would not intervene" in Indochina. But William Duiker's research suggests that "had the negotiations collapsed, the White House might have felt compelled to provide naval and air forces in a multinational defense of the area" (*Sacred War*, 94). David Anderson has also pointed out that "Eisenhower's interest in Radford's air strike plan suggests that the president was prepared to commit U.S. air power to Indochina, provided that his preconditions were met" (*Trapped by Success*, 38).

79 Duiker, *Communist Road to Power in Vietnam*, 173; Kolko, *Anatomy of a War*, 63.

80 Lockhart, *Nation in Arms*. Marilyn Young has observed: "On the basis of a nationalist appeal that was at the same time revolutionary, the government of Vietnam had organized and inspired a poor, untrained, ill-equipped population to fight and ultimately win against a far better equipped and trained" French army (*Vietnam Wars*, 35).

81 Dunn, *First Vietnam War*; Dunn, "First Vietnam War," 17–41.

82 For more comparisons between the French Indochina War and the British Malayan War, see Dalloz, *War in Indo-china*, 204.

83 Bodard, *Quicksand War*, 3.

84 Chen diary entry, Sept. 6, 1950, *Chen Geng riji (xu)*, 22.

85 Chen diary entry, Oct. 15, 1950, ibid., 35.

CHAPTER THREE

1 Chae-Jin Lee, *Communist China's Policy toward Laos*, 24–26.

2 Ibid., 27–30; Devillers, "Laotian Conflict in Perspective," 37–51; Brown and Zasloff, *Apprentice Revolutionaries*, 61.

3 Mao's talk with Souvanna Phouma, Aug. 21, 1956, *Mao waijiao wenxun*, 242–44. See also Pei Jianzhang, *Zhonghua renmin gongheguo waijiaoshi*, 153–56.

4 Zhou's talk with Souvanna Phouma, Aug. 21, 1956, *Zhou waijiao dashiji*, 156; *Zhou nianpu*, 1:612.

5 Zhou's talk with Souvanna Phouma, Aug. 25, 1956, *Zhou waijiao dashiji*, 156–57; *Zhou nianpu*, 1:612.

6 Zhou to Ho Chi Minh, Aug. 27, 1956, *Zhou nianpu*, 1:613–14.

7 Pei Jianzhang, *Zhonghua renmin gongheguo waijiaoshi*, 148; Roger M. Smith, *Cambodia's Foreign Policy*, 80; Leifer, *Cambodia*, 63; Chandler, *Tragedy of Cambodian History*, 80; Osborne, *Sihanouk*, 96.

8 Pei Jianzhang, *Zhonghua renmin gongheguo waijiaoshi*, 147–52; Xue Mouhong and Pei Jianzhang, *Dangdai Zhongguo waijiao*, 169–70. Kirk, *Wider War*, 48. For summaries of China's policy toward Cambodia, see Gurtov, *China and Southeast Asia*, ch. 3, and Armstrong, *Revolutionary Diplomacy*, ch. 6.

9 Duiker, *China and Vietnam*, 51–52.

10 Chae-Jin Lee, *Communist China's Policy toward Laos*, 31. On the shift in China's policy toward the independent Third World governments, particularly in Asia and the Middle East, around 1953, see Harding, "China and the Third World," 260–61, and Levine, "China in Asia," 116.

11 Quoted in Ang Cheng Guan, *Vietnamese Communists' Relations with China and the Second Indochina Conflict*, 17.

12 Ibid.; Osborne, *Sihanouk*, 96; Roger M. Smith, *Cambodia's Foreign Policy*, 80; Leifer, *Cambodia*, 63.

13 Duiker, *Sacred War*, 95–97; Guo Ming, *ZhongYue guanxi yanbian sishinian*, 62–63.

14 Kolko, *Anatomy of a War*, 69; Post, *Revolution, Socialism and Nationalism in Viet Nam*, 1:262; Pike, *History of Vietnamese Communism*, 103.

15 Guo Ming, *ZhongYue guanxi yanbian sishinian*, 65; Pei Jianzhang, *Zhonghua renmin gongheguo waijiaoshi*, 94.

16 Pei Jianzhang, *Zhonghua renmin gongheguo waijiaoshi*, 94; Hoang Van Hoan, *Canghai yisu*, 267.

17 Zhou to Luo, Fang, and Qiao, Oct. 8, 1954, *Zhou nianpu*, 1:417.

18 Post, *Revolution, Socialism and Nationalism in Viet Nam*, 1:262, 292; Olsen, *Solidarity and National Revolution*," 34.

19 Olsen, *Solidarity and National Revolution*, 33–34.

20 Buttinger, *Vietnam*, 422–23.

21 Pei Jianzhang, *Zhonghua renmin gongheguo waijiaoshi*, 91–95; *Zhou nianpu*, 1:489; Thayer, *War by Other Means*, 35.

22 Zhou to Luo Guibo, Fang Yi, and Qiao Xiaoguang, Jan. 18, 1955, *Zhou nianpu*, 1:442.

23 Olsen, *Solidarity and National Revolution*, 34–40.

24 Thayer, *War by Other Means*, 35–36; Olsen, *Solidarity and National Revolution*, 45–47.

25 According to an American source, by 1961 Beijing had provided over $600 million in aid to Hanoi. See Duiker, *China and Vietnam*, 41.

26 *Zhongguo junshi guwentuan*, 125–26.

27 Ibid., 127–28.

28 Ibid., 130–31.

29 Ibid., 126–27, 142. On October 16, 1955, Mao personally selected Peng Dehuai, Chen Geng, and Wei Guoqing as members of the Chinese delegation for the forthcoming discussions during Giap's second visit. See Mao to Liu Shaoqi, Zhou Enlai, Zhu De, and Deng Xiaoping, Oct. 16, 1955, *Mao wengao*, 5:419. Chen Geng, deputy defense minister, was not mentioned during Giap's first visit. Clearly, Mao wanted to present a stronger Chinese team to talk with Giap during his second trip.

30 *Zhongguo junshi guwentuan*, 142–43.

31 Duiker, *China and Vietnam*, 41. In 1956 Mao launched a campaign to let "one hundred flowers bloom" in the field of culture and "one hundred schools of thought contend" in the field of science.

32 White, "Peasants and the Party in the Vietnamese Revolution," 40.

33 Kolko, *Anatomy of a War*, 60–61; Hoang Van Hoan, *Canghai yisu*, 280–81. The number of executions during the land reform campaign has always been controversial. Edwin Moïse's study in *Land Reform in China and North Vietnam* remains the most careful assessment.

34 Duiker, *Sacred War*, 98.

35 Hoang Van Hoan, *Canghai yisu*, 281–85. Hoan argued that the Vietnamese Land Reform Committee, not the Chinese advisers, were responsible for the errors of the land reform program. Clearly, Hoan's pro-Chinese inclination colored his views.

36 On Catholic opposition to the land reform, see Porter, *Vietnam*, 39.

37 Post, *Revolution, Socialism and Nationalism in Viet Nam*, 2:366–67; Duiker, *China and Vietnam*, 41. According to David Elliott, since the late 1950s, the Vietnamese Communists "have been more inclined toward the Soviet model, at least in such areas as industrial management, bureaucratic procedures, and legal structures. The Soviet Union helped establish many of the scientific and technical institutions in the DRV, and Soviet academicians had an important influence on the State Scientific Commission, set up in late 1958" ("Institutionalizing the Revolution," 209).

38 Porter, *Vietnam*, 114–15. On the VWP's efforts to use collective leadership as a method to sustain its claim to legitimacy, see Vasavakul, "Vietnam," 257–89. I am grateful to Mark Bradley for pointing out this source to me.

39 Shi Zhongquan, *Zhou Enlai de zhuoyue fengxian*, 286–87.

40 Report by officials (unidentified) from the International Liaison Department of the CCP Central Committee at a national conference on foreign affairs in Beijing, Apr. 19, 1963, in Q3124, J77, JPA. On the Vietnamese party's leadership style, which emphasized consensus and unity over confrontation and dispute, see Porter, *Vietnam*, 114–18.

41 Duiker, *Sacred War*, 99–100.

42 Guo Ming, *ZhongYue guanxi yanbian sishinian*, 65.

43 *Zhou nianpu*, 1:489.

44 Zhou's talk with the Burmese ambassador, June 30, 1955, *Zhou waijiao dashiji*, 117.

45 Duiker, *Sacred War*, 109–10.

46 Nogee and Donaldson, *Soviet Foreign Policy since World War II*, 27–32.

47 Duiker, *Sacred War*, 111; Thayer, *War by Other Means*, 63.

48 Porter, "Vietnam and the Socialist Camp," 237–38; Thayer, *War by Other Means*, 63–67.

49 Shi Zhongquan, *Zhou Enlai de zhuoyue fengxian*, 286–87.

50 Ibid. For Zhou's visit to Hanoi, see also *Zhou waijiao dashiji*, 169–70, and *Zhou nianpu*, 1:639–41. According to Carlyle Thayer, Zhou's trip was occasioned partly by problems in the relationship between Chinese advisers in the DRV and their Vietnamese hosts. Thayer based his remarks on interviews with Huynh Kim Khanh, who had had conversations with high-ranking DRV officials. See *War by Other Means*, 213.

51 *Zhou waijiao dashiji*, 170; *Zhou nianpu*, 1:640; Duiker, *China and Vietnam*, 40.

52 *Zhou nianpu*, 1:640.

53 Zagoria, *Vietnam Triangle*, 102–4. According to Carlyle Thayer, in 1958 Moscow surpassed Beijing as Hanoi's number one provider of economic assistance (*War by Other Means*, 161).

54 Olsen, *Solidarity and National Revolution*, 91–96. See also Thayer, *War by Other Means*, 159–60.

55 Ho to Mao, Sept. 8, 1958, and Mao to Ho, Sept. 10, 1958, *Mao wengao*, 7:413.

56 Porter, "Vietnam and the Socialist Camp," 240.

57 Guo Ming, *ZhongYue guanxi yanbian sishinian*, 66.

58 Hoang Van Hoan, "Distortion of Facts about Militant Friendship between Viet Nam and China Is Impermissible," 15.

59 Porter, "Vietnam and the Socialist Camp," 240.

60 Kolko, *Anatomy of a War*, 102–3. The decisions made at the Fifteenth Plenum in January 1959 were not implemented until May. See Duiker, *Sacred War*, 120–22.

61 Duiker, *U.S. Containment Policy and the Conflict in Indochina*, 265.

62 Mao made this remark to a group of Chinese students in Moscow in November 1957. See Spence, *Search for Modern China*, 576.

63 For Mao's criticism of Zhou Enlai's "opposition to adventurism" between 1957 and 1958, see Shi Zhongquan, *Zhou Enlai de zhuoyue fengxian*, 324–39, and Li Ping, *Kaiguo zongli Zhou Enlai*, 359–60.

64 Han Huaizhi and Tan Jingqiao, *Dangdai Zhongguo jundui de junshi gongzuo*, 1:577–78.

65 Gilks and Segal, *China and the Arms Trade*, 37; Garver, *Foreign Relations of the People's Republic of China*, 139.

66 Han Huaizhi and Tan Jingqiao, *Dangdai Zhongguo jundui de junshi gongzuo*, 1:578.

67 On Mao's handling of the 1958 bombardment of Quemoy, see Zhai, *Dragon, the Lion, and the Eagle*, ch. 9, and Wu Lengxi, *Yi Maozhuxi*, 73–92.

68 Zhou's meeting with Pham Van Dong, Oct. 17, 1959, *Zhou nianpu*, 2:262.

69 Zeng Sheng, *Zeng Sheng huiyilu*, 638–41.

70 Hoang Van Hoan, "Distortion of Facts about Militant Friendship between Viet Nam and China Is Impermissible," 15.

71 Guo Ming, *ZhongYue guanxi yanbian sishinian*, 67.

72 Thayer, *War by Other Means*, 188. On the relationship between the NLF and the VWP politburo in Hanoi, see Kahin, *Intervention*, 119–20.

73 Post, *Revolution, Socialism and Nationalism in Viet Nam*, 2:252–53.

74 *Zhou nianpu*, 2:291–92.

75 Zhou's talk with Pham Van Dong, May 11, 1960, ibid., 316–17. For the DRV's borrowing of the Chinese slogan of "producing more, quicker, better, and more economically" in mobilizing its working class, see Post, *Revolution, Socialism and Nationalism in Viet Nam*, 2:273.

76 Zhou's talks with the VWP delegation, May 12 and 13, 1960, *Zhou nianpu*, 2:317–18. On North Vietnam's agricultural collectivization between 1958 and 1960, see Pike, *History of Vietnamese Communism*, 102; Porter, *Vietnam*, 116–17; and Post, *Revolution, Socialism and Nationalism in Viet Nam*, 2:254–55.

77 Porter, *Vietnam*, 49.

78 Report by officials (unidentified) from the International Liaison Department of the CCP Central Committee at a national conference on foreign affairs in Beijing, Apr. 19, 1963, in Q3124, J177, JPA.

79 Quoted in Fall, *Two Viet-Nams*, 161.

80 Zhou's talk with the VWP delegation, May 11, 1960, *Zhou nianpu*, 2:317.

81 On India's role in Indochina, see SarDesai, *Indian Foreign Policy in Cambodia, Laos, and Vietnam*, 239, 243; Thakur, *Peacekeeping in Vietnam*; and Thakur and Thayer, *Soviet Relations with India and Vietnam*, 231–68.

82 For the origins and early development of the Sino-Soviet dispute, see Chai Chengwen, Huang Zhengji, and Zhang Changjin, *Sanda tupo*, 275–92; Zagoria, *Sino-Soviet Conflict*; Hudson, Lowenthal, and MacFarquhar, *Sino-Soviet Dispute*; and Westad, *Brothers in Arms*.

83 Ma Qibin, *Zhongguo gongchandang zhizheng sishinian*, 187; Chai Chengwen, Huang Zhengji, and Zhang Changjin, *Sanda tupo*, 292–93; Yan Mingfu, "Peng Zhen zai Bujialesite huiyi shang," 71–86. As Russian interpreter, Yan Mingfu accompanied Peng Zhen to the Bucharest Conference. See also MacFarquhar, *Origins of the Cultural Revolution*, 2:274–78.

84 Suny, *Soviet Experiment*, 412.

85 Olsen, *Solidarity and National Revolution*, 112–13; Bukharkin, "Moscow and Ho Chi Minh," 22–23. At the Bucharest Conference, the North Vietnamese delegates, together with the representatives of the North Korean, Japanese, and Indonesian parties, urged bloc unity instead of joining Khrushchev in attacking the Chinese. See Yan Mingfu, "Peng Zhen zai Bujialesite huiyi shang," 71–86.

86 *Zhou nianpu*, 2:338; *Liu nianpu*, 2:492.

87 Mao's talk with Ho was summarized in Chen Yi's report at the Fourth National Conference on Foreign Affairs on Aug. 14, 1960, Q3124, J103, JPA. See also Yang Kuisong, "Zouxiang polie," 92.

88 Gu Longsheng, *Mao Zedong jingji nianpu*, 520.

89 Chen Yi's report at the Fourth National Conference on Foreign Affairs, Aug. 14, 1960, Q3124, J103, JPA.

90 The Editorial Team on "the Record of Mao Zedong's International Contacts," *Mao Zedong*, 58–59. Noting the Hungarian press report of Ho Chi Minh's presence at the Hungarian Exhibition in Moscow on August 15, 1960, the British scholar P. J. Honey discussed Ho's visit to the Soviet Union in his 1963 study of the Vietnamese-Chinese-Soviet Communist relationship. Without knowing about Ho's trips to Beijing before and after his journey to Moscow, Honey speculated that the VWP leader "went to the Soviet Union to conclude an agreement with Khrushchev," whereby Ho would receive

massive Soviet aid and technical assistance for the DRV's industrialization and Khrushchev would secure Vietnamese support in the Sino-Soviet rift. See *Communism in North Vietnam*, 76–78. New Chinese revelations about Ho's mediation trips to Beijing and Moscow have rendered Honey's speculation untenable.

91 Hoang Van Hoan accompanied Ho Chi Minh on his trip to Moscow. In his memoirs, Hoan blamed Khrushchev's "intransigence in opposing China" for the failure of Ho's effort. Again, Hoan's pro-Chinese bias warped his perspective. See Hoang Van Hoan, *Canghai yisu*, 290.

92 Olsen, *Solidarity and National Revolution*, 121–22.

93 Hong Zuojun, "Fengyu qianzaiqing," 21–39.

94 Duiker, *Sacred War*, 128; Duiker, "Seeds of the Dragon," 334.

95 Porter, *Vietnam*, 48.

96 Duiker, "Seeds of the Dragon," 334.

97 Duiker, *U.S. Containment Policy and the Conflict in Indochina*, 266; Duiker, *Sacred War*, 128.

98 Olsen, *Solidarity and National Revolution*, 124.

99 Ibid., 123.

100 Ma Qibin, *Zhongguo gongchandang zhizheng sishinian*, 193; Dittmer, *Sino-Soviet Normalization and Its International Implications*, 108; Whiting, "Sino-Soviet Split," 518.

101 French Communist Party leader Maurice Thorez told his Central Committee that Hanoi "upheld a conciliatory viewpoint" at the Moscow meeting. See Smyser, *Independent Vietnamese*, 43.

102 Yan Mingfu, "Wo suo zhidao de liangci Mosike huiyi he Hu Qiaomu," 155. Yan Mingfu was a translator for the Chinese delegation at the 1960 Moscow conference. See also Yang Kuisong, "Zouxiang polie," 94–96.

103 Quoted in Li Yueran, *Waijiao wutan shang de xinZhongguo lingxiu*, 207. Li Yueran was also a translator for the Chinese delegation at the Moscow meeting.

104 Porter, "Vietnam and the Socialist Camp," 245. According to William Duiker (*Communist Road to Power in Vietnam*, 402), when Liu Shaoqi walked out of the meeting hall in protest of Soviet speeches and returned to the Chinese embassy, Khrushchev asked Ho Chi Minh to persuade him to return. The North Vietnamese leader consented, and the dispute was papered over temporarily. See also Whiting, "Sino-Soviet Split," 518.

105 On August 21, 1961, Zhou Enlai talked with Ung Van Khiem, foreign minister of the DRV, in Beijing about Ho's mediation of the Soviet-Albanian rift. See *Zhou nianpu*, 2:428.

106 Zhou's talk with Ho Chi Minh and Le Duan, Oct. 12, 1961, ibid., 440.

107 Ibid., 440–41; Chai Chengwen, Huang Zhengji, and Zhang Changjin, *Sanda tupo*, 295; Khrushchev, *Khrushchev Remembers: The Last Testament*, 507.

108 R. B. Smith, *International History of the Vietnam War*, 2:36.

109 Ibid., 45.

CHAPTER FOUR

1 Goldstein, *American Policy toward Laos*; Timothy Castle, *At War in the Shadow of Vietnam*.

2 Chae-Jin Lee, *Communist China's Policy toward Laos*, 34–38; Brown and Zasloff, *Apprentice Revolutionaries*, 61–62.

3 Dommen, *Conflict in Laos*, 94–111; R. B. Smith, *International History of the Vietnam War*, 1:163; Timothy Castle, *At War in the Shadow of Vietnam*, 17.

4 Feingold, "Opium and Politics in Laos," 322–39; Garver, *Foreign Relations of the People's Republic of China*, 292.

5 Luo Guibo's speech at the Second National Conference on Foreign Affairs, Mar. 4, 1959, Q3124, J087, JPA.

6 *Shijie zhishi*, no. 6 (1959): 24–25.

7 *Zhou nianpu*, 2:258–59.

8 Dommen, *Conflict in Laos*, 143–48; Hall, "Laos Neutralization Agreement," 437.

9 Chen Yi's speech at the Fourth National Conference on Foreign Affairs, Aug. 14, 1960, Q3124, J103, JPA.

10 *Shijie zhishi*, no. 17 (1960): 8.

11 For Ho Chi Minh's conversation with Mao concerning Sino-Soviet differences on August 10, 1960, see the Editorial Group of "the Record of Mao Zedong's International Contacts," *Mao Zedong*, 58–59.

12 Chen Yi's speeches at the Fourth National Conference on Foreign Affairs, Aug. 12 and 14, 1960, Q3124, J103, JPA.

13 Dommen, *Conflict in Laos*, 148–65; Hall, "Laos Neutralization Agreement," 437–38.

14 Zhou's talk with the Soviet chargé d'affaires, Dec. 9, 1960, *Zhou waijiao dashiji*, 295.

15 Dommen, *Conflict in Laos*, 165–70; Hall, "Laos Neutralization Agreement," 438.

16 Zhou's talks with Tran Tu Binh, Dec. 12 and 16, 1960, *Zhou waijiao dashiji*, 295–96.

17 Dommen, *Conflict in Laos*, 163.

18 Thee, *Notes of a Witness*, 128.

19 Ai Lingyao, "Zhongguo yuanLao kangMei de guanghui pianzhang," 37.

20 Zhou's talk with Ne Win, Jan. 5, 1961, *Zhou waijiao dashiji*, 300.

21 Zhou's talk with the DRV Economic Delegation, Jan. 31, 1961, *Zhou nianpu*, 2:388.

22 Zhou's talk with U Nu, Apr. 12, 1961, *Zhou waijiao dashiji*, 307.

23 Zhang Yan's speech on the Geneva Conference on Laos at the National Conference on Foreign Affairs, Dec. 1961, Q3124, J123, JPA. In private, Chinese officials noted that Pathet Lao troops were incapable of conducting battles of annihilation. The reason for this ineffectiveness, they contended, was the "restriction of Buddhism" on the Lao people, who "were afraid of seeing blood." The Chinese believed that time was required to train and transform Pathet Lao soldiers. See Liao Chengzhi's internal speech on international affairs, Feb. 21, 1962, Q3124, J147, JPA.

24 Yang Shengqun and Tian Songnian, *Gongheguo zhongda juece de lailong qumai*, 358–63; MacFarquhar, *Origins of the Cultural Revolution*, 3:13–19.

25 *Zhou nianpu*, 2:400.

26 Ibid., 403.

27 For Chen's career, see Hu Shiyan, *Chen Yi zhuan*. Roderick MacFarquhar mentions Chen's early close connections with Mao, Liu Shaoqi, Zhou Enlai, and Deng Xiaoping as a possible reason for his being chosen as foreign minister. MacFarquhar, *Origins of the Cultural Revolution*, 2:75.

28 The information in this and the following paragraph is from Wu Lengxi, "Chen Yi tongzhi zai Rineiwa huiyi shang," 152–65. Wu Lengxi served as press spokesman for the

Chinese delegation at the Geneva Conference. See Li Yueran, *Waijiao wutan shang de xinZhongguo lingxiu*, 216–17. Between 1949 and 1964, Li Yueran served as a Russian-language interpreter for Chinese leaders. He attended the Geneva Conference. See Chen Xiaolu, "Chen Yi and China's Diplomacy," 102–3.

29 Wu Lengxi, "Chen Yi tongzhi zai Rineiwa huiyi shang," 154; Hu Shiyan, *Chen Yi zhuan*, 558–59.

30 Chen Xiaolu, "Chen Yi and China's Diplomacy," 103.

31 For Zhang Hanfu's career, see Geng Biao, "Huiyi xinZhongguo jiechu de waijiaojia Zhang Hanfu tongzhi."

32 For biographical information about Qiao Guanhua, see Zhang Hanzhi, *Wo yu Qiao Guanhua*. See also Cao Junjie, *Zhongguo liangQiao*, 179–274.

33 Lall, *How Communist China Negotiates*, 1–3, 12. Chae-Jin Lee argued that by sending the largest delegation to Geneva, the Chinese were intent on "demonstrating their growing power and status" (*Communist China's Policy toward Laos*, 81). To train cadres was another motivation.

34 Crozier, "Peking and the Laotian Crisis: An Interim Appraisal," 129.

35 In November 1961, the Chinese Economic and Cultural Mission was established in Khang Khay, which served as an important instrument of Beijing's policy in dealing with the Pathet Lao. The director of the mission was He Wei, China's ambassador to Hanoi. Aside from its economic and cultural functions, the mission also directed a group of military advisers attached to the Pathet Lao. See Liu Chun, "Quzhe de Zhong-Lao jianjiao yu shouci chushi Laowo," 7–14. Liu Chun was deputy director of the mission and became China's ambassador to Laos in October 1962.

36 *Zhou nianpu*, 2:407.

37 Brown and Zasloff, *Apprentice Revolutionaries*, 79.

38 Hall, "Laos Neutralization Agreement," 446.

39 Brown and Zasloff, *Apprentice Revolutionaries*, 80.

40 Hall, "Laos Neutralization Agreement," 446.

41 Ronning, *Memoir of China in Revolution*, 251. Ronning was deputy to Howard Green, Canadian foreign minister, at the Geneva Conference.

42 Chae-Jin Lee, *Communist China's Policy toward Laos*, 80; Wu Lengxi, "Chen Yi tongzhi zai Rineiwa huiyi shang," 154–55.

43 Wu Lengxi, "Chen Yi tongzhi zai Rineiwa huiyi shang," 155; Xue Mouhong and Pei Jianzhang, *Dangdai Zhongguo waijiao*, 164; Lall, *How Communist China Negotiates*, 50–54; Chae-Jin Lee, *Communist China's Policy toward Laos*, 81. Brian Crozier argued that "one of the Chinese objectives at the Geneva conference has been to humiliate the United States" ("Peking and the Laotian Crisis: An Interim Appraisal," 135).

44 Xue Mouhong and Pei Jianzhang, *Dangdai Zhongguo waijiao*, 165; Wu Lengxi, "Chen Yi tongzhi zai Rineiwa huiyi shang," 157; Chae-Jin Lee, *Communist China's Policy toward Laos*, 81.

45 Liu Shufa, *Chen Yi nianpu*, 2:877–78. On Chen's rebuttal of the Franco-American draft, see Lall, *How Communist China Negotiates*, 84–89. Without knowing the real motivations of the Chinese delegates, Lall was puzzled by the "contradictory meanings" of Chen's remarks. He wrote: "It must have been clear to Ch'en Yi that if the agreement was to be acceptable to all it would have to contain at least some of the concepts embodied in the Franco-American proposals. Since these words were spoken a few seconds after his

reaffirmation of resolute opposition to the Franco-American draft, Ch'en Yi was show-ing his capacity to make seemingly radical shifts of position, and by doing so was diminishing the seriousness of the Chinese position in the negotiation" (*How Communist China Negotiates*, 87).

46 Hu Shiyan, *Chen Yi zhuan*, 562.

47 Brown and Zasloff, *Apprentice Revolutionaries*, 82.

48 Zhou's talk with Leng Ngeth, July 10, 1961, *Zhou waijiao dashiji*, 316.

49 Zhou's talk with Quinim Pholsena and Phoumi Vongvichit, Oct. 21, 1961, ibid., 325. Pholsena and Vongvichit were the heads of the Royal Lao Government's and the Lao Patriotic Front's delegations to the Geneva Conference, respectively.

50 Zhang Yan's speech on the Geneva Conference on Laos at the National Conference on Foreign Affairs, Dec. 1961, Q3124, J123, JPA. Unaware of the inner calculations of Chinese leaders, Arthur Lall claimed that later in the conference China "abandoned" its "most forthright and apparently adamant" position of abolishing SEATO (*How Communist China Negotiates*, 86).

51 Chae-Jin Lee, *Communist China's Policy toward Laos*, 87.

52 Zhou's talk with Souphanouvong, Jan. 28, 1962, *Zhou waijiao dashiji*, 329. Souphanou-vong was on his way back to Laos from Geneva. Hoang Van Hoan was also present during the conversation.

53 Phoumi had deployed troops in Nam Tha with the hope of provoking a Communist assault and seizure of the city, which in turn would lead to American military interven-tion on his side and U.S. rejection of Souvanna Phouma and the neutralists. See Toye, *Laos*, 182–83. Hugh Toye was a British military attaché in Laos between 1960 and 1962. See also Goldstein, *American Policy toward Laos*, 256, and Timothy Castle, *At War in the Shadow of Vietnam*, 45.

54 Ai Lingyao, "Zhongguo yuanLao kangMei de guanghui pianzhang," 37.

55 According to Hugh Toye, the American advisers in the area dismissed the charge that Chinese soldiers had supported the Pathet Lao seizure of Nam Tha (*Laos*, 182). Hanoi later acknowledged that it "coordinated" the Nam Tha operation. See Stuart-Fox, *History of Laos*, 221 n. 59.

56 Brown and Zasloff, *Apprentice Revolutionaries*, 84–85; Hall, "Laos Neutralization Agree-ment," 447; Beschloss, *Crisis Years*, 397.

57 Chen Yi recognized that the Pathet Lao victory at Nam Tha made possible the political agreement in Laos (Chen Yi's report on the Geneva Conference on Laos, Aug. 1962, Q3124, J147, JPA). See also Chen Xiaolu, "Chen Yi and China's Diplomacy," 103.

58 Brown and Zasloff, *Apprentice Revolutionaries*, 85–86; Hall, "Laos Neutralization Agree-ment," 452.

59 During his stopover in Moscow on his way to Geneva in May 1961, Soviet foreign minister Andrei Gromyko expressed the wish to cooperate with China at Geneva. See Li Yueran, *Waijiao wutan shang de xinZhongguo lingxiu*, 217.

60 See Jay Taylor, *China and Southeast Asia*, 21.

61 Lall, *How Communist China Negotiates*, 51.

62 Chen Yi's report on the Geneva Conference on Laos, Aug. 1962, Q3124, J147, JPA; Zhang Yan's speech on the Geneva Conference on Laos at the National Conference on Foreign Affairs, Dec. 1961, Q3124, J123, JPA.

63 Zhang Yan's speech on the Geneva Conference on Laos at the National Conference on Foreign Affairs, Dec. 1961, Q3124, J123, JPA. Chester Ronning observed that "from among the problem areas involving the United States in confrontation with the Soviet Union," Kennedy and Khrushchev "had selected Laos as a sort of pilot project in détente" (*Memoir of China in Revolution*, 252).

64 Summary Record of White House Meeting on Laos, Jan. 23, 1961, Vietnam/Laos Collection (Porter-Perry-Prados Donation), Box 1, National Security Archives, Washington, D.C.

65 Beschloss, *Crisis Years*, 231.

66 Addis is quoted in Ang Cheng Guan, *Vietnamese Communists' Relations with China and the Second Indochina Conflict*, 218.

67 Chae-Jin Lee, *Communist China's Policy toward Laos*, 91.

68 Hu Shiyan, *Chen Yi zhuan*, 562.

69 Zhai, "China and the Geneva Conference of 1954."

70 Chae-Jin Lee, *Communist China's Policy toward Laos*, 91.

71 Describing Beijing's performance at the Laos conference, Roderick MacFarquhar wrote: "The Chinese took a far harder line publicly than the Russians, and their combination of tough rhetoric and covert support for the pro-communist forces, laced with a willingness to compromise when necessary, would in the end suggest that Beijing's way of dealing with the Americans was more effective than Moscow's" (*Origins of the Cultural Revolution*, 3:124).

72 Devillers, "Laotian Conflict in Perspective," 41; Hall, "Laos Neutralization Agreement," 435; Toye, *Laos*, 85; Langer and Zasloff, *North Vietnam and the Pathet Lao*, 49–54.

73 Maneli, *War of the Vanquished*, 192.

74 R. B. Smith, *International History of the Vietnam War*, 1:168–69.

75 Thee, *Notes of a Witness*, 128–31; Brown and Zasloff, *Apprentice Revolutionaries*, 81–82.

76 Chen Shuliang, "Huiyi jiejue Laowo wenti de Rineiwa huiyi he Yinduzhina renmin huiyi," 12–19. Ung Van Khiem was foreign minister of the DRV and the head of the DRV delegation to the Geneva Conference. Hoang Van Hoan was director of the International Liaison Department of the VWP and also head of the party's CP38 Commission in charge of Laotian and Cambodian affairs. He served as an adviser to the DRV delegation at Geneva. In 1979, he defected to Beijing after the break of relations between the DRV and the PRC.

77 According to a U.S. source, North Vietnam had about 9,000 combat troops in Laos in early 1962. See memorandum, Colonel Howard L. Burris to Vice President Lyndon Johnson, Feb. 5, 1962, Vietnam/Laos Collection (Porter-Perry-Prados Donation), Box 1, National Security Archives, Washington, D.C.

78 Zhang Yan's speech on the Geneva Conference on Laos at the National Conference on Foreign Affairs, Dec. 1961, Q3124, J123, JPA. In a conversation with Ung Van Khiem on July 22, 1962, U.S. representative W. Averell Harriman again asked whether there were North Vietnam military forces in Laos. Khiem replied that Souvanna Phouma's government had requested military aid and that the DRV had provided military trainers and military specialists to assist Souvanna's armies. But he stopped short of admitting the presence of North Vietnamese military units in Laos. Harriman felt, however, that Khiem's answer "was an improvement in candor over statements which had been made earlier at the Conference, when Mr. Pushkin had refused to confirm that there were

North Vietnamese military personnel in Laos" (Memorandum of conversation, July 22, 1962, Harriman Papers, Special Files: Public Services, Box 519, Library of Congress, Washington, D.C.).

79 Chen Yi's report on the Geneva Conference on Laos, Aug. 1962, Q3124, J147, JPA.
80 Chen Shuliang, "Huiyi jiejue Laowo wenti de Rineiwa huiyi he Yinduzhina renmin huiyi," 15.
81 Chae-Jin Lee, *Communist China's Policy toward Laos*, 91.
82 On the American and North Vietnamese presence in Laos after the conclusion of the 1962 Geneva Agreement, see Thee, *Notes of a Witness*, 303–13; Hall, "Laos Neutralization Agreement," 455; and Porter, "After Geneva," 179–212.
83 Prados, *Hidden History of the Vietnam War*, 231; Sandra Taylor, "Laos," 75.
84 Stuart-Fox, *History of Laos*, 153.
85 Veljko Micunovic, Yugoslavian ambassador to the United States, had a correct perception of Moscow's difference with Beijing and Hanoi over Laos when he said to U.S. secretary of state Dean Rusk on April 19, 1963, that the Soviet Union wished to stabilize the situation in Laos, but China and North Vietnam did not. See *FRUS, 1961–1963*, 24:994.
86 Hannah, *Key to Failure*, 37–38.
87 Timothy Castle, *At War in the Shadow of Vietnam*, 48.
88 Thee, *Notes of a Witness*, 325, 328–29.

CHAPTER FIVE

1 Herring, *America's Longest War*, 86; Prados, *Hidden History of the Vietnam War*, 23.
2 For Pham Van Dong's visit to China, see *Zhou waijiao dashiji*, 313–14. The remarks by Mao and Zhou are quoted in Guo Ming, *ZhongYue guanxi yanbian sishinian*, 67.
3 R. B. Smith, *International History of the Vietnam War*, 2:38; Porter, "Vietnam and the Socialist Camp," 247.
4 Herring, *America's Longest War*, 88.
5 R. B. Smith, *International History of the Vietnam War*, 2:38.
6 Zhang Yan's speech at the National Conference on Foreign Affairs, Dec. 1961, Q3124, J123, JPA.
7 Bui Tin, *Following Ho Chi Minh*, 45. Bui Tin also recalled that PLA chief of staff Luo Ruiqing, a member in the delegation, told him that if the Vietnamese provoked the Americans into retaliatory attacks close to the Chinese border, the Chinese would have to intervene as had occurred in Korea (ibid.). But *Peking Review*, Dec. 22, 1961, which reported on the composition and activities of the Ye mission, did not mention Luo.
8 MacFarquhar, *Origins of the Cultural Revolution*, 3:3.
9 Herring, *America's Longest War*, 95; Schulzinger, *Time for War*, 113.
10 For an establishment biography of Wang, see Xu Zehao, *Wang Jiaxiang zhuan*.
11 Ibid., 554–57. According to Wang Li, Liu Shaoqi endorsed Wang Jiaxiang's ideas (*Xianchang lishi*, 21). Wang Li had extensive discussions with Wang Jiaxiang in 1960 about the starvation in rural areas. He later became a key figure in the Cultural Revolution.
12 Wang Li, *Xianchang lishi*, 21; Cong Jin, *Quzhe fazhan de suiyue*, 500–502; Zhu Zhongli, *Liming yu wanxia*, 394–96. Zhu Zhongli is the wife of Wang Jiaxiang. See also Bachman, "Structure and Process in the Making of Chinese Foreign Policy," 43–44.

13 Ma Qibin, *Zhongguo gongchandang zhizheng sishinian*, 213; Cong Jin, *Quzhe fazhan de suiyue*, 502; Zhu Zhongli, *Liming yu wanxia*, 396–99; MacFarquhar, *Origins of the Cultural Revolution*, 3:274–81.

14 MacFarquhar, *Origins of the Cultural Revolution*, 3:281–83.

15 Xue Mouhong and Pei Jianzhang, *Dangdai Zhongguo waijiao*, 159; Guo Ming, *ZhongYue guanxi yanbian sishinian*, 69; Wang Xiangen, *YuanYue kangMei shilu*, 25. Wang Xiangen was a secretary at the headquarters of the PLA Engineering Corps in the late 1970s.

16 Viewing the PRC's economic failure and the exodus of refugees from the mainland to Hong Kong as signs of an internal disintegration, Chiang Kai-shek believed that 1962 was the best time to recover the mainland. Accordingly, he ordered his generals to make preparations to attack the PRC. But Washington opposed Chiang's plan. For recollections by Chiang's former lieutenants, see *Liu Anqi xiansheng fangwen jilu*, 195–96. Liu An-chi was commander in chief of the Nationalist Army in 1962. See also *Ni Yuxi xiansheng fangwen jilu*, 219. Ni Yue-si was commander in chief of the Nationalist navy in 1962.

17 About 60,000 Kazakhs fled to the Soviet Union, evidently lured by the higher living standards among their ethnic brothers there. On the Xinjiang incidents, see MacFarquhar, *Origins of the Cultural Revolution*, 3:239.

18 Report, the CCP Central Military Commission to Mao, Aug. 10, 1962, *Mao wengao*, 10:156. For a detailed discussion of the 1962 war preparations involving Mao, Defense Minister Lin Biao, and Chief of Staff Luo Ruiqing, see Huang Yao and Zhang Mingzhe, *Luo Ruiqing zhuan*, 368–76. This book, based on documents from the Central Archives and the Archives of the Central Military Commission, the Committee on National Defense, Science, and Industry, and the Ministry of Public Security, is the official biography of Luo.

19 Zhou's talk with Giap, Oct. 5, 1962, *Zhou nianpu*, 2:501.

20 Zhou's talk with the DRV military delegation, Oct. 7, 1962, ibid., 501–2.

21 Xue Mouhong and Pei Jianzhang, *Dangdai Zhongguo waijiao*, 159; Qu Aiguo, Bao Mingrong, and Xiao Zuyao, *YuanYue kangMei*, 8.

22 Xue Mouhong and Pei Jianzhang, *Dangdai Zhongguo waijiao*, 159; Qu Aiguo, Bao Mingrong, and Xiao Zuyao, *YuanYue kangMei*, 8.

23 *Liu nianpu*, 2:577.

24 Herring, *America's Longest War*, 105–8; Schulzinger, *Time for War*, 119.

25 For Mao's statement, see *Renmin ribao* (People's Daily), Aug. 30, 1963.

26 Tong Xiaopeng, *Fengyu sishinian*, 2:220–21. This book is a biography of Zhou Enlai by a longtime associate of the Chinese premier. Tong Xiaopeng participated in the Conghua meeting.

27 Steven Levine has observed that "in the early 1960s . . . the Chinese appeared to be assuming the role of catalyst in a loose grouping of Communist and radical states—the PRC, North Korea, North Vietnam, Cambodia, and Indonesia . . . to weaken, break up, or prevent the emergence of Asian states with an actual or presumptive anti-China bias" ("China in Asia," 118).

Although there is no indication that Communists from Thailand participated in the Conghua meeting, the politburo of the Thai Communist Party had adopted in August 1963 "a resolution to start preparations for creating revolutionary bases in jungle areas." Quoted in R. B. Smith, *International History of the Vietnam War*, 178.

28 On Chinese-Indonesian relations, see Mozingo, *Chinese Policy toward Indonesia*.

29 Zhang Yan's speech at the National Conference on Foreign Affairs, 1964, Q3124, J291, JPA.

30 There is little revelation in the recently released Chinese sources on Beijing's role in the September 30, 1965, coup in Indonesia.

31 According to the Vietnamese *White Paper*, 30, in 1963 the CCP proposed the formation of a new bloc of eleven Communist parties "in an attempt to seize the leadership of world revolution and to form a new Communist International dominated by Peking," but Hanoi opposed the idea because it did not want to see the socialist camp split. See also Post, *Revolution, Socialism and Nationalism in Viet Nam*, 3:164.

32 For Liu's visit to North Korea, see *Liu nianpu*, 2:580–81.

33 Hughes to Rusk, Oct. 22, 1963, in *FRUS, 1961–1963*, 4:418–19.

34 Quoted in Burchett, *Vietnam*, 216.

35 Liu Tianye et al., *Li Tianyou jiangjun zhuan*, 381–85; Li Ke, "Zhongguo renmin yuanYue kangFa de yeji biaobing qingshi," 30.

36 Duiker, *Communist Road to Power in Vietnam*, 239–41; King Chen, "North Vietnam in the Sino-Soviet Dispute," 1034. According to Cecil Currey, Le Duan and Nguyen Chi Thanh were advocates of a quick conclusion to the struggle in the south and taking advantage of the murder of Diem and chaos in Saigon, while Vo Nguyen Giap and Truong Chinh remained committed to the strategy of protracted war. See *Victory at Any Cost*, 243.

37 Mao to Ho Chi Minh, Dec. 27, 1963, *Mao wengao*, 10:465–66.

38 Hu Zhengqing, *Yige waijiaoguan de riji*, 5. Hu Zhengqing was a member of the CCP Work Team. Before going to Laos in 1965, he was a PLA officer stationed in Hengyang, Hunan province. His diaries are valuable because they not only describe the selection, organization, and purposes of the work team and provide important glimpses into the conditions and operations of the Pathet Lao but also illuminate the specific dilemmas confronting the Chinese advisers in Laos as a result of the special relationship between the VWP and the LPP. On Kaysone Phomvihane's visit to Beijing, see also Quan Yanchi and Du Weidong, *Gongheguo mishi*, ch. 1.

39 Hu Zhengqing, *Yige waijiaoguan de riji*, 5–6.

40 Ibid., 1–166.

41 Ibid. On the role of North Vietnam in Laos, see also Langer and Zasloff, *North Vietnam and the Pathet Lao*, 106–80.

42 Hu Zhengqing, *Yige waijiaoguan de riji*, 1–166.

43 Gaiduk, *Soviet Union and the Vietnam War*, 5. In a discussion with the Japanese Communist Party delegation led by Secretary-General Miyamoto Kenji on March 3, 1966, Deng Xiaoping claimed: "In 1962, when the guerrilla struggle began in South Vietnam, Vietnam asked the Soviet Union for arms supplies, but was refused; but China, supporting the struggle in South Vietnam, did its utmost to send all weapons stored in China in support of the struggle in South Vietnam." See Kojima, *Record of the Talks between the Japanese Communist Party and the Communist Party of China*, 81.

44 Porter, "Vietnam and the Socialist Camp," 248.

45 Bui Tin, *Following Ho Chi Minh*, 44–45.

46 Only the North Korean Communist delegation defended the Chinese position in open speeches. In his address to the Czechoslovak Party Congress, the North Korean delegate

Lee Chu-yon praised the Chinese revolution and the CCP and disapproved the practice of using one party's congress to attack another party (Wu Xiuquan, *Huiyi yu huainian*, 356). See also Griffith, *Sino-Soviet Rift*, 83.

47 Wu Xiuquan, *Huiyi yu huainian*, 351–52.

48 Porter, "Vietnam and the Socialist Camp," 248–49. Ken Post observed that in early 1963, "the Vietnamese gave signs of drawing closer to the Chinese position, although never absolutely and always obliquely" (*Revolution, Socialism and Nationalism in Viet Nam*, 3:151).

49 Quoted in Post, *Revolution, Socialism and Nationalism in Viet Nam*, 3:152. See also Zagoria, *Vietnam Triangle*, 109.

50 Post, *Revolution, Socialism and Nationalism in Viet Nam*, 3:152.

51 Gu Longsheng, *Mao Zedong jingji nianpu*, 581–82.

52 *Renmin ribao* (People's Daily), July 31, 1963. See also Griffith, *Sino-Soviet Rift*, 162–63.

53 Porter, "Vietnam and the Socialist Camp," 249. See also Zagoria, *Vietnam Triangle*, 109–10.

54 Quoted in King Chen, "North Vietnam in the Sino-Soviet Dispute," 1030–31. See also Zagoria, *Vietnam Triangle*, 109–10.

55 Quoted in King Chen, "North Vietnam in the Sino-Soviet Dispute," 1031–32.

56 Le Duan's speech to the Central Committee meeting was later published in *Hoc Tap* (Feb. 1964). Quoted in Porter, "Vietnam and the Socialist Camp," 250–51. Duan's praise of Mao's theory was deleted from this speech when it was reprinted in the 1977 edition of his writings.

57 Hoang Van Hoan, *Canghai yisu*, 293.

58 "Balance of Forces and Strategic Offensive," *Hoc Tap*, Jan. 1964. Quoted in King Chen, "North Vietnam in the Sino-Soviet Dispute," 1034.

59 R. B. Smith, *International History of the Vietnam War*, 2:226.

60 Quoted in Moïse, *Tonkin Gulf and the Escalation of the Vietnam War*, 48–49.

61 Stowe, "'Revisionism' in Vietnam," 6. According to a Chinese source, the DRV-Czechoslovak joint statement caused a "heated debate" within North Vietnam, and the VWP later issued several articles to refute the idea of peaceful coexistence. See Report by officials (unidentified) from the International Liaison Department of the CCP Central Committee at a national conference on foreign affairs in Beijing, Apr. 19, 1963, in Q3124, J177, JPA.

62 Bui Tin, *Following Ho Chi Minh*, 54–56; Moïse, *Tonkin Gulf and the Escalation of the Vietnam War*, 49. On Hoang Minh Chinh's background, see Stowe, "'Revisionism' in Vietnam."

63 Maneli, *War of the Vanquished*, 174–75, 180; Moïse, *Tonkin Gulf and the Escalation of the Vietnam War*, 49.

64 Ilya Gaiduk wrote that the DRV delegation "went to Moscow on a kind of reconnaissance mission, to determine the Soviet position" (*Soviet Union and the Vietnam War*, 8).

65 Hoang Van Hoan, *Canghai yisu*, 294.

66 Mao's talk with Le Duan, Jan. 30, 1964, quoted in Li Jie, "60 niandai Zhongguo guonei jushi de bianhua yu ZhongMei guanxi," 266.

67 On the organization and preparation of the nine polemics, see MacFarquhar, *Origins of the Cultural Revolution*, 3:360–64.

68 Gaiduk, *Soviet Union and the Vietnam War*, 8–9. See also Pike, *Vietnam and the Soviet Union*, 73.

69 Quoted in Pike, *Vietnam and the Soviet Union*, 73–74.

70 Zagoria, *Vietnam Triangle*, 111.

71 Pike, *Vietnam and the Soviet Union*, 74.

72 Gaiduk, *Soviet Union and the Vietnam War*, 10.

73 Bui Tin, *Following Ho Chi Minh*, 48–53.

74 Post, *Revolution, Socialism and Nationalism in Viet Nam*, 3:11, 50–52. In his discussion of the postliberation political system in North Vietnam, the Vietnam specialist David Elliott characterized the Soviet model as the administrative state, "a designation which implies hierarchy, formalism, a tendency towards bureaucratic solutions to policy problems, and a reluctance to encourage unstructured mass participation in government." Quoted in ibid., 11.

75 For China's internal developments between 1960 and 1966, see Spence, *Search for Modern China*, 590–609, and Gray, *Rebellions and Revolutions*, 326–36.

CHAPTER SIX

1 Herring, *America's Longest War*, 131–33.

2 Sandra Taylor, "Laos," 73–90; Timothy Castle, *At War in the Shadow of Vietnam*, 70–72; Prados, *Hidden History of the Vietnam War*, 232.

3 *Zhou waijiao dashiji*, 410–11.

4 Zhou's talk with Ne Win, July 10, 1964, *Zhou nianpu*, 2:655.

5 *Zhou waijiao dashiji*, 411. See also *Zhou nianpu*, 2:650.

6 Quoted in Li Danhui, "ZhongSu guanxi yu Zhongguo de yuanYue kangMei," 112.

7 Xue Mouhong and Pei Jianzhang, *Dangdai Zhongguo waijiao*, 159; Qu Aiguo, Bao Mingrong, and Xiao Zuyao, *YuanYue kangMei*, 9.

8 Present at the meetings were Zhou Enlai, Chen Yi, Wu Xiuquan, Yang Chengwu, and Tong Xiaopeng of the CCP; Ho Chi Minh, Le Duan, Truong Chinh, Pham Van Dong, Vo Nguyen Giap, Nguyen Chi Thanh, Hoang Van Hoan, and Van Tien Dung of the VWP; and Kaysone Phomvihane, Prince Souphanouvong, Nouhak Phoumsavan, and Phoumi Vongvichit of the LPP (*Zhou waijiao dashiji*, 413; Tong Xiaopeng, *Fengyu sishinian*, 2:220–21).

9 In July 1964, Mao, Liu Shaoqi, and Zhou Enlai instructed that China should increase the supply of military materials to the Pathet Lao and be ready to cover all the logistical needs of the Pathet Lao forces. See Han Huaizhi and Tan Jingqiao, *Dangdai Zhongguo jundui de junshi gongzuo*, 1:560.

10 Li Ke and Hao Shengzhang, *Wenhua dageming zhong de renmin jiefangjun*, 408; Qu Aiguo, Bao Mingrong, and Xiao Zuyao, *YuanYue kangMei*, 9.

11 "77 Conversations," 74.

12 Wang Dinglie and Lin Hu, *Dangdai Zhongguo kongjun*, 384; Qu Aiguo, Bao Mingrong, and Xiao Zuyao, *YuanYue kangMei*, 10; Chen Jian, "China's Involvement in the Vietnam War," 364.

13 Whiting, "How We Almost Went to War with China," 76; Gurtov and Byong-Moo Hwang, *China under Threat*, 160–61.

14 Li Ke, "Zhongguo renmin yuanYue kangMei de yeji biaobing qingshi," 30.

15 Mao's talk with Pham Van Dong and Hoang Van Hoan, Oct. 5, 1964, in "77 Conversations," 74–77.

16 Gurtov and Byong-Moo Hwang, *China under Threat*, 162; Herring, *America's Longest War*, 143–45.

17 Han Huaizhi and Tan Jingqiao, *Dangdai Zhongguo jundui de junshi gongzuo*, 1:539–40; Li Ke and Hao Shengzhang, *Wenhua dageming zhong de renmin jiefangjun*, 415; Guo Ming, *ZhongYue guanxi yanbian sishinian*, 69–70; Li Ke, "Zhongguo renmin yuanYue kangMei de yeji biaobing qingshi," 31.

18 Han Huaizhi and Tan Jingqiao, *Dangdai Zhongguo jundui de junshi gongzuo*, 1:539–40; Wang Xiangen, *YuanYue kangMei shilu*, 44; Li Ke, "Zhongguo renmin yuanYue kangMei de yeji biaobing qingshi," 31.

19 Xue Mouhong and Pei Jianzhang, *Dangdai Zhongguo waijiao*, 161.

20 Wang Xiangen, *YuanYue kangMei shilu*, 45.

21 Ibid., 35, 44; Li Ke and Hao Shengzhang, *Wenhua dageming zhong de renmin jiefangjun*, 422. R. B. Smith dates the Ho-Mao meeting at May 16–17. His source is the diary of Ho's personal secretary. See R. B. Smith, *International History of the Vietnam War*, 3:139.

22 Wang Xiangen, *YuanYue kangMei shilu*, 46–48; the CCP Central Documentary Research Department and the PLA Military Science Academy, *Zhou Enlai junshi wenxuan*, 4:527–29.

23 Li Ke and Hao Shengzhang, *Wenhua dageming zhong de renmin jiefangjun*, 417.

24 *White Paper*, 33. According to Luu Doan Huynh, a senior research fellow at the International Relations Institute of the Ministry of Foreign Affairs of Vietnam, Beijing informed Hanoi in June 1965 that it would not be able to defend North Vietnam from U.S. air attacks. Quoted in Whiting, "China's Role in the Vietnam War," 71–76.

25 *Beijing Review*, Nov. 30, 1979, 14; Xue Mouhong and Pei Jianzhang, *Dangdai Zhongguo waijiao*, 161; Qu Aiguo, Bao Mingrong, and Xiao Zuyao, *YuanYue kangMei*, 12.

26 My interview with researchers at the PLA Military Science Academy, Beijing, July 2, 1996.

27 Guo Ming, *ZhongYue guanxi yanbian sishinian*, 71; Li Ke and Hao Shengzhang, *Wenhua dageming zhong de renmin jiefangjun*, 427.

28 Li Ke and Hao Shengzhang, *Wenhua dageming zhong de renmin jiefangjun*, 410–11.

29 *Mao wengao*, 11:478.

30 Li Ke and Hao Shengzhang, *Wenhua dageming zhong de renmin jiefangjun*, 410.

31 Ibid., 412–14.

32 Li Ke, "Zhongguo renmin yuanYue kangMei de yeji biaobing qingshi," 31; Guo Ming, *ZhongYue guanxi yanbian sishinian*, 69.

33 According to the French scholar Marie Alexandrine Martin, on November 25, 1965, General Lon Nol, chief of staff of the Royal Khmer armed forces, visited Beijing on Sihanouk's orders and concluded with Luo Ruiqing a military treaty, which stipulated: "(1) Cambodia would permit the passage and the refuge of Vietnamese combatants in the border regions, granting them protection if necessary and permitting them to establish command posts; (2) Cambodia would permit the passage of material coming from China and intended for Vietnam." See Martin, *Cambodia*, 92–93. For a Chinese account of Beijing's use of Sihanoukville to send military supplies to the NLF between 1966 and 1967, see Kang Daisha, "Zai Jianpuzhai de rizi," 482–83. Kang Daisha is the wife of Chen Shuliang, who was China's ambassador to Cambodia between 1962 and 1967.

34 Gilks and Segal, *China and the Arms Trade*, 50.

35 Sihanouk worked out an arrangement with Beijing and Hanoi in 1964 to retain 10 percent of the Chinese weapons delivered to the Vietnamese through Sihanoukville.

Additional fees were charged for transporting food and other goods to the Vietnamese border in Cambodian army trucks and private vehicles contracted for that purpose. Many officers who had profited by trading with the Vietnamese Communists later supported General Lon Nol's coup against Sihanouk in 1970. See Chanda, *Brother Enemy*, 420, and Chandler, *Tragedy of Cambodian History*, 140.

36 Li Ke and Hao Shengzhang, *Wenhua dageming zhong de renmin jiefangjun*, 416; Chen Jian, "China's Involvement in the Vietnam War," 378–79.

37 Whiting, *Chinese Calculus of Deterrence*, 186; Whiting, "Forecasting Chinese Foreign Policy," 506–23.

38 Quoted in Schulzinger, "Johnson Administration, China, and the Vietnam War," 149–50.

39 *Zhou waijiao dashiji*, 445; *Zhou nianpu*, 2:723; Xue Mouhong and Pei Jianzhang, *Dangdai Zhongguo waijiao*, 160–61.

40 The strains in U.S.-Pakistani relations as a result of Karachi's deepening ties to Beijing between 1964 and 1965 are covered in detail in McMahon, *Cold War on the Periphery*, 309–24.

41 *Zhou nianpu*, 2:736.

42 Editorial note, *FRUS, 1964–1968*, 2:700–701.

43 Bundy to Rusk, June 5, 1965, ibid., 729. See also Schulzinger, "Johnson Administration, China, and the Vietnam War," 150. On William Bundy's role in the making of U.S. policy toward Vietnam, see Bird, *Color of Truth*.

44 Notes of meeting, July 22, 1965, in *FRUS, 1964–1968*, 3:215. See also Schulzinger, "Johnson Administration, China, and the Vietnam War," 151.

45 Garver, "Chinese Threat in the Vietnam War," 75.

46 Kenneth Young, *Negotiating with the Chinese Communists*, 270; Rogers, "Sino-American Relations and the Vietnam War," 298.

47 Schulzinger, "Johnson Administration, China, and the Vietnam War," 150; Rogers, "Sino-American Relations and the Vietnam War," 310–11. According to Anatoly Dobrynin, the Soviet ambassador to the United States, Walt Rostow, President Johnson's national security adviser, told him in June 1966 that a tacit understanding had been established between Washington and Beijing: "The United States would not attack or bomb mainland China, and China would at least not use its armed forces to interfere in the Vietnam War" (*In Confidence*, 142).

48 For Mao's view of the United States, see his January 12, 1964, statement in support of the struggle of the Panamanian people in *Mao wengao*, 11:6–7.

49 Quoted in Sun Dongsheng, "Woguo jingji jianshe zhanlue bujiu de dazhuanbian," 44.

50 Ma Qibin et al., *Zhongguo gongchandang zhizheng sishinian*, 248; *Mao wengao*, 11:103–4.

51 *Mao wengao*, 11:103–4.

52 Mao's talk with Pham Van Dong, Nov. 17, 1968, *Mao waijiao wenxuan*, 582.

53 Mao to Wang Dongxing, Aug. 6, 1964, *Mao wengao*, 11:120.

54 Yuan Dejin, "Lun xinZhongguo chengli hou Mao Zedong zhanzheng yu heping lilun de yanbian," 36.

55 On the origins, development, and consequences of the Third Front, see Naughton, "Third Front," 351–86.

56 For the text of the report, see *Dangde wenxian*, no. 3 (1995): 34–35.

57 Mao to Luo and Yang, Aug. 12, 1964, ibid., 33. See also *Mao wengao*, 11:126–27.

58 For the text of the Special Committee report of August 19, 1964, see *Dangde wenxian*, no. 3 (1995): 33–34.

59 Mao's remarks are quoted in Sun Dongsheng, "Woguo jingji jianshe zhanlue bujiu de dazhuanbian," 45.

60 Ibid., 44.

61 Naughton, "Third Front," 368.

62 Mao's talk with He Long, Luo Ruiqing, and Yang Chengwu, Apr. 28, 1965, in *Mao junshi wenji*, 6:404.

63 For Snow's version of his talk with Mao, see Snow, *Long Revolution*, 215–16. For the Chinese version, see *Mao waijiao wenxuan*, 544–62.

64 Li Ke and Hao Shengzhang, *Wenhua dageming zhong de renmin jiefangjun*, 341.

65 Ibid., 341–42; *Mao junshi wenji*, 6:403.

66 Lin Hu, *Kunjun shi*, 188.

67 *Liu nianpu*, 2:618.

68 *Mao wengao*, 11:359–60.

69 Zhou's talk with Spiro Koleka, May 9, 1965, *Zhou waijiao dashiji*, 455.

70 Liu Shaoqi's speech at the war planning meeting of the Central Military Commission, May 19, 1965, in *Dangde wenxian*, no. 3 (1995): 40.

71 The CCP Central Documentary Research Department, *Zhu De nianpu*, 537–38.

72 Ra'anan, "Peking's Foreign Policy 'Debate,'" 23–71; Zagoria, "Strategic Debate in Peking," 237–68; Yahuda, "Kremlinology and the Chinese Strategic Debate," 32–75; Harding, "Making of Chinese Military Power," 361–85; Lieberthal, "Great Leap Forward and the Split in the Yan'an Leadership," 129–30.

73 Barry Naughton has made a similar criticism in "Third Front," 370–71.

74 Lin Biao, "Long Live the Victory of People's War," 9–30.

75 Xu Yan, *Junshijia Mao Zedong*, 149; Huang Yao, *Sanci danan busi de Luo Ruiqing Dajiang*, 263, 265, 270–71. This book is based on sources from the Central Archives, the PLA General Staff Archives, and the Ministry of Public Security Archives.

76 On the Luo-Lin dispute, see Huang Yao, *Sanci danan busi de Luo Ruiqing Dajiang*, chs. 24–34, and Huang Yao and Zhang Mingzhe, *Luo Ruiqing zhuan*, chs. 13–15. Roderick MacFarquhar also reports that he has found no evidence that views on Vietnam policy played any role in the purge of officials in 1965 (*Origins of the Cultural Revolution*, 3:377).

77 For a critique of the Western assumption that politics was about policy in China, see Teiwes and Sun, *Tragedy of Lin Biao*, 164–65.

78 Michael Hunt has also criticized the emphasis on factions to account for Chinese foreign policy formation. He poses this question: "Does the factional model transpose on China the competitive ethos of American politics and underestimate the restraining authoritarian and hierarchical qualities of China's political culture?" See Hunt, "CCP Foreign Policy," 170.

79 Mao to Yang Chengwu and Lei Yingfu, Jan. 30, 1965, *Mao junshi wenji*, 6:402.

80 Thomson, "On the Making of U.S. China Policy," 236; Tucker, "Threats, Opportunities, and Frustrations in East Asia," 103.

81 McNamara, *In Retrospect*, 215.

82 On the role of Mao's united front doctrine in China's foreign policy, see Armstrong, *Revolutionary Diplomacy*.

83 For Mao's statements on the "Two Intermediate Zones," see *Mao waijiao wenxuan*, 506–9. See also Chi Aiping, "Mao Zedong guoji zhanlue sixiang de yanbian," 46–52, and Li Jie, "Mao Zedong guoji zhanlue sixiang yanjiu," 1–16.

84 Mao Zedong, "Talks with the American Correspondent Anna Louise Strong," in *Selected Works of Mao Tse-tung*, 4:99.

85 On China's policy toward Angola and Mozambique, see Jackson, "China's Third World Foreign Policy," 387–422. On Beijing's efforts to woo Sihanouk during the late 1950s and early 1960s, see Wang Youping, "Qu Jinbian zhixing teshu shiming," 66–82. Wang Youping was China's ambassador to Cambodia in 1958–62. On Chinese-Indonesian relations, see Mozingo, *Chinese Policy toward Indonesia*. On Beijing's economic and military aid to Cuba in the early 1960s, see Lin Ping and Ji Ni, "Bujuan de kaituo zhe," 150–51.

   During his visit to Morocco in December 1963, Zhou Enlai heard a report from Chinese ambassador Yang Qiliang regarding China's contacts with African nationalist organizations based in that country. According to Yang, many African nationalist groups had offices and military training camps in Morocco and the Chinese embassy maintained close and friendly relations with them. Zhou commended Yang for his work. See Yang Qiliang, "Dui Zhou zongli liangci chufang de huiyi ji qita," 332.

86 On Beijing's attempt to divide the Soviet-led bloc, see Hoxha, *Reflections on China*, and Halliday, *Artful Albanian*, ch. 5. For an overview of Chinese-Albanian relations, see Fan Chengzuo, "ZhongA guanxi de 'chun xia jiu dong,'" 50–52. Fan Chengzuo is a former ambassador to Albania.

87 Mao's talk with the Chilean Journalist Delegation, June 23, 1964, *Mao waijiao wenxuan*, 529–33.

88 Mao's talk with delegates from Asia, Africa, and Oceania on July 9, 1964, ibid., 534–39.

89 On anti-imperialism in Chinese foreign policy, see Van Ness, *Revolution and Chinese Foreign Policy*, and Friedman, "Anti-Imperialism in Chinese Foreign Policy."

90 On the Chinese foreign policy setbacks in 1965 and their impact on China's internal development, see Garver, *Foreign Relations of the People's Republic of China*, 152–57.

91 McNamara, *In Retrospect*, 215.

92 The CCP delegation included about sixty members, an indication of the importance Beijing attached to the mission. See MacFarquhar, *Origins of the Cultural Revolution*, 3:364–65, and Gurtov and Byong-Moo Hwang, *China under Threat*, 161.

93 For a detailed, first-hand account of Zhou Enlai's visit to Moscow, see Yu Zhan, "Yici buxunchang de shiming." Yu Zhan was director of the Department of the Soviet Union and Eastern Europe of the Chinese Foreign Ministry in 1964. He accompanied Zhou to Moscow. See also Gu Yongzhong and Liu Yansheng, *He Long zhuan*, 530–33.

94 *Zhou waijiao dashiji*, 428.

95 Zhou's talk with Ho Chi Minh and Le Duan, Mar. 1, 1965, in ibid., 438.

96 R. B. Smith, *International History of the Vietnam War*, 3:54.

97 *White Paper*, 30. See also Chanda, "Secrets of Former Friends," 38–39. I have not seen any Chinese material that confirms the Vietnamese claim.

98 Xie Yixian, *Zhongguo waijiao shi*, 344. According to the Russian scholar Vladislav Zubok, Kosygin represented the "China Lobby" within the Soviet leadership, which wanted to restore Sino-Soviet unity and placed its hopes on Zhou Enlai. Other members of the lobby included Mikhail Suslov, a party secretary, and Alexander Shelepin, a

former KGB chief. One of the purposes of Kosygin's Beijing trip was to "clarify misunderstandings" with the Chinese. After the failure of the visit, the China Lobby "calmed down." See Zubok, "Unwrapping the Enigma," 165–66. According to Georgi Arbatov, the debacle of the Kosygin mission made Soviet leaders realize that they could not easily mend fences with the Chinese without abandoning fundamental principles of domestic and international policies. See Arbatov, *System*, 113.

99 *Peking Review*, Mar. 11, 1966, 5.

100 Dittmer, *Sino-Soviet Normalization and Its International Implications*, 334.

101 Xie Yixian, *Zhongguo waijiao shi*, 345.

102 Ibid., 346–48; *Peking Review*, May 6, 1966, 25–26; Lawson, *Sino-Vietnamese Conflict*, 167.

103 For detailed coverage of the chaos in Guangxi between 1967 and 1968 and Zhou Enlai's efforts to restore order there, see Jiao Hongguang, " 'Wenge' zhong Zhou Enlai chuli Guangxi wenti deng youguan qingkuang," 73–76. Jiao Hongguang was an air force officer in the Guangzhou Military District during the Cultural Revolution. He participated in Zhou Enlai's meetings with the Red Guards' representatives from Guangxi between 1967 and 1968. See also *Zhou nianpu*, 3:161, 166, 181–82, 189–90, 200, 207, 215, 220–22, 232.

104 Douglas Pike describes Hanoi's strategy to put the Sino-Soviet dispute to its own use in service of its war as "the alternating tilt gambit." See Pike, *Vietnam and the Soviet Union*, 54–55.

105 For Mao's reaction to Dulles's policy, see Bo Yibo, *Ruogan zhongda juece yu shijian de huigu*, 2:1137–57.

106 Lieberthal, "Great Leap Forward and the Split in the Yan'an Leadership," 143.

107 On Mao's attempt to use the escalation of the Indochina conflict to radicalize China's political and social life, see Chen Jian, "China's Involvement in the Vietnam War," 361–65.

108 Wang Xiangen, *YuanYue kangMei shilu*, 60–68.

109 Li Weixian, "YuanYue kangMei fangkong zuozhan 300 tian," 19–23. Li Weixian was a deputy commander of a Chinese antiaircraft artillery division, which was dispatched to North Vietnam in October 1966.

110 Zhao Xuemei, "Qinli jianwen," 25–30. Zhao Xuemei was a Chinese engineering soldier in North Vietnam between 1965 and 1968.

111 Wang Xiangen, *YuanYue kangMei shilu*, 74–75.

112 Guo Ming, *ZhongYue guanxi yanbian sishinian*, 102.

113 "77 Conversations," 94–98. The Le Duan delegation was making a stopover in Beijing after attending the Twenty-third Congress of the Soviet Communist Party.

114 Cong Jin, *Quzhe fazhan de suiyue*, 607.

115 *Mao wengao*, 11:394–95.

116 Kojima, *Record of the Talks between the Japanese Communist Party and the Communist Party of China*.

117 Quoted in Zagoria, *Vietnam Triangle*, 112. On Hanoi's delicate act of distancing itself from Beijing in Soviet eyes while simultaneously using the NLF's diplomats to placate China, see Brigham, *Guerrilla Diplomacy*, ch. 4.

118 Lawson, *Sino-Vietnamese Conflict*, 165.

119 Zagoria, *Vietnam Triangle*, 112; Sulzberger, *Age of Mediocrity*, 323–24.

120 Summers, *On Strategy*, 93–94, 96.
121 Garver, "Chinese Threat in the Vietnam War," 75.

CHAPTER SEVEN

1 On Soviet goals in Vietnam, see Gaiduk, *Soviet Union and the Vietnam War*, and Dobrynin, *In Confidence*, 128–40.
2 Xie Yixian, *Zhongguo waijiao shi*, 344.
3 Chinese Foreign Ministry memo, "A Conversation Outline: Refuting the Argument That 'China Blocked the Soviet Aid to Vietnam,'" Apr. 1, 1965, Q3124, J235, JPA. This memo was distributed by the Foreign Affairs Office of the State Council on April 6, 1965, to provincial foreign affairs committees as an explanation of China's position on the Vietnam question.
4 Marilyn Young, *Vietnam Wars*, 153.
5 According to a biographer of Harold Wilson, the Walker trip was designed "to distract attention from Britain's continuing support for the United States." The prime minister had a penchant for "activity" as opposed to real executive "action." See Morgan, *Harold Wilson*, 277.
6 *Zhou waijiao dashiji*, 444.
7 Xie Yixian, *Zhongguo waijiao shi*, 340.
8 Cooper, *Lost Crusade*, 329.
9 R. B. Smith, *International History of the Vietnam War*, 3:60–61, 105–9; Herring, *Secret Diplomacy of the Vietnam War*, 829. The idea of convening an international conference on Cambodia dated back to 1962 in the wake of the border dispute between Cambodia and Thailand; Sihanouk wanted such a conference to guarantee the borders of Cambodia as defined on nineteenth-century French maps. While China supported Sihanouk's proposal, the United States, Thailand, and South Vietnam opposed it. See Leifer, "Cambodia and China," 345.
10 *Zhou waijiao dashiji*, 450.
11 Herring, *Secret Diplomacy of the Vietnam War*, 46. McNamara recalled that the administration found all but the third point of Hanoi's terms acceptable. See McNamara, *In Retrospect*, 181–82.
12 Xie Yixian, *Zhongguo waijiao shi*, 338. For U Thant's peace moves between 1964 and 1965, see Cooper, *Lost Crusade*, 327–28; Herring, *LBJ and Vietnam*, 91–94; Gardner, *Pay Any Price*, 145–46; and U Thant, *View from the UN*, 57–84.
13 Quoted in Xie Yixian, *Zhongguo waijiao shi*, 339.
14 Herring, *Secret Diplomacy of the Vietnam War*, 49, 831; Xie Yixian, *Zhongguo waijiao shi*, 339. On India's role in Indochina before 1964, see SarDesai, *Indian Foreign Policy in Cambodia, Laos, and Vietnam*.
15 Herring, *Secret Diplomacy of the Vietnam War*, 45–47.
16 *Shijie zhishi*, June 10, 1965, 5–8. For Hanoi's response to the MAYFLOWER initiative, see Brigham, "Vietnamese-American Peace Negotiations," 377–95.
17 Xie Yixian, *Zhongguo waijiao shi*, 340–41; R. B. Smith, *International History of the Vietnam War*, 3:154; Morgan, *Harold Wilson*, 277; Wilson, *Personal Record*, 108–13; Barbara Castle, *Castle Diaries*, 37, 40–41.
18 Xiong Xianghui, *Lishi de Zhujiao*, 151–57.

19 Xie Yixian, *Zhongguo waijiao shi*, 341.

20 Thompson, *Ghana's Foreign Policy*, 409–11.

21 Chinese Foreign Ministry circular, "Talks between the Ghanaian Mission and the Vietnamese," Aug. 3, 1965, Q3124, J123, JPA. This circular, along with two other circulars quoted later in this chapter, was distributed by the CCP Central Committee to its regional bureaus and provincial committees on August 24, 1965, as an instruction of China's position regarding peace negotiations over Vietnam.

22 Chinese Foreign Ministry circular, "Talks between the Ghanaian Mission and the Vietnamese," Aug. 3, 1965, Q3124, J123, JPA. The circular's summary of the Vietnamese position during the discussions with the Ghanaian mission was based on a Vietnamese report.

23 Thompson, *Ghana's Foreign Policy*, 411.

24 *Shijie zhishi*, July 10, 1965, 10–12.

25 Chinese Foreign Ministry circular, "On 'Peace Talk' Activities over Vietnam," Aug. 19, 1965, Q3124, J123, JPA.

26 Chinese Foreign Ministry circular, "Malraux's Visit to China," Aug. 12, 1965, Q3124, J123, JPA. For Malraux's account of his 1965 visit to China, see Malraux, *Anti-memoirs*, 325–80. The book, however, makes no mention of Malraux's suggestion of redividing Vietnam. In the words of Jean Lacouture, Malraux's proposal was "the most wildly improbable idea that ever emerged from the brain of a novelist." See Lacouture, *Andre Malraux*, 431. On Paris's Vietnam policy, see Sullivan, *France's Vietnam Policy*, and Costigliola, *France and the United States*, ch. 4.

27 *Peking Review*, Sept. 3, 1965, 5–6.

28 Ibid., Sept. 30, 1965, 29–31.

29 Kang Daisha, "Zai Jianpuzhai de rizi," 477–78.

30 Herring, *LBJ and Vietnam*, 100.

31 Michalowski, "Polish Secret Peace Initiatives in Vietnam," 241, 258–59; Gaiduk, *Soviet Union and the Vietnam War*, 83–84; Radvanyi, *Delusion and Reality*, 125–26.

32 For an excerpt of Michalowski's memoirs, see Hershberg, "Central and East European Documents on the Vietnam War." See also Radvanyi, *Delusion and Reality*, 126–27.

33 Hershberg, "Central and East European Documents on the Vietnam War."

34 Michalowski believed that Ho's negative attitude toward negotiations was related to the strong Chinese pressure. See ibid.

35 Ibid.; Gaiduk, *Soviet Union and the Vietnam War*, 84. No details have been revealed from either the Russian or Vietnamese archives regarding Shelepin's talks with the North Vietnamese. On this issue, Janos Radvanyi wrote:

> There was . . . complete agreement between the Soviet and Vietnamese negotiators regarding the American peace proposal. When this question came up during negotiations, Ho Chi Minh explained . . . that the military situation in the South was not yet considered favorable for a start of negotiations with the Americans. He did not discount the possibility of future negotiations: he viewed diplomatic maneuvering as but another form of revolutionary fighting . . . and he hinted that possibly in two or three years the DRV might be ready to . . . start negotiations. Shelepin made no attempt to modify the Vietnamese position. . . . He completely agreed with Ho. (Radvanyi, *Delusion and Reality*, 165)

Radvanyi based his account on reports by the Hungarian embassy in Hanoi as well as information Budapest received from Moscow through party channels.

36 *Shijie zhishi*, Feb. 10, 1966, 4–5; *Peking Review*, Feb. 18, 1966, 10.

37 Wang Bingnan's speech at the National Conference on Foreign Affairs, Feb. 11, 1966, Q3124, J270, JPA. Wang was a deputy foreign minister who participated in the Li-Shelepin talks.

38 Radvanyi, *Delusion and Reality*, 167.

39 Kojima, *Record of the Talks between the Japanese Communist Party and the Communist Party of China*, 156–57.

40 Quoted in Zagoria, *Vietnam Triangle*, 144.

41 Thompson, *Ghana's Foreign Policy*, 412.

42 *Zhou nianpu*, 3:13.

43 Thompson, *Ghana's Foreign Policy*, 413. In Beijing, Nkrumah held five talks with Zhou Enlai between February 24 and 28. See *Zhou waijiao dashiji*, 490.

44 Herring, *LBJ and Vietnam*, 104; Sulzberger, *Age of Mediocrity*, 349; Dallek, *Flawed Giant*, 389. According to Henry Cabot Lodge, U.S. ambassador to South Vietnam, Lewandowski "was terribly worried about China," and Western diplomats believed that "it was China's influence which was making Hanoi so intransigent." See Lodge to the State Department, July 24, 1966, *FRUS, 1964–1968*, 4:528–29.

45 Herring, *America's Longest War*, 185; Marilyn Young, *Vietnam Wars*, 180; Dallek, *Flawed Giant*, 389.

46 Memo of conversations between Stoessel and Michalowski, Dec. 13 and 14, 1967, *FRUS, 1964–1968*, 17:359–60. U.S. officials were clearly frustrated by China's attack on the American peace moves. On January 17, 1966, Arthur J. Goldberg, U.S. representative to the United Nations, said: "There are a few voices that say America is engaged in a propaganda maneuver. When that voice comes from Peiping, it can be dismissed for what it is worth." See U.S. Department of States, *Department of States Bulletin* (Feb. 7, 1966), 200.

47 Zhou's talk with Nyerere, June 4, 1965, *Zhou waijiao dashiji*, 460.

48 On Mao's fear of Soviet-American domination of the world between 1963 and 1969, see Garver, "Tet Offensive and Sino-Vietnamese Relations," 55–59.

49 For the English version of the commentary, see *Peking Review*, Feb. 18, 1966, 6–12.

50 *Zhou waijiao dashiji*, 493; Keith, *Diplomacy of Zhou Enlai*, 158.

51 Keith, *Diplomacy of Zhou Enlai*, 157.

52 On Hanoi's approach to negotiations, see Porter, *Peace Denied*, 1–33; Goodman, *Lost Peace*, 11–12; and Duiker, *Sacred War*, 191–92.

53 Brigham, "Vietnamese-American Peace Negotiations," 391–92.

54 Thies, *When Governments Collide*, 198; Herring, *LBJ and Vietnam*, 108; Oberdorfer, *Tet!*, 68–69.

55 Truong Nhu Tang, *Journal of a Vietcong*, 194. Truong Nhu Tang was minister of justice of the Provisional Revolutionary Government between 1969 and 1975.

56 Chinese Foreign Ministry circular, "On 'Peace Talk' Activities over Vietnam," Aug. 19, 1965, Q3124, J123, JPA.

57 Mao's talk with the DRV party and government delegation, Oct. 20, 1965, *Mao waijiao wenxuan*, 570–73. Pham Van Dong came to Beijing after completing a visit to Moscow. It is possible that he had discussed with the Soviets the issue of negotiations and reported this discussion to Mao and other Chinese leaders.

58 Brigham, "Vietnamese-American Peace Negotiations," 385–89.

59 Kojima, *Record of the Talks between the Japanese Communist Party and the Communist Party of China*, 116.

60 *Zhou waijiao dashiji* (487) mentions Zhou's talks with Nguyen Duy Trinh on December 18–19, 1965, but provides no detail of them.

61 "77 Conversations," 92.

62 Gaiduk, *Soviet Union and the Vietnam War*, 109. *Zhou waijiao dashiji* does not mention Zhou's talk with Le Duan in October–November 1966.

63 Herring, *America's Longest War*, 185. According to Anatoly Dobrynin, the Soviet ambassador to the United States, in early 1967 Hanoi secretly asked the Soviets to use the British government to put pressure on Washington to reach a peaceful solution in Vietnam. See Dobrynin, *In Confidence*, 155.

64 Zhou's talks with Pham Van Dong and Vo Nguyen Giap, Apr. 7, 1967, *Zhou waijiao dashiji*, 509–10.

65 The document consists of an unidentified cadre's notes taken from a high-level indoctrination course in 1967. Cited in Duiker, *Sacred War*, 193–94.

66 Zhou's talk with Pham Van Dong, Apr. 10, 1967, *Zhou waijiao dashiji*, 510.

67 Zhou's talk with Pham Van Dong, Apr. 11, 1967, ibid., 510–11.

68 Cited in Gaiduk, *Soviet Union and the Vietnam War*, 109.

69 Herring, *America's Longest War*, 226–27; Duiker, *Sacred War*, 215–16.

70 Herring, *America's Longest War*, 230; Duiker, *Sacred War*, 216.

71 Hoang Van Hoan, *Canghai yisu*, 308; Hoang Van Hoan, "Distortion of Facts about Militant Friendship between Viet Nam and China Is Impermissible," 18. Hoang Van Hoan was also in Beijing at the time for a rest cure.

72 "77 Conversations," 123–29.

73 Zhou's talk with Xuan Thuy, May 7, 1968, *Zhou waijiao dashiji*, 524.

74 Herring, *America's Longest War*, 231.

75 "77 Conversations," 137–38.

76 Herring, *America's Longest War*, 237.

77 "77 Conversations," 138–40.

78 During this same period, Hanoi censored China's references to the "peace talks fraud" and the "bombing halt hoax." See Jay Taylor, *China and Southeast Asia*, 61, and Hoang Van Hoan, "Distortion of Facts about Militant Friendship between Viet Nam and China Is Impermissible," 18.

79 Mao's talk with Pham Van Dong, Nov. 17, 1968, *Mao waijiao wenxuan*, 580–83.

80 Lawson, *Sino-Vietnamese Conflict*, 216; Jay Taylor, *China and Southeast Asia*, 63.

81 F. Charles Parker, *Vietnam*, 224.

82 Lawson, *Sino-Vietnamese Conflict*, 216. Hanoi's endorsement of the Soviet invasion of Czechoslovakia greatly upset the Chinese. The North Vietnamese delegation at Beijing's October 1 celebrations that year was ranked behind the Australian Communist Party. See Jay Taylor, *China and Southeast Asia*, 61.

83 Lawson, *Sino-Vietnamese Conflict*, 217.

84 Zhou's talk with Ion Gheorghe Maurer, Sept. 7, 1969, *Zhou waijiao dashiji*, 538–39.

85 American officials believed that the Chinese had blocked peace talks between North Vietnam and Washington. Rusk said in 1966 that China "will not talk or do anything. Peking has actively intruded on any talks between Hanoi and [the] U.S. Hanoi appears

to be somewhere between Moscow and Peking—but closer to Peking" (Notes of meeting, Jan. 28, 1966, *FRUS, 1964–1968*, 4:179).

86 Gaiduk, *Soviet Union and the Vietnam War*, 16.

87 Kissinger, *White House Years*, 749. Between 1969 and 1972, Soviet diplomats in Paris met regularly with the DRV delegation to discuss developments in the peace negotiations. The North Vietnamese kept Moscow informed not only of the official sessions but also of private meetings between Xuan Thuy, Le Duc Tho, and Kissinger. See Gaiduk, *Soviet Union and the Vietnam War*, 221.

88 Wilson, *Personal Record*, 205–6.

CHAPTER EIGHT

1 Kolko, *Anatomy of a War*, 279; Duiker, *Sacred War*, 208.

2 Mao Zedong, "On Protracted War," 187–267. See also Garver, "Tet Offensive and Sino-Vietnamese Relations," 46–52.

3 Garver, "Tet Offensive and Sino-Vietnamese Relations," 46–52. On how Hanoi's strategy differed from Mao's military principles, see Elliott, "Hanoi's Strategy in the Second Indochina War," 66–94.

4 *White Paper*, 33.

5 In a 1973 talk with Le Duan and Pham Van Dong, Mao blamed Defense Minister Lin Biao for insisting on guerrilla war in Vietnam while claiming that he himself had been hoping that "you would conduct a mobile war so that you could annihilate part of the enemy force." Quoted in Chen Donglin and Du Pu, *Zhonghua renmin gongheguo shilu*, 919.

6 Xie Yixian, *Zhongguo waijiao shi*, 360. This source does not mention the exact date of Mao's remarks.

7 Zhou's talk with Ho Chi Minh, Feb. 7, 1968, *Zhou nianpu*, 3:217.

8 For further discussions of Beijing's calculations in insisting on a protracted people's war in Vietnam, see Dittmer, *Sino-Soviet Normalization and Its International Implications*, 198, and Ross, *Indochina Tangle*, 23.

9 Herring, *America's Longest War*, 208–28; Duiker, *Sacred War*, 212–16.

10 Li Ke and Hao Shengzhang, *Wenhua dageming zhong de renmin jiefangjun*, 426; Qu Aiguo, Bao Mingrong, and Xiao Zuyao, *YuanYue kangMei*, 13.

11 Zhou's talk with Pham Hung and Hoang Van Thai, Apr. 21, 1969, *Zhou waijiao dashiji*, 535, and *Zhou nianpu*, 3:293.

12 Li Ke and Hao Shengzhang, *Wenhua dageming zhong de renmin jiefangjun*, 416. According to the Vietnamese *White Paper*, in 1968, when discussing aid to the DRV for 1969, Beijing cut its aid by 20 percent of the 1968 figure. See *White Paper*, 37.

13 Han Huaizhi and Tan Jingqiao, *Dangdai Zhongguo jundui de junshi gongzuo*, 1:562–74; Ai Lingyao, "Zhongguo yuanLao kangMei de guanghui pianzhang," 38–41.

14 Lemnitzer memorandum, Jan. 13, 1969, National Security File, Country File: Laos, Box 272, Lyndon Johnson Papers, Lyndon B. Johnson Library, Austin, Tex.

15 Quan Yanchi and Du Weidong, *Gongheguo mishi*, 250–51. See also Chen Jian, "China's Involvement in the Vietnam War," 383–84.

16 Porter, "Vietnamese Policy and the Indochina Crisis," 79.

17 Herring, *America's Longest War*, 248.

18 Xue Mouhong and Pei Jianzhang, *Dangdai Zhongguo waijiao*, 219; Xiong Xianghui, *Lishi de Zhujiao*, 189–90; Cohen, *America's Response to China*, 196–97; Ross, *Negotiating Cooperation*, 32–33.

19 Xiong Xianghui, *Lishi de Zhujiao*, 173–204; Ross, *Negotiating Cooperation*, 30–31.

20 Gong Li, *Kuayue honggou*, 49; Harding, *Fragile Relationship*, 38.

21 Xue Mouhong and Pei Jianzhang, *Dangdai Zhongguo waijiao*, 219; Harding, *Fragile Relationship*, 38.

22 Robert Ross has perceptively assessed the impact of the Cambodian invasion on Mao's individual sensitivities, but his contention that the incident "played into the hands" of the Lin Biao group, who had continuously stressed the American threat, is less convincing. See Ross, *Negotiating Cooperation*, 34. I have not seen any Chinese document that indicates Lin's exploitation of the Cambodian crisis to oppose the Sino-American dialogue.

23 In fact, the Samlaut rebellion was primarily a localized action. David Chandler writes that the revolt "sprang from local grievances against injustice and social change, corruption, and ham-fisted government behavior" and that the participants "did not respond to orders from the CPK central committee" (*Tragedy of Cambodian History*, 166). According to Milton Osborne, the rebellion "was more an outbreak of largely spontaneous resistance to government actions than the first orchestrated challenge from the radicals" (*Sihanouk*, 191). Cambodia and Kampuchea represent, respectively, English and Khmer pronunciations of the same word. The fullest account of the Samlaut rebellion is contained in Kiernan, "Samlaut Rebellion."

24 "77 Conversations," 101–4.

25 Ibid., 107–14; *Zhou waijiao dashiji* (510–11) records Zhou's conversations with Pham Van Dong on April 10–11, 1967, but it only includes their talks on the war in South Vietnam and is silent on the Cambodian issue.

26 *Black Paper*, 25–26. It should be noted that this pamphlet, believed to have been authored primarily by Pol Pot, was issued after the break of relations between the Khmer Rouge and Vietnam. It is thus a highly emotional and bitterly worded tract with a strong anti-Vietnamese bias, but it does reveal a number of specific facts regarding Vietnamese–Khmer Rouge interactions.

   According to Western sources, after his visit to Hanoi, Pol Pot traveled to China and spent four months or more there, including a period when CCP secretary-general Deng Xiaoping worked with him. See Heder, "Kampuchea's Armed Struggle," 6–7, and Kiernan, *How Pol Pot Came to Power*, 219–24.

27 Porter, "Vietnamese Communist Policy toward Kampuchea," 78–79.

28 Gilks, *Breakdown of the Sino-Vietnamese Alliance*, 52.

29 Chandler, *Tragedy of Cambodian History*, 171. On the first two years of Pol Pot's revolutionary warfare, see Kiernan, *How Pol Pot Came to Power*, 268–88; Heder, "Kampuchea's Armed Struggle," 13–14; and Etcheson, *Rise and Demise of Democratic Kampuchea*, 82–84.

30 Chandler, *Tragedy of Cambodian History*, 171–74; Heder, "Kampuchea's Armed Struggle," 14.

31 "77 Conversations," 135–37. The Cambodian hostility increased when more North Vietnamese regular units moved into Cambodia in mid-1968 following the Tet offensive. These troops were more recognizable as foreigners than the previous NLF units on

Cambodian soil, and they often acted more abrasively toward the local population. See Chandler, *Tragedy of Cambodian History*, 160.

32 "77 Conversations," 135–37.

33 According to William Duiker, in 1968, Pol Pot, after a visit to China, launched an armed rebellion against Sihanouk. See Duiker, *China and Vietnam*, 53. Duiker drew upon his interview with Kong Korn, deputy foreign minister of the People's Republic of Kampuchea, on December 18, 1985. Kong Korn claimed that Beijing instigated the insurrection.

34 Armstrong, *Revolutionary Diplomacy*, 209.

35 Kissinger, *White House Years*, 250–51. See also Duiker, *China and Vietnam*, 53.

36 Etcheson, *Rise and Demise of Democratic Kampuchea*, 234.

37 Chandler, *Tragedy of Cambodian History*, 184.

38 "77 Conversations," 158–59.

39 *Black Paper*, 32–34; Porter, "Vietnamese Communist Policy toward Kampuchea," 82–84.

40 Chandler, *Tragedy of Cambodian History*, 191–94. According to Marie Alexandrine Martin, while in France, "Sihanouk asked his prime minister to organize popular anti-Vietnamese demonstrations in support of his initiatives with the two Communist giants" (*Cambodia*, 122–23).

41 Zhou's talk with Nay Valentin, Mar. 14, 1970, *Zhou waijiao dashiji*, 548, and *Zhou nianpu*, 3:354.

42 Zhou's talk with the North Korean ambassador, Mar. 16, 1970, *Zhou waijiao dashiji*, 548–49.

43 Sihanouk, *My War with the CIA*, 24–25. Written after Sihanouk's deposition, this book has a strong anti-American tone.

44 Papp, *Vietnam*, 160; Duiker, *China and Vietnam*, 53.

45 Sihanouk, *My War with the CIA*, 26–27; Chandler, *Tragedy of Cambodian History*, 197.

46 Sihanouk, *My War with the CIA*, 27.

47 Zhou's talk with Sihanouk, Mar. 19, 1970, *Zhou nianpu*, 3:356. See also *Zhou waijiao dashiji*, 549.

48 *Zhou nianpu*, 3:356.

49 Ibid.

50 "77 Conversations," 160–62. Pol Pot later claimed that he participated in the Zhou-Dong negotiations and had been in Hanoi beforehand. See Chandler, *Tragedy of Cambodian History*, 200. According to the *Black Paper* (35), when the March 18 coup occurred, the CPK delegation led by Pol Pot was holding discussions with the CCP in Beijing, but Sihanouk was not aware of this development.

51 Chandler, *Tragedy of Cambodian History*, 200.

52 Ibid.

53 *Zhou waijiao dashiji* (549) mentions the Zhou-Dong meeting on March 22 but does not include its contents.

54 Zhou's talk with Sihanouk, Mar. 22, 1970, *Zhou nianpu*, 3:356. See also *Zhou waijiao dashiji*, 549.

55 Chandler, *Tragedy of Cambodian History*, 200–201; Martin, *Cambodia*, 135–36.

56 Martin, *Cambodia*, 136. According to Anne Gilks, the Chinese, in deference to Sihanouk's sensitivities, did not inform him of Pol Pot's presence in Beijing (*Breakdown of the Sino-Vietnamese Alliance*, 55).

57 Jay Taylor, *China and Southeast Asia*, 151–52; Lawson, *Sino-Vietnamese Conflict*, 196; R. B. Smith, "International Setting of the Cambodia Crisis," 330.

58 Zhou made his remarks in Pyongyang at the welcome banquet hosted by Kim Il Sung. See Xie Yixian, *Zhongguo waijiao shi*, 354.

59 Jay Taylor, *China and Southeast Asia*, 152–53; Lawson, *Sino-Vietnamese Conflict*, 196; Armstrong, *Revolutionary Diplomacy*, 210; Gilks, *Breakdown of the Sino-Vietnamese Alliance*, 54. In 1973 Zhou Enlai told Henry Kissinger that it was Lon Nol who wanted to maintain diplomatic relations with China after his coup against Sihanouk. According to Zhou, at the beginning, Lon Nol promised that he would permit the use of Sihanouk-ville to transport weapons to South Vietnam. Zhou informed Kissinger that China "rejected" Lon Nol because he had engaged in "subversive activities" and made "unreasonable and unjust" policies. See memorandum of conversation between Zhou and Kissinger, Feb. 16, 1973, in Burr, *Kissinger Transcripts*, 103–9 (quotations from 106).

After returning to Beijing in May 1970, Kang Maozhao became head of the Cambodian office in the Chinese Foreign Ministry. The office, established on March 19, 1970, was responsible for coordinating Sihanouk's activities in China. Kang supervised a staff of about twelve people. See Kang Maozhao, "Zai peiban Xihanuke qingwang de rizili," 31–32.

60 Kissinger, *White House Years*, 448–57; Gilks, *Breakdown of the Sino-Vietnamese Alliance*, 54; R. B. Smith, "International Setting of the Cambodia Crisis," 319; Kirk, *Wider War*, 46–47.

61 *Beijing Review*, Mar. 13, 1970, 13.

62 Gilks, *Breakdown of the Sino-Vietnamese Alliance*, 54.

63 Zhou's talk with Sihanouk, Mar. 28, 1970, *Zhou waijiao dashiji*, 550.

64 Gilks, *Breakdown of the Sino-Vietnamese Alliance*, 56.

65 Before the summit opened, Chinese vice foreign minister Han Nianlong led a team of officials to Guangzhou to make arrangements. See Zhang Qing, "Qingshen yizhong ershi zai," 155. Zhang Qing was an official in the Asian Department of the Chinese Foreign Ministry at the time. He went with Han to Guangzhou.

66 Zhang Qing, "Qingshen yizhong ershi zai," 155. The author did not explain the nature of the differences between Pham Van Dong and Sihanouk. The actual proceedings of the summit remain murky and controversial. According to Western accounts, China and Sihanouk wanted to establish a permanent organization to coordinate activities, but Hanoi opposed this proposal because the organization was presumably to be located in China. The North Vietnamese intended that the conference serve only propaganda purposes and not get involved in planning operations. See Jay Taylor, *China and Southeast Asia*, 156, and Lawson, *Sino-Vietnamese Conflict*, 198. Anne Gilks, on the other hand, writes that "the conference did not create a joint military command, which would have considerably strengthened Vietnam's influence over the NUFK" (*Breakdown of the Sino-Vietnamese Alliance*, 57). Gilks implies that the initiative for a joint military command hailed from Hanoi.

67 Xie Yixian, *Zhongguo waijiao shi*, 356–57; Papp, *Vietnam*, 161.

68 Truong Nhu Tang, *Journal of a Vietcong*, 147.

69 *Zhou waijiao dashiji*, 552; Xie Yixian, *Zhongguo waijiao shi*, 357.

70 The Editorial Team on "the Record of Mao Zedong's International Contacts," *Mao Zedong guoji jiaowang lu*, 66–68.

71 Xue Mouhong and Pei Jianzhang, *Dangdai Zhongguo waijiao*, 219; Gong Li, *Kuayue honggou*, 56–57.

72 As Kissinger pointed out to Nixon at the time, Mao's speech "makes no threats, offers no commitments, is not personally abusive toward you, and avoids positions on contentious bilateral issues." Absent in Mao's address was the usual phrase about China being a "rear area" for the Indochinese struggle. See Kissinger, *White House Years*, 695.

73 Chai Chengwen, Huang Zhengji, and Zhang Changjin, *Sanda tupo*, 243.

74 Gilks, *Breakdown of the Sino-Vietnamese Alliance*, 58–62; Chandler, *Tragedy of Cambodian History*, 205–10; Jay Taylor, *China and Southeast Asia*, 156; Martin, *Cambodia*, 142.

CHAPTER NINE

1 Xue Mouhong and Pei Jianzhang, *Dangdai Zhongguo waijiao*, 219–20; Gong Li, *Kuayue honggou*, 66; Cohen, *America's Response to China*, 197.

2 "77 Conversations," 176.

3 Ibid.

4 Herring, *America's Longest War*, 265; Marilyn Young, *Vietnam Wars*, 253; Stuart-Fox, *History of Laos*, 143–44; Kimball, *Nixon's Vietnam War*, 241–48.

5 Quoted in Kissinger, *White House Years*, 706–7.

6 Kissinger, *White House Years*, 706. Kissinger again noted that Beijing's criticisms "carefully avoided personal attacks on Nixon." See also Garthoff, *Détente and Confrontation*, 288.

7 Gong Li, *Kuayue honggou*, 69.

8 Zhou's talk with the DRV party and government delegation, Mar. 7, 1971, *Zhou waijiao dashiji*, 580–81. See also *Zhou nianpu*, 3:441–42.

9 "77 Conversations," 178–80.

10 Garthoff, *Détente and Confrontation*, 288.

11 Xue Mouhong and Pei Jianzhang, *Dangdai Zhongguo waijiao*, 220–21.

12 Gong Li, *Kuayue honggou*, 105. The author does not identify the officials who had reservations. According to the conventional view in the West, Lin Biao opposed improving relations with the United States because a continuation of the "dual enemy" approach would benefit his constituency, the military. But there is no evidence in the newly available Chinese sources that supports such a hypothesis.

13 Gong Li, *Kuayue honggou*, 102–7.

14 Li Ke and Hao Shengzhang, *Wenhua dageming zhong de renmin jiefangjun*, 416; Gilks, *Breakdown of the Sino-Vietnamese Alliance*, 74. George McT. Kahin observed that during his trip to the DRV in September 1972, nearly all of the hundreds of trucks he saw on the roads between Hanoi and the China border were of Chinese make, and oil and gasoline pipelines had been constructed across the border deep into Vietnam ("Nixon and the PRG's 7 Points," 66).

15 *White Paper*, 41.

16 The Diplomatic History Research Office of the PRC Foreign Ministry, *XinZhongguo waijiao fengyun*, 2:41–42; Xue Mouhong and Pei Jianzhang, *Dangdai Zhongguo waijiao*, 221–22; Zhang Guang, "Dakai ZhongMei guanxi damen de lishi beijing yu jingguo," 59.

17 The Diplomatic History Research Office of the PRC Foreign Ministry, *XinZhongguo waijiao fengyun*, 2:41–42.

18 Ross, *Negotiating Cooperation*, 40.

19 *Zhou waijiao dashiji*, 596.

20 *White Paper*, 40.

21 Kahin, "Nixon and the PRG's Seven Points," 47–70; Luu Doan Huynh, "The Seven-Point Proposal of the PRG (July 1, 1971) and the U.S. Reaction," 198–202.

22 Cited in Papp, *Vietnam*, 166.

23 Garver, "Sino-Vietnamese Conflict and the Sino-American Rapprochement," 454.

24 Papp, *Vietnam*, 164–65. Whitlam met with Zhou Enlai in Beijing on July 5. The official account of Zhou's diplomacy mentions their meeting but provides no detail about the conversation. See *Zhou waijiao dashiji*, 595.

25 Papp, *Vietnam*, 164–65.

26 *Zhou nianpu*, 3:469–70.

27 Hersh, *Price of Power*, 442. Hersh's account was based on his interview with North Vietnamese deputy foreign minister Nguyen Co Thach in Hanoi in August 1979. Thach had been present with Pham Van Dong in Beijing in November 1971. See also Duiker, *Sacred War*, 234.

28 *Zhou nianpu*, 3:497.

29 Yun Shui, *Chushi qiguo jishi*, 136. This book is based primarily on Wang Youping's recollections. After the first formal meeting with Pham Van Dong on November 21, Zhou Enlai blamed Deputy Foreign Minister Han Nianlong, who was in charge of arranging Dong's visit, for not including in the meeting's agenda China's appreciation for the DRV's support for its representation in the United Nations (ibid., 136–37).

30 Ross, *Negotiating Cooperation*, 49; Walters, *Silent Missions*, 545–46.

31 The Diplomatic History Research Office of the PRC Foreign Ministry, *XinZhongguo waijiao fengyun*, 3:71–82.

32 Ross, *Negotiating Cooperation*, 49. Ross's account was based on his interview with Haig.

33 The Diplomatic History Research Office of the PRC Foreign Ministry, *XinZhongguo waijiao fengyun*, 3:73–75.

34 *White Paper*, 43. See also Gilks, *Breakdown of the Sino-Vietnamese Alliance*, 84.

35 Gaiduk, *Soviet Union and the Vietnam War*, 232.

36 Zhang Guang, "Dakai ZhongMei guanxi damen de lishi beijing yu jingguo," 62.

37 Kissinger, *White House Years*, 1087.

38 For the text of the Shanghai Communiqué, see Harding, *Fragile Relationship*, appendix B, 373–77. Sihanouk was unhappy with Beijing's decision to invite Nixon, his arch enemy, to visit China. Unwilling to stay in the same city with Nixon, Sihanouk left Beijing for Hanoi before the American president's arrival on February 21, and he did not return to China until after Nixon's departure. See Kang Maozhao. "Zai peiban Xihanuke qingwang de rizili," 35–36.

39 Yun Shui, *Chushi qiguo jishi*, 138.

40 Guo Ming, *ZhongYue guanxi yanbian sishinian*, 102–3.

41 Quoted in Duiker, *China and Vietnam*, 59.

42 Quoted in "Memorandum on Vice-Premier Li Xiannian's Talks with Premier Pham Van Dong," 18.

43 DRV deputy foreign minister Nguyen Co Thach's testimony, Oct. 8, 1978, quoted in Porter, "Vietnamese Policy and the Indochina Crisis," 74.

44 *White Paper*, 41.

45 Yun Shui, *Chushi qiguo jishi*, 138.

46 Duiker, *China and Vietnam*, 59.

47 Duiker, *Sacred War*, 234.

48 Truong Nhu Tang, *Journal of a Vietcong*, 204.

49 Turley, *Second Indochina War*, 138–39; Duiker, *Sacred War*, 234–35.

50 Herring, *America's Longest War*, 271–74; Marilyn Young, *Vietnam Wars*, 269–71.

51 Zhou's talk with Nguyen Tien, Apr. 14, 1972, *Zhou waijiao dashiji*, 627.

52 *Haijun shi*, 178.

53 *Peking Review*, May 19, 1972.

54 *Haijun shi*, 178–82; Li Zuyi and Jia Xiaoguang, "YuanYue kangMei saolei zuezhan jishi."
   According to another Chinese source, the Chinese minesweepers cleared forty-two
   mines independently and five mines in cooperation with North Vietnamese troops. See
   Li Ke and Hao Shengzhang, *Wenhua dageming zhong de renmin jiefangjun*, 426.

55 Li Ke and Hao Shengzhang, *Wenhua dageming zhong de renmin jiefangjun*, 426; Garver,
   "Sino-Vietnamese Conflict and the Sino-American Rapprochement," 456.

56 Garthoff, *Détente and Confrontation*, 290.

57 Gaiduk, *Soviet Union and the Vietnam War*, 236, 290n; Kissinger, *White House Years*,
   1151. According to Georgi Arbatov, after the U.S. mining of Haiphong, the Soviet leadership met on May 9 and 10 to discuss whether to cancel the Soviet-American summit.
   Although many high officials called for a cancellation, the decision to hold the summit
   was upheld. See Arbatov, *System*, 176–77.

58 Garthoff, *Détente and Confrontation*, 291.

59 Herring, *America's Longest War*, 275.

60 Duiker, *Sacred War*, 235–37; Marilyn Young, *Vietnam Wars*, 273; Schulzinger, *Time for
   War*, 298–99. According to Jeffrey Kimball, North Vietnamese leaders explained their
   dropping of the demand for Thieu's removal as the playing of an "ace up their sleeve";
   namely, once the United States was ready by mid-1972 to formally agree to withdraw all
   of its remaining troops, they threw in their card—abandoning their long-standing
   insistence on Thieu's removal—in order to prod the Nixon administration to conclude a
   settlement. Once the Americans were gone, it would be easier to deal with Thieu. See
   Kimball, "Russia's Vietnam War," 161.

61 Herring, *America's Longest War*, 276–77.

62 Hersh, *Price of Power*, 442; Duiker, *Sacred War*, 234. According to Luu Doan Huynh,
   Mao advised Pham Van Dong that Thieu should be kept in office and negotiated with.
   See Kahin, "Nixon and the PRG's Seven Points," 66. See also Garver, "Sino-Vietnamese
   Conflict and the Sino-American Rapprochement," 459–60.

63 Garver, "Sino-Vietnamese Conflict and the Sino-American Rapprochement," 460.

64 Zhou's talk with Le Duc Tho, July 12, 1972, *Zhou waijiao dashiji*, 637; "77 Conversations,"
   182–84.

65 Garthoff, *Détente and Confrontation*, 292.

66 Herring, *America's Longest War*, 277; Marilyn Young, *Vietnam Wars*, 275–76; Kimball,
   Nixon's Vietnam War, 342. In private, Kissinger called Thieu "a complete SOB." See
   Haldeman, *Haldeman Diaries*, 558.

67 Herring, *America's Longest War*, 278–80; Marilyn Young, *Vietnam Wars*, 278; Kimball,
   Nixon's Vietnam War, 364–66.

68 Gilks, *Breakdown of the Sino-Vietnamese Alliance*, 89; Herring, *America's Longest War*, 280.

69 Mao's talk with Nguyen Thi Binh, Dec. 29, 1972, quoted in Chen Donglin and Du Pu, *Zhonghua renmin gongheguo shilu*, 878.

70 Zhou's talk with Truong Chinh, Dec. 31, 1972, *Zhou waijiao dashiji*, 659.

71 Zhou's talk with Le Duc Tho, Jan. 3, 1973, ibid., 660.

72 Herring, *America's Longest War*, 281; Marilyn Young, *Vietnam Wars*, 279; Kimball, *Nixon's Vietnam War*, 366–68.

73 Zhou's talk with Sihanouk, Jan. 24, 1973, *Zhou waijiao dashiji*, 662.

74 Zhou's talk with Penn Nouth, Feb. 2, 1973, ibid., 663.

75 Hoang Van Hoan, "Distortion of Facts about Militant Friendship between Viet Nam and China Is Impermissible," 19. See also Garver, "Sino-Vietnamese Conflict and the Sino-American Rapprochement," 461.

76 "77 Conversations," 187–91; Chanda, *Brother Enemy*, 27. See also *White Paper*, 48.

77 Garver, "Sino-Vietnamese Conflict and the Sino-American Rapprochement," 462.

78 Kissinger, *White House Years*, 1383; Gilks, *Breakdown of the Sino-Vietnamese Alliance*, 91.

79 Gilks, *Breakdown of the Sino-Vietnamese Alliance*, 94; Brown and Zasloff, "Pathet Lao and the Politics of Reconciliation in Laos," 259–63; Stuart-Fox, *History of Laos*, 156–58.

80 Gilks, *Breakdown of the Sino-Vietnamese Alliance*, 94–95.

81 Xue Mouhong and Pei Jianzhang, *Dangdai Zhongguo waijiao*, 272–74; Duiker, *China and Vietnam*, 60–61.

82 Chanda, *Brother Enemy*, 20; Evans and Rowley, *Red Brotherhood at War*, 44–45.

83 Xue Mouhong and Pei Jianzhang, *Dangdai Zhongguo waijiao*, 270; "Memorandum on Vice-Premier Li Xiannian's Talks with Premier Pham Van Dong," 20.

84 *Zhou nianpu*, 3:644–45. For Ye Jianying's role in Beijing's decision making during the Paracels crisis, see Fan Shuo, *Ye Jianying zhuan*, 614–17. On China's operations in the South China Sea in January 1974, some writers have speculated about the division within the Beijing leadership. For instance, Anne Gilks writes that the moderates led by Zhou Enlai, "who were more sensible to the subtleties of international politics and the management of triangular relations, may have recognized that a less heavy-handed policy toward Hanoi might offer the best way to counter Soviet influence. Conversely, the radicals, disdainful of geopolitics, may have fuelled Hanoi's suspicions of Chinese expansionism by their strident nationalism during the Paracels crisis in January 1974" (Gilks, *Breakdown of the Sino-Vietnamese Alliance*, 117). There is no evidence in recently released Chinese sources to support Gilks's hypothesis. In fact, new documents from Zhou Enlai's archives indicate that the Chinese premier was the principal organizer behind China's seizure of the Paracel Islands.

85 *Zhou nianpu*, 3:645.

86 Chanda, *Brother Enemy*, 21.

87 Quoted in ibid., 21.

88 Xue Mouhong and Pei Jianzhang, *Dangdai Zhongguo waijiao*, 271.

89 Pye, "China Factor in Southeast Asia," 230.

90 Xue Mouhong and Pei Jianzhang, *Dangdai Zhongguo waijiao*, 274–75; Gilks, *Breakdown of the Sino-Vietnamese Alliance*, 114–15; Duiker, *China and Vietnam*, 61; Porter, "Vietnamese Policy and the Indochina Crisis," 83–84.

91 Gilks, *Breakdown of the Sino-Vietnamese Alliance*, 115.

92 *Zhou waijiao dashiji*, 693–94; Gilks, *Breakdown of the Sino-Vietnamese Alliance*, 118.

93 Truong Nhu Tang, *Journal of a Vietcong*, 249.

94 Ibid., 256–57; see also Gilks, *Breakdown of the Sino-Vietnamese Alliance*, 121.

95 Memorandums of conversation between Zhou and Kissinger, Feb. 16 and 18, 1973, and Kissinger's memorandum for Nixon, Mar. 2, 1973, in Burr, *Kissinger Transcripts*, 103–17. Commenting on the situation in Cambodia, Zhou Enlai told David Bruce, the head of the U.S. liaison office in Beijing, on May 18, 1973, that "the only way to find a solution was for the parties concerned to implement fully all the subsidiary clauses of Article 20" of the Paris Peace Agreement, which required the withdrawal of all foreign troops from Cambodia (and Laos). Zhou indicated his objection to Hanoi's domination of Indochina by declaring that China wanted to see Cambodia become "more peaceful, neutral, and independent than ever before." See Kissinger, *Years of Upheaval*, 350–51, and Gilks, *Breakdown of the Sino-Vietnamese Alliance*, 108.

96 Snepp, *Decent Interval*, 97; Martin, *Cambodia*, 143–44.

97 Chandler, *Tragedy of Cambodian History*, 226; Kiernan, *How Pol Pot Came to Power*, 372–73; Gilks, *Breakdown of the Sino-Vietnamese Alliance*, 109.

98 *Zhou waijiao dashiji*, 699–700. During his meeting with Zhou Enlai, Khieu Samphan gave the Chinese premier a grenade launcher as a gift. See Shawcross, *Sideshow*, 336.

99 Gilks, *Breakdown of the Sino-Vietnamese Alliance*, 125–26; Duiker, *China and Vietnam*, 60.

100 Shawcross, *Sideshow*, 344; Chandler, *Tragedy of Cambodian History*, 233. In talks with Secretary of State Kissinger in Beijing in November 1974, Vice Premier Deng Xiaoping declared that China supported both Sihanouk and the Khmer Rouge and that it was "not reliable" for the United States "to place its hopes on Lon Nol." He rejected Kissinger's proposal for a new Cambodian coalition involving Sihanouk and some of Lon Nol's supporters. See memorandums of conversation between Deng and Kissinger, Nov. 26 and 27, 1974, in Burr, *Kissinger Transcripts*, 293, 311–12.

101 *Haijun shi*, 182. See also Shawcross, *Sideshow*, 347–48, and Kiernan, *How Pol Pot Came to Power*, 412. In August 1975, following the liberation of Phnom Penh, the Khmer Rouge asked China to help clear mines in the Mekong to restore traffic. Between May and June 1976, the Chinese minesweeping team successfully removed all the remaining mines in the river. See *Haijun shi*, 182–83.

102 Chanda, *Brother Enemy*, 11–14; Kiernan, *How Pol Pot Came to Power*, 414.

103 Xue Mouhong and Pei Jianzhang, *Dangdai Zhongguo waijiao*, 283.

104 Quoted in Chanda, *Brother Enemy*, 16.

105 On Stalin's euphoria about the victory of the Chinese Communist Party, see Gaddis, *We Now Know*, 66–68.

106 "77 Conversations," 194; Cheng Zhongyuan, "Mao Zedong de sanxiang zhishi he Deng Xiaoping zhuchi de 1975 nian zhengdun," 66.

107 Chanda, *Brother Enemy*, 17; *Zhou waijiao dashiji*, 712; *Zhou nianpu*, 3:717.

108 Chanda, *Brother Enemy*, 17.

109 "77 Conversations," 194.

110 Porter, "Vietnamese Policy and the Indochina Crisis," 77. See also the editor's note to "Memorandum on Vice-Premier Li Xiannian's Talks with Premier Pham Van Dong," 17.

111 Chanda, *Brother Enemy*, 27.

112 "77 Conversations," 194–95.

113 Quoted in Chanda, *Brother Enemy*, 28.

114 Porter, "Vietnamese Policy and the Indochina Crisis," 78; Chanda, *Brother Enemy*, 28; Evans and Rowley, *Red Brotherhood at War*, 44.

CONCLUSION

1 Snyder, "Security Dilemma in Alliance Politics." Hope Harrison has made a similar discovery of the entrapment and abandonment syndrome in the Soviet–East German alliance. See Harrison, "Ulbricht and the Concrete 'Rose.'"

2 Ang Cheng Guan has also emphasized the existence of mutual need in the Chinese-DRV relationship. See his *Vietnamese Communists' Relations with China and the Second Indochina Conflict*, 233–34.

3 On the Soviet role in connecting the DRV with the West and the United Nations, see Gaiduk, *Soviet Union and the Vietnam War*, 75–78.

4 For a critique of Mao's sense of superiority in dealing with the Vietnamese, see Chen Jian, "China's Involvement in the Vietnam War," 386.

5 According to Huynh Kim Khanh, the designation of the Indochinese Communist Party was imposed by a Comintern instruction in late 1929 and adopted reluctantly in 1930 by the previously separated Communist units in Vietnam (*Vietnamese Communism*, 123–29). See also Brown, "Indochinese Federation Idea," 85–86.

6 For a highly useful definition of ideology, see Hunt, *Ideology and U.S. Foreign Policy*.

7 My discussion of the three sources of Mao's ideology is borrowed from Levine, "Perception and Ideology in Chinese Foreign Policy," 33.

8 On the role of the justice motive in international affairs, see Welch, *Justice and the Genesis of War*.

9 For recent works that stress the role of ideology in Communist foreign policy, see Chen Jian, *China's Road to the Korean War*; Mastny, *Cold War and Soviet Insecurity*; Gaddis, *We Now Know*; Sheng, *Battling Western Imperialism*; Macdonald, "Communist Bloc Expansion in the Early Cold War"; Nichols, "Lessons from the New History of the Cold War"; and Gould-Davis, "Rethinking the Role of Ideology in International Politics during the Cold War."

10 On the role of domestic mobilization in Mao's decision to bombard Quemoy in 1958, see Christensen, *Useful Adversaries*.

11 On Chinese-Soviet competition in Cuba, see Prozumenschikov, "Sino-Indian Conflict, the Cuban Missile Crisis, and the Sino-Soviet Split."

12 On the effects of anti-Sovietism on China's relations with its Asian neighbors during the 1970s, see Levine, "China in Asia," 123–24.

13 Westad, "Secrets of the Second World," 269.

14 Gaddis, *We Now Know*, 289.

BIBLIOGRAPHY

CHINESE-LANGUAGE SOURCES

Archives

Nanjing
  Jiangsu Provincial Archives
    Collection of the Foreign Affairs Office of the Jiangsu Provincial Government

Party History Journals

Dangdai Zhongguoshi yanjiu (Studies on Contemporary Chinese History). Beijing.
Dangde wenxian (Party Documents). Beijing.
Dangshi yanjiu ziliao (Party History Research Materials). Beijing.
Dangshi tongxun (Party History Bulletin). Beijing.
Dangshi yanjiu (Studies on Party History). Beijing.
Junshi lishi (Military History). Beijing.
Junshi shilin (Military History Circles). Beijing.
Renwu (Biographical Sketches). Beijing.
Shijie zhishi (World Knowledge). Beijing.
Waijiao xueyuan xuebao (Journal of Foreign Affairs College). Beijing.
Wenxian he yanjiu (Documents and Research). Beijing.
Zhonggong dangshi yanjiu (Studies on CCP History). Beijing.
Zhonggong dangshi ziliao (Materials on CCP History). Beijing.

Books and Articles

Ai Lingyao. "Zhongguo yuanLao kangMei de guanghui pianzhang" (The Glorious Chapter of China's Assistance to Laos against the United States). *Junshi lishi*, no. 1 (1990): 37–41.
Bo Yibo. *Ruogan zhongda juece yu shijian de huigu* (Recollections of Certain Important Decisions and Events). 2 vols. Beijing: Zhonggong zhongyang dangxiao chubanshe, 1991–93.
Cao Junjie, ed. *Zhongguo liangQiao: Hu Qiaomu, Qiao Guanhua zhuanlue* (Two Qiaos of China: Brief Biographies of Hu Qiaomu and Qiao Guanhua). Nanjing: Jiangsu renmin chubanshe, 1996.

The CCP Central Documentary Research Department, ed. *Jianguo yilai Mao Zedong wengao* (Mao Zedong's Manuscripts since the Founding of the Country). 13 vols. Beijing: Zhongyang wenxian chubanshe, 1987–98.

——. *Liu Shaoqi nianpu, 1898–1969* (A Chronicle of Liu Shaoqi's Life, 1898–1969). 2 vols. Beijing: Zhongyang wenxian chubanshe, 1996.

——. *Zhou Enlai nianpu, 1949–1976* (A Chronicle of Zhou Enlai's Life, 1949–1976). 3 vols. Beijing: Zhongyang wenxian chubanshe, 1997.

——. *Zhu De nianpu* (A Chronicle of Zhu De's Life). Beijing: Renmin chubanshe, 1986.

The CCP Central Documentary Research Department and the PLA Military Science Academy, eds. *Mao Zedong junshi wenji* (Collection of Mao Zedong's Military Writings). 6 vols. Beijing: Junshi kexue chubanshe and Zhongyang wenxian chubanshe, 1993.

——. *Zhou Enlai junshi wenxuan* (Selected Military Writings of Zhou Enlai). 4 vols. Beijing: Renmin chubanshe, 1997.

Chai Chengwen, Huang Zhengji, and Zhang Changjin. *Sanda tupo: XinZhongguo zouxiang shijie de baogao* (Three Breakthroughs: A Report on New China's Road to the World). Beijing: Jiefangjun chubanshe, 1994.

Chai Chengwen and Zhao Yongtian. *Banmendian tanpan* (Panmunjom Negotiations). Beijing: Jiefangjun chubanshe, 1989.

Chen Donglin and Du Pu, eds. *Zhonghua renmin gongheguo shilu: disanjuan (xia) Neiluan yu kangzheng—"Wenhua dageming" de shinian, 1972–1976* (A Factual Record of the People's Republic of China: Volume 3 (Part 2), Internal Disturbance and Rebellion—The Ten Years of the "Great Cultural Revolution," 1972–1976). Changchun: Jilin renmin chubanshe, 1994.

Chen Geng riji (xu) (Chen Geng Diaries, supplement). Beijing: Jiefangjun chubanshe, 1984.

Chen Shuliang. "Huiyi jiejue Laowo wenti de Rineiwa huiyi he Yinduzhina renmin huiyi" (Recalling the Geneva Conference on Laos and the Indochinese Peoples' Conference). *Waijiao xueyuan xuebao*, no. 3 (1988): 12–19.

Cheng Hua, ed. *Zhou Enlai he tade mishumen* (Zhou Enlai and His Secretaries). Beijing: Zhongguo guangbo dianshi chubanshe, 1992.

Cheng Xiangjun, ed. *Nu waijiaoguan* (Women Diplomats). Beijing: Renmin tiyu chubanshe, 1995.

Cheng Zhongyuan. "Mao Zedong de sanxiang zhishi he Deng Xiaoping zhuchi de 1975 nian zhengdun" (Mao Zedong's Three Instructions and the 1975 Rectification Directed by Deng Xiaoping). *Dangdai Zhongguoshi yanjiu*, no. 1 (1997): 63–78.

Chi Aiping. "Mao Zedong guoji zhanlue sixiang de yanbian" (The Evolution of Mao Zedong's International Strategic Thought). *Dangde wenxian*, no. 3 (1994): 46–52.

Cong Jin. *Quzhe fazhan de suiyue* (Years of Distorted Development). Zhengzhou: Henan renmin chubanshe, 1989.

The Diplomatic History Research Office of the PRC Foreign Ministry, ed. *Dangdai Zhongguo shijie waijiao shengya* (Diplomatic Careers of Contemporary Chinese Diplomats). 5 vols. Beijing: Shijie zhishi chubanshe, 1995–97.

——. *Huainian Chen Yi* (In Memory of Chen Yi). Beijing: Shijie zhishi chubanshe, 1991.

——. *Mao Zedong waijiao sixiang yanjiu* (Studies on Mao Zedong's Diplomatic Thought). Beijing: Shijie zhishi chubanshe, 1994.

——. *XinZhongguo waijiao fengyun* (Diplomatic Turbulence of New China). 4 vols. Beijing: Shijie zhishi chubanshe, 1990–96.

——. *Yanjiu Zhou Enlai: Waijiao sixiang yu shijian* (Studies on Zhou Enlai: Diplomatic Thought and Practice). Beijing: Shijie zhishi chubanshe, 1989.

——. *Zhou Enlai waijiao huodong dashiji, 1949–1975* (A Chronicle of Zhou Enlai's Diplomatic Activities, 1949–1975). Beijing: Shijie zhishi chubanshe, 1993.

The Editorial Team on the History of the CMAG, ed. *Zhongguo junshi guwentuan yuanYue kangFa douzheng shishi* (Historical Facts about the Role of the Chinese Military Advisory Group in the Struggle of Aiding Vietnam and Resisting France). Beijing: Jiefangjun chubanshe, 1990.

The Editorial Team on "the Record of Mao Zedong's International Contacts," ed. *Mao Zedong guoji jiaowang lu* (The Record of Mao Zedong's International Contacts). Beijing: Zhonggong dangshi chubanshe, 1995.

Fan Chengzuo. "ZhongA guanxi de 'chun xia jiu dong' " (The "Spring, Summer, Autumn, and Winter" in Chinese-Albanian Relations). *Waijiao xueyuan xuebao*, no. 3 (1993): 50–52.

Fan Shuo, chief ed. *Ye Jianying zhuan* (Biography of Ye Jianying). Beijing: Dangdai Zhongguo chubanshe, 1995.

Fu Hao and Li Tongcheng, eds. *Zhongguo waijiaoguan congshu: Kaiqi guomen— Waijiaoguan de fengcai* (Chinese Diplomats Series: Opening the Gate of the Country— The Glory of Diplomats). Beijing: Zhongguo huaqiao chubanshe, 1995.

Gao Hongdi. "Jiefang zhanzheng shiqi Zhongguo gongchandang zai Xianggang de caijing gongzuo" (The CCP's Financial and Economic Work in Hong Kong during the Period of the War of Liberation). *Zhonggong dangshi ziliao*, no. 54 (July 1995): 92–101.

Geng Biao. "Huiyi xinZhongguo jiechu de waijiaojia Zhang Hanfu tongzhi" (Recalling Comrade Zhang Hanfu, an Outstanding Diplomat of New China). *Renmin ribao* (Sept. 3, 1987), 5.

Gong Li. *Kuayue honggou: 1969–1979 nian Zhong Mei guanxi de yanbian* (Crossing the Chasm: The Evolution of Sino-American Relations, 1969–1979). Zhengzhou: Henan renmin chubanshe, 1992.

Gu Longsheng, ed. *Mao Zedong jingji nianpu* (A Chronicle of Mao Zedong's Economic Activities). Beijing: Zhonggong zhongyang dangxiao chubanshe, 1993.

Gu Yongzhong and Liu Yansheng, chief eds. *He Long zhuan* (Biography of He Long). Beijing: Dangdai Zhongguo chubanshe, 1993.

Guo Ming, ed. *ZhongYue guanxi yanbian sishinian* (The Evolution of Sino-Vietnamese Relations over the Last Forty Years). Nanning: Guangxi renmin chubanshe, 1991.

Guoji zhanlue yanjiu jijinhui, ed. *Huanqiu tongci liangre: Yidai lingxiumen de guoji zhanlue sixiang* (Everything Is the Same in the World: The International Strategic Thinking of a Generation of Leaders). Beijing: Zhongyang wenxian chubanshe, 1993.

Haijun shi (History of the Navy). Beijing: Jiefangjun chubanshe, 1989.

Han Huaizhi and Tan Jingqiao, chief eds. *Dangdai Zhongguo jundui de junshi gongzuo* (Contemporary Military Work of the Chinese Armed Forces). 2 vols. Beijing, Zhongguo shehui kexue chubanshe, 1989.

He Jingxiu et al., eds. *Mianhuai Liu Shaoqi* (Remembering Liu Shaoqi). Beijing: Zhongyang wenxian chubanshe, 1988.

He Yanhong. "Qingyi shensihai: Ji Zhou Enlai yu Hu Zhiming de jiaowang" (Friendship as Deep as the Sea: Zhou Enlai's Associations with Ho Chi Minh). *Renwu*, no. 4 (1991): 5–12.

Hoang Van Hoan. *Canghai yisu: Hoang Van Hoan geming huiyilu* (A Drop in the Ocean: Hoang Van Hoan's Revolutionary Reminiscences). Beijing: Jiefangjun chubanshe, 1987.

Hong Zuojun. "Fengyu qianzaiqing: Hu Zhiming yu YueZhong liangguo renmin" (Long-Term Friendship: Ho Chi Minh and the Peoples of Vietnam and China). *Renwu*, no. 2 (1994): 21–39.

Hu Shiyan, chief ed. *Chen Yi zhuan* (Biography of Chen Yi). Beijing: Dangdai Zhongguo chubanshe, 1991.

Hu Zhengqing. *Yige waijiaoguan de riji* (The Diaries of a Diplomat). Jinan: Huanghe chubanshe, 1991.

Huang Yao. *Sanci danan busi de Luo Ruiqing Dajiang* (Senior General Luo Ruiqing Who Survived Three Deaths). Beijing: Zhonggong dangshi chubanshe, 1994.

Huang Yao and Zhang Mingzhe. *Luo Ruiqing zhuan* (Biography of Luo Ruiqing). Beijing: Dangdai Zhongguo chubanshe, 1996.

Huang Zheng. *Hu Zhiming yu Zhongguo* (Ho Chi Minh and China). Beijing: Jiefangjun chubanshe, 1987.

———. *Liu Shaoqi yisheng* (Life of Liu Shaoqi). Beijing: Zhongyang wenxian chubanshe, 1995.

Jiang Changbin and Robert Ross, eds. *1955–1971 nian de ZhongMei guanxi: Huanhe zhiqian: lengzhan chongtu yu kezhi de zai tantao* (Sino-American Relations, 1955–1971: A Re-Examination of Cold War Conflict and Restraint before Bilateral Détente). Beijing: Shijie zhishi chubanshe, 1998.

Jiang Ying. "Yuenan zhanzheng yu Zhongguo duiMei zhengce" (The Vietnam War and China's Policy toward the United States). In Jiang and Ross, eds., *1955–1971 nian de ZhongMei guanxi: Huanhe*, 99–137.

Jiao Hongguang. " 'Wenge' zhong Zhou Enlai chuli Guangxi wenti deng youguan qingkuang" (Facts about Zhou Enlai's Handling of the Guangxi Problem during the "Cultural Revolution"). *Dangde wenxian*, no. 3 (1996): 73–76.

Jiefangjun jiangling zhuan (Biographies of the Generals of the Liberation Army). Vol. 3. Beijing: Jiefangjun chubanshe, 1986.

Kang Daisha. "Zai Jianpuzhai de rizi" (My Days in Cambodia). In Cheng, ed., *Nu waijiaoguan*, 482–83.

Kang Maozhao. "Zai peiban Xihanuke qingwang de rizili" (In the Days of Accompanying Prince Sihanouk). *Bainianchao* (Hundred Year Tide), no. 2 (1999): 31–38.

Li Danhui. "ZhongSu guanxi yu Zhongguo de yuanYue kangMei" (Sino-Soviet Relations and China's Assistance to the DRV against the United States). *Dangdai Zhongguoshi yanjiu*, no. 3 (1998): 111–26.

Li Haiwen. "Zhou Enlai zai Rineiwa huiyi qijian wei huifu Induzhina heping jinxing de nuli" (Zhou Enlai's Effort to Restore Peace in Indochina during the Geneva Conference). *Dangde wenxian*, no. 1 (1997): 57–61.

Li Jie. "Mao Zedong guoji zhanlue sixiang yanjiu" (Study on Mao Zedong's International Strategic Thought). In the International Strategic Studies Foundation, ed., *Huanqiu tongci liangre*, 1–16.

———. "60 niandai Zhongguo guonei jushi de bianhua yu ZhongMei guanxi" (Changes in China's Domestic Situation in the 1960s and Sino-U.S. Relations). In Jiang and Ross, eds., *1955–1971 nian de ZhongMei guanxi: Huanhe*, 256–97.

Li Jing and Li Haiwen, eds. *Zhou Enlai jiaoyou lu* (A Record of Zhou Enlai's Circle of Friends). Beijing: Zhonggong zhongyang dangxiao chubanshe, 1995.

Li Ke. "Zhongguo renmin yuanYue kangFa de yeji biaobing qingshi" (The Indelible Mark on History of Chines Assistance to Vietnam against the United States). *Junshi lishi*, no. 4 (1989): 30–35.

Li Ke and Hao Shengzhang. *Wenhua dageming zhong de renmin jiefangjun* (The People's Liberation Army during the Great Cultural Revolution). Beijing: Zhonggong dangshi ziliao chubanshe, 1989.

Li Lianqing. *Da waijiaojia Zhou Enlai, dierbu: Shezhan Rineiwa* (Master Diplomat Zhou Enlai, Vol. 2: Oral Fight at Geneva). Hong Kong: Tiandi tushu, 1994.

Li Ping. *Kaiguo zongli Zhou Enlai* (First Premier Zhou Enlai). Beijing: Zhonggong zhongyang dangxiao chubanshe, 1994.

Li Weixian. "YuanYue kangMei fangkong zuozhan 300 tian" (300 Days of Antiaircraft Combat during Assistance to Vietnam against the United States). *Junshi shilin*, no. 3 (1991): 19–23.

Li Yueran. *Waijiao wutan shang de xinZhongguo lingxiu* (New China's Leaders on the Diplomatic Stage). Beijing: Jiefangjun chubanshe, 1989.

Li Zuyi and Jia Xiaoguang. "YuanYue kangMei saolei zuezhan jishi" (Record of Minesweeping Operations during Assistance to Vietnam against the United States). *Junshi shilin*, no. 5 (1992): 12–16.

Lin Hu, chief ed. *Kunjun shi* (History of the Air Force). Beijing: Jiefangjun chubanshe, 1989.

Lin Ping and Ji Ni. "Bujuan de kaituo zhe, gengyunzhe: Zhou zongli yu ladingmeizhou" (An Indefatigable Pioneer and Cultivator: Premier Zhou and Latin America). In The Diplomatic History Research Office of the PRC Foreign Ministry, ed., *Yanjiu Zhou Enlai*, 147–56.

Liu Anqi xiansheng fangwen jilu (The Reminiscences of Mr. Liu An-chi). Interviewed by Chang Yu-fa and Chen Tsun-kung and recorded by Huang Ming-ming. Taipei: Institute of Modern History, Academia Sinica, 1991.

Liu Chun. "Quzhe de ZhongLao jianjiao yu shouci chushi Laowo" (The Bumpy Process of Establishing Diplomatic Relations between China and Laos and My First Mission to Laos). In *Waijiao xueyuan xuebao*, no. 2 (1989): 7–14.

Liu Shufa, chief ed. *Chen Yi nianpu* (A Chronicle of Chen Yi's Life). 2 vols. Beijing: Renmin chubanshe, 1995.

Liu Tianye et al. *Li Tianyou jiangjun zhuan* (Biography of General Li Tianyou). Beijing: Jiefangjun chubanshe, 1993.

Liu Zhende. *Wo wei Shaoqi dang mishu* (I Served as Secretary for Shaoqi). Beijing: Zhongyang wenxian chubanshe, 1994.

Lu Dingyi. *Lu Dingyi wenji* (Collection of Lu Dingyi's Writings). Beijing: Renmin chubanshe, 1992.

Luo Guibo. "Lishi de huigu: Zhongguo yuanYue kangFa yu ZhongYue liangdang liangguo guanxi jishi" (Recalling History: A Factual Account of China's Assistance to Vietnam against the French and Relations between the Two Parties and Two Countries of China and Vietnam). In Fu and Li, eds., *Zhongguo waijiaoguan congshu*, 150–76.

——. "Shaoqi tongzhi paiwo chushi Yuenan" (Comrade Shaoqi Sent Me to Vietnam). In He Jingxiu et al., eds., *Mianhuai Liu Shaoqi*, 233–42.

Ma Qibin et al. *Zhongguo gongchandang zhizheng sishinian, 1949–1989* (The Forty Years of the Chinese Communist Party in Power, 1949–1989). Beijing: Zhonggong dangshi ziliao chubanshe, 1989.

Mu Xin, ed. *Ji Chen Geng jiangjun* (Commemorating General Chen Geng). Changsha: Hunan renmin chubanshe, 1984.

Ni Yuxi xiansheng fangwen jilu (The Reminiscences of Adm. Ni Yue-si). Interviewed and recorded by Chang Li. Taipei: Institute of Modern History, Academia Sinica, 1991.

Pei Jianzhang, chief ed. *Zhonghua renmin gongheguo waijiaoshi, 1949–1956* (Diplomatic History of the People's Republic of China, 1949–1956). Beijing: Shijie zhishi chubanshe, 1994.

The PRC Foreign Ministry and the CCP Central Documentary Research Department, eds. *Mao Zedong waijiao wenxuan* (Selected Diplomatic Works of Mao Zedong). Beijing: Zhongyang wenxian chubanshe and Shijie zhishi chubanshe, 1994.

———. *Zhou Enlai waijiao wenxuan* (Selected Diplomatic Works of Zhou Enlai). Beijing: Zhongyang wenxian chubanshe, 1990.

Qu Aiguo, Bao Mingrong, and Xiao Zuyao. *YuanYue kangMei: Zhongguo zhiyuan budui zai yuenan* (Assist Vietnam and Resist America: Chinese Support Troops in the DRV). Beijing: Junshi kexue chubanshe, 1995.

Qu Xing. "Shilun Mao Zedong guanyu ZhongFa guanxi de zhanlue sixiang" (A Tentative Analysis of Mao Zedong's Strategic Thought Regarding Sino-French Relations). In The Diplomatic History Research Office of the PRC Foreign Ministry, ed., *Mao Zedong waijiao sixiang yanjiu*, 239–55.

———. "Shilun 1954 nian Rineiwa huiyi shang de Zhou Enlai waijiao" (A Tentative Analysis of Zhou Enlai's Diplomacy at the 1954 Geneva Conference). In The Diplomatic History Research Office of the PRC Foreign Ministry, ed., *Yanjiu Zhou Enlai*, 253–68.

Quan Yanchi and Du Weidong. *Gongheguo mishi* (Secret Envoys of the Republic). Beijing: Guangming ribao chubanshe, 1990.

Shi Yingfu. *Mimi chubing yare conglin: YuanYue kangMei jishi* (Secret Warfare in Subtropical Jungles: A Record of Assistance to Vietnam against the United States). Beijing: Jiefangjun wenyi chubanshe, 1990.

Shi Yinhong. *Meiguo zai Yuenan de ganshe he zhanzheng, 1954–1968* (America's Intervention and War in Vietnam, 1954–1968). Beijing: Shijie zhishi chubanshe, 1993.

Shi Zhe. "Rineiwa huiyi sanyi" (Random Recollections of the Geneva Conference). *Renwu*, no. 1 (1989): 37–44.

———. *Zai lishi juren shenbian: Shi Zhe huiyilu* (At the Side of Historical Giants: Shi Zhe Memoirs). Beijing: Zhongyang wenxian chubanshe, 1991.

Shi Zhongquan. *Zhou Enlai de zhuoyue fengxian* (Zhou Enlai's Brilliant Contributions). Beijing: Zhonggong zhongyang dangxiao chubanshe, 1993.

"Shixian Yazhou heping he anquan de genben daolu" (The Basic Route to the Realization of Peace and Security in Asia). *Shijie zhishi* (May 20, 1954), 3.

Sun Dongsheng. "Woguo jingji jianshe zhanlue bujiu de dazhuanbian: Sanxian jianshe juece xingcheng shulue" (The Great Transformation in the Strategic Planning of Our Country's Economic Construction: A Brief Description of the Decision Making on the Construction of the Third Front). *Dangde wenxian*, no. 3 (1995): 42–48.

Tian Zengpei and Wang Taiping, eds. *Lao waijiaoguan huiyi Zhou Enlai* (Veteran Diplomats Remember Zhou Enlai). Beijing: Shijie zhishi chubanshe, 1998.

Tong Xiaopeng. *Fengyu sishinian* (Forty Years of Winds and Rains). 2 vols. Beijing: Zhongyang wenxian chubanshe, 1994–96.

Wang Bingnan. *ZhongMei huitan jiunian huigu* (Recollections of the Nine-Year Sino-American Talks). Beijing: Shijie zhishi chubanshe, 1985.

Wang Dinglie and Lin Hu, chief eds. *Dangdai Zhongguo kongjun* (Contemporary Chinese Air Force). Beijing: Zhongguo shehui kexue chubanshe, 1989.

Wang Li. *Xianchang lishi: Wenhua da geming jishi* (Present at Historical Scenes: Events of the Great Cultural Revolution). New York: Oxford University Press, 1993.

Wang Xiangen. *YuanYue kangMei shilu* (A Factual Record of Assistance to Vietnam against the United States). Beijing: Guoji wenhua chuban gongsi, 1990.

Wang Youping. "Qu Jinbian zhixing teshu shiming" (On a Special Assignment to Phnom Penh). In The Diplomatic History Research Office of the PRC Foreign Ministry, ed., *Dangdai Zhongguo shijie waijiao shengya*, 1:66–82.

Wu Jilin. "Yiduan xianwei renzhi de yuanYue kangFa lishi" (Unknown History about the Assistance to Vietnam against France). *Junshi lishi*, no. 6 (1994): 23–26.

Wu Lengxi. "Chen Yi tongzhi zai Rineiwa huiyi shang" (Comrade Chen Yi at the Geneva Conference). In The Diplomatic History Research Office of the PRC Foreign Ministry, ed., *Huainian Chen Yi*, 152–65.

———. *Yi Maozhuxi* (Recalling Chairman Mao). Beijing: Xinhua chubanshe, 1995.

Wu Xiuquan. *Huiyi yu huainian* (Recollections and Memories). Beijing: Zhonggong zhongyang dangxiao chubanshe, 1991.

———. *Zai waijiaobu banian de jingli* (Eight-Year Experience in the Ministry of Foreign Affairs). Beijing: Shijie zhishi chubanshe, 1983.

Xie Yixian, ed. *Zhongguo waijiao shi: Zhonghua renmin gongheguo shiqi, 1949–1979* (A Diplomatic History of China: The Period of the People's Republic of China, 1949–1979). Zhengzhou: Henan renmin chubanshe, 1988.

Xiong Xianghui. *Lishi de Zhujiao: Huiyi Mao Zedong, Zhou Enlai ji Silaoshuai* (Historical Footnotes: Remembering Mao Zedong, Zhou Enlai as well as Four Old Marshals). Beijing: Zhonggong zhongyang dangxiao chubanshe, 1995.

Xu Peilan and Zheng Pengfei. *Chen Geng jiangjun zhuan* (Biography of General Chen Geng). Beijing: Jiefangjun chubanshe, 1988.

Xu Yan. *Junshijia Mao Zedong* (Military Strategist Mao Zedong). Beijing: Zhongyang wenxian chubanshe, 1995.

———. "Ximie Induzhina zhanhuo de zhuoyue lishi: Shilun Zhonggong zhongyang guanyu yuanYue kangFa ji heping jiejue Induzhina zhanzheng de fangzhen jiqi shishi" (The Remarkable History of Extinguishing the Flames of the Indochina War: A Tentative Analysis of the CCP Central Committee's Principle and Practice of Aiding Vietnam against France and Making a Peaceful Settlement of the Indochina War). *Dangde wenxian*, no. 5 (1992): 20–25.

Xu Zehao. *Wang Jiaxiang zhuan* (Biography of Wang Jiaxiang). Beijing: Dangdai Zhongguo chubanshe, 1996.

Xu Zhongliang. "Renmin jiefangjun lishi shang de waiji jiangjun: Hong Shui Shao Jiang" (Foreign-Born Generals in the PLA: Major General Hong Thuy). *Junshi lishi*, no. 4 (1991): 17–18.

Xue Mouhong and Pei Jianzhang, chief eds. *Dangdai Zhongguo waijiao* (Contemporary Chinese Diplomacy). Beijing: Zhongguo shehui kexue chubanshe, 1990.

Yan Mingfu. "Peng Zhen zai Bujialesite huiyi shang" (Peng Zhen at the Bucharest Meeting). *Dangdai Zhongguoshi yanjiu*, no. 3 (1998): 71–86.

——. "Wo suo zhidao de liangci Mosike huiyi he Hu Qiaomu" (What I Know about the Two Moscow Conferences and Hu Qiaomu). In Yang et al., *Wo suo zhidao de Hu Qiaomu*, 133–58.

Yang Kuisong. "Zouxiang polie (1960–1963): Zhonggong zhongyang ruhe miandui ZhongSu guanxi weiji" (The Path toward the Split: How the CCP Central Committee Confronted the Crisis in Sino-Soviet Relations, 1960–1963). *Dangdai Zhongguoshi yanjiu*, no. 3 (1998): 87–99.

Yang Qiliang. "Dui Zhou zongli liangci chufang de huiyi ji qita" (My Recollections of Premier Zhou's Two Foreign Visits and Other Matters). In The Diplomatic History Research Office of the PRC Foreign Ministry, ed., *Yanjiu Zhou Enlai*, 328–35.

Yang Shangkun et al. *Wo suo zhidao de Hu Qiaomu* (What I Know of Hu Qiaomu). Beijing: Dangdai Zhongguo chubanshe, 1997.

Yang Shengqun and Tian Songnian, eds. *Gongheguo zhongda juece de lailong qumai (1949–1965)* (The Causes and Effects of Important Decisions of the Republic, 1949–1965). Nanjing: Jiangsu renmin chubanshe, 1995.

"Yazhou renmin de yuanwang shi juedui burong hushi de" (The Aspiration of the Asian People Can Not Absolutely Be Ignored). *Shijie zhishi* (June 5, 1954), 3.

Yuan Dejin. "Lun xinZhongguo chengli hou Mao Zedong zhanzheng yu heping lilun de yanbian" (The Evolution of Mao Zedong's Theory of War and Peace since the Founding of New China). *Junshi lishi*, no. 4 (1994).

Yun Shui. *Chushi qiguo jishi: jiangjun dashi Wang Youping* (Record of Diplomatic Missions to Seven Countries: General Ambassador Wang Youping). Beijing: Shijie zhishi chubanshe, 1996.

Yu Zhan. "Yici buxunchang de shiming: Yi Zhou Enlai zuihou yici fangwen Sulian" (An Unusual Visit: Remembering Zhou Enlai's Last Visit to the Soviet Union). *Dangde wenxian*, no. 2 (1992): 85–91.

Zeng Sheng. *Zeng Sheng huiyilu* (Memoirs of Zeng Sheng). Beijing: Jiefangjun chubanshe, 1992.

Zhang Baijia. "Biandong zhong de guoji huanjing yu Zhongguo duiMei zhengce (1954–1970)" (The Changing International Scene and China's Policies toward the United States, 1954–1970). In Jiang and Ross, eds., *1955–1971 nian de ZhongMei guanxi: Huanhe*, 175–208.

Zhang Dequn. "YuanYue guwentuan gongzuo suoyi" (Random Recollections of the Work of the Advisory Group in Vietnam). *Zhonggong dangshi ziliao*, no. 54 (July 1995): 71–76.

Zhang Guang. "Dakai ZhongMei guanxi damen de lishi beijing yu jingguo" (The Historical Background and Process of the Opening of Sino-American Relations). *Waijiao xueyuan xuebao*, no. 2 (1991): 54–63.

Zhang Hanzhi et al. *Wo yu Qiao Guanhua* (My Encounters with Qiao Guanhua). Beijing: Zhongguo qingnian chubanshe, 1994.

Zhang Qing. "Qingshen yizhong ershi zai: Zhou Enlai yu Xihanuke jiaowang shilu" (Twenty Years of Deep Friendship: A Record of Zhou Enlai's Contacts with Sihanouk). In Tian and Wang, eds., *Lao waijiaoguan huiyi Zhou Enlai*, 150–74.

Zhao Xuemei. "Qinli jianwen" (My Personal Experiences and Observations). *Junshi shilin*, no. 5 (1990): 25–30.

Zhu Yuanshi. "Liu Shaoqi 1949 nian mimi fangSu" (Liu Shaoqi's Secret Visit to the Soviet Union in 1949). *Dangde Wenxian*, no. 3 (1991): 74–89.

Zhu Zhongli. *Liming yu wanxia: Wang Jiaxiang wenxue zhuanji* (Dawn and Dusk: A Literary Biography of Wang Jiaxiang). Beijing: Jiefangjun chubanshe, 1986.

ENGLISH-LANGUAGE SOURCES

Archives

Austin, Texas
  Lyndon B. Johnson Library
    Lyndon Johnson Papers (National Security Files)
Washington, D.C.
  Library of Congress
    W. Averell Harriman Papers
  National Security Archives
    The Vietnam/Laos Collection (Porter-Perry-Prados Donation)

Oral History Interviews

Reischauer, Edwin O. Lyndon B. Johnson Library, Austin, Tx.
Thomson, James C. Jr. Lyndon B. Johnson Library, Austin, Tx.

Government Documents

Pentagon Papers (Gravel Edition). Boston: Beacon Press, 1971.
Public Papers of the Presidents: Dwight D. Eisenhower, 1953–1961. Washington, D.C.: Government Printing Office, 1960–61.
Public Papers of the Presidents: Harry S. Truman, 1945–1953. Washington, D.C.: Government Printing Office, 1961–66.
Public Papers of the Presidents: John F. Kennedy, 1961–1963. Washington, D.C.: Government Printing Office, 1962–64.
Public Papers of the Presidents: Lyndon B. Johnson, 1963–1969. Washington, D.C.: Government Printing Office, 1965–69.
Public Papers of the Presidents: Richard M. Nixon, 1969–1974. Washington, D.C.: Government Printing Office, 1970–75.
U.S. Department of States. *Department of States Bulletin.* Washington, D.C.: Government Printing Office, 1950–75.
——. *Foreign Relations of the United States, 1950–1968.* Washington, D.C.: Government Printing Office, 1976–98.

Books, Articles, and Papers

Accinelli, Robert. *Crisis and Commitment: United States Policy toward Taiwan, 1950–1955.* Chapel Hill: University of North Carolina Press, 1996.
Adams, Nina S., and Alfred W. McCoy, eds. *Laos: War and Revolution.* New York: Harper & Row, 1970.
Alagappa, Muthiah, ed. *Political Legitimacy in Southeast Asia: The Quest for Moral Authority.* Stanford: Stanford University Press, 1995.

Allen, Douglas, and Ngo Vinh Long, eds. *Coming to Terms: Indochina, the United States, and the War.* Boulder: Westview Press, 1991.

Amer, Ramses. "The Ethnic Vietnamese in Cambodia: A Minority at Risk?" *Contemporary Southeast Asia* 16 (September 1994): 210–38.

———. "Vietnam and Its Neighbours: The Border Dispute Dimension." *Contemporary Southeast Asia* 17 (December 1995): 298–318.

Anderson, David L. *Trapped by Success: The Eisenhower Administration and Vietnam, 1953–61.* New York: Columbia University Press, 1991.

Ang Cheng Guan. "Decision-Making Leading to the Tet Offensive (1968)—The Vietnamese Communist Perspective." *Journal of Contemporary History* 33 (July 1998): 341–53.

———. *Vietnamese Communists' Relations with China and the Second Indochina Conflict, 1956–1962.* Jefferson, N.C.: McFarland, 1997.

Arbatov, Georgi. *The System: An Insider's Life in Soviet Politics.* New York: Random House, 1992.

Armstrong, J. D. *Revolution and World Order: The Revolutionary State in International Society.* Oxford: Clarendon Press, 1993.

———. *Revolutionary Diplomacy: Chinese Foreign Policy and the United Front Doctrine.* Berkeley: University of California Press, 1977.

Bachman, David. "Structure and Process in the Making of Chinese Foreign Policy." In Kim, ed., *China and the World: Chinese Foreign Policy Faces the New Millennium,* 34–54.

Ball, S. J. *The Cold War: An International History, 1947–1991.* London: Arnold, 1998.

Barnett, Anthony, and John Pilger. *Aftermath: The Struggle of Cambodia and Vietnam.* London: New Statesman, 1982.

Barnouin, Barbara, and Yu Changgen. *Chinese Foreign Policy during the Cultural Revolution.* London: Kegan Paul International, 1998.

Barrett, David M., ed. *Lyndon B. Johnson's Vietnam Papers: A Documentary Collection.* College Station: Texas A&M University Press, 1997.

———. *Uncertain Warriors: Lyndon Johnson and His Vietnam Advisers.* Lawrence: University Press of Kansas, 1993.

Becker, Elizabeth. *When the War Was Over: The Voices of Cambodia's Revolution and Its People.* New York: Simon and Schuster, 1986.

Berman, Larry. *Lyndon Johnson's War: The Road to Stalemate in Vietnam.* New York: W. W. Norton, 1989.

———. *Planning a Tragedy.* New York: W. W. Norton, 1982.

Berman, William C. *William Fulbright and the Vietnam War: The Dissent of a Political Realist.* Kent: Kent State University Press, 1988.

Beschloss, Michael R. *The Crisis Years: Kennedy and Khrushchev, 1960–1963.* New York: Edward Burlingame Books, 1991.

Billings-Yun, Melanie. *Decision against War: Eisenhower and Dien Bien Phu, 1954.* New York: Columbia University Press, 1988.

Bird, Kai. *The Color of Truth: McGeorge Bundy and William Bundy Brothers in Arms.* New York: Simon and Schuster, 1998.

Black Paper: Facts and Evidences of the Acts of Aggression and Annexation of Vietnam against Kampuchea. Phnom Penh: Department of Press and Information of the Ministry of Foreign Affairs of Democratic Kampuchea, September 1978.

Blair, Anne E. *Lodge in Vietnam: A Patriot Abroad.* New Haven: Yale University Press, 1995.

Bodard, Lucien. *The Quicksand War: Prelude to Vietnam*. Boston: Little, Brown, 1967.

Boudarel, Georges. "Influences and Idiosyncracies in the Line and Practice of the Vietnam Communist Party." In Turley, ed., *Vietnamese Communism in Comparative Perspective*, 137–69.

Bradley, Mark. "Imagining America: The United States in Radical Vietnamese Anticolonial Discourse." *Journal of American–East Asian Relations* 4 (Winter 1995): 299–329.

———. "An Improbable Opportunity: America and the Democratic Republic of Vietnam's 1947 Initiative." In Werner and Huynh, eds., *The Vietnam War*, 3–23.

Bradley, Mark, and Robert K. Brigham. "Vietnamese Archives and Scholarship on the Cold War Period: Two Reports." Cold War International History Project Working Paper No. 7. Washington, D.C.: Woodrow Wilson International Center for Scholars, 1993.

Brands, H. W. *What America Owes the World: The Struggle for the Soul of Foreign Policy*. New York: Cambridge University Press, 1998.

Brigham, Robert K. *Guerrilla Diplomacy: The NLF's Foreign Relations and the Viet Nam War*. Ithaca: Cornell University Press, 1999.

———. "The NLF and the Tet Offensive." In Gilbert and Head, eds., *The Tet Offensive*, 63–72.

———. "Vietnamese-American Peace Negotiations: The Failed 1965 Initiatives." *Journal of American–East Asian Relations* 4 (Winter 1995): 377–95.

Brown, MacAlister. "The Indochinese Federation Idea: Learning from History." In Zasloff, ed., *Postwar Indochina*, 77–101.

Brown, MacAlister, and Joseph J. Zasloff. *Apprentice Revolutionaries: The Communist Movement in Laos, 1930–1985*. Stanford: Hoover Institution Press, 1986.

———. "The Pathet Lao and the Politics of Reconciliation in Laos, 1973–1974." In Zasloff and Brown, eds., *Communism in Indochina*, 259–82.

Bui Tin. *Following Ho Chi Minh: The Memoirs of a North Vietnamese Colonel*. London: Hurst & Company, 1995.

Bukharkin, Igor. "Moscow and Ho Chi Minh, 1945–1969." Paper delivered at the Cold War International History Project, University of Hong Kong conference on "The Cold War in Asia," Jan. 1996.

Bundy, William. *A Tangled Web: The Making of Foreign Policy in the Nixon Presidency*. New York: Hill and Wang, 1998.

Burchett, Wilfred G. *Vietnam: Inside Story of the Guerilla War*. 3rd ed. New York: International Publishers, 1968.

Burr, William, ed. *The Kissinger Transcripts: The Top Secret Talks with Beijing and Moscow*. New York: The New Press, 1999.

Buttinger, Joseph. *Vietnam: A Political History*. New York: Praeger, 1968.

Buzzanco, Robert. *Masters of War: Military Dissent and Politics in the Vietnam Era*. New York: Cambridge University Press, 1996.

Cable, James. *The Geneva Conference of 1954 on Indochina*. London: Macmillan, 1986.

Cameron, Allan W. "The Soviet Union and Vietnam: The Origins of Involvement." In Duncan, ed., *Soviet Policy in Developing Countries*, 166–205.

Castle, Barbara. *The Castle Diaries, 1964–70*. London: Weidenfeld and Nicolson, 1984.

Castle, Timothy N. *At War in the Shadow of Vietnam: U.S. Military Aid to the Royal Lao Government, 1955–1975*. New York: Columbia University Press, 1993.

Chanda, Nayan. *Brother Enemy: The War after the War*. New York: Macmillan, 1986.

———. "Secrets of Former Friends." *Far Eastern Economic Review* June 15, 1979, 38–39.

Chandler, David P. *Brother Number One: A Political Biography of Pol Pot*. Boulder: Westview, 1992.

———. *The Tragedy of Cambodian History: Politics, War, and Revolution since 1945*. New Haven: Yale University Press, 1991.

Chandler, David P., and Ben Kiernan, eds. *Revolution and Its Aftermath in Kampuchea: Eight Essays*. New Haven: Yale University Southeast Asia Studies, Monograph Series No. 5, 1983.

———. *Vietnam and China, 1938–1954*. Princeton: Princeton University Press, 1969.

Chen Jian. "China and the First Indo-China War, 1950–54." *China Quarterly*, no. 133 (March 1993): 85–110.

———. "China's Involvement in the Vietnam War, 1964–69." *China Quarterly*, no. 142 (June 1995): 357–87.

———. *China's Road to the Korean War: The Making of the Sino-American Confrontation*. New York: Columbia University Press, 1994.

Chen, King. "North Vietnam in the Sino-Soviet Dispute, 1962–64." *Asian Survey* 4 (September 1964): 1023–36.

———. *Vietnam and China, 1938–1954*. Princeton: Princeton University Press, 1969.

Chen Xiaolu. "Chen Yi and China's Diplomacy." In Hunt and Niu, eds., *Toward a History of Chinese Communist Foreign Relations*, 89–112.

Christensen, Thomas J. *Useful Adversaries: Grand Strategy, Domestic Mobilization, and Sino-American Conflict, 1947–1958*. Princeton: Princeton University Press, 1996.

Cohen, Warren I. *America's Response to China: A History of Sino-American Relations*. 3rd ed. New York: Columbia University Press, 1990.

———, ed. *Pacific Passage: The Study of American–East Asian Relations on the Eve of the Twenty-First Century*. New York: Columbia University Press, 1996.

Cohen, Warren I., and Nancy Bernkopf Tucker, eds. *Lyndon Johnson Confronts the World: American Foreign Policy, 1963–1968*. Cambridge: Cambridge University Press, 1994.

Colvin, John. *Giap: Volcano under Snow*. New York: Soho Press, 1996.

Cooper, Chester L. *The Lost Crusade: America in Vietnam*. New York: Dodd, Mead & Company, 1970.

Costigliola, Frank. *France and the United States: The Cold Alliance since World War II*. New York: Twayne Publishers, 1992.

Crozier, Brian. "Peking and the Laotian Crisis: An Interim Appraisal." *China Quarterly* (July–September 1961): 128–37.

———. "Peking and the Laotian Crisis: A Further Appraisal." *China Quarterly* (July–September 1962): 116–23.

Currey, Cecil B. *Victory at Any Cost: The Genius of Viet Nam's Gen. Vo Nguyen Giap*. Washington: Brassey's, 1997.

Dallek, Robert. *Flawed Giant: Lyndon Johnson and His Times, 1961–1973*. New York: Oxford University Press, 1998.

Dalloz, Jacques. *The War in Indo-China, 1945–54*. Dublin: Gill & Macmillan, 1987.

Deac, Wilfred P. *Road to the Killing Fields: The Cambodian War of 1970–1975*. College Station: Texas A&M University Press, 1997.

Devillers, Philippe. "The Laotian Conflict in Perspective." In Adams and McCoy, eds., *Laos*, 37–51.

DiLeo, David L. *George Ball, Vietnam, and the Rethinking of Containment*. Chapel Hill: University of North Carolina Press, 1991.

Dirlik, Arif, Paul Healy, and Nick Knight, eds. *Critical Perspectives on Mao Zedong's Thought*. Atlantic Highlands, N.J.: Humanities Press, 1997.

Dittmer, Lowell. *Sino-Soviet Normalization and Its International Implications, 1945–1990*. Seattle: University of Washington Press, 1992.

Dittmer, Lowell, and Samuel Kim, eds. *China's Quest for National Identity*. Ithaca: Cornell University Press, 1993.

Dobrynin, Anatoly. *In Confidence: Moscow's Ambassador to America's Six Cold War Presidents (1962–1986)*. New York: Times Books, 1995.

Dommen, Arthur J. *Conflict in Laos: The Politics of Neutralization*. Rev. ed. New York: Praeger, 1971.

Duiker, William J. *China and Vietnam: The Roots of Conflict*. Berkeley: Institute of East Asian Studies, University of California, 1986.

——. *The Communist Road to Power in Vietnam*. 2nd ed. Boulder: Westview Press, 1996.

——. *Sacred War: Nationalism and Revolution in a Divided Vietnam*. New York: McGraw-Hill, 1995.

——. "Seeds of the Dragon: The Influence of the Maoist Model in Vietnam." In Dirlik, Healy, and Knight, eds., *Critical Perspectives on Mao Zedong's Thought*, 313–41.

——. *U.S. Containment Policy and the Conflict in Indochina*. Stanford: Stanford University Press, 1994.

——. *Vietnam: Revolution in Transition*. 2nd ed. Boulder: Westview Press, 1995.

——. "Waging Revolutionary War: The Evolution of Hanoi's Strategy in the South, 1959–1965." In Werner and Huynh, eds., *The Vietnam War*, 24–36.

Duncan, W. Raymond, ed. *Soviet Policy in Developing Countries*. Waltham, Mass.: Ginn-Blaisdell, 1970.

Duncanson, Dennis. "The Legacy of Ho Chi Minh." *Asian Affairs* 23 (February 1992): 49–62.

Dunn, Peter M. *The First Vietnam War*. New York: St. Martin's Press, 1985.

——. "The First Vietnam War: Aftershocks in the East." In Errington and McKercher, eds., *The Vietnam War as History*, 17–41.

Eden, Anthony. *Full Circle: The Memoirs of Anthony Eden*. Boston: Houghton Mifflin, 1960.

Elliott, David W. P. "Hanoi's Strategy in the Second Indochina War." In Werner and Huynh, eds., *The Vietnam War*, 66–94.

——. "Institutionalizing the Revolution: Vietnam's Search for a Model of Development." In Turley, ed., *Vietnamese Communism in Comparative Perspective*, 199–223.

——. "Political Integration in North Vietnam: The Cooperativization Period." In Zasloff and Brown, eds., *Communism in Indochina*, 165–93.

——, ed. *The Third Indochina Conflict*. Boulder: Westview Press, 1981.

Ellison, Herbert J., ed. *The Sino-Soviet Conflict: A Global Perspective*. Seattle: University of Washington Press, 1982.

Engelbert, Thomas, and Christopher E. Goscha. *Falling out of Touch: A Study on Vietnamese Communist Policy towards an Emerging Cambodian Communist Movement, 1930–1975*. Clayton Victoria, Australia: Center of Southeast Asian Studies, Monash University, 1995.

Errington, Elizabeth Jane, and B. J. C. McKercher, eds. *The Vietnam War as History*. New York: Praeger, 1990.

Etcheson, Craig. *The Rise and Demise of Democratic Kampuchea*. Boulder: Westview Press, 1984.

Evans, Grant, and Kelvin Rowley. *Red Brotherhood at War: Indochina since the Fall of Saigon*. London: Verso, 1984.

Fairbank, John King, ed. *The Chinese World Order: Traditional China's Foreign Relations*. Cambridge, Mass.: Harvard University Press, 1968.

Fall, Bernard B. *The Two Viet-Nams: A Political and Military Analysis*. 2nd rev. ed. New York: Praeger, 1967.

Feingold, David. "Opium and Politics in Laos." In Adams and McCoy, eds., *Laos*, 322–39.

Fetzer, James. "Clinging to Containment: China Policy." In Paterson, ed., *Kennedy's Quest for Victory*, 178–97.

FitzGerald, Frances. *Fire in the Lake: The Vietnamese and the Americans in Vietnam*. New York: Vintage Books, 1989.

Foot, Rosemary. *The Practice of Power: U.S. Relations with China since 1949*. Oxford: Clarendon Press, 1995.

Freeman, Nick. "Fighting the 'Non-Attributable War' in Laos: A Review Article." *Contemporary Southeast Asia* 17 (March 1996): 430–42.

Friedman, Edward. "Anti-Imperialism in Chinese Foreign Policy." In Kim, ed., *China and the World: Chinese Foreign Relations in the Post Cold War Era*, 60–74.

Frings, K. Viviane. "Rewriting Cambodian History to 'Adapt' It to a New Political Context: The Kampuchean People's Revolutionary Party's Historiography (1979–1991)." *Modern Asian Studies* 31 (1997): 807–46.

Funnell, Victor C. "Vietnam and the Sino-Soviet Conflict, 1965–1976." *Studies in Comparative Communism* 11 (Spring/Summer 1978): 142–69.

Gaddis, John Lewis. *We Now Know: Rethinking Cold War History*. Oxford: Clarendon Press, 1997.

Gaiduk, Ilya V. "Soviet Policy towards U.S. Participation in the Vietnam War." *History* (1996): 40–54.

———. *The Soviet Union and the Vietnam War*. Chicago: Ivan R. Dee, 1996.

———. "The Vietnam War and Soviet-American Relations, 1964–1973: New Russian Evidence." *Cold War International History Project Bulletin*, nos. 6–7 (Winter 1995–96): 232, 250–58.

Gardner, Lloyd C. *Approaching Vietnam: From World War II through Dien Bien Phu, 1941–1954*. New York: W. W. Norton, 1988.

———. *Pay Any Price: Lyndon Johnson and the Wars for Vietnam*. Chicago: Ivan R. Dee, 1995.

Garson, Robert. *The United States and China since 1949: A Troubled Affair*. Madison, N.J.: Fairleigh Dickinson University Press, 1994.

Garthoff, Raymond L. *Détente and Confrontation: American-Soviet Relations from Nixon to Reagan*. Rev. ed. Washington, D.C.: Brookings Institution, 1994.

Garver, John W. *China's Decision for Rapprochement with the United States, 1968–1971*. Boulder: Westview, 1982.

———. "The Chinese Threat in the Vietnam War." *Parameters* 22 (Spring 1992): 73–85.

———. *Foreign Relations of the People's Republic of China*. Eaglewood Cliffs, N.J.: Prentice-Hall, 1993.

——. "Polemics, Paradigms, Responsibility, and the Origins of the U.S.-PRC Confrontation in the 1950s." *Journal of American–East Asian Relations* 3 (Spring 1994): 1–34.

——. *The Sino-American Alliance: Nationalist China and American Cold War Strategy in Asia.* Armonk, N.Y.: M. E. Sharpe, 1997.

——. "Sino-Vietnamese Conflict and the Sino-American Rapprochement." *Political Science Quarterly* 96 (Fall 1981): 445–64.

——. "The Tet Offensive and Sino-Vietnamese Relations." In Gilbert and Head, eds., *The Tet Offensive*, 46–52.

George, Alexander L., Philip J. Farley, and Alexander Dallin, eds. *U.S.-Soviet Security Cooperation: Achievements, Failures, Lessons.* New York: Oxford University Press, 1988.

Gibbons, William Conrad. *The U.S. Government and the Vietnam War: Executive and Legislative Roles and Relationships.* 3 vols. Princeton: Princeton University Press, 1986–89.

Gilbert, Marc Jason, and William Head, eds. *The Tet Offensive.* Westport, Conn.: Praeger, 1996.

Gilks, Anne. *The Breakdown of the Sino-Vietnamese Alliance, 1970–1979.* Berkeley: Institute of East Asian Studies, University of California, 1992.

Gilks, Anne, and Gerald Segal. *China and the Arms Trade.* New York: St. Martin's, 1985.

Goldstein, Martin E. *American Policy toward Laos.* Cranbury, N.J.: Fairleigh Dickinson University Press, 1973.

Goncharov, Sergei N., John W. Lewis, and Xue Litai. *Uncertain Partners: Stalin, Mao, and the Korean War.* Stanford: Stanford University Press, 1993.

Goodman, Allan E. *The Lost Peace: America's Search for a Negotiated Settlement of the Vietnam War.* Stanford: Hoover Institution Press, 1978.

Gould-Davis, Nigel. "Rethinking the Role of Ideology in International Politics during the Cold War." *Journal of Cold War Studies* 1 (Winter 1999): 90–109.

Gray, Jack. *Rebellions and Revolutions: China from the 1800s to the 1980s.* New York: Oxford University Press, 1990.

Green, Marshall, John H. Holdridge, and William N. Stokes. *War and Peace with China: First-Hand Experiences in the Foreign Services of the United States.* Bethesda, Md.: Diplomatic and Consular Officers, Retired (DACOR) Press, 1994.

Griffith, William E. *The Sino-Soviet Rift.* Cambridge: MIT Press, 1964.

Gurtov, Melvin. *China and Southeast Asia: The Politics of Survival.* Baltimore: Johns Hopkins University Press, 1971.

——. *The First Vietnam Crisis: Chinese Communist Strategy and United States Involvement, 1953–1954.* New York: Columbia University Press, 1967.

Gurtov, Melvin, and Byong-Moo Hwang. *China under Threat: The Politics of Strategy and Diplomacy.* Baltimore: Johns Hopkins University Press, 1980.

Haldeman, H. R. *The Haldeman Diaries: Inside the Nixon White House.* New York: G. P. Putnam's Sons, 1994.

Hall, David K. "The Laos Neutralization Agreement, 1962." In George, Farley, and Dallin, eds., *U.S.-Soviet Security Cooperation*, 435–65.

Halliday, Jon, ed. *The Artful Albanian: Memoirs of Enver Hoxha.* London: Chatto & Windus, 1986.

Halpern, A. M., ed. *Policies toward China: Views from Six Continents*. New York: McGraw-Hill, 1965.

Hamilton, Donald W. *The Art of Insurgency: American Military Policy and the Failure of Strategy in Southeast Asia*. Westport, Conn.: Praeger, 1998.

Hamilton-Merritt, Jane. *Tragic Mountains: The Hmong, the Americans, and the Secret Wars for Laos, 1942–1992*. Bloomington: Indiana University Press, 1993.

Hammond, William M. *Reporting Vietnam: Media and Military at War*. Lawrence: University Press of Kansas, 1998.

Hannah, Norman. *The Key to Failure: Laos and the Vietnam War*. Lanham, Md.: Madison Books, 1987.

Harding, Harry. "China and the Third World: From Revolution to Containment." In Solomon, ed., *The China Factor*, 257–95.

———. *A Fragile Relationship: The United States and China since 1972*. Washington, D.C.: Brookings Institution, 1992.

———. "The Making of Chinese Military Power." In Whitson, ed., *The Military and Political Power in China in the 1970s*, 361–85.

———, ed. *China's Foreign Relations in the 1980s*. New Haven: Yale University Press, 1984.

Harrison, Hope M. "Ulbricht and the Concrete 'Rose': New Archival Evidence on the Dynamics of Soviet–East German Relations and the Berlin Crisis, 1958–1961." Cold War International History Project Working Paper No. 5. Washington, D.C.: Woodrow Wilson International Center for Scholars, 1993.

He Di. " 'The Last Campaign to Unify China': The CCP's Unmaterialized Plan to Liberate Taiwan, 1949–1950." *Chinese Historians* 5 (Spring 1992): 1–16.

Heder, Stephen. "Kampuchea's Armed Struggle: The Origins of an Independent Revolution." *Bulletin of Concerned Asian Scholars* 11 (1979): 2–23.

Hendrickson, Paul. *The Living and the Dead: Robert McNamara and Five Lives of a Lost War*. New York: Alfred A. Knopf, 1996.

Herring, George C. *America's Longest War: The United States and Vietnam, 1950–1975*. 3rd ed. New York: McGraw-Hill, 1996.

———. *LBJ and Vietnam: A Different Kind of War*. Austin: University of Texas Press, 1994.

———, ed. *The Secret Diplomacy of the Vietnam War: The Negotiating Volumes of the Pentagon Papers*. Austin: University of Texas Press, 1983.

Hersh, Seymour M. *The Price of Power: Kissinger in the Nixon White House*. New York: Summit Books, 1983.

Hershberg, James G., ed. "Central and East European Documents on the Vietnam War: Sample Materials from Polish, Hungary, and East German Sources." Washington, D.C.: Wilson Center Cold War International History Project, 1997.

Hilsman, Roger. *To Move a Nation: The Politics of Foreign Policy in the Administration of John F. Kennedy*. New York: Dell, 1964.

Hoang Van Hoan. "Distortion of Facts about Militant Friendship between Viet Nam and China Is Impermissible." *Beijing Review*, December 7, 1979, 11–23.

Hogan, Michael J. *A Cross of Iron: Harry S. Truman and the Origins of the National Security State, 1945–1954*. New York: Cambridge University Press, 1998.

Holdridge, John H. *Crossing the Divide: An Insider's Account of the Normalization of U.S.-China Relations*. Lanham, Md.: Rowman & Littlefield, 1997.

Holloway, David. *Stalin and the Bomb: The Soviet Union and Atomic Energy, 1939–1956*. New Haven: Yale University Press, 1994.

Honey, P. J. *Communism in North Vietnam: Its Role in the Sino-Soviet Dispute*. Cambridge: MIT Press, 1963.

Hood, Steven J. *Dragons Entangled: Indochina and the China-Vietnam War*. Armonk, N.Y.: M. E. Sharpe, 1992.

Hoxha, Enver. *Reflections on China*. 2 vols. Tirana: 8 Nentori, 1979.

Hudson, G. F., Richard Lowenthal, and Roderick MacFarquhar. *The Sino-Soviet Dispute*. New York: Praeger, 1961.

Hunt, Michael H. "Beijing and the Korean Crisis, June 1950–June 1951." *Political Science Quarterly* 107 (Fall 1992): 453–78.

———. "CCP Foreign Policy: 'Normalizing the Field.' " In Hunt and Niu, eds., *Toward a History of Chinese Communist Foreign Relations*, 163–91.

———. "Chinese Foreign Relations in Historical Perspective." In Harding, ed., *China's Foreign Relations in the 1980s*, 1–42.

———. *The Genesis of Chinese Communist Foreign Policy*. New York: Columbia University Press, 1996.

———. *Ideology and U.S. Foreign Policy*. New Haven: Yale University Press, 1987.

———. *Lyndon Johnson's War: America's Cold War Crusade in Vietnam, 1945–1968*. New York: Hill and Wang, 1996.

Hunt, Michael H., and Niu Jun, eds. *Toward a History of Chinese Communist Foreign Relations, 1920s–1960s: Personalities and Interpretive Approaches*. Washington, D.C.: Woodrow Wilson International Center for Scholars Asia Program, 1995.

Huynh Kim Khanh. *Vietnamese Communism, 1925–1945*. Ithaca: Cornell University Press, 1982.

Irving, R. E. M. *The First Indochina War: French and American Policy, 1945–54*. London: Croom Helm Ltd., 1975.

Isaacson, Walter. *Kissinger: A Biography*. New York: Simon and Schuster, 1992.

Jackson, Steven F. "China's Third World Foreign Policy: The Case of Angola and Mozambique, 1961–93." *China Quarterly*, no. 143 (June 1995): 387–422.

Jervis, Robert. *System Effects: Complexity in Political and Social Life*. Princeton: Princeton University Press, 1997.

Johnston, Alastair Iain. *Cultural Realism: Strategic Culture and Grand Strategy in Chinese History*. Princeton: Princeton University Press, 1995.

Kahin, George McT. *Intervention: How America Became Involved in Vietnam*. New York: Doubleday, 1986.

———. "Nixon and the PRG's Seven Points." In Werner and Hunt, eds., *The American War in Vietnam*, 47–70.

Kaplan, Lawrence S., Denise Artaud, and Mark R. Rubin, eds. *Dien Bien Phu and the Crisis of Franco-American Relations, 1954–1955*. Wilmington, Del.: Scholarly Resources, 1990.

Karnow, Stanley. *Vietnam: A History*. New York: Viking, 1983.

Kaznacheev, Aleksandr. *Inside a Soviet Embassy: Experiences of a Russian Diplomat in Burma*. Philadelphia: J. B. Lippincott Company, 1962.

Keith, Ronald C. *The Diplomacy of Zhou Enlai*. New York: St. Martin's Press, 1989.

Khong, Yuen Foong. *Analogies at War: Korea, Munich, Dien Bien Phu, and the Vietnam Decisions of 1965*. Princeton: Princeton University Press, 1992.

Khrushchev, Nikita S. *Khrushchev Remembers*. Boston: Little, Brown, 1970.

———. *Khrushchev Remembers: The Glasnost Tapes*. Boston: Little, Brown, 1990.

———. *Khrushchev Remembers: The Last Testament*. Boston: Little, Brown, 1974.

Kiernan, Ben. *How Pol Pot Came to Power: A History of Communism in Kampuchea, 1930–1975*. London: Verso, 1985.

———. "The Samlaut Rebellion, 1967–68." In Kiernan and Chanthou Boua, eds., *Peasants and Politics in Kampuchea*, 166–205.

Kiernan, Ben, and Chanthou Boua, eds. *Peasants and Politics in Kampuchea, 1942–1981*. London: Zed Press, 1982.

Kim, Samuel S., ed. *China and the World: Chinese Foreign Relations in the Post Cold War Era*. 3rd ed. Boulder: Westview Press, 1994.

———, ed. *China and the World: Chinese Foreign Policy Faces the New Millennium*. 4th ed. Boulder: Westview Press, 1998.

Kimball, Jeffrey. *Nixon's Vietnam War*. Lawrence: University Press of Kansas, 1998.

———. "Russia's Vietnam War." *Reviews in American History* 25 (March 1997): 157–62.

Kirk, Donald. *Wider War: The Struggle for Cambodia, Thailand, and Laos*. New York: Praeger, 1971.

Kissinger, Henry. *White House Years*. Boston: Little, Brown, 1979.

———. *Years of Renewal*. New York: Simon and Schuster, 1999.

———. *Years of Upheaval*. Boston: Little, Brown, 1982.

Kojima, Masaru, ed. *The Record of the Talks between the Japanese Communist Party and the Communist Party of China: How Mao Zedong Scrapped the Joint Communiqué*. Tokyo: Central Committee of the Japanese Communist Party, 1980.

Kolko, Gabriel. *Anatomy of a War: Vietnam, the United States, and the Modern Historical Experience*. New York: Pantheon Books, 1985.

Kunz, Diane B., ed. *The Diplomacy of the Crucial Decade: American Foreign Relations during the 1960s*. New York: Columbia University Press, 1994.

Lacouture, Jean. *Andre Malraux*. New York: Pantheon Books, 1975.

Lall, Arthur. *How Communist China Negotiates*. New York: Columbia University Press, 1968.

Langer, Paul F., and Joseph J. Zasloff. *North Vietnam and the Pathet Lao: Partners in the Struggle for Laos*. Cambridge, Mass.: Harvard University Press, 1970.

Lawson, Eugene K. *The Sino-Vietnamese Conflict*. New York: Praeger, 1984.

Lee, Chae-Jin. *China and Korea: Dynamic Relations*. Stanford: Hoover Institution Press, 1996.

———. *Communist China's Policy toward Laos: A Case Study, 1954–67*. Lawrence: Center for East Asian Studies, University of Kansas, 1970.

Lee, Steven Hugh. *Outposts of Empire: Korea, Vietnam, and the Origins of the Cold War in Asia, 1949–1954*. Montreal: McGill-Queens University Press, 1995.

Leffler, Melvyn P. "The Cold War: What Do 'We Now Know'?" *American Historical Review* (April 1999): 501–24.

———. *A Preponderance of Power: National Security, the Truman Administration, and the Cold War*. Stanford: Stanford University Press, 1992.

Leifer, Michael. "Cambodia and China: Neutralism, 'Neutrality,' and National Security." In Halpern, ed., *Policies toward China*, 329–47.

———. *Cambodia: The Search for Security*. New York: Praeger, 1967.

Levine, Steven I. "China in Asia: The PRC as a Regional Power." In Harding, ed., *China's Foreign Relations in the 1980s*, 107–45.

———. "Perception and Ideology in Chinese Foreign Policy." In Robinson and Shambaugh, eds., *Chinese Foreign Policy*, 30–46.

Lieberthal, Kenneth. "The Great Leap Forward and the Split in the Yan'an Leadership, 1958–65." In MacFarquhar, ed., *The Politics of China*, 87–147.

Li Haiwen. "Restoring Peace in Indochina at the Geneva Conference." Paper delivered at the Cold War International History Project, University of Hong Kong conference, "The Cold War in Asia," January 1996.

Li Zhisui. *The Private Life of Chairman Mao*. Translated by Tai Hung-chao. New York: Random House, 1994.

Lin Biao. "Long Live the Victory of People's War." *Peking Review*, Sept. 3, 1965, 9–30.

Lockhart, Greg. "Constructing the Vietnam War: Review Article." *Contemporary Southeast Asia* 18 (December 1996): 320–36.

———. *Nation in Arms: The Origins of the People's Army of Vietnam*. London: Allen and Unwin, 1991.

Logevall, Fredrik. *Choosing War: The Lost Chance for Peace and the Escalation of War in Vietnam*. Berkeley: University of California Press, 1999.

———. "De Gaulle, Neutralization, and American Involvement in Vietnam, 1963–1964." *Pacific Historical Review* 61 (February 1992): 69–102.

———. "The Swedish-American Conflict over Vietnam." *Diplomatic History* 17 (Summer 1993): 421–45.

Lomperis, Timothy J. *From People's War to People's Rule: Insurgency, Intervention, and the Lessons of Vietnam*. Chapel Hill: University of North Carolina Press, 1996.

Lowe, Peter, ed. *The Vietnam War*. New York: St Martin's, 1998.

Luu Doan Huynh. "The Seven-Point Proposal of the PRG (July 1, 1971) and the U.S. Reaction." In Werner and Huynh, eds., *The Vietnam War*, 198–202.

Macdonald, Douglas J. "Communist Bloc Expansion in the Early Cold War: Challenging Realism, Refuting Revisionism." *International Security* 20 (Winter 1995–96): 152–88.

MacFarquhar, Roderick. *The Origins of the Cultural Revolution*. Vol. 1, *Contradictions among the People, 1956–1957*. New York: Columbia University Press, 1974.

———. *The Origins of the Cultural Revolution*. Vol. 2, *The Great Leap Forward, 1958–1960*. New York: Columbia University Press, 1983.

———. *The Origins of the Cultural Revolution*. Vol. 3, *The Coming of the Cataclysm, 1961–1966*. New York: Columbia University Press, 1997.

———, ed. *The Politics of China, 1949–1989*. Cambridge: Cambridge University Press, 1993.

MacFarquhar, Roderick, and John K. Fairbank, eds. *The Cambridge History of China*. Vol. 14, *The People's Republic, Part I: The Emergence of Revolutionary China, 1949–1965*. Cambridge: Cambridge University Press, 1987.

McMahon, Robert J. *The Cold War on the Periphery: The United States, India, and Pakistan*. New York: Columbia University Press, 1994.

———. *The Limits of Empire: The United States and Southeast Asia since World War II*. New York: Columbia University Press, 1999.

McMaster, H. R. *Dereliction of Duty: Lyndon Johnson, Robert McNamara, the Joint Chiefs of Staff, and the Lies that Led to Vietnam*. New York: HarperCollins, 1997.

McNamara, Robert S. *In Retrospect: The Tragedy and Lessons of Vietnam*. New York: Random House, 1995.

McNamara, Robert S., James G. Blight, and Robert K. Brigham. *Argument without End: In Search of Answers to the Vietnam Tragedy*. New York: Public Affairs, 1999.

Malraux, Andre. *Anti-Memoirs*. New York: Holt, Rinehart and Winston, 1968.

Mancall, Mark. *China at the Center: 300 Years of Foreign Policy*. New York: Free Press, 1984.

Maneli, Mieczyslaw. *War of the Vanquished*. Translated by Maria de Gorgey. New York: Harper & Row, 1971.

Mao Zedong. "On Protracted War." In Mao, *Selected Military Writings*, 187–267.

——. *Selected Military Writings of Mao Tse-tung*. Beijing: Foreign Languages Press, 1967.

——. *Selected Works of Mao Tse-tung*. 4 vols. Beijing: Foreign Languages Press, 1965.

Marr, David G. *Vietnamese Anticolonialism, 1885–1925*. Berkeley: University of California Press, 1971.

——. *Vietnamese Tradition on Trial, 1920–1945*. Berkeley: University of California Press, 1981.

——. *Vietnam 1945: The Quest for Power*. Berkeley: University of California Press, 1995.

Martin, Marie Alexanderine. *Cambodia: A Shattered Society*. Berkeley: University of California Press, 1994.

Mastny, Vojtech. *The Cold War and Soviet Insecurity: The Stalin Years*. New York: Oxford University Press, 1996.

Meisner, Maurice. *Mao's China and After: A History of the People's Republic*. New York: Free Press, 1986.

"Memorandum on Vice-Premier Li Xiannian's Talks with Premier Pham Van Dong, June 10, 1977." *Beijing Review*, March 30, 1979, 17–22.

Michalowski, Jerzy. "Polish Secret Peace Initiatives in Vietnam." *Cold War International History Project Bulletin*, nos. 6–7 (Winter 1995–96): 241, 258–59.

Miller, D. B., ed. *Peasants and Politics: Grass Roots Reaction to Change in Asia*. New York: St. Martin's Press, 1978.

Ministry of Foreign Affairs of the Socialist Republic of Viet Nam. *The Truth about Vietnam-China Relations over the Last Thirty Years*. Hanoi: 1979.

Mirsky, Jonathan, and Stephen E. Stonefield. "The Nam Tha Crisis: Kennedy and the New Frontier on the Brink." In Adams and McCoy, eds., *Laos*, 155–78.

Moïse, Edwin E. *Land Reform in China and North Vietnam: Consolidating the Revolution at the Village Level*. Chapel Hill: University of North Carolina Press, 1983.

——. *Tonkin Gulf and the Escalation of the Vietnam War*. Chapel Hill: University of North Carolina Press, 1996.

Morgan, Austen. *Harold Wilson*. London: Pluto Press, 1992.

Morris, Stephen J. "The Soviet-Chinese-Vietnamese Triangle in the 1970s: The View from Moscow." Cold War International History Project Working Paper No. 25. Washington, D.C.: Woodrow Wilson International Center for Scholars, 1999.

——. *Why Vietnam Invaded Cambodia: Political Culture and the Causes of War*. Stanford: Stanford University Press, 1999.

Mozingo, David. *Chinese Policy toward Indonesia, 1949–1967*. Ithaca: Cornell University Press, 1976.

Munroe, Donald J. *The Imperial Style of Inquiry in Twentieth-Century China: The Emergence of New Approaches*. Ann Arbor: Center for Chinese Studies, University of Michigan, 1996.

Nathan, Andrew J., and Robert S. Ross. *The Great Wall and the Empty Fortress: China's Search for Security*. New York: W. W. Norton, 1997.

Naughton, Barry. "The Third Front: Defence Industrialization in the Chinese Interior." *China Quarterly*, no. 115 (September 1988): 351–86.

Nelson, Keith L. *The Making of Détente: Soviet-American Relations in the Shadow of Vietnam*. Baltimore: Johns Hopkins University Press, 1995.

Ngo Vinh Long. "The Tet Offensive and Its Aftermath." In Werner and Hunt, eds., *The American War in Vietnam*, 23–45.

Nguyen Vu Tung. "Coping with the United States: Hanoi's Search for an Effective Strategy." In Lowe, ed., *The Vietnam War*, 30–61.

Nichols, Thomas M. "Lessons from the New History of the Cold War." *International Journal* 53 (Autumn 1998): 661–86.

Ninkovich, Frank. *Modernity and Power: A History of the Domino Theory in the Twentieth Century*. Chicago: University of Chicago Press, 1994.

Nogee, Joseph L., and Robert H. Donaldson. *Soviet Foreign Policy since World War II*. 3rd ed. New York: Pergamon Press, 1988.

Nordell, John R., Jr. *The Undetected Enemy: French and American Miscalculations at Dien Bien Phu*. College Station: Texas A&M University Press, 1995.

O'Ballance, Edgar. *The Indo-China War, 1945–1954: A Study in Guerilla Warfare*. London: Faber and Faber, 1964.

Oberdorfer, Don. *Tet!* Garden City, N.Y.: Doubleday, 1971.

Olsen, Mari. *Solidarity and National Revolution: The Soviet Union and the Vietnamese Communists, 1954–1960*. Oslo: Institutt for Forsvarsstudier, 1997.

Osborne, Milton. *Sihanouk: Prince of Light, Prince of Darkness*. Honolulu: University of Hawaii Press, 1994.

Papp, Daniel S. *Vietnam: The View from Moscow, Peking, Washington*. Jefferson, N.C.: McFarland, 1981.

Parker, Alastair. "International Aspects of the Vietnam War." In Lowe, ed., *The Vietnam War*, 196–218.

Parker, F. Charles, IV. *Vietnam: Strategy for a Stalemate*. New York: Paragon Books, 1989.

Parker, James E., Jr. *Codename Mule: Fighting the Secret War in Laos for the CIA*. Annapolis, Md.: Naval Institute Press, 1995.

Paterson, Thomas G., ed. *Kennedy's Quest for Victory: American Foreign Policy, 1961–1963*. New York: Oxford University Press, 1989.

Pike, Douglas. *History of Vietnamese Communism, 1925–1976*. Stanford: Hoover Institution Press, 1978.

——. "The Impact of the Sino-Soviet Dispute on Southeast Asia." In Ellison, ed., *The Sino-Soviet Conflict*, 185–205.

——. *Vietnam and the Soviet Union: Anatomy of an Alliance*. Boulder: Westview, 1987.

Porter, Gareth. "After Geneva: Subverting Laotian Neutrality." In Adams and McCoy, eds., *Laos*, 179–212.

——. *A Peace Denied: The United States, Vietnam, and the Paris Agreement*. Bloomington: Indiana University Press, 1975.

——. *Vietnam: The Politics of Bureaucratic Socialism*. Ithaca: Cornell University Press, 1993.

——. "Vietnam and the Socialist Camp: Center or Periphery?" In Turley, ed., *Vietnamese Communism in Comparative Perspective*, 225–64.

———. "Vietnamese Communist Policy toward Kampuchea, 1930–1970." In Chandler and Kiernan, eds., *Revolution and Its Aftermath in Kampuchea*, 57–98.

———. "Vietnamese Policy and the Indochina Crisis." In Elliott, ed., *The Third Indochina Conflict*, 69–137.

Post, Ken. *Revolution, Socialism and Nationalism in Viet Nam*. 5 vols. Belmont, Calif.: Wadsworth Publishing Company, 1989.

Prados, John. *The Blood Road: The Ho Chi Minh Trail and the Vietnam War*. New York: John Wiley & Sons, Inc., 1999.

———. *The Hidden History of the Vietnam War*. Chicago: Ivan R. Dee, 1995.

———. "Looking at the War from Both Sides Now." *VVA Veteran* 17 (August–September 1997): 29–31.

Prozumenschikov, M. Y. "The Sino-Indian Conflict, the Cuban Missile Crisis, and the Sino-Soviet Split, October 1962: New Evidence from the Russian Archives." *Cold War International History Project Bulletin*, nos. 8–9 (Winter 1996–97): 251–57.

Pye, Lucian W. "The China Factor in Southeast Asia." In Solomon, ed., *The China Factor*, 216–56.

Quinn-Fudge, Sophie. "Ho Chi Minh: New Perspectives from the Comintern Files." *Viet Nam Forum* 14 (1993): 61–81.

Ra'anan, Uri. "Peking's Foreign Policy 'Debate,' 1965–1966." In Tsou, ed., *China in Crisis*, 23–71.

Race, Jeffrey. *War Comes to Long An: Revolutionary Conflict in a Vietnamese Province*. Berkeley: University of California Press, 1972.

Radvanyi, Janos. *Delusion and Reality: Gambits, Hoaxes, and Diplomatic One-Upmanship in Vietnam*. South Bend, Ind.: Gateway Editions, 1978.

Richter, James G. *Khrushchev's Double Bind: International Pressures and Domestic Coalition Politics*. Baltimore: The Johns Hopkins University Press, 1994.

Roberts, Priscilla, ed. *Sino-American Relations since 1900*. Hong Kong: University of Hong Kong, 1991.

Robinson, Thomas W., and David Shambaugh, eds. *Chinese Foreign Policy: Theory and Practice*. Oxford: Clarendon Press, 1994.

Rogers, Frank E. "Sino-American Relations and the Vietnam War, 1964–66." *China Quarterly*, no. 66 (June 1976): 293–314.

Rogers, Robert F. "Policy Differences within the Hanoi Leadership." *Studies in Comparative Communism* 9 (Spring–Summer 1976): 108–28.

Ronning, Chester. *A Memoir of China in Revolution: From the Boxer Rebellion to the People's Republic*. New York: Pantheon, 1974.

Ross, Robert S. *The Indochina Tangle: China's Vietnam Policy, 1975–1979*. New York: Columbia University Press, 1988.

———. *Negotiating Cooperation: The United States and China, 1969–1989*. Stanford: Stanford University Press, 1995.

Rudenstine, David. *The Day the Presses Stopped: A History of the Pentagon Papers Case*. Berkeley: University of California Press, 1996.

Salisbury, Harrison E. *To Peking and Beyond: A Report on the New Asia*. New York: Quadrangle, 1973.

SarDesai, D. R. *Indian Foreign Policy in Cambodia, Laos, and Vietnam, 1947–1964*. Berkeley: University of California Press, 1968.

Schaller, Michael. *Altered States: The United States and Japan since the Occupation*. New York: Oxford University Press, 1997.

——. *The United States and China in the Twentieth Century*. 2nd ed. New York: Oxford University Press, 1990.

Schoenhals, Michael. *Doing Things with Words in Chinese Politics: Five Case Studies*. Berkeley: Institute of East Asian Studies, University of California, 1992.

Schulzinger, Robert D. "The Johnson Administration, China, and the Vietnam War." In Jiang and Ross, eds., *1955–1971 nian de ZhongMei guanxi: Huanhe*, 138–74.

——. *A Time for War: The United States and Vietnam, 1941–1975*. New York: Oxford University Press, 1997.

Schurmann, Franz. *The Logic of World Power: An Inquiry into the Origins, Currents, and Contradictions of World Politics*. New York: Pantheon Books, 1974.

Schwab, Orrin. *Defending the Free World: John F. Kennedy, Lyndon Johnson, and the Vietnam War, 1961–1965*. Westport, Conn.: Praeger, 1998.

Shao, Kuo-kang. *Zhou Enlai and the Foundations of Chinese Foreign Policy*. New York: St. Martin's Press, 1996.

——. "Zhou Enlai's Diplomacy and the Neutralization of Indo-China, 1954–55." *China Quarterly*, no. 107 (September 1986): 483–504.

Shapley, Deborah. *Promise and Power: The Life and Times of Robert McNamara*. Boston: Little, Brown, 1993.

Shawcross, William. *The Quality of Mercy: Cambodia, Holocaust and Modern Conscience*. New York: Simon and Schuster, 1984.

——. *Sideshow: Kissinger, Nixon and the Destruction of Cambodia*. New York: Simon and Schuster, 1979.

Sheng, Michael M. *Battling Western Imperialism: Mao, Stalin, and the United States*. Princeton: Princeton University Press, 1997.

Showalter, Dennis E. "Dien Bien Phu in Three Cultures." *War & Society* 16 (October 1998): 93–108.

Sihanouk, Norodom. *My War with the CIA: Cambodia's Fight for Survival*. London: Penguin Books, 1973.

Simmons, Robert R. *The Strained Alliance: Peking, Pyongyang, Moscow and the Politics of the Korean Civil War*. New York: Free Press, 1975.

Skocpol, Theda. *States and Social Revolutions: A Comparative Analysis of France, Russia, and China*. Cambridge: Cambridge University Press, 1979.

Smith, R. B. "China and Southeast Asia: The Revolutionary Perspective, 1951." *Journal of Southeast Asian Studies* 19 (March 1988): 97–110.

——. "The Foundation of the Indochinese Communist Party, 1929–1930." *Modern Asian Studies* 32 (October 1998): 769–805.

——. *An International History of the Vietnam War*. 3 vols. New York: St. Martin's Press, 1983–91.

——. "The International Setting of the Cambodia Crisis, 1969–1970." *International History Review* 18 (May 1996): 303–35.

Smith, Roger M. *Cambodia's Foreign Policy*. Ithaca: Cornell University Press, 1965.

Smyser, W. R. *The Independent Vietnamese: Vietnamese Communism between Russia and China, 1956–1969*. Athens: Ohio University Center for International Studies, 1980.

Snepp, Frank. *Decent Interval: An Insider's Account of Saigon's Indecent End Told by the CIA's Chief Strategy Analyst in Vietnam*. New York: Random House, 1977.

Snow, Edgar. *The Long Revolution*. New York: Random House, 1971.

Snyder, Glenn H. *Alliance Politics*. Ithaca: Cornell University Press, 1997.

——. "The Security Dilemma in Alliance Politics." *World Politics* (July 1984): 461–95.

Solomon, Richard H., ed. *The China Factor: Sino-American Relations and the Global Scene*. Eaglewood Cliffs, N.J.: Prentice-Hall, 1981.

Spector, Ronald H. *After Tet: The Bloodiest Year in Vietnam*. New York: Vintage, 1993.

Spence, Jonathan D. *The Search for Modern China*. New York: W. W. Norton, 1990.

Stowe, Judy. " 'Revisionism' in Vietnam." Paper presented at the workshop "Recasting the International History of the Vietnam War," the Woodrow Wilson International Center for Scholars, March 26, 1998.

Stuart-Fox, Martin. *A History of Laos*. Cambridge: Cambridge University Press, 1997.

Stueck, William. *The Korean War: An International History*. Princeton: Princeton University Press, 1995.

Sullivan, M. P. *France's Vietnam Policy: A Study in Franco-American Relations*. Westport, Conn.: Greenwood Press, 1978.

Sulzberger, C. L. *An Age of Mediocrity: Memoirs and Diaries, 1963–1972*. New York: Macmillan, 1973.

Summers, Harry G., Jr. *On Strategy: A Critical Analysis of the Vietnam War*. New York: Dell, 1982.

Sun Tzu. *The Art of War*. Translated by Samuel B. Griffith. New York: Oxford University Press, 1963.

Suny, Ronald Grigor. *The Soviet Experiment: Russia, the USSR, and the Successor States*. New York: Oxford University Press, 1998.

Szulc, Tad. *The Illusion of Peace: Foreign Policy in the Nixon Years*. New York: Vikings, 1978.

Tai, Hue-Tam Ho. *Radicalism and the Origins of the Vietnamese Revolution*. Cambridge, Mass.: Harvard University Press, 1992.

Taubman, William. "Khrushchev vs. Mao: A Preliminary Sketch of the Role of Personality in the Sino-Soviet Split." *Cold War International History Project Bulletin*, Issues 8–9 (Winter 1996–97): 243–48.

Taylor, Jay. *China and Southeast Asia: Peking's Relations with Revolutionary Movements*. Expanded and updated edition. New York: Praeger, 1976.

Taylor, Keith W. "China and Vietnam: Looking for a New Version of an Old Relationship." In Werner and Huynh, eds., *The Vietnam War*, 271–85.

Taylor, Sandra C. "Laos: The Escalation of a Secret War." In Errington and McKercher, eds., *The Vietnam War as History*.

Teiwes, Frederick C. "The Establishment and Consolidation of the New Regime, 1949–57." In MacFarquhar, ed., *The Politics of China*, 69–73.

Teiwes, Frederick C., and Warren Sun. *The Tragedy of Lin Biao: Riding the Tiger during the Cultural Revolution*. Honolulu: University of Hawaii Press, 1996.

Thakur, Ramesh. *Peacekeeping in Vietnam: Canada, India, Poland, and the International Commission*. Edmonton: University of Alberta Press, 1984.

Thakur, Ramesh, and Carlyle A. Thayer. *Soviet Relations with India and Vietnam*. New York: St. Martin's Press, 1992.

Thant, U. *View from the UN*. Garden City, N.Y.: Doubleday, 1978.

Thayer, Carlyle A. *War by Other Means: National Liberation and Revolution in Viet-Nam, 1954–60*. Sydney: Allen & Unwin, 1989.

Thee, Marek. *Notes of a Witness: Laos and the Second Indochina War*. New York: Random House, 1973.

Thies, Wallace J. *When Governments Collide: Coercion and Diplomacy in the Vietnam Conflict, 1964–1968*. Berkeley: University of California Press, 1980.

Thompson, W. Scott. *Ghana's Foreign Policy, 1957–1966: Diplomacy, Ideology, and the New State*. Princeton: Princeton University Press, 1969.

Thomson, James C., Jr. "On the Making of U.S. China Policy, 1961–69: A Study in Bureaucratic Politics." *China Quarterly*, no. 50 (April–June 1972): 220–43.

Topping, Seymour. *Journey between Two Chinas*. New York: Harper & Row, 1972.

Toye, Hugh. *Laos: Buffer State or Battleground*. London: Oxford University Press, 1968.

Trachtenberg, Marc. *A Constructed Peace: The Making of the European Settlement, 1945–1963*. Princeton: Princeton University Press, 1999.

Tran Van Tra. "Tet: The 1968 General Offensive and General Uprising." In Werner and Huynh, eds., *The Vietnam War*, 37–65.

Truong Buu Lam. "Intervention versus Tribute in Sino-Vietnamese Relations, 1788–1790." In Fairbank, ed., *The Chinese World Order*, 165–79.

Truong Chinh. *Primer for Revolt: The Communist Takeover in Viet-Nam*. With an introduction and notes by Bernard B. Fall. New York: Praeger, 1963.

Truong Nhu Tang. *Journal of a Vietcong*. London: Jonathan Cape, 1985.

Tsou, Tang, ed. *China in Crisis*. Vol. 2. Chicago: University of Chicago Press, 1968.

Tucker, Nancy Bernkopf. "Threats, Opportunities, and Frustrations in East Asia." In Cohen and Tucker, eds., *Lyndon Johnson Confronts the World*, 99–134.

Turley, William S. *The Second Indochina War: A Short Political and Military History, 1954–1975*. Boulder: Westview Press, 1986.

———, ed. *Vietnamese Communism in Comparative Perspective*. Boulder: Westview Press, 1980.

Turton, Andrew, Jonathan Fast, and Malcolm Caldwell, eds. *Thailand: Roots of Conflict*. Nottingham: Spokesman, 1978.

Usowski, Peter S. "Intelligence Estimates and U.S. Policy toward Laos, 1960–63." *Intelligence and National Security* 6 (April 1991): 367–94.

U Thant. *View from the UN*. Garden City, N.Y.: Doubleday, 1978.

VanDemark, Brian. *Into the Quagmire: Lyndon Johnson and the Escalation of the Vietnam War*. New York: Oxford University Press, 1991.

Vandiver, Frank E. *Shadows of Vietnam: Lyndon Johnson's Wars*. College Station: Texas A&M University Press, 1997.

Van Ness, Peter. "China and the Third World: Patterns of Engagement and Indifference." In Kim, ed., *China and the World: Chinese Foreign Policy Faces the New Millennium*, 151–68.

———. *Revolution and Chinese Foreign Policy: Peking's Support for Wars of National Liberation*. Berkeley: University of California Press, 1970.

Vasavakul, Theveeporn. "Vietnam: The Changing Models of Legitimation." In Alagappa, ed., *Political Legitimacy in Southeast Asia*, 257–89.

Vo Nguyen Giap. *People's War, People's Army: The Viet Cong Insurrection Manual for Underdeveloped Countries*. New York: Praeger, 1962.

Waldron, Arthur. "From Nonexistent to Almost Normal: U.S.-China Relations in the 1960s." In Kunz, ed., *The Diplomacy of the Crucial Decade*, 219–50.

Walters, Vernon A. *Silent Missions*. Garden City, N.Y.: Doubleday, 1978.

Warner, Roger. *Back Fire: The CIA's Secret War in Laos and Its Link to the War in Vietnam*. New York: Simon and Schuster, 1995.

Wehrle, Edmund F. " 'A Good, Bad Deal': John F. Kennedy, W. Averell Harriman, and the Neutralization of Laos, 1961–1962." *Pacific Historical Review* 67 (August 1998): 349–77.

Welch, David A. *Justice and the Genesis of War*. New York: Cambridge University Press, 1993.

Werner, Jayne S., and David Hunt, eds. *The American War in Vietnam*. Ithaca: Southeast Asia Program, Cornell University, 1993.

Werner, Jayne S., and Luu Doan Huynh, eds. *The Vietnam War: Vietnamese and American Perspectives*. Armonk, N.Y.: M. E. Sharpe, 1993.

Westad, Odd Arne. *Cold War and Revolution: Soviet-American Rivalry and the Origins of the Chinese Civil War, 1944–1946*. New York: Columbia University Press, 1993.

———. "Secrets of the Second World: The Russian Archives and the Reinterpretation of Cold War History." *Diplomatic History* 21 (Spring 1997): 259–71.

———, ed. *Brothers in Arms: The Rise and Fall of the Sino-Soviet Alliance, 1945–1963*. Washington, D.C.: Woodrow Wilson Center Press and Stanford, Stanford University Press, 1998.

———. *The Fall of Détente: Soviet-American Relations during the Carter Years*. Oslo: Scandinavian University Press, 1997.

Westad, Odd Arne, Chen Jian, Stein Tonnesson, Nguyen Vu Tung, and James G. Hershberg, eds. "77 Conversations between Chinese and Foreign Leaders on the Wars in Indochina, 1964–1977." Cold War International History Project Working Paper No. 22. Washington, D.C.: Woodrow Wilson International Center for Scholars, 1998.

White, Christine Pelzer. "The Peasants and the Party in the Vietnamese Revolution." In Miller, ed., *Peasants and Politics*, 19–48.

Whiting, Allen S. "China's Role in the Vietnam War." In Werner and Hunt, eds., *The American War in Vietnam*, 71–76.

———. *The Chinese Calculus of Deterrence: India and Indochina*. Ann Arbor: University of Michigan Press, 1975.

———. "Forecasting Chinese Foreign Policy: IR Theory vs. the Fortune Cookie." In Robinson and Shambaugh, eds., *Chinese Foreign Policy*, 506–23.

———. "How We Almost Went to War with China." *Look*, April 29, 1969, 76–77, 79.

———. "The Sino-Soviet Split." In MacFarquhar and Fairbank, eds., *The Cambridge History of China*, 478–538.

Whitson, William, ed. *The Military and Political Power in China in the 1970s*. New York: Praeger, 1973.

Wilson, Harold. *A Personal Record: The Labour Government, 1964–1970*. Boston: Little, Brown, 1971.

Wohlforth, William Curti. *The Elusive Balance: Power and Perceptions during the Cold War*. Ithaca: Cornell University Press, 1993.

Woods, Randall Bennett. *Fulbright: A Biography*. New York: Cambridge University Press, 1995.

Woodside, Alexander Barton. *Vietnam and the Chinese Model: A Comparative Study of*

Nguyen and Ch'ing Civil Government in the First Half of the Nineteenth Century. Cambridge, Mass.: Harvard University Press, 1971.

Yahuda, Michael. "Chinese Foreign Policy after 1963: The Maoist Phases." *China Quarterly*, no. 36 (October–December 1968): 93–113.

———. "Kremlinology and the Chinese Strategic Debate, 1965–66." *China Quarterly*, no. 49 (January–March 1972): 32–75.

Young, Kenneth T. *Negotiating with the Chinese Communists: The United States Experience, 1953–1967*. New York: McGraw-Hill, 1968.

Young, Marilyn B. *The Vietnam Wars, 1945–1990*. New York: HarperPerennial, 1991.

Zagoria, Donald S. *The Sino-Soviet Conflict, 1956–1961*. New York: Atheneum, 1964.

———. "The Strategic Debate in Peking." In Tsou, ed., *China in Crisis*, 237–68.

———. *Vietnam Triangle: Moscow, Peking, Hanoi*. New York: Pegasus, 1967.

Zasloff, Joseph J., ed. *Postwar Indochina: Old Enemies and New Allies*. Washington, D.C.: Foreign Service Institute of the U.S. State Department, 1988.

Zasloff, Joseph J., and MacAlister Brown, eds. *Communism in Indochina: New Perspectives*. Lexington, Mass.: Lexington Books, D. C. Heath, 1975.

Zhai, Qiang. "Beijing and the Vietnam Conflict, 1964–1965: New Chinese Evidence." *Cold War International History Project Bulletin*, nos. 6–7 (Winter 1995–96): 233–50.

———. "China and the Geneva Conference of 1954." *China Quarterly*, no. 129 (March 1992): 103–22.

———. *The Dragon, the Lion, and the Eagle: Chinese-British-American Relations, 1949–1958*. Kent: Kent State University Press, 1994.

———. "Opposing Negotiations: China and the Vietnam Peace Talks, 1965–1968." *Pacific Historical Review* 68, no. 1 (February 1999): 21–49.

———. "Transplanting the Chinese Model: Chinese Military Advisers and the First Vietnam War, 1950–1954." *Journal of Military History* 57 (October 1993): 689–715.

Zhang, Shu Guang. *Deterrence and Strategic Culture: Chinese-American Confrontations, 1949–1958*. Ithaca: Cornell University Press, 1992.

———. *Mao's Military Romanticism: China and the Korean War, 1950–1953*. Lawrence: University Press of Kansas, 1995.

Zhang, Xiaoming. "The Vietnam War, 1964–1969: A Chinese Perspective." *Journal of Military History* 60 (October 1996): 731–62.

Zheng, Shiping. *Party vs. State in Post-1949 China: The Institutional Dilemma*. Cambridge: Cambridge University Press, 1997.

Zubok, Vladislav M. "Unwrapping the Enigma: What Was Behind the Soviet Challenge in the 1960s?" In Kunz, ed., *The Diplomacy of the Crucial Decade*, 149–82.

Zubok, Vladislav, and Constantine Pleshakov. *Inside the Kremlin's Cold War: From Stalin to Khrushchev*. Cambridge, Mass.: Harvard University Press, 1996.

INDEX

101); aid to DRV, 69–71, 73–74, 135, 137, 179–80, 195–96, 207, 261 (n. 14); and Vietnamese reunification, 77–81; recognition of NLF, 83; aid to Pathet Lao, 96, 180, 247 (n. 9); reaction to Gulf of Tonkin incident, 132; dispute with DRV, 152–55, 171, 172, 173, 175, 177–78, 197–98, 208–15, 217–18, 260 (n. 66); policy toward Vietnam peace talks, 157–68; insistence on protracted war in Vietnam, 170–71, 175, 178; competition with DRV in Laos, 180–81, 220; opening to U.S., 181–82, 193; competition with DRV in Cambodia, 184, 190, 192, 211, 213; response to Sihanouk's overthrow, 186–92, 260 (n. 59); aid to Khmer Rouge, 212, 213

Chinese Communist Party Central Military Commission, 36, 37, 45, 116, 143, 209; and Dien Bien Phu battle, 46–47

Chinese Communist Party Hong Kong Sub-Bureau, 12

Chinese Economic and Cultural Mission, 131, 240 (n. 35)

Chinese Military Advisory Group (CMAG), 29, 33–34, 63, 73–74; creation of, 19; and Northwest campaign (1952), 36–38; and Vietnamese land reform (1953), 40–41; and Dien Bien Phu battle, 46–49

Chinese Political Advisory Group (CPAG), 35; and Vietnamese land reform (1953), 39

Chinh huan (political campaign), 35

Chongqing, 100, 163

Clifford, Clark, 179

Columbia University, 99

Cominform, 23

Comintern, 99

Commonwealth Peace Mission, 160

Communist Party of Kampuchea (CPK), 183, 184. *See also* Khmer Rouge

Conghua, 117, 190

Crozier, Brian, 100

Cuba, 147, 222

Cultural Revolution, 150–52, 154, 167–68

Czechoslovakia, 174

Danang, 133, 211

Day River, 34

De Gaulle, Charles, 146, 162, 163

De Lattre de Tassigny, General Jean, 33

Deng Xiaoping, 6, 83, 114–15, 129, 150–51, 154, 165, 209, 213–14; and Sino-Soviet dispute, 152–53; and China's policy toward Cambodia, 265 (n. 100)

Deng Yifan, 19

Dien Bien Phu, 41–42, 45–49, 55, 59, 63, 64, 104

Dong Khe, 29, 31

Duan Suquan, 121–22

Duiker, William J., 31, 202, 233 (n. 78)

Dulles, John Foster, 54, 62, 151

Eden, Anthony, 57, 106

Eisenhower, Dwight D., 112

Eisenhower administration, 44, 205; policy toward Laos, 92–93, 95–96

Ely, General Paul, 49

Engels, Friedrich, 25–26

European Defense Community, 52, 58

Expressen (Swedish newspaper), 46

Fang Yi, 70

First Regiment of the Southern Guangdong People's Force, 11–12

Five Principles of Peaceful Coexistence, 54–55, 66–68, 79

France, 13, 15–16, 37, 46–47, 50, 54–56, 59–61, 87, 96, 99, 173, 175

French Communist Party, 5, 13, 33

Gaddis, John Lewis, 21, 222

Gaiduk, Ilya, 128

Garver, John W., 139, 155, 207

Geneva Accords (1954), 62, 63, 66, 69, 72, 73, 75, 77, 89, 92, 93, 94, 102, 103, 107, 161, 162

Geneva Accords (1962), 105, 110, 130, 208

Geneva Conference (1954), 56–57, 64, 65,

66, 69, 72, 75, 92, 100, 109, 200, 217; Chinese role in, 50–63; Soviet role in, 52
Geneva Conference on Laos, 91; Sino-Soviet relations at, 105–7; Sino-Vietnamese relations at, 107–10
Ghana, 160, 165, 175
Godunov, N. I., 86
Goldberg, Arthur J., 255 (n. 46)
Gordon Walker, Patrick, 158, 159, 160, 253 (n. 5)
Great Leap Forward, 5, 81, 84, 89, 97, 111, 114, 115, 129, 151
Green Berets (U.S. Special Forces), 112
Gromyko, Andrei, 53, 106, 164, 241 (n. 59)
Guangdong, 11, 12, 113, 117
Guangxi, 11, 16, 17, 20, 22, 23, 28, 29, 47, 98, 137, 150
Guangzhou, 10, 26, 190
Gulf of Tonkin incident, 132, 150, 152; China's reaction to, 140, 142
Gushev, General, 74

Haig, Alexander M., 199
Hainan Island, 137, 143
Haiphong, 44, 60, 73, 165; U.S. mining of, 203
Han Nianlong, 260 (n. 65), 262 (n. 29)
Hanoi, 11, 12, 33, 34, 44, 48, 60, 69, 82, 83, 89, 96, 100, 113, 126, 164, 165, 166
Harriman, W. Averell, 110, 163, 242 (n. 78)
He Long, 142, 148–49
He Wei, 240 (n. 35)
Ho Chi Minh, 1, 4, 6, 13, 20, 23, 24, 34, 35, 36, 66, 69, 70, 74, 79, 94, 98, 108, 117, 120, 123, 132, 133–34, 147, 149, 161, 164, 172, 178, 214; early relationship with CCP, 5, 10–11; and creation of Viet Minh, 11; and establishment of DRV, 11; visits Soviet Union (1950), 17; and border campaign (1950), 26, 32, 33; and Northwest campaign (1952), 37–38; and Navarre plan, 44–45; on negotiations with France, 46; and Geneva Conference (1954), 51, 58, 59–60, 62; visits China (1955), 71, 77; visits Soviet Union (1955), 72–73; and land

reform, 75, 76; on reunification, 77; reaction to Taiwan Strait crisis (1958), 80; reaction to Sino-Soviet dispute, 86–91, 218, 237–38 (n. 90), 238 (n. 104); reaction to Kong Le's coup, 95; visits China (1962), 116; death of, 174
Ho Chi Minh Trail, 95, 122, 128, 194
Hoa Binh, 31
Hoang Hoa Tham I (operation), 33
Hoang Hoa Tham II (operation), 34
Hoang Minh Chinh, 126
Hoang Quoc Viet, 201
Hoang Van Hoan, 11, 12, 17–18, 19, 75, 80, 83, 108, 123, 125, 133, 172, 207, 214, 242 (n. 76), 247 (n. 8)
Hoang Van Thai, 29, 179
Hoc Tap (Study), 124, 125
Hong Kong, 11
Hong Thuy (Vo Nguyen Bac), 19
Hongqi (Red Flag), 167
Hu Qiaomu, 23
Hu Zhengqing, 8, 121, 245 (n. 38)
Huan Xiang, 100
Huang Hua, 50, 165
Huang Jingwen, 11, 12
Huang Kecheng, 48
Hughes, Thomas L., 120
Humphrey, Hubert, 163
Hunan, 26
Hundred Flowers Campaign, 75

Ieng Sary, 192, 212, 213
India, 87, 94, 99, 114, 116, 127, 147, 175; peace proposal on Vietnam, 160
Indochina. *See* Cambodia; Laos; Vietnam, Democratic Republic of
Indochinese Communist Party (ICP), 11, 61, 220
Indonesian Communist Party (PKI), 117, 119
International Control Commission (ICC), 85, 103, 107, 109

Japan, 11, 23, 54, 100, 144
Japanese Communist Party, 23
Johnson, General Harold K., 139

Liu Ningyi, 114

Liu Shaoqi, 6, 8, 13, 21, 22, 35, 90, 115, 119, 129, 143, 151, 154, 162, 165, 169–70, 243 (n. 11); relationship with Ho Chi Minh, 5, 10, 16, 38; and Chinese aid to Viet Minh, 18, 19, 23, 25; and border campaign (1950), 26; on Viet Minh's financial mismanagement, 36; and Northwest campaign (1952), 37; visits DRV (1963), 117, 124; promises aid to DRV, 133, 134; on China's war preparation, 144; meets with Sihanouk (1965), 163

Liuzhou, 58, 60, 62

Lon Nol, 183, 188, 189, 211, 218, 260 (n. 59); coup against Sihanouk, 187; relationship with China, 248 (n. 33)

London School of Economics, 100

Long Cheng, 190

Lu Dingyi, 21

Lu Huixiang, 191

Luang Prabang, 43, 45, 48

Luo Guibo, 6, 15, 18, 19, 23, 25, 29, 35, 64, 70, 80, 93; as head of CPAG, 35; and Northwest campaign (1952), 36–38; and Vietnamese land reform, 40–41; and Navarre plan, 44–46

Luo Ruiqing, 82, 132, 133, 134, 137, 141, 142, 144, 145, 243 (n. 7), 244 (n. 18), 248 (n. 33); visits DRV (1963), 117

Ly Bich Son, 13, 15

MacDonald, Malcolm, 108

MacFarquhar, Roderick, 115

McNamara, Robert S., 146, 148, 179; reaction to DRV's Four Points peace plan, 253 (n. 11)

Mai Van Bo, 210

Malaya, 22, 59, 94, 119; Communist insurrection in, 64

Malenkov, Georgi M., 60

Malinovsky, Rodion Y., 149

Malraux, Andre, 162, 254 (n. 26)

Manchuria, 12

Maneli, Mieczyslaw, 107, 126

Mao Khe, 34

Mao Zedong, 3, 6, 8, 13, 18, 24, 26, 34, 39,

42, 50, 69, 76, 84, 112, 117, 120, 145, 162, 164, 210, 212, 219–20; worldview of, 4, 20–21, 221; and Geneva Conference (1954), 4; and Geneva Conference on Laos, 4–5, 99; and China's recognition of DRV, 15; relationship with Ho Chi Minh, 16, 17, 87, 88; and CMAG, 19, 23, 25; and perception of threats, 20, 140–41, 143, 146; and border campaign (1950), 32; and Dien Bien Phu battle, 45–48; meets with Souvanna Phouma (1956), 66; meets with Sihanouk (1956), 67; and Taiwan Strait crisis (1958), 80, 81; dispute with Soviet Union, 86, 87, 90, 123, 124, 127, 148–51, 153–54, 167; view of Vietnamese–Pathet Lao relationship, 108–9; criticism of Wang Jiaxiang, 114–16; view of PKI, 119; reaction to U.S. escalation of war in Vietnam (1964), 131, 132, 133, 135–37, 140–41; view of national liberation movements, 146–48; meets with Sihanouk (1965), 163; and Vietnam peace talks, 173; on protracted people's war, 177, 178; reaction to U.S. invasion of Cambodia, 191; opening to U.S., 193, 195, 198; on U.S. withdrawal from Vietnam, 196; urges DRV to end the war, 204–5, 206, 263 (n. 62); reaction to Paris Peace Agreement, 206; meets with Pol Pot (1975), 212–13

Martin, Graham, 213

Marx, Karl, 21, 25, 26, 213

Maurer, Ion Gheorghe, 174

Mei Jiasheng, 19

Mekong River, 180, 212, 265 (n. 101)

Mendès-France, Pierre, 57, 58, 60, 61, 62

Michalowski, Jerzy, 164, 166

Micunovic, Veljko, 243 (n. 85)

Midway Island, 181

Mikoyan, Anastas I., 78

Military Assistance Advisory Group (MAAG), 112

Military Assistance Command, Vietnam, 114

Ming Tombs (Shisanling) Reservoir, 140

Miyamoto Kenji, 154, 169

policy toward DRV, 72–73, 77, 78, 79–80, 149, 150, 157–58, 214; policy toward Laos, 96, 98, 100, 110; competition with China in Cambodia, 187, 190; reaction to U.S. mining of Haiphong, 204, 263 (n. 57)

Spratleys (Nansha), 209, 210

Spring Offensive, 202–4; U.S. reaction to, 203; China's reaction to, 203

Stalin, Joseph V., 3, 21, 26, 33, 79, 91, 213; and Vietnam, 13, 15, 17; endorses China's role in Vietnam, 22; and Northwest campaign (1952), 37; meets with Ho Chi Minh (1952), 38

Stoessel, Walter J., Jr., 166, 182

Strong, Anna Louise, 146

Stuart-Fox, Martin, 110

Su Yu, 48

Sukarno, 119, 147

Summers, Harry G., 155, 156

Summit Meeting of the Indochinese Peoples (1970), 190–91, 192, 260 (n. 66)

Sun Zi (Sun Tzu), 28

Suslov, Mikhail, 251 (n. 98)

Taiwan, 20, 50, 93, 116, 144, 196, 201

Tang Caiyou, 11, 12

Tap Chi Quan Doi Nhan Dan (PAVN's monthly journal), 126

Tet offensive, 168, 171, 176–79; China's reaction to, 177–79

Thai Nguyen, 29, 31

Thailand, 18, 59, 68, 93, 94, 95, 96, 97, 104, 109, 162, 180; China's concerns about, 94

That Khe, 31

Thayer, Carlyle, 83

Thee, Marek, 96

Third Front, 141, 142, 144

Third National Congress (VWP), 88–89

Thompson, Llewellyn, 106

Tito, Joseph Broz, 91, 124, 125, 147, 148, 163, 184

Tong Xiaopeng, 8, 247 (n. 8)

Tovmassian, Suren A., 126

Tran Dang Khoa, 16

Tran Tu Binh, 96, 162

Truman, Harry S., 44

Truman administration, 139

Truong Chinh, 25, 32, 38, 126, 206; and land reform, 42, 75, 76; and Sino-Soviet dispute, 123

Truong Nhu Tang, 210

Truong Son Ra mountain, 162

U Nu, 97

U Thant, 160, 163, 164

Ung Van Khiem, 108, 126, 242 (nn. 76, 78)

Unger, Leonard, 110

United Nations, 53, 79, 81, 95, 97, 100, 105, 160, 162, 175, 199

United States, 47, 50, 53, 55, 60, 62, 87, 88, 91, 114, 117, 118; policy toward Laos, 92–93, 109, 110, 131; policy toward DRV, 130; invasion of Cambodia, 182

United States Operations Mission (USOM), 92

Ussuri River, 181

Van Tien Dung, 131, 132, 134, 247 (n. 8)

Vang Pao, 122, 190

Vienna, 106

Viet Bac, 31, 36

Viet Minh, 5; and border campaign (1950), 26–33; and Navarre plan, 43–46

Vietnam, Democratic Republic of (DRV), 1; tax reform (1951), 36, 230 (n. 109); land reform, 38–42, 75–76; famine in, 70; adoption of Soviet model of development, 76, 89, 128–29, 235 (n. 37); policy toward Sino-Indian conflict, 85–86; policy toward Sino-Soviet dispute, 86–91, 122–29, 149, 151, 154, 252 (n. 117); dispute with China, 152–55, 171, 172, 173, 175, 177–78, 197–98, 208–15, 217–18, 260 (n. 66); Four Points peace plan, 159, 170; peace strategy, 168; policy toward Cambodia, 183–84, 188–89; reaction to China's opening to U.S., 197–98, 201–2; agricultural collectivization in, 237 (n. 76)

Vietnam, Republic of, 112, 117, 119, 120

Vietnam Workers' Party (VWP), 36, 69,

91, 260 (n. 59); on Soviet threats, 194; and China's opening to U.S., 195, 199; discusses Vietnam with Kissinger, 196; discusses Vietnam with Nixon, 200; reaction to U.S. mining of Haiphong, 203; reaction to Paris Peace Agreement, 206–7; role in China's seizure of Paracel Islands, 209–10, 264 (n. 84)